Indians in the United States and Canada

 A COMPARATIVE HISTORY

Roger L. Nichols

University of Nebraska Press   Lincoln & London

© 1998 by the University of Nebraska Press
All rights reserved
Manufactured in the United States of America

⊗

First Bison Books printing: 1999
Most recenting printing indicated
by the last digit below:
10 9 8 7 6 5 4 3 2 1

Library of Congress Cataloging-in-Publication Data
Nichols, Roger L.
Indians in the United States and Canada:
a comparative history / Roger L. Nichols.
p.   cm.
Includes bibliographical references and index.
ISBN 0-8032-3341-8 (cl: alk. paper)
ISBN 0-8032-8377-6 (pa: alk. paper)
1. Indians of North America—History 2. Indians
of North America—Canada—History. I. Title.
E77.N554 1998 971'.00497—dc21 97-31596 CIP

TO JEFFREY R. NICHOLS

Contents

Maps and Plates

Seminole family, 1910.

File Hills Indian Colony Band, ca. 1915.

Cree Indian children attending Anglican Church Missionary School, 1945.

Chief Joseph John from Tofino, Vancouver Island, British Columbia.

Zuñi winter ceremony, 1917.

Negotiations during the 1973 Wounded Knee incident.

Acknowledgments

This project began in 1983 with many of the usual assumptions that books-to-be carry. Namely that it would be completed quickly, would be of modest size, and would have an audience waiting eagerly for it to appear. The process has been more complex than anticipated, as several factors combined to lengthen the research and writing phases considerably. Getting acquainted thoroughly with the historiography of a second country proved to be a long process. Publishing six other books in the meantime did nothing to help completion either. Then, too, the project has changed direction frequently over the years thanks to my broadening knowledge and the suggestions of friends and colleagues.

Many people have helped at each step along the way. In particular, faculty, friends, and colleagues assisted willingly in many ways. William T. Jackson suggested the need for comparative study, making it sound challenging and interesting. William T. Hagan had considered work on the same topic but stepped aside graciously when he learned of my interest. Leonard Dinnerstein, Peter Iverson, and James Ronda all read and commented on parts of the manuscript as it evolved. John Leslie of the Canadian Treaties and Historical Research Office welcomed me and allowed complete access to valuable files there. Staff at the Library of Congress Reader Service Division and Photographic Archives provided valuable assistance. Staff at the National Library of Canada and the National Archives of Canada guided me to needed documents and photographs.

My own institution, the University of Arizona, helped in many ways. I began the research in 1983–84 while on a sabbatical leave from my teaching duties there. The interlibrary loan office staff repeatedly located items not available locally. History Department staff Patricia Foreman, James Lombardo, and Mary Sue Passe all prepared various drafts of the manuscript. Office Manager Julie Nagle provided for computer assistance during the final phases of manuscript preparation.

Others helped too. The University of Nebraska Press staff worked with me throughout the process. Copyeditor Larry Hamberlin caught and corrected many errors and omissions that had crept into the final draft. Both of the scholarly readers raised important questions, sharpened the focus, and forced me to reconsider questionable ideas and data. As always my wife, Marilyn J. Nichols, read parts of the manuscript more than anyone should have to. She questioned the ideas and construction frequently, saving me from muddled prose and errors of logic.

All of these people and institutions have my sincere appreciation for this assistance. If errors remain despite their efforts, they are mine.

Introduction

In 1513, when Europeans first reached North America, between five and ten million native people lived in what are now the United States and Canada. During the next several centuries American Indian populations fell drastically because several million Europeans invaded, overrunning and often destroying the tribal societies. This long-running multiracial encounter brought violence and warfare that alternated with periods of peace. Whatever the circumstances, the interlopers seized land and resources that the Indians considered their own. Often trade, cooperation, and goodwill coexisted with greed, brutality, and violence. In these circumstances ethnocentrism, misunderstanding, miscalculation, incompetence, and criminality all played central roles as they poisoned relations between tribal peoples and the intruding Europeans.

From the sixteenth through the nineteenth centuries, similar things happened in many parts of the world as the Europeans penetrated parts of Africa, Australia, New Zealand, and South America as well. In each place the specific events varied, but generally the invaders strove to take physical control of the region and to subjugate the local populations. Indigenous peoples, however, resisted the newcomers with great skill much of the time. Plainly what happened in North America resembled similar events elsewhere. Frontier encounters became common.[1] In most cases the Europeans prevailed and came to direct the societies that emerged from these conflicts. That certainly describes the results in North America, Australia, and New Zealand.

Disease marched well ahead of many European interlopers, felling thousands, perhaps millions, of the indigenous people. Higher levels of technology, including metal tools, firearms, wheeled vehicles, and domesticated animals, gave the intruders material advantages. More hierarchically organized political, economic, and military structures also operated on the Europeans' side. In differing frontier settings around the world, then, the invading groups often seemed to hold the most advantageous positions. They used their skills of communicating on paper to seal agreements with tribal peoples. The plagues and other medical disasters that decimated the Indians, Maoris, and Australian Aborigines seemed to pass them by. With these advantages on their side, the whites pushed forward, greedily taking possession or control whenever possible.

Despite this, many Indian societies in the United States and Canada did not disappear. Certainly some did, while others combined ranks with their neighbors or fled beyond the immediate reach of the intruders. During that process changes swept through the Indian tribes and bands. At times these brought incredible transformations among the villagers, while under other circumstances Indians merely added some white ideas or customs to their own. Nevertheless, the evidence analyzed for this study shows a distinct pattern that occurred repeatedly between 1513 and the present in what is now the United States and Canada. It includes five stages: tribal independence, or even supremacy over the Europeans; a gradual shift to Indian-white equality; the reduction of the tribes to a position of dependency on the colonial or national government in each region; the further descent of Indian people to marginality at the fringes of the majority society; and for some, a resurgence of cultural nationalism, economic recovery, and political awareness and influence. By no means was this model universal, but the pattern occurred with such frequency that it is useful and effective as a means through which to examine the experiences of tribal peoples in each of the two countries.

The motivation for writing this study of white and Indian relationships in the two countries came partly from hearing a 1977 address urging those in the audience to consider research projects on comparative frontier issues. Other projects occupied my interests at the time, so the speaker's suggestions had to wait. Then, reading for something else, I encountered a striking coincidence. In 1969 Vine Deloria Jr., a Standing Rock Sioux, published *Custer Died for Your Sins*. This popular and devastating critique of white destructive impacts on tribal experiences in the United States was the first of his articulate and influential books on these issues. What struck me was that during that same year, 1969, Harold Cardinal, a Canadian Cree, published *The Unjust Society*, often making similar criticisms about government actions and ideas in Canada. Both of these writers discussed the cultural destruction of North American Indian societies and the processes through which they had lost their homelands. To me the appearance of these two moving books in the same year indicated that the time was ripe for a comparative analysis of Indian experiences in the two countries.[2]

Having decided to begin this project, it became apparent quickly that comparative history is a strange undertaking. People call for such studies repeatedly. The few in existence receive much praise, but not many scholars actually attempt such complex projects. This is certainly obvious when one examines histories of North American issues. For generations writers in the United States and Canada have inundated both societies with a flood of materials on native peoples. Biographies of leaders, ethnologies of individual groups, and studies of policies, customs, economies, and warfare line the library shelves in both countries. Certainly a few broad studies address issues of Indian affairs in both countries, but when measured against the total outpourings of scholars and popular writers, the amount of comparative writing is limited indeed.[3]

There are many reasons for this. To do comparative history well, one must be thoroughly familiar with the issues and historiography in more than one society. The story of Indian affairs in the United States and Canada includes an overwhelming amount and variety of data. As a result this study has depended almost entirely on published primary materials and existing secondary literature. Comparative studies also present major organizational difficulties. When looking at North American developments, one has to consider the policies and actions of five governments—Spain, France, Great Britain, Canada, and the United States—as well as the actions of the Hudson's Bay Company, which was on the scene for two full centuries. Moreover, hundreds of Indian societies occupied the region, having developed many levels of economic, political, and social organization. As a result, their perceptions of and initiatives toward the Europeans differed widely.

The five-century time span and wide variety of issues forces one to avoid a heavy dependence on specificity. Instead, this account paints the events in broad strokes, using specific examples to illustrate general issues. The book's central goals are straightforward. For the era stretching from 1513 through the 1860s it examines most of the events as a series of frontier encounters, that is, actions taken in zones of interethnic competition and conflict. The modern era is considered through the concept of the emerging and then the modern state. Throughout these eras the narrative compares and contrasts the experiences of tribal peoples with the ideas and actions of the intruders in what are now the United States and Canada. It examines the roles played by native peoples and the long-term results of the interracial contacts in each.

Certainly fundamental similarities and differences existed in both societies, and the narrative develops these. However, the rivalries between and among the Europeans never provided a significant basis for explaining the difficulties between Indians and whites. Rather, the vast gulf that lay between the native peoples and the invaders proved central in these events. From the start the Europeans shared most basic elements of their culture. They practiced some variety of Christianity, accepted individual private property and top-down political structures, looked to their governments to settle group and individual disputes, enjoyed a level of technology at least somewhat more advanced than the Indians', and possessed highly developed ethnocentrism. In almost every instance these values and practices brought them into direct competition if not conflict with the native people in North America.

The invasion of North America, conquest and attempted incorporation of the tribal peoples, and subsequent development of the United States and Canada as modern, multiracial societies provide the framework for this analysis. Frequent variations occurred, but the general patterns that evolved proved remarkably parallel. Throughout the entire five-century period the nature of interracial contacts changed only moderately. The cultural and technological gaps between the competing groups continued to produce difficulties between them. By the twentieth century the emerging continental societies in each nation dealt with Indian groups in ever more similar ways.

This study provides data and examples to illuminate facets of the settlement process that affected many parts of the early modern world. Nearly all regions saw friction and violence between immigrant and incoming groups and resident peoples. Where the Europeans succeeded, the majority populations either incorporated the minority groups into their society or kept them subjugated and at the fringes of the majority communities. In the United States and Canada the story is far more complex than merely narrating how evil whites abused honorable Indians or some other version of the victimization approach. Certainly there is plenty of blame to assign, but it is important to reject simplistic versions of the events. What in fact happened is that several societies with widely differing values and practices collided. The result was a vast tragedy. How and why that occurred and what its results brought carry this analysis down to the present.

Comparing the rich fabric of human experience in two diverse but neighboring societies provides an opportunity to achieve an understanding of current ethnic issues in both the United States and Canada. Present demands such as tribal sovereignty—even independence—claims to vast portions of territory, and requests for recognition as distinct tribes from the descendants of groups long thought to be extinct have caught many people in both societies by surprise. This narrative provides the data needed to assess such events. It demonstrates clearly that, despite the frequent differences and variations, the Indian-white story in Canada resembles that in the United States closely. That resemblance suggests that human motivations and actions remain less varied than past events seem to indicate. Although designed as only a pioneering study, this book analyzes the significant issues in the Indian history of both nations. Presumably others will build upon the foundation laid here to expand the scope of comparative study of North American Indian issues.

Indian groups at time of European contact

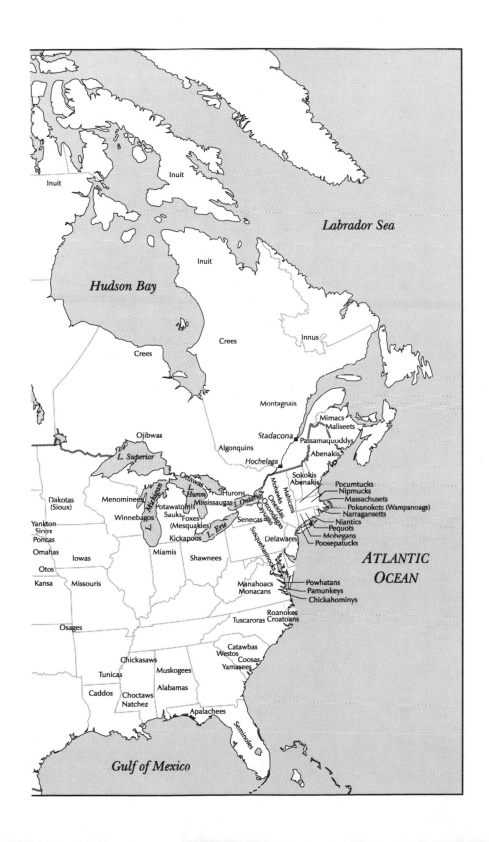

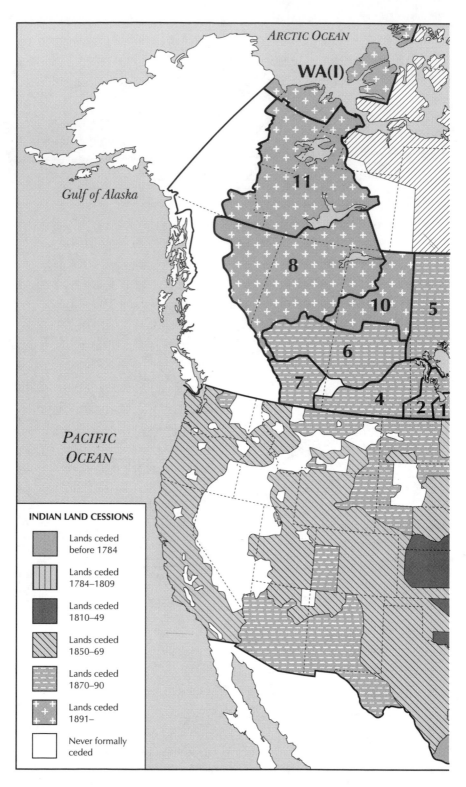

ARCTIC OCEAN

WA(I)

Gulf of Alaska

11

8

10

5

6

7

4

2 1

PACIFIC
OCEAN

INDIAN LAND CESSIONS

Lands ceded
before 1784

Lands ceded
1784–1809

Lands ceded
1810–49

Lands ceded
1850–69

Lands ceded
1870–90

Lands ceded
1891–

Never formally
ceded

Land cessions and Nunavut

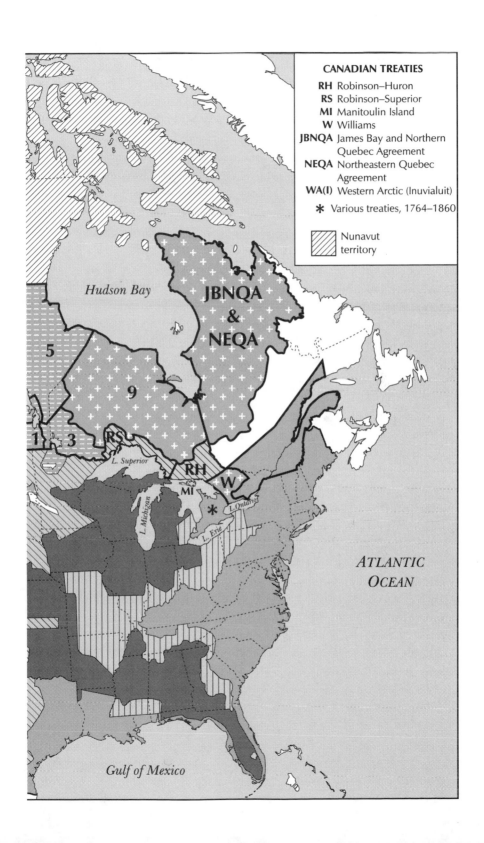

CANADIAN TREATIES

RH Robinson–Huron
RS Robinson–Superior
MI Manitoulin Island
W Williams
JBNQA James Bay and Northern Quebec Agreement
NEQA Northeastern Quebec Agreement
WA(I) Western Arctic (Inuvialuit)
✳ Various treaties, 1764–1860

Nunavut territory

JBNQA & NEQA

Hudson Bay

5

9

1   3   RS

L. Superior

RH

W

MI

✳

L. Michigan

L. Ontario

L. Erie

ATLANTIC OCEAN

Gulf of Mexico

ARCTIC
OCEAN

Gulf of Alaska

Ft. Chipewyan †

■ Ft. Simpson
†Metlakatla
Stuart Lake †

Williams Lake †

Nootka †
Ft. Victoria ■

Lethbridge †

■ Ft. Vancouver
St. Ignatius
†
St. Peter †
St. Paul †

■ Ft. Hall

Ft. Laramie ■

PACIFIC
OCEAN

Ft. Kearny ■

San Gerónimo de Taos †

San Esteban de Ácoma †

Ft. Sill ■

† San Pedro y San Pablo

San Antonio
missions †

Missions and forts

Labrador Sea

Hudson Bay

Lorette †
Sillery †
Bécancour †
Saint-François †
Caughnawaga † Norridgewock †

L. Superior
Sault Ste. Marie Wikwemikong
Ft. Mackinac The Narrows
Manitowaning St. Regis
Ft. Snelling Saugeen Ft. Frontenac
New Ulm Coldwater
Walpole Island Ft. Niagara Ft. Stanwix
L. Michigan Ft. Detroit Six Nations
Ft. Dearborn L. Erie Ft. McIntosh
Ft. Miami
Ft. Wayne Ft. Pitt
Ft. Atkinson Ft. Recovery
Ft. Washington
Ft. Leavenworth
Ft. Finney
Ft. Christanna

ATLANTIC
OCEAN

Ft. Loudoun
Ft. Smith Ft. Prince George
Ft. Toulouse
Ft. Jackson Santa Catalina
Ft. Rosalie Ft. Mims San Mateo
San Augustín

Gulf of Mexico

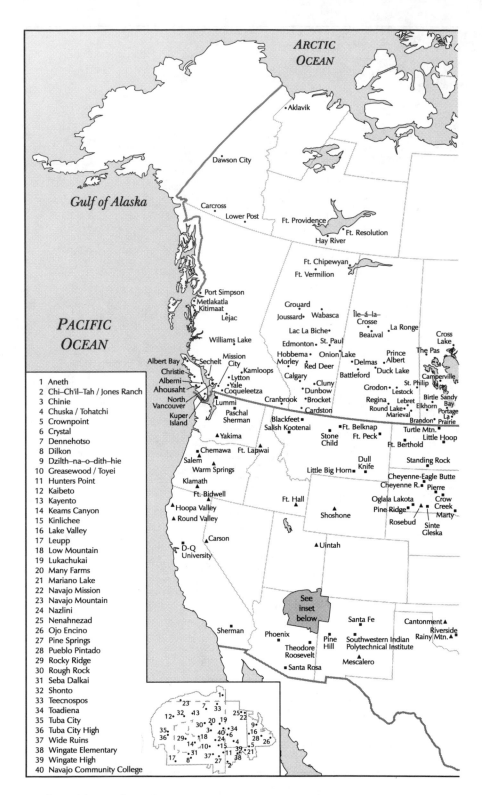

ARCTIC
OCEAN

· Aklavik

Dawson City

Gulf of Alaska

Carcross
Lower Post
Ft. Providence
Hay River · Ft. Resolution

Ft. Chipewyan
Ft. Vermilion

PACIFIC
OCEAN

· Port Simpson
· Metlakatla
Kitimaat
Lejac

Grouard · Wabasca
Joussard · Île–á–la–
Crosse
Lac La Biche · La Ronge
Beauval
Williams Lake Edmonton· St. Paul
Hobbema · Onion Lake Prince
Albert Bay Morley Red Deer · Delmas Albert
Christie Mission City Calgary · Cluny Battleford Duck Lake St. Philip
Alberni Lytton · Dunbow Grodon· Lestock Camperville
Ahousaht Yale · Coqueleetza Regina· Lebret Birtle Sandy
North Cranbrook · Brocket Round Lake· Elkhorn Bay
Vancouver Lummi · Cardston Marieval Portage La
Kuper Paschal Brandon· Prairie
Island Sherman Blackfeet Ft. Belknap Turtle Mtn.
Salish Kootenai Stone Little Hoop
▲ Yakima Child Ft. Peck Ft. Berthold
· Chemawa Ft. Lapwai Dull Standing Rock
Salem Knife
Warm Springs ▲ Little Big Horn· Cheyenne-Eagle Butte
Klamath Cheyenne R.· Pierre
Ft. Bidwell Ft. Hall Oglala Lakota Crow
▲ Hoopa Valley Pine Ridge Creek
▲ Round Valley Shoshone Rosebud Marty
Sinte
· Carson Gleska
D-Q ▲ Uintah
University

See
inset
below Santa Fe Cantonment ▲
Riverside
· Sherman Pine Rainy Mtn. ▲
Phoenix Hill Southwestern Indian
Theodore Polytechnical Institute
Roosevelt Mescalero
· Santa Rosa

1 Aneth
2 Chi–Ch'il–Tah / Jones Ranch
3 Chinie
4 Chuska / Tohatchi
5 Crownpoint
6 Crystal
7 Dennehotso
8 Dilkon
9 Dzilth–na–o–dith–hie
10 Greasewood / Toyei
11 Hunters Point
12 Kaibeto
13 Kayento
14 Keams Canyon
15 Kinlichee
16 Lake Valley
17 Leupp
18 Low Mountain
19 Lukachukai
20 Many Farms
21 Mariano Lake
22 Navajo Mission
23 Navajo Mountain
24 Nazlini
25 Nenahnezad
26 Ojo Encino
27 Pine Springs
28 Pueblo Pintado
29 Rocky Ridge
30 Rough Rock
31 Seba Dalkai
32 Shonto
33 Teecnospos
34 Toadiena
35 Tuba City
36 Tuba City High
37 Wide Ruins
38 Wingate Elementary
39 Wingate High
40 Navajo Community College

North American Indian schools in the late twentieth century

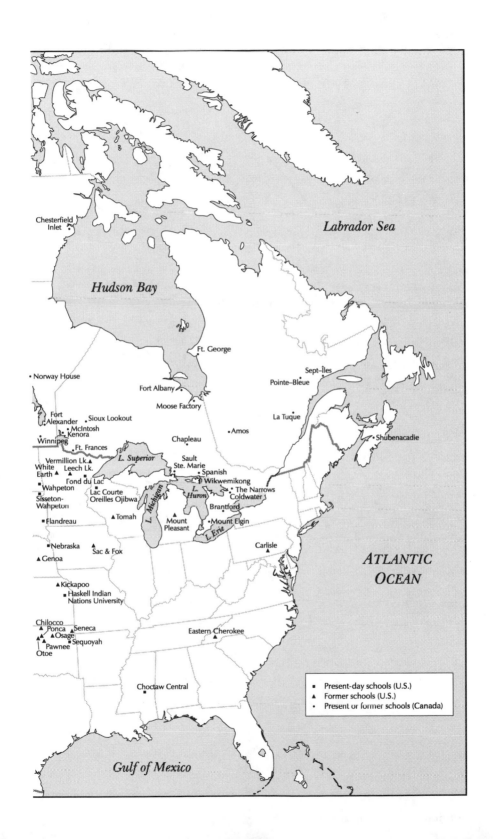

Chesterfield
Inlet

Labrador Sea

Hudson Bay

Ft. George

• Norway House

Sept-Îles

Fort Albany

Pointe–Bleue

Fort
Alexander   • Sioux Lookout
    • McIntosh
    • Kenora
Winnipeg •
    • Ft. Frances

Moose Factory

La Tuque

Amos

• Shubenacadie

Chapleau

L. Superior

Sault
Ste. Marie

Vermillion Lk.▲
White   Leech Lk.▲
Earth ▲
■   ʃond du Lac
Wahpeton ■

• Spanish

Lac Courte
Oreilles Ojibwa

Ð Wikwemikong

L.
Huron

The Narrows
Coldwater •

Sisseton-
Wahpeton ■

Brantford

▲ Tomah

L. Michigan

▲   •Mount Elgin
Mount
Pleasant

■ Flandreau

L. Erie

■ Nebraska

Sac & Fox ▲

Carlisle ▲

ATLANTIC
OCEAN

▲ Genoa

▲ Kickapoo
■ Haskell Indian
Nations University

Chilocco
Ponca ▲
▲ ▲ Seneca
Pawnee ▲ ▲ Osage
Otoe   ▲ Sequoyah

Eastern Cherokee ▲

Choctaw Central •

■   Present-day schools (U.S.)
▲   Former schools (U.S.)
•   Present or former schools (Canada)

Gulf of Mexico

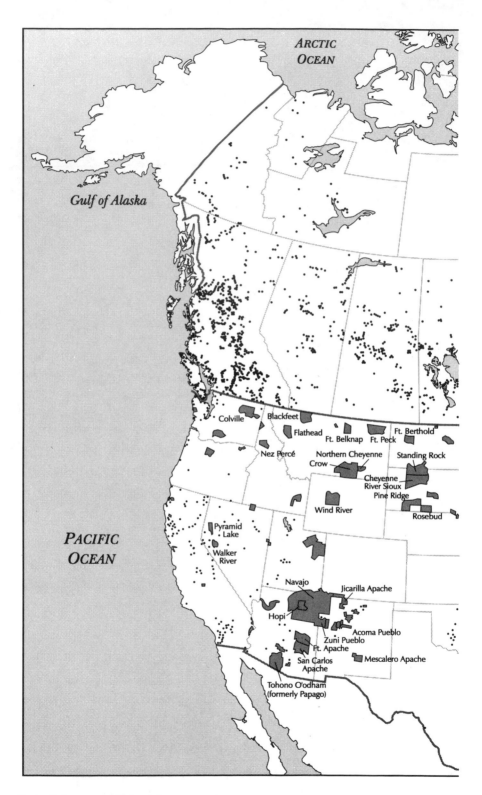

ARCTIC
OCEAN

Gulf of Alaska

PACIFIC
OCEAN

Colville   Blackfeet
        Flathead   Ft. Berthold
            Ft. Belknap   Ft. Peck
Nez Percé   Standing Rock
        Northern Cheyenne
Crow   Cheyenne
                         River Sioux
                          Pine Ridge
        Wind River
                              Rosebud

Pyramid
Lake

Walker
River

        Navajo   Jicarilla Apache

Hopi   Acoma Pueblo
                    Zuni Pueblo
                    Ft. Apache   Mescalero Apache
San Carlos
Apache

Tohono O'odham
(formerly Papago)

Present-day reservations and reserves

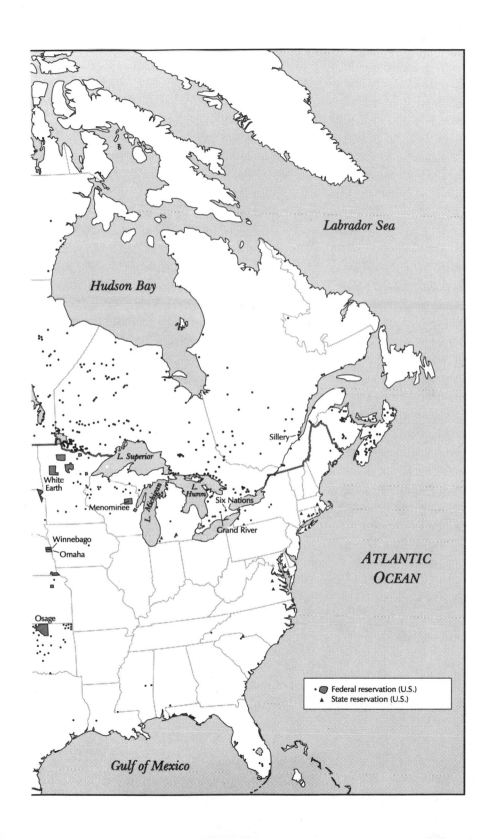

Labrador Sea

Hudson Bay

L. Superior

Sillery

White
Earth

L. Huron

Menominee

L. Michigan

Six Nations

Grand River

Winnebago

Omaha

ATLANTIC
OCEAN

Osage

• ⬟ Federal reservation (U.S.)
▲ State reservation (U.S.)

Gulf of Mexico

INDIANS IN
THE UNITED STATES
AND CANADA

1 Indians Meet the Spanish, French, and Dutch, 1513–1701

 THEIR ANCESTORS MIGRATED east from Siberia into Alaska and then south into the rest of North America some twelve thousand to fourteen thousand or more years before any Europeans "discovered" the continent at the end of the fifteenth century. During those millennia the people now known as Indians developed hundreds of societies with differing languages, social practices, and adaptations to their local environments. In eastern Canada the Laurentian Iroquoians supplemented their gardening with hunting and fishing near their Saint Lawrence Valley towns. Their Algonquian neighbors hunted and gathered along the north shores of the great river while the populous agricultural Hurons lived to the West. South in Florida and along the Gulf Coast much larger Indian societies would encounter the Spanish early in the sixteenth century. Agricultural people such as the Coosa, Apalachee, and Natchez had developed large and complex societies based on rich soil, plenty of rainfall, and a mild climate. Farther west beyond the plains a variety of smaller groups inhabited the semiarid and arid part of the Southwest, where Zuni, Hopi, and other pueblo dwellers all had well-established permanent settlements.[1] Wherever and however these people lived in 1500, they could not escape some contact with the Europeans who probed the continent repeatedly.

The entire native world differed drastically from that of the Europeans. There were no empires or kingdoms and probably only a few loose confederacies with which to deal. Even most groups now recognized as tribes or nations developed those identities after 1500 and often as a result of contact with the invaders.

Usually Indians lived in village societies with only limited cultural ties to people who used their language and who shared broad social practices. The Christian view of nature placed humans outside and above it. Resources existed for humanity's benefit. God ruled from beyond the earth. While Indian groups held many differing ideas and practices, they shared a more reverent approach to nature. Animals, trees, and other living things as well as the sun, moon, and sky all possessed spiritual powers recognized as important for day-to-day actions and for help in making decisions. A shaman or spiritual leader helped interpret these forces and conducted needed ceremonies to keep people healthy and their lives in balance with the other forces of nature.

Most Indian groups lacked the formal hierarchy Europeans took for granted. Civil chiefs, usually older men, made local decisions after often lengthy discussion brought consensus. There were no elections, and if some villagers rejected their leaders' decisions they could always leave the community. Social rather than governmental pressure brought acceptance and obedience to the agreed-upon behaviors in the village. During times of crisis war chiefs directed village affairs. Women played only a modest role in public affairs, focusing most of their efforts on crucial needs such as food production, clothing, and shelter. Children learned necessary skills from a variety of adults in the village. Shaming and ridicule rather than corporal punishment enforced discipline. Although local economies varied, most included some combination of agriculture, hunting, and fishing as well as gathering and trade. Frequent sharing and the expectation that good leaders helped those in need limited wide extremes of wealth. In fact, among some groups people considered those who gave away much of their goods as successful.

Clearly, with at least six hundred different groups on the scene in 1500, generalizations are difficult at best. Yet it is clear that Indian life differed widely from that of the incoming Europeans. Technological differences make this point most vividly. Some coastal groups used large, well-constructed boats, but they rarely ventured beyond sight of land. Europeans ships, however, served as miniature movable communities. They carried the goods needed to keep people alive for weeks, even months at times. Metal implements differentiated Old and New World societies too. Iron, steel, brass, and copper implements usually worked better and lasted longer than the Indian implements of wood, bone, or stone. Gunpowder, metal weapons, and body armor often gave the newcomers an immediate military advantage over Indian arrows, war clubs, and wooden shields. Having domesticated animals allowed the Spanish in particular to march hundreds of miles or more with their own mobile food supply. True,

Indian hunters knew their environment well and proved to be exceptionally good providers, but hunting involved a high degree of chance when contrasted to herding tame animals. Having access to horses and dogs also helped the Europeans gain military victory when they might not otherwise have done so. Written records allowed them to record, and perhaps to alter, agreements made with local Indian leaders.[2]

Like the native groups, the Europeans differed among themselves. Yet they shared many basic ideas and practices too. All of them lived during an era of growing nationalism, continuing religious quarrels, and bitter economic competition. Highly ethnocentric, they saw themselves and their institutions as the pinnacle of civilization. All four of the early colonizing powers—Spain, France, Holland, and England—had experienced bitter, protracted religious wars and turmoil. Each seemed to consider itself as clearly superior to its European neighbors and certainly more "civilized" than the native peoples of North America. Whether the result of religious nationalism as in Spain, a quest for trade and markets as for the Dutch and French, or the bumbling and halfhearted efforts that characterized English actions, all four powers saw exploration and colony founding as important for national self-esteem and power.

Attitudes of superiority, whether the result of Spanish success against the Moors or English victories in Ireland, crossed the Atlantic with the Europeans. Christianity, usually a particularly chauvinist brand of it, stood out in stark contrast to the religious ideas and practices of the Indians. Their accumulated knowledge of science, geography, and technology all added to European feelings that God really was on their side. Despite repeated early failures and disasters, the invaders rarely seem to have questioned that their destiny might not include grabbing large chunks of the continent and subduing the resident peoples they encountered. They came for God, glory, adventure, wealth, fame, or perhaps mere opportunity to escape difficult lives at home. Whatever their reasons, when they arrived in North America during the sixteenth or seventeenth centuries they encountered a world foreign to their experience—a place with vast resources, many opportunities, and strange, unknown peoples, who, in some cases, presented the most difficult challenges of all.

The Spanish opened the story with the 1513 expedition of Juan Ponce de Léon from Puerto Rico to Florida. Seeking riches, slaves, or perhaps the legendary "fountain of youth," he found none of them. Instead, in 1521, on his second trip to Florida, an Indian arrow gave him a mortal wound. Other wealth seekers followed, often seizing native people and carrying them off into slavery in the Caribbean. Spanish ships ranged north up the eastern coast at least as far as

Chesapeake Bay, and west along the Gulf Coast as far as Texas. Everywhere they went these early explorers brought misery and destruction to the Indians they met. Cabeza de Vaca offers the only exception to this dismal record, and then only because he lacked the power to abuse his hosts. At least in the Southeast, news of the kidnapping, rape, robbery, and warfare the Europeans brought spread quickly, and by the middle of the sixteenth century many Indians either fled or resisted Spanish incursions.[3]

While the Spaniards got to North America first, Jacques Cartier's explorations in the Saint Lawrence Valley of eastern Canada preceded their major land expeditions farther to the south. The Frenchman avoided much of the Spaniards' open brutality and greed, but his dealings with the northern tribes barely remained peaceable. By the time he got to eastern Canada the tribal peoples there had opened informal trading with the European fishing vessels along the coast. Despite these early contacts, Cartier knew little about the native peoples when he crossed the Atlantic, as his early actions toward them demonstrate.

In early July 1534, while he sailed in the Gulf of Saint Lawrence, Indian canoes approached his ship for trade. When efforts to wave the unwelcome visitors away failed, the Frenchman ordered the ship's cannons fired in an effort to frighten them. When the Indians continued their approach, the sailors "shot off two fire-lances which scattered among them and frightened them so much that they began to paddle off."[4] Once Cartier realized that the Indians came to trade he allowed some Montagnais to board the "vessels as freely as if they had been Frenchmen." By late July 1534 the Frenchman had met a large number of Indians who had descended the Saint Lawrence to fish for mackerel. These people happily accepted the beads, combs, and small knives that Cartier's people handed out. They had little to trade but welcomed the manufactured goods and told Cartier of settlements and possible riches far up the Saint Lawrence Valley. Instead of showing gratitude for that information, the explorer kidnapped two sons of Donnacona, chief of Stadacona, a village near present-day Quebec City.[5]

Although Cartier's kidnapping damaged relations with the Indians, his captives proved useful back in France, where they told stories of rich settlements and kingdoms in the Canadian interior. These tales brought increased support for continuing exploration as the explorer had hoped. In 1535 Cartier led a squadron of three ships up the Saint Lawrence to Stadacona. There he made a winter camp and announced his intention to proceed farther upriver despite the obvious reluctance of his Iroquoian neighbors. Ignorant of local Indian practices, he failed to ask permission of nearby villagers before setting up his camp and ignored the need to meet with Chief Donnacona and to make at least a ceremonial alliance with him. His actions angered the villagers who viewed French actions as discourteous and threatening to their economic well-being.[6]

Unaware that by custom his hosts claimed the right to control who might ascend the river or to collect tolls from those who did, he led his party to a larger Indian settlement called Hochelaga near present-day Montreal. There the villagers welcomed the French happily as Cartier handed out small presents. Despite the Hochelagans' warm reception, the explorer hesitated. Because his base camp at Stadacona lay closer to the Atlantic, he returned downstream that same day. At Donnacona's village the French experienced a difficult winter. The chief's sons had warned their father not to trust the visitors, while the French grew increasingly suspicious of the Indians. By midwinter Cartier had established a policy of noncontact with the Indians. His worst fears seemed to come true when scurvy broke out among his men by midwinter, but when the Indians learned of the whites' difficulty they taught them how to make a medicinal tea from white cedar bark and conifer needles to cure that disease. In addition, the Indians traded food to the French for metal goods, chiefly knives and awls. As the winter ended, the treacherous Cartier kidnapped Donnacona, his sons, and several other Indians and took them back to France, where all but one of the captives died.[7] This action antagonized the villagers without gaining any particular advantage for the explorers.

In France Chief Donnacona's descriptions of rich kingdoms of the interior convinced French officials to launch another expedition to North America. This time they planned to establish a resident colony under the command of Jean-François de La Rocque, sieur de Roberval, with Cartier serving as pilot for the expedition. In May 1541 Cartier set out with several hundred colonists. Once at the destination he set up his camp at Cap Rouge, a short distance upstream from Stadacona. After two bad experiences with the French, the Indians greeted the invaders sullenly. When Cartier claimed that the chief and the other villagers had decided to remain in France rather than admitting that they had died, the Indians said little but clearly disbelieved his story. Relations between Indians and French deteriorated quickly, and during the 1541–42 winter the Stadaconans and their tribal neighbors raided his camp repeatedly. Later evidence suggests that the villagers may have killed as many as thirty-five of the French that winter. In the spring of 1542, after telling Roberval that the Indian threat made successful settlement unlikely, Cartier led the survivors back to France. Undeterred, Roberval brought still more would-be settlers up the Saint Lawrence. Scurvy and starvation defeated this effort, too, and in 1543 the French returned home, abandoning settlement in North America for more than sixty years.[8]

These first tentative French efforts at exploration and trade brought few positive results other than laying a firm basis for that nation's later imperial claims to a part of North America. The Iroquoians' attitudes toward the Europeans ranged from cautious welcome, a willingness to trade, and some efforts to help the newcomers to misunderstanding, suspicion, and open hostility. The kidnappings complicated relations between the invaders and the local population. Indians objected when the Europeans ignored or broke the local economic and diplomatic customs to push into the interior. Cartier's failure to get Indian permission to locate settlements near existing Indian villages did nothing to endear the French to the Indians either, but at least in those cases the intruders could plead ignorance. When Cartier failed to find usable water routes to the west or to open a profitable trade, these early explorations proved unproductive. With high costs in both men and goods and no immediate economic return in view, the French government withdrew its support without learning much from these experiences. By the time the French returned to the Saint Lawrence region sixty years later, the descendants of the resident villagers had left the area, so even the Indians retained little knowledge of these matters.

SPANISH FORAYS IN THE SOUTH AND WEST

Like the French, Spanish exploration came under the direct oversight of the royal government. Yet because the Crown begrudged spending large sums for New World ventures, it contracted with *adelantados* or what the English would call proprietors to direct specific actions in America. These men expected to gain wealth, power, and perhaps public offices if they succeeded. So when they set out to enrich themselves, spread Christianity, and bring new regions under Spanish control, their efforts resembled the goals of their European competitors.

A few years after Ponce de Léon's death in 1521, the Spanish renewed their interest in North America, their effort coming at the same time that the French entered the Saint Lawrence Valley. After several small probing actions along the east coast of Florida, in the summer of 1539 Hernando de Soto brought a force of some six hundred men to Tampa Bay. From there he began a four-year march of attempted conquest and destruction as his men crisscrossed parts of the Southeast. That region was one of thickly settled villages belonging to a variety of chiefdoms. At each stop de Soto enslaved enough people to keep his force supplied with laborers. As word of Spanish atrocities spread, most of the villagers in his path fled or resisted. Although his men enjoyed superior weaponry and body armor, as well as having horses and dogs to help, Indian attacks gradually weakened the invaders. In May 1542, while on the lower Mississippi River, de Soto died. His faltering expedition struggled back to the Gulf of Mexico and from there continued south to Mexico.[9]

While de Soto and his men butchered villagers in the Southeast, reports of Indian wealth in the southwestern deserts reached Mexico City. There, in 1538, Viceroy Antonio de Mendoza sent a small party led by the Franciscan Fray Marcos de Niza north to investigate. A year later the priest returned with tales of Cibola and other rich Indian cities. Soon the viceroy appointed Francisco Vasquez de Coronado to lead an expedition north. He, in turn, gathered a well-equipped force of at least three hundred Spaniards and one thousand Indians. In 1540 the party began its trek into what is now the United States.

To their dismay, they learned that Fray Marcos was either a liar or deluded. There was no truth to his stories of large cities with easy riches to be found. Nevertheless, optimism and greed persuaded Coronado to continue. First he captured the Zuni village that Fray Marcos had called Cibola and used it as his headquarters. From there he sent out reconnaissance parties. Then he moved the main force east and camped near present-day Albuquerque. During the 1540–41 winter the nearby pueblo peoples fought with Coronado's men repeatedly, as the invaders destroyed at least a dozen villages and forced hundreds of survivors to flee. In early 1541 Coronado marched east seeking the land of Quivira. After crossing parts of Texas and Oklahoma, the tired explorers halted in central Kansas not more than three hundred miles from where de Soto's men, then in Arkansas and having found nothing they recognized as wealth, were preparing to turn back. Later that year Coronado was injured and decided to return to Mexico City. In 1542 he led his weary followers back south. They returned with plenty of geographic information but little booty.[10]

That same year, 1542, Juan Rodriguez Cabrillo commanded a small fleet of three ships while exploring the California coast. His voyage continued Spanish efforts in the Pacific begun in 1513 when Balboa first sighted that ocean. For several decades authorities in Mexico had sent mariners north, but Cabrillo, a veteran warrior, was the first to get as far as California. By September the ships landed at present-day San Diego, where the explorers met Indians bearing news of Coronado's actions farther east. After surviving an Indian attack his first night ashore, Cabrillo met peaceably with the Ipai people the next day. Then he headed north to Catalina Island, where the sailors spent the winter. There, in

January 1543, he died from an injury. His chief pilot continued the voyage north to southern Oregon, but dwindling supplies and heavy seas persuaded him to return to Mexico.[11]

These three expeditions constituted only the most spectacular Spanish actions in what is now the United States. Other explorers, clerics, and wealth seekers continued to probe the land. In doing so they brought misery, disease, and destruction to many of the Indian peoples they met. At the same time they gathered much information about the land and its resources as well as bringing back stories, legends, lies, and incorrect data about the places they had visited. Yet throughout the first half of the sixteenth century they established little permanent presence north of Mexico. Spanish diplomats and cartographers might color vast parts of the map their national color, but such actions represented mostly wishful thinking. For native people in the affected regions Spanish knowledge and claims meant little at the time. As they pillaged the countryside, however, the invaders brought fatal diseases such as malaria and smallpox as well as a host of other illnesses. These, far more than Spanish arms or destruction, brought disaster to the Indians.

Several decades later Spain renewed its efforts to colonize Florida and other parts of the Atlantic Coast. Responding in part to threats to their Caribbean shipping posed by English and French raiders as well as the continuing search for wealth, and a water route to Asia, in 1565 the government acted. It authorized Pedro Menendez de Avilés to direct settlement in Florida and sent him with over one thousand men to accomplish that objective. Once there he built a line of forts stretching from near present-day Miami north to what is now South Carolina. He also sent subordinates to establish other forts and settlements in the Southeast. For several years soldiers crossed Florida, meeting Indians, seeking wealth, and learning about the land.

Avilés strove to accomplish his goals without antagonizing the villagers, going so far as to marry the sister of one of the chiefs. Still, difficulties between the Spanish and their Indian neighbors arose repeatedly. Hungry soldiers seized food and abused native women. Before long several of the larger tribes, having come to view the invaders as a threat, began raiding smaller settlements. In 1568 one tribe helped French raiders sack Fort San Mateo. At that point the Spanish leaders asked for permission to launch a "war of fire and blood" in which "those taken alive shall be sold as slaves" in the island colonies of the Caribbean.[12] This request illustrates the Spaniards' continuing willingness to destroy or enslave their enemies, whether Moors in Spain, other Europeans in competing colonies, or Indians. No such war took place. Instead, further skirmishing with the Indians and British raids along the coast reduced the Spanish hold on Florida to Saint Augustine and a few tiny missions by the end of the century.

While secular leaders spoke of destroying Indians, Jesuit missionaries labored to bring Christianity and Spanish practices to several Florida groups. Despite their early optimism, within a few years their mission plans lay in ruins. At first the missionaries gave food to the large numbers of children who listened to their preaching. When the food supply ended, however, so did the children's attention. Next, the Jesuits mocked the ideas of the village shamans, angering their hosts repeatedly. By the late 1560s the Indians came to ignore or oppose the missionaries' efforts. In fact, they attacked the settlements repeatedly hoping to destroy their unwanted neighbors. At the same time European epidemics swept through the Florida tribes as new pathogens struck down large numbers of Indians. With officials at home busy with other matters, affairs in Florida got little attention, and by the end of the decade Spanish efforts faced collapse.[13]

Three decades later, would-be Spanish settlers moved north along the Rio Grande in present-day New Mexico. Led by Juan de Oñate, this effort proved more successful and permanent than its predecessors. The settlers proceeded up the river valley, stopping to meet Pueblo leaders just north of Albuquerque. Continuing beyond Santa Fe they took over an Indian village, renamed it San Juan, and used this as their headquarters for the next ten years. Oñate's settlement concluded several decades of interest in New Mexico by both church and government officials. His force of some five hundred people, including priests, women, and children, laid the foundation for the continuing Spanish presence in New Mexico during the seventeenth century.

Yet these pioneers clung to their precarious base only with difficulty. Almost immediately troubles with the Indians erupted. During the first winter the hungry Spaniards forced them to provide food and clothing. Some men abused Indian women. In retaliation Acoma Pueblo warriors killed eleven of the soldiers. Oñate demanded their surrender, and when the Indians refused, his tiny force of seventy-two men scaled the mesa. In three days of heavy fighting the soldiers killed some eight hundred men, women, and children, taking the rest of the people captive. When the fighting ended the victors cut off one foot of each adult male, enslaved those between the ages of twelve and twenty-five, and turned the children over to the priests for instruction. These brutal acts broke immediate Indian resistance but did nothing to improve conditions for either whites or Indians. The Spanish settlement grew slowly as poverty, isolation, and continued danger from the tribes inhibited further immigration. Thus after nearly a century of efforts in the southern regions of the present-day United States, the Spanish hold on the region was weak at best.[14]

THE RISE OF THE SAINT LAWRENCE FUR TRADE

Far to the northeast the French returned to North America, as fishermen and would-be fur traders frequented the coast of what is now Maritime Canada and penetrated the lower Saint Lawrence River Valley. There, by the 1580s, an informal trade developed when each summer the Algonquian people of the region gathered to fish and enjoy the pleasant weather along the great river. The hunters brought their surplus furs and hides, and by 1600, or perhaps slightly earlier, an annual fur trade had developed. As the profits rose, professional fur traders supplanted the fishermen, but the Indians grew more skilled in the trade too. Hundreds of them gathered at Tadoussac, near the mouth of the Saguenay River, refusing to barter until several French ships had arrived so that they could play one group of traders against the others to get the best prices for their furs.[15]

Seeking to establish a recognized French presence there, King Henry IV tried to encourage colonization and settlement through grants to successful merchants. These men differed from their Spanish competitors. They appear not to have seen themselves as instruments of national expansion or Christian evangelization. Because they saw their actions in financial terms they rarely lived up to their commitments to the government. As a result, the French succeeded through this mechanism, but just barely. In 1603 Henry IV granted a ten-year trade monopoly to Pierre du Guast, sieur de Monts, and appointed him a vice admiral and lieutenant governor of New France. In return he expected de Monts to transport and support some sixty French settlers who were to provide the basis for the first permanent French settlement in North America.[16] From the start nobody tried to enforce that part of the agreement. As a result, the settlements lacked the coercive power of the Spanish because New France had too few settlers to impose its demands on the Indians.

Despite his knowledge and experience, the new admiral and his cartographer, Samuel de Champlain, chose to establish the outpost on the Atlantic Coast. After a disastrous first year the survivors moved in 1605 to what became Port Royal on the Bay of Fundy, but Acadia, as the region became known, presented few opportunities for major colonial development. Nevertheless, French settlement continued there even as authorities shifted some efforts to the Saint Lawrence Valley.[17] There they chose the fur trade as the economic base for the new settlements. In doing so the French became partners with and even dependents of the Indians because the native Canadians' environmental knowledge, hunting skills, and willingness to cooperate made them crucial. Not only did they provide the beaver and other pelts, but the tribal people greatly outnumbered the French. This made it relatively easy for the villagers to dictate both the terms and methods of the evolving trade.

Contrary to popular belief, the fur trade did not arise solely from European efforts. Often the Indians initiated it themselves. For generations tribal people had exchanged their surplus goods with others, and dealing with Europeans merely enlarged the number of trading partners they accepted. The agricultural bands bartered corn, tobacco, and other items for the fish, meat, hides, and furs their hunting neighbors offered. Luxury goods such as copper or wampum beads passed from one village to another as well. In this context the Indians saw the newcomers as just another group in their existing economic system.

At first the Europeans accepted furs and hides of all sorts, varying from the pelts of highly prized martin to the hides of larger animals such as deer, moose, and bear. After 1580, as the fashions in Europe changed, the beaver became central to the fur business. First the Indian hunters killed and skinned the animals. Then the village women scraped the flesh side of each pelt clean, trimmed each into a rectangular shape, and sewed them together into loose-fitting robes with the fur side worn in, next to the body. Their scraping and the natural oils from the wearers' bodies loosened the long outer hairs of the pelts, leaving the short inner hair for furriers to use in making a high-quality felt for beaver hats. Because the Saint Lawrence peoples had always hunted the beaver for its meat and fur, the new trade with Europeans at first disturbed their lives little. For the nearby agricultural tribes, however, the fur trade brought immediate changes. As the men spent more time away from the villages hunting, the women had to assume some of their domestic work. Also, the increasing numbers of pelts needing to be processed took the women away from their food production and child rearing. For both the hunters and farmers the trade brought a rapid shift from their traditional economic patterns to dependency on the Europeans for the prized trade goods. Whether they recognized this as a danger or not remains uncertain, but seeing the utility of metal tools, cooking utensils, weapons, and European fabrics, they exchanged furs and hides willingly for them.[18]

To the Indians furs were commonplace, while the whites' goods were not. So they gave furs, which had only a modest value to them, for cloth and metal items they considered valuable, usually thinking that they had benefited from the exchange. Often within just a few years the trade became central to tribal life. By the 1630s one of the missionaries reported that he could not keep from laughing at the Indians' wry perception of the trade. "In truth, my brother," one warrior told him, "the Beaver does everything to perfection. He makes for us kettles, axes, swords, knives, and gives us drink and food without the trouble of cultivating the ground."[19] Clearly by that time, at least along the Atlantic Coast, the trade had brought fundamental changes to Indian life.

It is impossible to overestimate the impact of the trade on the Indian world. Existing economic patterns and the diplomatic relationships they represented changed drastically during the first and second generations of trade with the French. Those Indians chosen as trade captains by the French, those who controlled trade routes, and band or village chiefs all gained wealth because of the gifts they got from the French during the pretrade ceremonies. This enhanced their status within the village because they now had more goods to share. Some people even relocated their villages and hunting territories in order to benefit more fully from the new trade. Several Huron bands joined the Huron Confederacy between 1580 and 1610 in order to have access to the trade.[20] The enlarging and strengthening of the Huron Confederacy is just one example of the impact enlarged commerce brought to the tribal world. The new political links among the Huron brought all of them into the ongoing hostilities with the Senecas, Onondagas, Oneidas, and Mohawks in present-day New York. As trade increased and men carried furs and European goods across the countryside, older localism eroded. Indians traveled far from home, met new people, and extended their diplomatic and exchange networks. While all of this affected village life, social customs, and local economies, often the changes came slowly, at a pace dictated by village customs and Indian desires.[21]

Each tribe or even village claimed the right to prohibit others from traveling through its territory or to levy a toll on those it allowed to pass. For example, as late as 1650, when a canoe brigade of Huron traders led by a Jesuit priest tried to force its way beyond an Algonquin village on the Ottawa River without paying a toll, the local chieftain objected. Enraged at the Hurons' breach of tribal custom, he ordered his warriors to hang the priest "from a tree by the arm-pits." Having shocked the Huron traders by mistreating the cleric, he told the unfortunate Frenchman "that the French were not the masters of his country; and that in it he alone was acknowledged as chief."[22] Such monopolies weakened gradually, but only after intense French pressure and with great Indian reluctance.

The Canadian tribes manipulated their relations with the Europeans in several ways. Far from acting as innocents in the trade, they controlled it through shrewd bargaining. Champlain reported that in 1611 the native traders refused to exchange their furs with the first ship that reached Tadoussac that year.

Instead, he complained that they "waited until several ships had arrived in order to get our wares more cheaply. Thus those people are mistaken who think that by coming first they can do better business; for the Indians are now too sharp and crafty."[23]

In addition to skillful bargaining, as early as 1610 the Canadian Indians forced the French to accept tribal customs. Huron leaders proved so central to successful trade that they demanded that all negotiations be conducted in their language. When they visited the French each summer, the two held an intricate ceremony that reaffirmed their diplomatic alliance. The chiefs made large gifts to the Europeans while giving lengthy speeches asking for high-quality goods and fair prices. When the Indians finished their speeches the French responded, complimenting their guests, thanking them for the rich presents, and offering them goods and food in return. Only after these elaborate rituals ended did any real barter take place. Even then, the Indians refused to haggle over prices. They demanded that the French accept their furs and give them the manufactured goods they wanted. The Indians understood the concept of profit, but for some decades they continued to look at the trade in their own customary terms—that is, as an exchange of gifts among friends rather than as bargaining among rivals.[24]

Because French dependence on the fur trade and their small population meant that they had little need for land, their situation was unlike that of the Spanish or the later English settlements to the south. Settlers from both those European powers posed a physical threat to the Indians and were active competitors for the land and its resources. On the other hand, having the Indians as allies and trading partners was central to French actions; thus, whatever misgivings the newcomers had, they worked closely with their tribal neighbors for economic success. While Indian wars racked New France repeatedly during the seventeenth century, usually the conflicts were not with their trading partners or close neighbors. Rather, they were with the Iroquois tribes of present-day New York and the Mesquakies of central Wisconsin, both of whom the French saw as threats to the fur trade. From the first the French realized that they needed to retain good relations with the Indians living north of the Saint Lawrence River, who had access to more and better furs than did the people south of that river. The Iroquois, who saw the French siding with their trade rivals and longtime enemies as well as threatening their diplomatic supremacy in the region, turned to raiding when other tactics failed. The causes for the Indian-French conflicts, then, usually varied widely from those of tribes who fought against the Spanish or the English during the seventeenth century.[25]

The first successful French settlement along the Saint Lawrence began in

1607, when word came from France that although de Monts had lost his fur trade monopoly along the coast, he had permission to establish a new post on the Saint Lawrence. Bypassing the oft-used trade center at Tadoussac, at the mouth of the Saguenay River, in July 1608 Champlain led a small group of French traders to the site of present-day Quebec City. It seems likely that the Montagnais, who controlled the Indian side of the fur trade farther downriver, agreed to let the whites pass through their region in exchange for getting more weapons and armed Frenchmen between themselves and the marauding bands of Iroquois warriors from the south and west. In any case, the Europeans built a rude outpost that became Quebec. It included "three connected barracks, eighteen feet by fifteen feet, a large storehouse, and a pigeon loft, all surrounded by a palisade with a cannon mounted at the corners and a fifteen-foot moat complete with drawbridge."[26] Each summer traders arrived to swell the small population, which usually remained under twenty men for most of the year. The residents tended a few small vegetable gardens but spent most of their time cutting firewood for the long winters, while remaining dependent on France for food, clothing, and trade goods.[27]

From the start Champlain and de Monts had considered how to ensure dependable cooperation from their trading partners. No sooner had the French begun erecting their stockade at Quebec than local Indians urged Champlain to prove the strength of his word by sending some of his men along on a raid against the Iroquois, and he appears to have agreed to do so. In early July 1609 the French leader and two companions joined a combined raiding party of Montagnais, Algonquins, and Hurons as it moved south. Near the southern tip of Lake Champlain they intercepted some two hundred Mohawks on their way north. To the delight of his tribal companions, Champlain and his men led a successful attack on the larger Mohawk force and dealt them a crushing defeat, killing nearly fifty men and taking another dozen captive. The next year the French and their Indian partners attacked the Mohawks again. This time they overran a fortified camp, killing or capturing most of the one hundred men there. These one-sided victories gave Champlain a distinct edge over his fur-trade rivals, described by the Indians as "women who wish only to make war on our beavers."[28]

Despite the poor quality of French weapons, they proved decisive in giving the northern tribes a temporary advantage over their longtime Iroquois enemies. In 1611 some of the Algonquins and the Hurons brought their furs to the Lachine Rapids for trade. For the next several years Champlain remained in France, but in 1615 he returned to find the Hurons organizing another raiding party and learned that they wanted him to accompany them one more time. He visited their country and, without realizing the ceremonial significance of his actions, concluded alliances with the village leaders. In early September the war party traveled south to attack the Senecas. Their siege of a large fortified village failed, and during the attack Champlain suffered a painful wound. On their return the Hurons insisted that Champlain recuperate at their villages during the next winter, and in 1616 several chiefs accompanied the explorer back to Quebec for further talks. These early attacks against the Iroquois were tied to Indian customs and served as retaliation against the targeted groups for earlier incidents. While these French actions did not begin any new wars, they enmeshed the Europeans in ongoing rivalries and conflicts.[29]

While the French may have enjoyed the strengthened ties with their trading partners because of their successful intervention against the Mohawks and Senecas, they probably wanted to trade with the Iroquois as well as with the Canadian Indians. Certainly the Mohawks sought to open trade with the French as well as with their Dutch neighbors in order to get more favorable prices from the Europeans. Both the French and the Mohawks, however, also had important reasons for avoiding such commerce. If they concluded peace, the tribes living north of the Saint Lawrence might want to trade in Albany rather than Quebec, thus threatening the near monopoly the French enjoyed in dealing with the northern groups. The Mohawks also feared peace. It would allow the northern tribes, having access to more and better furs, to deal with the Dutch, weakening the Mohawk position as middlemen. So both sides saw peace and cooperation as an ideal, but neither proved willing to take the risks that a true cessation of hostilities might bring. Throughout the seventeenth century the French traded with the Montagnais, Algonquins, and Hurons, while the Iroquois maintained their commercial relations with the Dutch and later the English. The two groups used each other as a potential threat to trade and stability while practicing almost continuous raiding for generations.[30]

The ongoing raids and wars that pitted the northern Indians and their French allies against the Five Nations of the Iroquois Confederacy had many causes. Just prior to French settlement along the Saint Lawrence, perhaps as late as 1600, the Mohawks had ousted some of the agricultural people who lived along that river. When Champlain agreed to aid his trading partners against the Iroquois he embroiled the colonists in a continuing conflict. Within only a few decades, however, the motivations for the raids shifted somewhat. Gradually the Hurons, Montagnais, and other Algonquians to the north increased their supplies of European goods. To the south the Susquehannocks and others acquired similar trade goods from the Dutch, Swedes, or English. The Iroquois tribes found themselves living between or near other Indian groups who seemed to be growing more powerful through hunting and trade with the whites.

Although the Iroquois also traded with the Dutch, their home country lacked a good supply of fur-bearing animals, and the pelts available to them lacked the quality their rivals to the north gathered. In addition, the New York tribes had sedentary, agricultural neighbors, preventing them from trading their surplus corn or other foodstuffs for meat, hides, or pelts. With little opportunity to hunt and little experience as traders, they saw their situation as deteriorating when compared to their tribal neighbors'. In any long-term competition their situation appeared bleak. So, to hold their own against their enemies, the Mohawks in particular decided to turn to raiding and robbery. If successful, this would obtain European goods or high-quality furs that could be traded to the whites.[31] That, in turn, would strengthen their power and influence among the nearby tribes.

Even though the Europeans helped them fight the Iroquois and provided coveted trade goods, the Indians in New France remained unimpressed by most things French. Because the groups living on the Atlantic had encountered the invaders the longest, they held the most negative ideas. To them, the bearded whites had ugly, doglike faces, but they came to accept this peculiarity. Soon they learned not to trust the traders and repeatedly defended themselves, telling the whites that "we are not thieves, like you."[32] These same people considered themselves braver and more intelligent than the French. Farther inland, groups such as the Huron reacted similarly. They assumed their own intellectual superiority, and as a result European technology brought little credit to its bearers. Rather, the Hurons assigned magical powers to the devices or to those who had them. To those missionaries who criticized their customs, the villagers pointed out the inconsistencies between what the priests taught and how the rest of the population acted. They disliked French food, rejected the whites' medical practices as far inferior to their own, and soon came to avoid the hospital at Quebec, calling it a house of death.[33]

Often, from the start, French imperial actions in North America differed from those of their European competitors. At least in Canada they did not demand valuable land as did the Spanish and English. While the Spanish sought to control all aspects of tribal life, the French hoped for peace and profits from the fur trade. When they located their trade center at Quebec, the invaders chose a region with virtually no permanent Indian settlements. Thus the tribal people had no reason to view the Europeans as competitors for the land. The few Indians who lived in their immediate vicinity carried out little if any agriculture. This meant that usually the French met the native groups primarily as missionaries or traders, and each of these enterprises required Indian cooperation. Obviously this differed from Spanish efforts to demand obedience and to extract wealth from them, from English demands for agricultural land, or from the heavy-handed actions of the Dutch.

For the Indians in each region these different approaches shaped their relations with the intruding Europeans too. Along the Saint Lawrence the Algonquins and Montagnais increased their traditional hunting of fur bearers and continued their gathering and fishing economies. From the French they enjoyed some fur trade benefits as well as some housing, food, and clothing if they accepted the whites' invitations to live at one of the Indian reserves. For sedentary, agricultural people such as the Hurons, the European invasion brought increased prosperity for a time and helped strengthen and enlarge their confederacy. These things occurred without any territorial loss because the French had little interest in land and their few small settlements remained tied to the Saint Lawrence, miles from the rich agricultural fields of the Hurons. As a result, the peoples of the region looked upon their French neighbors as allies who provided valuable markets for their furs and foodstuffs and who supplied them with manufactured goods that improved their standard of living.

For French purposes it was fortunate that so few Indians lived in their immediate vicinity, because the Europeans took nearly a half century to get more than a few hundred people to New France. In 1608 Champlain left twenty men to winter at Quebec, and by the next spring only eight had survived. The population at the outpost varied according to season and year, but for the decade 1618–28 it fluctuated between sixty and eighty-one people. In 1627 all of New France including both the Saint Lawrence settlement and Acadia on the Atlantic Coast included only 106 people. When Lewis and Thomas Kirke led English forces against Quebec in 1628–29, the defenders had little hope of victory. A relief expedition sent out by the French company brought some two hundred settlers in an attempt to run Kirke's blockade of the Saint Lawrence at Tadoussac, but these were captured. Left with a garrison of only seventy-five hungry people at Quebec in July 1629, Champlain surrendered the colony he had led for two decades.[34]

THE NEW NETHERLAND COLONY

While the French struggled for control of the Saint Lawrence Valley, the Dutch began their colonial settlements in present-day New York and New Jersey along the Hudson and Delaware Rivers. Their ships carried traders around the world, and after Henry Hudson explored the river that bears his name in New York, business followed quickly. At first individual traders visited Indian villages on the coastal islands as well as on the bays and estuaries that carried them beyond the shoreline. Hoping to profit by regulating the growing trade, the Dutch States-General chartered the Dutch West India Company, modeled on the highly successful East India Company then in operation. By 1624 the company brought settlers to the region, building Fort Orange near present-day Albany. From the start the Dutch came well prepared to do business in this new environment. They chose their locations with care, equipped the settlers and traders with the goods they needed, and urged careful diplomacy when dealing with the local Indians. They also appear to have recognized tribal landownership and repeatedly purchased land from the nearby tribes. One scholar suggests that they did this to give their own land claims validity when competing with other Europeans who claimed much of North America through prior exploration.[35]

Operating out of Fort Orange, Dutch traders joined the Algonquian Mahicans, who then dominated the upper Hudson River Valley in a profitable trade. In 1626, as Champlain had done earlier in New France, they joined their partners in a raid against the Mohawks. Instead of victory, however, the Dutch and their allies stumbled into a successful Mohawk ambush. After that the traders abandoned their partners, and the Iroquois swept the Mahicans from the region at least temporarily.[36] That brought the intruding Europeans to a policy of neutrality and a grudging peace and trade with the Mohawks. This commerce provided the Iroquoians with the firearms they used so successfully against the Hurons and the French some decades later. By the early 1630s the West India Company decided to expand the Dutch settlements, and it began transporting townspeople and farmers to what became New Netherland. This brought immediate pressures on the nearby Indians to sell ever more of their lands and provided accessible targets for Indian discontent.

During the 1640s the relationship between the Dutch and the nearby tribes shifted drastically. Because of their desire for European goods the tribal people hunted the local fur bearers to near extinction. At that point the Indians came to be seen as people who occupied valuable farmlands and as a threat to the growth and safety of the colony rather than as useful partners in a profitable trade. Still, the local tribes continued to produce the most and highest-quality wampum beads then used as trade currency and to make belts to record tribal history or signal diplomatic actions among the tribes. Frequently Dutch *bosch loopers*, unregulated traders living among Indians, robbed and cheated villages, causing tribal anger and retaliation against the Dutch. Such events spread fear among the Dutch pioneers who asked the authorities for protection or military action against the nearby Indians.

By the mid-1640s difficulties in the fur trade, continuing interracial violence, and Dutch high-handedness brought the situation to a boil, resulting in Governor Kieft's War. From the beginning of his administration Willem Kieft carried out anti-Indian actions. He encouraged settlers to take more land. As that happened, Dutch-owned cattle and pigs overran Indian fields, damaging or destroying the villagers' crops. If Indians dared to resist or retaliate, Kieft struck back rapidly. In 1642 Dutch forces marched through local villages to intimidate the inhabitants. In February 1643 the Pavonia Massacre of villagers occurred. Figures of the casualties and deaths vary, but clearly this was a major Indian defeat. For the next year Dutch and English soldiers joined forces to destroy Indian encampments on Long Island and as far north as Connecticut. By 1644 the Europeans had broken the morale of the local tribes and forced them to accept a negotiated peace.[37]

At the negotiations one tribal leader denounced the victorious Dutch. When the Dutch first came, he said, "you left your people here with their goods; we traded with them . . . and cherished them . . . we gave them our daughters for companions, who have borne children and many Indians have sprung from the Swannekens [Dutch], and now you villainously massacre your own blood."[38] Despite that complaint, the Indians signed the peace accord. Yet continuing rumors of war, incidents in which Indians or Europeans were hurt or even killed, and the expanding Dutch agricultural population all kept relations between the two groups in turmoil. This continued until the 1660s, when the English seized control of New Netherland. For example, in 1660 Governor Peter Stuyvesant ordered the local tribes to surrender some of their children as hostages. When the Esopus tribe refused, Stuyvesant had several hundred of those Indians seized, and when tribal leaders still refused to submit, the governor sent the prisoners into slavery, working on Caribbean plantations.[39]

At least as important as their near destruction of the neighboring tribes, Dutch trading and diplomatic relations with the Mohawks remained significant for generations. Having lost in their first military encounter with those Iroquoian people, the New Netherlanders found themselves depending heavily on the Mohawks for their continued trade successes. At the same time, the Europeans had to ask these same allies for help in dealing with several fractious tribes nearer to the coast, but they did this with great reluctance. The result was that the Dutch never could control the fur trade with their powerful partners. Unlike the French, who could and did dominate their trading system much of the time, the Dutch had less success unless they worked closely with the Mohawks. This meant that the Europeans provided the Indians with large numbers of weapons and a continuing supply of shot and powder.

In some ways Dutch actions resembled those of the English who settled parts of the Atlantic Coast at about the same time. They traded, farmed enough for the taking of Indian lands to become a major issue, and fought bitter and destructive wars against their tribal neighbors. In fact, Captain John Underhill, who led joint English-Dutch forces during the 1643–44 war, had led some of the Puritan force that destroyed the Pequots less than a decade earlier. Like the English, Dutch authorities expressed an interest in bringing Christianity to the Indians, but their actions never met the level of their talk. The businessmen might learn tribal languages out of necessity, but there is little evidence that Dutch clerics spent much time doing it as a means of achieving Indian conversions. As an economic enterprise the New Netherland colony appears to have profited heavily through the early fur trade, but by the time the English conquered it, high costs had discouraged the Europeans investors. The most significant results of the Dutch colonial actions were the long-standing alliance between the Mohawks and the traders at Albany, and the Europeans' willingness to provide arms and munitions to these Indians. After their 1664 conquest of the colony, the English moved quickly to enter the imperial and fur trade competition with the French to the north and west.

CATHOLIC MISSIONS IN NEW FRANCE AND NEW SPAIN

In 1632, while the formidable Mohawk trade developed, the French returned to New France. Once the French regained Quebec under the Treaty of Saint-Germain-en-Laye of 1632, Champlain hurried back to rebuild the town. This time working with the Company of New France, or the Hundred Associates, the outcome should have differed from what occurred earlier. Organized in 1627, the company had to wait until France had regained the region before it began operations. In return for title to all the land and a trade monopoly, its obligations included having to bring at least 200 colonists a year to New France, and by 1643 it was to have transported at least 4,300 people there. As had been the case with earlier monopolies based on the fur trade, the Company of New France fell far short of these expectations. Several reasons limited French migration to the colony. Transporting settlers across the Atlantic proved expensive, and the company benefited little from their presence at Quebec; in fact, colonists often disrupted the trade. Their technology limited land clearance to one or two acres per person each year, so often the settlers had to depend on the company for survival, and the danger from Iroquois attacks continued for much of the seventeenth century. As a result figures for 1640 reveal a population at Quebec of between 350 and 360 people, including 82 soldiers and priests and some 64 families.[40] Clearly, despite the new organization and support, peopling the Canadian settlements proved difficult at best.

While France tried to lure permanent settlers to North America, those already at Quebec struggled to create a workable society and to deal with their Indian neighbors. Champlain had repeatedly called for missionaries to bring Christianity, and the church had responded in 1615 by sending four Recollet friars. From the start in New France the authorities saw the Indians as subjects and partners rather than enemies. So at least in theory they made every effort to incorporate the tribal people into the colonial society. Indians were to be acculturated and then converted to Christianity, and the missionaries set out immediately to accomplish these goals. The friars recognized that as long as their charges subsisted through hunting, gathering, and fishing there was little chance to change their lives or to incorporate them into the society of the colony. Therefore, hoping to "endeavor to make them men before we go about to make them Christians," the missionaries sought to persuade the Montagnais to settle near existing French posts.[41]

Champlain wanted to send the missionaries to live among the agricultural villagers too, and the Huron leaders quickly accepted his proposal. Apparently thinking that this was a continuation of the exchange of young men that had begun with the French in 1609, the Indians hoped that having more Europeans living among them would strengthen the whites' willingness to protect the villages from possible attack. The undermanned Recollets, however, remained in the Indian country only long enough to suffer its hardships but not long enough to see any results from their work. In addition to having too few men for the assignment, these Franciscans considered the Canadian tribes to be too "primitive" for conversion. It is highly unlikely that they had any effective translators. As a result, they reported that Indian culture lacked such basic concepts as set religious tenets or any organized religious authority, and the idea that teachers or leaders might regulate individual actions, the friars claimed, was foreign to native thinking.[42]

These early missionaries had only a modest impact on the local tribes. They urged Indians who lived as hunters to become farmers, but few did. They strove unsuccessfully to move French settlers into the Indian villages and to replace native culture and languages with French ideas and language. Because they failed to understand the logic of accepting gifts to settle disputes among the villagers, they objected to tribal ideas about justice. The Recollets did succeed in getting a few Indian boys to live with them—again, apparently because of tribal ideas about the exchange of young men and boys as an act binding the two groups together—but they reported having baptized fewer than fifty Indians, and usually those only when the people were dying. Thus when the Jesuits took charge of the New France mission work, the Recollets seem to have had few objections to relinquishing that particular field.[43]

The first Jesuits arrived in 1625, and when Champlain led the French back to Quebec in May 1633 these missionaries returned with him. Led by Father Paul Le Jeune, they began their mission in earnest. From their initial meetings with the tribal people, these new clerics accepted the idea that the two races would eventually join and that the native people would become acculturated French subjects. Both Champlain and the early missionaries encouraged intermarriage of French and Indians to bring the two peoples together. French-style education for children and later adults offered another path toward the general French objective of incorporating the native people into the invaders' society.[44] Except for sporadic official encouragement of intermarriage, the French goals resembled those of the Spanish to the south. While their purposes resembled each other, these two colonizing powers used differing tactics. The French depended largely on persuasion, but the Spanish tended to use force. The basic reason for the difference was twofold and simple. The former lacked enough people to compel Indian obedience. Also, the French economic base rested firmly on the fur trade, and that enterprise needed Indian partners, not subjects.

Europeans of whatever stripe often began their acculturative work among the adults, only to retreat in dismay and failure. When that happened they turned to schools for the children, hoping through them to influence the adults. From the start missionaries and educators throughout North America complained about the negative influence family and village life had on the children, and repeatedly they sought to separate the students from their parents. In theory this should have worked because tribal custom at the time included exchanging children and young men with allies and trading partners to strengthen the ties between the two societies, but by the 1630–40 era the movement of children and young people had become a one-way street. As one Montagnais chief complained, "You are continually asking us for our children, and you do not give yours; I do not know any family among us which keeps a Frenchman with it."[45]

Despite such objections by parents and village leaders, some Indian children did attend the French schools, but never as many as the missionaries had expected. Father Le Jeune focused most of his educational program on a boarding school or seminary at Quebec. Opened in 1636, the seminary had only five boys as the first students. During the few years the school remained open the Hurons, Algonquins, and Montagnais all sent children, boys aged ten to fourteen. Often the boys became depressed, and some fled to escape Jesuit discipline or because of homesickness.[46] From the start little went as the Jesuits had anticipated. Costs far exceeded their support as the boys literally wore their clothing to shreds in a few weeks. Unused to regular meals or European foods, they ate far more than was good for them, and before long the missionaries switched them back to a Huron diet. The drastic change from village life also took its toll on the boys as colds, influenza, and other respiratory illnesses struck repeatedly. Within the first two years two of the best students had died. In 1638 several of the new recruits objected to their enforced French lifestyle, stole a canoe, loaded it with food, and fled. Almost in despair the missionaries shifted their efforts and tried to induce young men in their early twenties to attend the seminary, but this too failed, and in 1642 they closed the seminaries at Quebec.[47]

Indian girls did not escape the French educational net either. In 1636 Le Jeune reported that several Indian girls were living in French homes at Quebec. Three years later a contingent of Ursuline sisters arrived and began active work with Indian girls. They too reported an almost complete lack of success. Marie de l'Incarnation complained of how little impact the order's school had among the Indians. Describing the girls as "only birds of passage" who stayed at the school briefly, she noted that their "savage humour" could not tolerate sadness or depression, and if either happened their parents took them home, fearing that otherwise the girls would die. At other times the girls went off "by whim or caprice; they climb our palisades like squirrels, which is as high as a stone wall, and go to run in the woods."[48] By the 1640s the Jesuits realized that their educational approach and curriculum offered little attraction for the Indian children. In fact, their goal of changing Indian society and beliefs through the children rested on a false premise. They had hoped to bring about conversions to Christianity by having the children teach their elders, but in Indian communities education went from the adults to the children—not the opposite direction. It was highly unlikely that the parents would change because of what their children told them about the wonders of French education or religion.[49]

With this in mind the Jesuits shifted their focus from children and young people to mature adult males. The change did not come easily or without doubts, but the pleading of a fifty-year-old Huron man to be admitted to the seminary caught their attention. Replying to their disparaging comments about his learning abilities, the Indian chided the missionaries for preferring children to adults. "Young people are not listened to in our country," he told them. "But men speak—they have solid understanding, and what they say is believed."[50] Recognizing the wisdom of this assertion, the Jesuits decided to drop their efforts with Indian boys and young men, so within the next few years their seminary shifted to teaching French children. The missionaries then agreed to teach individual adult Indians and to concentrate their work on respected leaders or more prominent males in the villages.

At the same time, the Jesuits decided to try other approaches to Indian conversion. In 1637 they had concluded that the hunting tribes could not survive and certainly could not be converted to Christianity unless they ended their nomadic wandering. Consequently, in 1637 the Jesuits founded what later became known as the first Indian reserve in Canada at Sillery, near Quebec. By this time they also had come to reject their earlier efforts to acculturate the Indians by replacing all aspects of their tribal culture. Based on ideas from their successful experiences in Asia, they decided to change only the things in tribal society that they considered to be anti-Christian, rather than trying to disrupt all aspects of Indian custom. By calling for changes in only limited areas of the tribal people's lives they hoped to find a basis for agreement between their wishes and Indian standards of morality. To do this they decided that it was better to segregate their Indian charges from the rest of the French and Indian population whenever possible.[51] Clearly at this point in their work the missionaries had begun to recognize the difficulties of achieving basic cultural changes.

The Jesuits named the Indian settlement for Noël Brûlart de Sillery, a member of the Company of the Hundred Associates, who donated money for it. In 1637 Sillery paid for twenty workmen to build a chapel and to prepare the fields for use by Indian farmers. The settlement began modestly in 1638 with just two Algonquin families, about twenty people, and a single one-room house. Yet that same year the missionaries reported having baptized thirty-two Indian converts, and another fifty-six the following year. Apparently the offer of housing, food, and clothing sounded good to the Montagnais of the region. By the late 1630s the nearby wildlife had been overhunted and the tribal people faced the dismal alternatives of migration or starvation. The price they had to pay to live at the new settlement was simple—accept Christianity and close Jesuit supervision.[52]

Like Spanish missions and the later "Praying Towns" of Massachusetts, the Sillery reserve grew out of the partial collapse of the native economy and the intruding whites' determination to segregate their Indian charges from the rest of the colonial society. Exactly why the tribal people accepted the French offer to settle at the mission is not clear. Few wanted to become farmers, and many continued their seminomadic existence at least part of each year. The Jesuits' motivation, however, was clear—they hoped that the reserve would keep their charges in one place long enough for Christianity to take hold. They also wanted to limit further contact with the French settlers and fur traders. Living in the Jesuit-dominated settlement offered no protection from the epidemics then sweeping through the Indian villages of New France, however, and in 1639 smallpox ravaged the Sillery dwellers. After the epidemic abated, the missionaries worked to rebuild the settlement. They recruited more Indians, and in 1641 the Ursulines from Quebec built a hospital at the reserve.[53]

Although the Jesuit-sponsored reserve survived the smallpox epidemic, other problems racked the community. Determined to control the life and society of the settlement, the missionaries fostered Christian domination in the village. While most of the Indians looked at Sillery more as a convenient camp and as a place to get food, Le Jeune and his associates held an election—certainly nothing that the reserve dwellers had ever experienced—and the Jesuits counted the votes. They ruled that the Christian group had won and established a local government at the village under Christian control. In their newfound zeal the converts proposed to exclude all non-Christian Indians from the settlement, but this did not occur. Instead, continuing disputes racked the village for the next several years. Nevertheless, by 1645 the mission register listed 167 Christian Indians. The next year the missionaries reported that the villagers were trying to farm, but a shortage of money for seeds and tools limited the results. Then, news of Iroquois raids that had destroyed the Huron villages to the west frightened the Montagnais and they fled, so that by 1649 only two Frenchmen remained at Sillery.[54]

In 1651 the Company of New France granted the seigneury of Sillery and fishing rights on the Saint Lawrence nearby to the Indians, under the direction of the Jesuits. The significant thing about this grant was that, while it gave a seigneurial title for the land to the native people who moved there, the missionaries retained actual control. As was often the case in both Canada and the United States, the Indians were not allowed to either sell or give away the land. The Jesuits could allow outsiders to fish or hunt in the area, but the real estate belonged to their charges. Repeated bouts of smallpox and continuing Iroquois raids kept most of the Montagnais from settling there. With few patients, the hospital closed and moved to Quebec in 1647, and nine years later fire destroyed the chapel and mission house. The Jesuits rebuilt the chapel in 1660 but in that same year began granting some of the land to white settlers. By the end of that decade the missionaries reported no further baptisms, and although the mission still cared for refugee groups, it never achieved its potential.[55]

In addition to their reserve at Sillery the Jesuits traveled into the Huron country, or Huronia, during the 1620s to begin their labors there. The twenty thousand or so Hurons lived in sedentary villages in southwestern Ontario between Lake Simcoe and Georgian Bay. There they produced annual surpluses of corn, which they used as the basis for a highly successful and wide-ranging trade with the tribes to the north and west. They moved quickly and by 1616 served as middlemen in the French fur trade. Between 1616 and 1629 the Hurons provided about two-thirds of the beaver pelts brought into the French posts on the Saint Lawrence, and they so dominated the trade that Huron became the accepted business language at the time. During the 1620s a few Jesuits lived among the Hurons briefly trying to learn their language, but they played an insignificant role there until 1632, when the French regained the Saint Lawrence. The Jesuits came back as well, and when the Huron traders arrived in Quebec during the summer of 1633 Champlain insisted that the Indians escort the missionaries to their home villages as a price of continuing their fur trade with the French. Huron leaders avoided taking any of the priests home with them that summer, but in 1634 priests and some workmen arrived in Huronia.[56]

The reintroduction of Jesuits into Huronia in 1634 opened a brief but vigorous period of missionary work there. That same year the clerics founded the mission of Saint Joseph, and within the next few years they expanded their efforts throughout the Huron country slowly. For most of the 1630s only a handful of missionaries lived among the villagers, and even then they stayed despite the Indians' bitter objections. Native shamans saw the Jesuits as rivals and blamed the epidemics of measles in 1634, influenza in 1636, and smallpox in 1639 on the intruders, calling them witches. Despite this opposition, the priests increased their presence in Huronia and in 1639 founded the Sainte Marie mission. This ambitious work included the usual chapel and housing for the missionaries, but they also built a hospital, mill, barns, and stables for livestock and erected a log-and-stone stockade around the buildings. At its height the Sainte Marie mission population numbered sixty-six people, including the priests, lay assistants, a surgeon, an apothecary, artisans, and servants. From this outpost the French clerics launched a full-scale assault on Huron life and society.[57]

During the epidemics nearly half of the Hurons died, and because the missionaries frequently baptized the dying, village shamans denounced the priests for killing Indians. This resentment, coupled with anger at having to be hosts for the "black robes" during the 1640s, did nothing to ease Jesuit-Huron relations.

The clerics' insistence upon European and Christian domination of the society fractured village life. Those native fur traders who accepted baptism saw that act as strengthening their kinship relations with the French, and some sought out this ceremony to aid their standing in the fur trade. Nonbaptized traders objected to what they considered unfair treatment when they reached Quebec. Traditional leaders and their supporters objected bitterly to Jesuit efforts to take control of their villages. Hostile headmen publicly denounced the missionaries and urged their followers to avoid meetings sponsored by the Jesuits. The most graphic example of Huron anger over clerical meddling occurred in late 1638 while the villagers tortured an Iroquois captive to death. After the Jesuits had baptized the victim, the village leaders had holes burned through his hands and feet to mock the crucifixion story, and when they killed the captive they hacked off one of his hands and threw it into the missionaries' cabin.[58]

Examples of Huron-Jesuit conflict abound for the 1635–45 era, but all indicate that the village elders recognized clearly what the French clerics were doing, and that they wanted no part in having their society torn apart by these strangers. In 1635 Huron leaders insisted that the missionaries remove the cross from atop their mission house because they believed that it had caused a crippling drought that summer. The following year, when an epidemic swept through one village the Jesuits displayed life-sized images of Jesus and the Virgin Mary, and Indian shamans blamed the sickness and deaths on the images. Reacting in fear because of the medical disaster, they attacked the clerics as witches and sorcerers.[59]

By 1640 the damage had been done. One half of the Hurons had died from epidemic disease. With the Indian society weakened badly, the Europeans tried to punish them for their opposition to the priests, an event one scholar calls "a turning point in French-Huron relations." Before this the Europeans privately were ready to ignore the Jesuit deaths at the hands of the Indians, but from 1640 on they saw the weakened Hurons as economically dependent on the fur trade and therefore on them. Taking advantage of this newfound confidence, the Jesuits proceeded to meddle openly in village affairs as well as to cooperate with the colonial authorities, who gave special trading preferences to baptized Huron traders at the expense of their traditional non-Christian neighbors. Then in 1641 they decided to reward the converts further by limiting the sale or distribution of firearms only to them. This action deprived most Huron warriors of muskets during the Iroquois wars that soon followed. In less than a decade this shortsighted policy helped bring about the total destruction of the Huron Confederacy and the Indian-French fur trade as it had developed in the preceding four decades, but at the time the colonial authorities saw their limit on muskets as yet another way to dominate the tribal people.[60]

During the 1640s the Huron-Jesuit friction increased steadily so that by 1645 an active anti-French rather than merely antimissionary group developed. Seeing Christianity as a threat to traditional Huron society, village leaders tied it to their trading alliance with the French. Thus, to survive some chiefs decided that they had to end their trading relationship with the French and even turned to the Iroquois as possible trade partners. This ploy failed, and the Jesuits continued making inroads within the villages. By 1648 as many as 15 percent of the Indians had accepted some degree of Christianity at one of the ten mission stations in Huronia, with many villages split between pro- and anti-Jesuit factions. That same year the clerics and their followers gained control of the major village that housed the center of the Huron Confederacy. The Christian chiefs refused to allow traditional ceremonies to be practiced and even appointed a Jesuit as headman of the village.[61] Clearly by the late 1640s these bitter disputes between Huron Christians and traditionalists had undermined chances for successful communal life. That and the loss of nearly one-half of the population to the epidemics of the 1630s shattered tribal unity and led to the precipitous collapse of the Huron Confederacy in 1649–50, when Iroquois raiders devastated Huron villages.

Far to the south, Spanish missionary efforts operated differently from those in New France. In Florida Jesuits had accompanied Avilés during the 1560s when they began work there. In the West, Coronado brought priests along too. By the 1590s Franciscans had taken over missionary work in the Spanish areas, expanding the efforts of their predecessors on both sides of the continent. In 1629 some thirty friars reached New Mexico, and almost immediately they spread out among the Indians there. By 1650 at least thirty chapels and mission houses stood as evidence of their labors. Schools taught children and adults Christian songs, parts of the catechism, and Catholic doctrine. Some people learned to read, write, and speak basic Spanish.[62]

Yet this apparent progress brought high costs to the Indians. As everywhere in America, the Europeans introduced new diseases, with often tragic results. To demonstrate Christian superiority, the priests strove to undermine native shamans and to disrupt local social and religious ceremonies. They created lasting bitterness when they openly destroyed medicine bundles, ceremonial masks, and other items central for native rituals. Like the French, the Spanish clerics could not imagine any genuine conversions among the Indians unless the villagers accepted European social values and practices as well. Thus they worked tirelessly to obliterate all customs that did not meet their view of civilized actions. They tried to break up plural marriages, hoped to have men and women accept traditional European tasks, and assumed that the villagers would learn Spanish. Although the missionaries brought new crops and domesticated animals as well as utensils and tools that, they assumed, would make the Indians' lives easier, that change did not happen. Rather, the Spaniards also brought excessive demands for labor and resources that disrupted village society and created bitter hatred throughout much of Spanish North America.

While seeming to accept the clerics' demands, Indians tried to expel their oppressors repeatedly. In New Mexico this led to the 1680 Pueblo Revolt, which brought the villages together against the invaders. Students of this event suggest that it resulted from a complex pattern of occurrences. Twenty years of drought had reduced crops and animal herds at the same time that the Spanish demanded that the Christian Indians stop trading with their nomadic neighbors. That, in turn, led to increased Apache and Navajo raiding as those groups tried to get items they lacked because of the trade cutoff. In the face of new raids and crop failures the villagers turned increasingly to their traditional religious ceremonies, infuriating the clerics, who responded harshly. After Spanish officials beat numerous native priests and hanged several others, Indian anger boiled over. Led by Popé, a religious leader from San Juan Pueblo, the native people launched a bloody multivillage attack that drove the Spaniards out of the region for a decade. It was not until 1694 that Diego de Vargas led a new host of soldiers and settlers to reoccupy the Rio Grande Valley towns. By 1700 the much-reduced Indians abandoned some of their pueblos and stopped trying to oust the Spaniards.[63]

In Florida the Franciscans found more chance of success because of the denser population. They took over mission work in the Southeast during the 1570s, when the Jesuits retreated from the area. By the middle of the seventeenth century Franciscan missions stretched north from Saint Augustine up the coast of present-day Georgia and west some 250 miles into the Florida panhandle. At that time seventy friars labored among the Indians teaching as many as ten thousand to twelve thousand people. The villagers appear to have accepted varying degrees of Christianity from the priests. At this distance their motivations appear dim, but certainly they included genuine conversions, economic motives, a fear of European diseases, dependence on manufactured goods, and certainly fear of how the Franciscans might treat them if they refused to cooperate. By 1675, just before the onset of an expanding English settlement at Charleston, the Spanish mission enterprise reached its height. The missionaries had been there for several generations, had acquainted thousands of Indians with their ideas, and had introduced the local population to new crops and livestock. Nevertheless, like other mission work in North America, this effort lacked a solid basis for long-term success. In 1675 the Choctaws revolted, driving the missionaries from the westernmost Florida missions and demonstrating the shaky foundation on which the entire operation stood.[64]

ESCALATING FRENCH-INDIAN TENSIONS

To the north the situation proved at least as complex. There the French, although they quarreled repeatedly with their Huron allies, faced the New York Iroquoian peoples, who, in 1641, asked for peace. At that point the New York Indians still hoped to persuade the French to build a trading post in their country as an alternative to the Dutch traders based at Albany. That did not happen because they failed to secure peace immediately. In 1645 the Mohawks agreed to stop their raids. They needed time to exchange prisoners with the nearby tribes, and they still hoped to open trade with the French.[65] The temporary peace that followed hurt both sides. Freed from the threat of Iroquois raids, tribes that traded with the French could bring their pelts south to the Dutch at Albany. That, in turn, hurt Iroquois traders, who could not compete with the high-quality furs their northern competitors offered. At the time both the French and the Iroquois came to recognize that a secure, long-term peace hurt them.

That dilemma vanished during 1649 when both the Senecas and the Mohawks launched devastating raids on the Huron villages. That year and the next they sent hundreds of well-armed warriors into Huron country, attacking and robbing the trading convoys and destroying the home villages too. Huron defenses collapsed immediately because they lacked sufficient firearms to oppose their heavily armed attackers. As a result the Mohawk and Seneca raiders swept through Huronia almost unopposed. The earlier failure of French diplomatic and economic policies to bring about peace with the Iroquoians on the one hand and their meddling in and disruption of Huron society on the other brought disaster as the terrified villagers fled.[66]

At the time, however, the French certainly did not anticipate this result. Rather, beginning with Champlain colonial leaders assumed that by tying the local tribes to them through a combination of missionary action and the fur trade they would be able to incorporate the Indians into French colonial society. The missionaries had looked forward to the same result, as Father Sagard noted when he wrote, "I had hoped to promote a peace between the Hurons and the Iroquois so that Christianity could be spread among them and to open the roads to trade with many nations."[67] The centrality of trade is clear when one realizes that by 1640, three decades after Quebec had been established, there were still less than four hundred Frenchmen in the colony. French efforts to acculturate the Indians failed, and throughout the period from 1633 to 1700 only fifteen years passed without conflict between the French or their tribal allies and the Iroquois. In fact, the Iroquois tribes destroyed their rivals systematically, beginning with the 1628 defeat and dispersion of the Mahicans near present-day Albany. Following that victory they obliterated the Huron Confederacy in 1649, the Neutrals in 1651, the Eries during the mid-1650s, and the Susquehannocks in 1676. Their raids proved so overwhelming that an Iroquois chief bragged that his men had kept the French and their allies so terrified that "they were not able to go over a door to pisse." Few in New France would have argued.[68]

While the French trading settlements clung to their Saint Lawrence base for survival, a tiny colonial society emerged. Colonial leaders gave the Indians considerable attention from the start because they considered them as partners. Because of their relative openness toward the tribesmen, the French talked about incorporating them into their colonial society as quickly as possible. For their part, the Indians had few objections to intermarriage, and the French, at least in theory, would solve the problems resulting from too few women in New France if they looked to their tribal neighbors for mates.[69] Fears of a population shortage in France persuaded early colonial officials that intermarriage offered more hope than migration from the mother country. Champlain's comments to the Hurons reflected these ideas when he assured the Indians that when they accepted the teachings of the missionaries the French would "go to live among them, marry their daughters, and teach them their arts and trades."[70] Just how much formal intermarriage took place is uncertain, but for generations some occurred among the Micmac on the Atlantic Coast, and many French traders and Indian women lived together in "marriages of the country" throughout the history of New France. Nevertheless, despite factors in both societies favoring such unions, only a modest number of formal marriages appear in the records for the early decades.[71]

In fact, in 1635 an official of the Company of New France chided the Montagnais living near Trois-Rivières for preferring their own people as marriage partners and for not accepting French mates. When the subject came up again a year later, one of the chiefs replied that when young Frenchmen lived with villagers and joined their war parties, then Indian girls would be happy to marry them. Here the Montagnais spokesman stated what should have been obvious. Until the French became successful hunters who could support a family, the women saw the Europeans as poor marriage prospects. Ignoring or misunderstanding the Indians' reluctance, colonial officers continued to mention intermarriage as a reasonable means of facing social issues such as a lack of population, an unbalanced sex ratio, and the need to convert Indians. By the 1640s the founders of the Montreal settlement still hoped that interracial marriage would hasten conversion of the nearby tribal people. To their disappointment neither the marriages nor the conversions took place.[72]

Having begun their trading colony with the idea that the Indians would become integrated into the French society, such issues as equality in law, assimilation or segregation, and fair treatment received some attention. During the first two decades so few Frenchmen lived along the Saint Lawrence that such questions rarely arose. Yet with Cardinal Richelieu's efforts to strengthen the nation's hold on New France in the late 1620s they could no longer be avoided. The charter of the Company of New France listed the conversion of the Indians to Christianity as its main goal and went so far as to state that converts who became practicing Catholics had full equality with all other French subjects as well as the rights of citizenship, and could even settle in France if they so wished. Certainly few if any Indians had any knowledge of what that meant, but at least in theory the company charter offered equality and protection for them.[73]

That such promises failed to translate into full or even partial equality is hardly surprising. From the start of New France, traders and clerics there as well as distant government officials and investors in Europe all sought to impose French control. For example, in 1627 one or several Montagnais killed two Frenchmen, and Champlain demanded that the local band leader provide hostages until the murderers surrendered. The headman agreed reluctantly and handed over three children, who remained in French hands through the winter. The next spring, when one of the accused appeared before Champlain, he defended himself saying that because the French had been killing Indians, proper Montagnais custom demanded that he retaliate to satisfy his clan and family obligations by avenging the loss of his kinsmen. Champlain dismissed his arguments and imprisoned him over the objections of the other tribesmen present. While in jail the man sickened; his relatives offered reparations to cover the blood of his victims according to Indian custom, but again Champlain rejected Indian legal custom. When the French needed food desperately that same year the Montagnais refused to provide any until the prisoner had been released. Thus the tribe enforced its code of justice on the Quebec settlement because of its strength and French weakness at the time.[74]

Unable or unwilling to grasp native legal theories, French civil and clerical

authorities angered the tribal people repeatedly. The whites demanded organized corporal punishment for individual guilt, while Indian custom called on
family members to seek satisfaction from or revenge on those who harmed
them or their kinsmen. The French dealt with the perpetrator, whereas the
tribal peopled focused on giving satisfaction to the victim. To the Indians the
European approach appeared as entirely too rigid and inflexible. Because it offered little that they thought was positive and inhibited what they saw as the
natural response to accidents or crimes, the Saint Lawrence tribes found little in
the French system to their liking.[75]

French indecision over whether integration or segregation best served the
goals of the church and state did little to overcome Indian resistance because of
their resentment of discriminatory actions. Frequently the chiefs complained
that French prejudice brought harsher standards than white traders received in
the application of economic regulations, liquor restrictions, and even the assignment of penance for those who were practicing Catholics. Thus in the Indians' view both the civil and church authorities treated them as less than
equals. Actually they perceived the situation accurately. Discrimination existed in all facets of life in New France despite claims to the contrary.

Discrimination occurred more often in the clerical operations of church, hospital, and school than elsewhere. The priests separated Indians and whites in religious processions, in church pews, and eventually even into separate churches.
School classrooms and dormitories remained segregated as well. Tribal people
resented these practices and reported that their children had heard one of the
priests say that "the French did not resemble them, and were not base as they."[76]
When Indians died at the Quebec hospital, the nuns there did not ring the bells
as they did when a French person died. An obvious example of segregation, and
one that caused considerable anger, occurred when the Jesuits refused to allow
the Hurons to bury the corpses of two Frenchmen in the village common grave
where the ceremonies surrounding the annual Feast of the Dead took place.
Even the Christian Hurons objected to the priests' decision, saying that if the
French really considered the Indians as equals they would have no objection to
burying their corpses with those of the villagers.[77]

In 1663 the government of France assumed direct control over affairs in New
France, and for the next century this imperial control tied affairs there closely to
those in Europe. While that occurred, the French colonial presence in America
grew rapidly, if unevenly, and although the fur trade remained important, its
goals became more diplomatic and military than economic. Despite orders to
the contrary from France, Jean-Baptiste Talon, the local intendant, sent fur

traders west under the guise of exploration; by 1670 traders had visited the Ojibwas living in the copper region of Lake Superior, the Shawnees, Wyandots, and Potawatomis on the south shores of Lake Erie, and the Winnebagos on the Green Bay portion of Lake Michigan. Two years later Talon and the newly appointed governor general, Louis Frontenac, dispatched Louis Jolliet and Jacques Marquette to find the Mississippi River, and before the decade ended René-Robert Cavelier, sieur de La Salle, reached the mouth of that stream. In 1673 the new governor ordered workers to the eastern end of Lake Ontario, where they built Fort Frontenac, well within Iroquois territory. The Mohawks objected to this encroachment but had their hands full in an intertribal war with the Mahicans to the east and the Andastes to the south, so for the time being they chose not to retaliate.[78]

During the next decade traders moved west, exploring and opening new trade with tribes south of the Great Lakes and in the Mississippi Valley. Posts near the southern end of Lake Michigan and west to the Mississippi River flourished, and at the same time the French pushed north to the shores of the James and Hudson Bays, where they ran into the beginnings of the British trade there. As the traders probed new regions and sought the mouth of the Mississippi, they brought much of the central area of North America under at least a vague French claim. They also established new relationships with such people not before encountered as the Sauks, Mesquakies, Illinois, and Sioux, scattered the population of New France across much of the continent, produced a vast but unwanted harvest of furs that drove prices down at a time when European demand had slackened, and laid the foundation for French settlement for the next seventy-five years.[79]

Some tribes welcomed this rapid expansion of French trade, but others paid dearly for it. During the late 1670s the Iroquois, having settled the ongoing wars with their eastern neighbors, again threatened New France and its Indian allies. The western Iroquois, led by the Senecas, viewed the expansion of the French trade network south and west of the Great Lakes as an invasion of their domain. Determined to disrupt the French advance and to strengthen their own role in the western fur trade, the Senecas gathered their forces for a new war. Unfortunately for the western tribes, Frontenac ignored the new menace. Then, in late 1680, with some six or seven hundred men, a Seneca-led force moved west. There they defeated the French and Illinois, destroyed one village completely, and took large numbers of prisoners. Their raids continued for the next several years as the French remained unwilling or unable to assist their allies.[80]

To the east the Mohawks quarreled with the French for other reasons. When they had made peace with colonial officials in the late 1660s, they agreed to allow Jesuit missionaries to live in their villages. The French treated Mohawk Christians well, giving them presents and favoring them in the fur trade. This helped the Jesuits to make converts quickly, and as they had done a generation earlier among the Hurons, the priests worked to divide the Indians by disrupting their local village customs. By 1680 at least four hundred Mohawks moved from their home villages into new settlements begun by the missionaries. The traditional Mohawks considered this to be a threat to tribal solidarity, even survival. Not only did their population drop, but they also worried that their Christian relatives would no longer participate in tribal ceremonies or live up to clan obligations. Eventually that would destroy the tribe. So when the Mohawks joined in the anti-French raids, often they did so for reasons of social self-preservation rather than for economics or diplomacy.[81]

One other factor, a custom known as the "mourning war," proved central to the continued Iroquois raids. Many tribes took prisoners to replace villagers who had died or been killed in battle. The practice fulfilled both personal and social needs within Iroquois society. When a person died the Indians believed that the family lost his or her power, so to prevent that they held a "requickening" ceremony at which they passed the power, obligations, and perhaps even the name of the deceased to another. Often captives served as the replacements, but if the family rejected adoption, the villagers tortured and killed the captive to gain satisfaction for their personal loss. These customs meant that young Iroquois males had to raid enemy villages repeatedly to get captives. In doing so they not only proved their personal bravery but, equally important, upheld their family and village obligations. As the tribes gained more firearms and fatalities rose, more raids became necessary to gather ever larger numbers of captives to replenish the shrinking village populations.[82]

Responding to this increasing Indian warfare, in 1684 a Canadian force at Fort Frontenac moved against the Iroquois in New York. When disease swept through the eleven-hundred-man army as it struggled through the forests, it collapsed as a fighting force. The Iroquois dictated a humiliating peace; the Indians allowed the French to retreat northward without attack, but they announced their determination to destroy the Europeans' allies, the Illinois tribe. Thus, as had happened to the Hurons a generation earlier, the Illinois paid dearly for their alliance and trade with the French. Repeated Iroquois raids crushed them, and the terrified survivors fled to join other tribes.[83]

The continuing Iroquois attacks, as well as growing efforts by the English traders at Albany to penetrate the French screen of forts and posts and open trade with the tribes of the west, forced the new governor, the Marquis de

Denonville, to act. He invaded Iroquois home territory in 1687, but the Seneca he hoped to defeat had fled, leaving his troops with little more to do than burn crops and lodges. The next year smallpox and measles ravaged New France, killing nearly 10 percent of the population, so Denonville turned from war to negotiations. The Iroquois seemed to accept his call for talks and promised to send their envoys the next spring. No one arrived until August 1689, when fifteen hundred warriors surprised and destroyed most of the small settlement of Lachine, just west of Montreal. The attackers killed many of the villagers and burned more than fifty buildings there. While the terrified French huddled in their stockade they heard the screams of the captives being burned to death just across the river.[84]

Although Frontenac soon returned as governor, his efforts to conclude a peace with the Iroquois failed too, and sporadic warfare and raiding continued for much of the rest of the century. Gradually the French altered their tactics by resorting to Indian-style ambushes and small-scale raids rather than marching large forces through the deserted forests. These changes enabled the colonists to surprise and defeat several Iroquois raiding parties and destroy Indian villages and crops with increasing frequency. By 1695 the Iroquois energies began to flag, and they tried to divide the French from their Ottawa allies in the west. To prevent that, officials in New France organized yet another major invasion of the Iroquois homeland. In 1696 the Canadians destroyed the northern and eastern villages of the Oneidas and Onondagas, and although few Indians died in this campaign, once again they lost much of their stored food and standing crops. When the English ignored their requests for assistance, the weakened Iroquois had little choice but to sue for peace.[85]

While peace did not come immediately, it helped to change Indian-European relations at the turn of the century. The seemingly endless war between the Iroquois and the French finally ended in 1701 when Frontenac's successor, Hector de Callières, concluded a treaty with them. The agreement included Iroquois promises to end further raids against the tribes allied to the French in the Ohio Valley and west into Wisconsin and Illinois, and to remain neutral in later French-British disputes. The treaty allowed them to turn their attention and raids to tribal people to the south and east all the way into Carolina. When the raids shifted to that region the western tribes had a chance to regroup, to leave the confederated villages Iroquois attacks had forced them to develop, and to regain some of their shattered confidence and independence. For the tribal people south of the Great Lakes the ending of Iroquois raids allowed them to rebuild their societies. Increasingly they modified and combined Indian and European customs, producing what one study labels a "middle ground" between the races. Within that new set of practices and ideas the fur trade continued to function as a major diplomatic and economic force.[86]

By 1701 tribal people in the French and other colonies had plenty of experience in dealing with the Europeans. In every region the invaders entered, disease and warfare reduced Indian numbers rapidly. There conflict arose between the resident people and the advancing pioneers and often took on interracial overtones. To the north the dispute was between the French and their Indian trading partners on the one hand and the competing Iroquois from New York on the other. There, during much of the century, the fighting resulted from intertribal competition, conflicting local customs, and economic issues rather than clearly racial ones. Before 1700, however, the Iroquois-French conflict had evolved into interracial warfare too. Yet it took more than a half century for that to happen, and then it did so primarily because neither group wished to conclude a lasting or meaningful peace.[87]

The tribes' experiences with French, Spanish, and Dutch ideas about landholding also differed substantially. Because the native peoples of the Saint Lawrence Valley practiced a nomadic hunting and gathering economy, the tiny French presence there had little impact on the local native population's land use. The Spanish, in contrast, tried to shape Indian production to their needs, and the Dutch in New Netherland settled in large numbers and often on land actually farmed by the villagers. In New France, when the clerics opened reserves along the Saint Lawrence their efforts brought tribal people into regions they had not occupied at the time of the Europeans' arrival. The Jesuit reserve at Sillery and their mission at Trois-Rivières illustrate this difference.[88]

Although all three European governments assumed ultimate sovereignty over the land and people of their colonial regions, their ideas differed, and that affected their dealings with the tribes. The Dutch claimed title to the lands and their resources through purchase. They recognized a vague Indian right of occupancy and sought to extinguish it through negotiation or purchase. The French, while claiming a similar right of sovereignty, assumed that the tribes would join the emerging colonial society. If that happened there was no need to purchase Indian land. A Spanish observer noted the peculiarity of this French dual approach to the Indians, observing that the tribes "were not absolutely subjects of the King of France, nor entirely independent of him."[89] The result of these differences meant that rather than pay tribute as they did in the Spanish settlements, the tribes of New France received valuable presents from the government each year. The issues of tribal sovereignty and landownership increasingly differentiated French, Spanish, and Dutch theories of dealing with the Indians during the remainder of the colonial era.

In the Saint Lawrence region, clerical influence played a significant role throughout the seventeenth century. Recollet fathers entered the Indian country almost as fast as did Champlain and his fellow traders. By the 1620s the Jesuits had arrived, and their work was central to relations with the tribes. Ursuline Nuns operated at least one hospital and several schools for Indian children. Protestants dominated the English colonies. In theory they worked to convert the tribes to Christianity, but in fact the clerics rarely left the settlements, few learned tribal languages, and those who worked actively with Indians usually dealt with the remnants of defeated or displaced tribes. The Franciscans operated scores of Spanish Indian missions. Education for tribal children and young people appears to have been spectacularly unsuccessful everywhere.

In many ways the intruding Europeans brought similar results to the tribes they encountered in North America, but for strikingly different reasons. Disease, warfare, dislocation, and cultural and economic disruption were endemic. Yet clear differences existed. The Dutch acted as invaders. They took the land and its resources, tried to subjugate the native people, and wanted almost no inclusion of Indians in their society, destroying or pushing aside the native people. The French, because they expected to dominate the region and to profit from tribal actions, fought few early wars of conquest. Rather, they campaigned to protect their economic trading partners and themselves and to keep open commerce on the streams of the Saint Lawrence Valley. They took little land through conquest, but tried to achieve voluntary incorporation of tribal people in their society. The Spanish assumed a right to dominate Indian peoples and demanded that the tribes accept inclusion in their colonial system.

After a century of settlement, trade, and warfare, the results of the Europeans' invasion were clear. Thousands of Indians had died of disease, dislocation, and warfare. By 1701 increased intertribal competition and warfare developed between the tribal allies of the competing Europeans. At the same time, cooperation within each trading network increased. Throughout this era the Europeans gained and kept ultimate control of most trade because they had the desired manufactured goods. While the tribes could and did withhold the skins as they tried to play one group of whites off against another, eventually their need for European goods forced them to trade. As a result of these developments, tribal systems lay shattered or badly disrupted, while the Europeans grew stronger and more solidly entrenched in the region.

2 Indians and English near the Chesapeake, 1570s–1670s

THE ENGLISH BEGAN their exploration of North America slightly before the French and Spanish, but following the efforts of John and Sebastian Cabot during the late fifteenth and early sixteenth centuries, they lapsed into inactivity. In fact, nearly three-quarters of a century passed before Sir Humphrey Gilbert and then Sir Walter Ralegh restarted British explorations. In 1583 Gilbert perished at sea, and in 1584 Ralegh dispatched two ships to investigate the southern coast of North America. Under the command of Philip Amadas and Arthur Barlowe, they reached the outer banks of Carolina near Roanoke Island in July of that year. That month members of the Roanoke and Croatoan tribes met the English peacefully. Then, in August, the English set sail for England with "two of the savages being lustie men, whose names were Wanchese and Manteo."[1] Apparently the village leaders agreed to send at least one of the two young men back with them, although there is some possibility that the intruders abducted Wanchese.[2] In any case, early relations between the tribal people and the whites proved relatively peaceful, but that was not to last.

The next spring Ralegh sent a fleet of seven ships carrying nearly six hundred men to North America. Although not all of this force reached its destination, much of it did, and with an invasion that size it was only a matter of time until violence occurred. By late June 1585 the first ship reached the outer banks and began exploring nearby islands and coastal regions. In mid-July, after the Indians visited one of the ships, the English realized that a silver cup belonging to Sir Richard Grenville was missing. Although the villagers denied having taken it, the Europeans destroyed the standing corn near their town and then burned the village to the ground.³ Despite their anger at the unexpected attack, there was no immediate retaliation, but sporadic violence between the invaders and the local people broke out. One of the Englishmen, deploring the preemptive attacks, wrote that "some of our companie towards the ende of the yeare [1585], shewed themselves too fierce, in slaying some of the people, in some towns, upon causes that on our part, might easily enough have been borne withall."⁴

That winter some of the English visited friendly tribes along the Chesapeake Bay while the rest remained on Roanoke Island. In March 1586 Governor William Lane, a former army officer, led the soldiers of the garrison inland to visit the Chowan tribe, which the English feared was about to launch an attack on them. After surprising the villagers, Lane spent several days there trying to learn about the nearby countryside. When he set off on his return to Roanoke, he seized the chief's son Skiko as a hostage and took him back to the settlement.⁵ This act did little to calm matters, and rumors of Indian alliances against the English circulated freely. The failure of a relief expedition expected to bring food for the invaders prompted Lane to raid the nearby village. On 1 June 1586 his forces attacked, killing and decapitating the chief and scattering the inhabitants. Having seen one local chief murdered, another man seized as a hostage, and their village and crops destroyed, the coastal people saw the Europeans as treacherous and dangerous people, and they fled inland, leaving the English without any dependable food source. As a result, in mid-June 1586 the discouraged colonists accepted passage back to England from Sir Francis Drake.⁶

The Indians had little chance to celebrate, however, because no sooner had Drake's ships set sail for England than Sir Richard Grenville arrived with more colonists and supplies. Disappointed that the colony had disbanded, Grenville decided to leave a token force of fifteen to eighteen men and then he, too, returned to Europe. These men fled after the Indians killed several later that summer. Those who survived the fight apparently died at sea. At least, they disappeared.⁷ In July 1587 the last group of settlers reached Roanoke when their pilot refused to take them further. The party of men, women, and children hardly finished building shelters when the leaders persuaded Governor John White to return to England for more colonists and supplies. Once there, war with Spain prevented him from returning to the settlement until 1590, by which time the colonists had disappeared. An authority on these events has concluded that it is likely that some of the colonists died, while the rest migrated to join Indians living along the Chesapeake Bay. Most of these were killed by the Powhatans some years later. The surviving children grew to adulthood as members of their particular Indian village, and so the colony vanished.[8]

Thus the early record of English colonial activity, like that of their European competitors, ended with economic failure, large-scale loss of life, and considerable violence. In this instance unprovoked attacks, kidnappings, and mutual suspicion alternated with friendship, trade, and shared efforts of people from each group trying to learn about the others. For the Indians the firsthand experiences with invading Europeans made them realize that these strangers were powerful but dangerous people who were anything but trustworthy, and whose actions frequently could not be understood. Nevertheless, the tribes maintained their edge in numerical superiority and wilderness skills over the bumbling intruders. For the English, the experiences seemed to have strengthened their ethnocentric tendencies. They viewed the natives as backward savages, dangerous people who failed to recognize that the European intruders had a superior culture, technology, organization, and religion. Clearly the first brief contacts for each of these groups proved mostly negative and set patterns of ideas and actions that continued for generations.

When efforts to launch actual settlements began at the beginning of the seventeenth century, relations between tribal people and the intruders followed the paths marked out decades earlier. Early in the seventeenth century, even before the first settlers reached Jamestown they met Indian hostility. In late April 1607 near Cape Henry at the mouth of the Chesapeake Bay the expedition under the command of Christopher Newport landed for a few hours. As they returned to their ships members of the Chesapeake tribe attacked and, fortunately for the Englishmen, succeeded only in wounding several of the men. Whatever its causes, in 1607 this assault seemed unprovoked to the whites and heightened their level of fear and suspicion of the Indians. Three days later the English ships entered the mouth of the James River and sailed inland about sixty miles to the site of what was to become Jamestown. There the local Paspahegh tribe seemed to welcome them, and so they cleared fields, cut trees for a stockade, and worked at erecting shelter. As soon as the Indians realized that these strangers had begun to "plant & fortefye, Then they fell to skyrmishing & killed 3 of" the colonists.[9] Small-scale raids and sniping continued for some days. Then on 26 May 160 warriors of the Powhatan Confederacy assaulted the stockade defenders and withdrew only after suffering heavy losses to English musket fire and a cannonade from the nearby ships.[10]

The attackers belonged to one of a number of Algonquian groups then living in the Virginia tidewater region. In the decade or so preceding the Jamestown landing, Powhatan, chief of the Pamunkey tribe, had extended his influence gradually over some thirty tribes and bands in the region. What came to be called the Powhatan Confederacy was actually more nearly a budding empire with Powhatan at its center. He drew other tribes and groups into his orbit through diplomacy, trade, intimidation, and warfare, and when the English landed he was still actively expanding his influence. The early attack on Jamestown appears to have been Powhatan's attempt to defend his territory from invading strangers. After being repulsed he decided that the newcomers might be of use to him against his tribal enemies.

The experience of this highly successful Indian leader with the whites illustrates vividly the patterns of relationships between the two races for generations. From the English he hoped to obtain metal and later both firearms and fighting men with whom he might march to the interior to defeat his Siouan enemies there.[11] Except for his perceived need for metal goods and firearms it seems clear that Powhatan felt superior to these bumbling intruders and perfectly capable of manipulating them for his own goals. The chief's difficulties arose from English unpredictability, the whites' incompetence at mere survival, and their assumption that the villagers could provide an unending supply of food. The Indians did not always have large surpluses and occasionally chose not to supply Europeans with as much or as wide a variety as the hungry whites desired. Frequently this led to violent attacks and efforts to force the villagers to surrender their food supplies. Clearly such actions strained Powhatan's ability to control the situation between the races. Particularly during the 1607–9 era alternating raids and counterraids, the taking of prisoners as temporary hostages and then their release, peaceful trade, and visits by whites to Indian towns and by Indians to Jamestown all kept the situation confused and tense, with neither the Indians nor the English having a clear understanding of the other's motivations or capabilities.

Powhatan was no fool, however, and he soon realized that the English represented a powerful force in his home region; thus he sought to use them for his benefit. For example, as early as the winter of 1607–8 he had tried to persuade the settlers to give him two cannons, but without success.[12] John Smith, the English military leader, reported smugly that the Indians planned to plant some captured gunpowder in order to raise their own supply, so clearly the local people recognized that the English had powerful items that would be of great use. The whites knew this as well and had stringent prohibitions on the trade or sale of firearms to the Indians; nevertheless, despite their best efforts to curtail such exchanges a small but steady stream of muskets, powder, and shot came into the hands of the villagers. Then in 1609 two German workers fled Jamestown with eight muskets, along with powder and shot, and presented these to the Indians. Although that was only a few weapons, the authorities denounced the runaways bitterly for bringing guns to the enemy. Later the Jamestown authorities would demand repeatedly that the Indians surrender all runaways, prisoners, and firearms to colonial authorities.[13]

By the time the Indians began to acquire guns the Jamestown colonists, following the aggressive leadership of John Smith, undertook a belligerent campaign to intimidate the nearby tribesmen. Recognizing the colonists' weakness, Smith hoped to end sporadic Indian attacks and to force agreements to supply the settlers with corn and other foodstuffs. During the winter of 1608–9 he demanded submission from whole villages, publicly humiliating Indian chiefs, taking hostages, and being coercive whenever he dealt with native leaders. On one foray the bellicose captain dragged a village headman into the nearby river, nearly drowning him, then threatened to decapitate the luckless chief. Finally Smith took him back to Jamestown to be held in chains as a hostage for the good behavior and cooperation of his home village. Of more significance was Smith's harsh treatment of Opechancanough, brother of Powhatan and leader of one of the major villages in the Indian confederacy. While at that village Smith threatened the chief with his loaded pistol in the presence of the armed village warriors. Then, according to the Englishman's account, he seized the startled Indian by the hair, demanding that the villagers load his boat with corn. If they refused, Smith threatened to fill the craft "with your dead carkases."[14] Whatever else this terror campaign may have done, it seems certain that threatening Opechancanough in front of his own warriors turned this native leader into a lifelong hater of the colonists, because he led the anti-English forces in coastal Virginia for the next half century.

Regardless of what the English might have thought, Powhatan recognized the growing danger that his aggressive neighbors represented to the Indian confederacy. At least according to John Smith, the native leader stated his fears that if he launched a major attack against the colonists he would "be so hunted by you that I can neither rest eat nor sleepe, but my tired men must watch, and if a twig but breake, everie one crie, there comes Captaine *Smith*: then must I flie I knowe not whether, and thus with miserable feare end my miserable life."[15] While the chief's statement may only show his efforts to lower English hostility or even to create a false sense of confidence among the whites, Smith's bragging demonstrates his confidence that in the long run the English would prevail. If the chieftain said anything of the sort, the conversation indicates Powhatan's awareness of the seriousness of the English threat. Not only did he want to avoid an all-out war with the Jamestown settlers, but he also had to avoid giving major offense to his Indian allies and tributaries lest they rebel against him and turn to the English for aid and support.

Certainly the English hoped and soon planned for that very development in their dealings with the coastal tribes. In 1609 the London Company issued a new directive for dealing with Powhatan. It recognized that the chief had not welcomed the English as neighbors and suggested that the newly appointed governor, Sir Thomas Gates, try to take the Indian leader captive. Should that not be possible, the Jamestown leaders were to induce the chief to accept a position as a tributary of the Crown. If that tactic failed, the orders called for Gates to try to weaken the Indian confederacy by getting the chiefs of the villages and tribes subordinate to Powhatan to "acknowledge no other Lord but King James."[16] Once that happened, company officials reasoned, it would be easier to persuade the chiefs to cooperate with the English by providing food for the settlers. In fact, the authors of these orders in faraway London supposed that the Indians would be so happy at being freed from their vassalage to Powhatan that they would willingly provide such tribute as corn, dye, hides, and skins, as well as working to clear the land for English use.[17] What the tribal people were to get from all this was not discussed.

At the same time Gates's orders called upon him to diligently "endeavour the conversion of the natives" to Christianity, "as the most pious and noble end of this plantation." To achieve this goal the company officials suggested that the colonists persuade the Indians to send some of their children to live in James- town "to be brought up in your language, and manners."[18] While under more peaceful circumstances the tribal people might have agreed to such an arrange- ment, they would have demanded in exchange for their own children that En- glish children move into their villages, where they would be taught Indian ways. This was a widespread tribal practice, but clearly such an exchange was farthest from the minds of Virginia Company officials. What the whites expected all along was the one-sided acculturation of the villagers to English society and thought, whereas the vast majority of Indians had little incentive or desire to make such a transformation. Interestingly, the instructions to bring Christian- ity to the Indians appeared again in the company instructions to Thomas de la Warr, Gates's successor.[19] Gates, however, was the first to receive such conflict- ing and unrealistic directions as trying to capture Powhatan, working to under- mine his confederacy, and convincing the villagers to feed and labor for the

English. If his efforts to achieve those goals failed and the Indians still refused to cooperate or tried to flee, the governor was ordered to capture the chiefs, headmen, and village religious leaders and take them to Jamestown, where some might be persuaded to adopt English ways and the rest could be killed.[20]

The combination of increasing English desperation and aggression, coupled with Powhatan's understanding of the Indian-white situation, raised tensions on both sides and led to repeated conflict. Although major fighting occurred only sporadically, the situation deteriorated to one of frequent raids against the English, and when those failed to dislodge the unwelcome colonists, the villagers tried to starve the invaders. If possible the Indians fled at the approach of colonial foraging or trading parties. When surprised in their villages they pleaded a lack of surplus food or provided as little as they thought they could convince the whites to accept. These tactics worked so well that by the winter of 1609–10 the colony faced collapse yet again. The settlers' ineptitude and unwillingness to raise their own food, poor crops among the Indians, and continued small raids and harassment of those Englishmen who left the settlement for any reason brought the colony to its knees. The Indians might well have prevailed as the colonists began to evacuate, but Lord de la Warr arrived at the last minute with more colonists and supplies as well as the determination to smash Indian resistance once and for all.[21]

THE FIRST ANGLO-POWHATAN WAR

With Captain Smith's campaign of calculated aggression, the new Virginia Company orders regarding Indian diplomacy, and Lord de la Warr's hope to defeat the local population on the one hand, and Powhatan's determination to resist continuing white encroachments on the other, by 1609–10 an undeclared war had commenced. In fact, a recent student of these affairs labels the years 1609–14 as those of the First Anglo-Powhatan War and views relations between the Virginia tribes and the Jamestown settlers as being in a state of at least semihostility throughout the era. There were few major battles, but rather sporadic raids, ambushes, attacks, and the taking of hostages by both sides. However, as one year slipped into the next and the invading whites obtained more and better firearms and more experience in campaigning against the Indians, the tide of battle shifted in their favor. Columns of heavily armed and armored Englishmen marched and countermarched across the tidewater region of Virginia. In particular they succeeded in almost clearing the James River Valley of Indian resistance as their murderous musket fire brought destruction and death to Indian fighting men whose arrows all too often glanced harmlessly off the whites' body armor. During these sporadic hostilities Pocahontas, daughter of the chief, became a hostage of the English. Despite her captivity, Powhatan did not agree to accepting peace with the English until 1614, when the combined weight of successive military defeats, high casualties, an attack on his own major village, and the complete failure of tribal religious practices to help the Indians defeat their enemies all convinced the chief to capitulate.[22]

During the war some of the tributary tribes broke away from the confederacy to make separate agreements with the English, further weakening the ability of the coastal tribes to resist the colonists' advance. When Powhatan and his allies accepted a one-sided peace agreement forced upon them by the Jamestown government, the aging chief surrendered his actual leadership of the confederation to his younger brothers. Soon the militant Opechancanough began an effort to regain supremacy over the English. To accomplish this he sought to obtain muskets and ammunition from the whites, and as early as 1615 some Indian warriors could use the firearms as well as the colonists. Throughout his life Opechancanough remained bitterly opposed to English expansion and used his considerable diplomatic and political skills in an effort to retain Indian control of the interracial situation in Virginia. For example, by 1616 colonial officials in Jamestown had received orders to try the more peaceful and less expensive tactic of offering English "civilization" and Christianity to the Indians rather than making war on them. The chief used the colonists' desire to spread their culture and religion among the villagers as a way to wheedle firearms out of the whites. He simply prohibited English efforts at acculturation and conversion of his people unless the interracial trade included muskets, lead, and powder.[23]

While the forces of the badly shaken Powhatan Confederacy struggled to regain their strength and confidence, the Jamestown settlers received directives from the Virginia Company that refocused their dealings with the Indians from diplomatic and military to cultural, and from conflict to cooperation. John Rolfe's marriage to Pocahontas and Powhatan's willingness to accept peace with the English seemed to bring a renewed sense of well-being to the whites. Even prior to the 1614 cessation of hostilities spokesmen for the Virginia Company had begun to call for a less violent approach to Indian affairs. Whether to deflect some of the continuing bad publicity, to cut costs by reducing military campaigning, or because they thought humanitarian means more advisable, these spokesmen urged that violence be avoided when possible. For example, Alexander Whitaker, writing in 1613, called for the colonists to "put on the bowells of compassion, and let the lamentable estate of these miserable people [the Indians] enter your consideration."[24] Even the irascible John Smith, who seemed to delight in bellicose treatment of the native people, admitted that despite Indian barbarity the villagers had "such government, as that their Magistrates for good commanding, and their people for due subjection and obeying, excell in many places that would be counted very civil."[25]

Such attitudes and continuing English ethnocentrism, which blinded the colonists to Indian reluctance to surrender or exchange their culture for that of the whites, led to missionary and educational activities among the tribes of coastal Virginia. In 1619 the first Virginia legislature required each settlement to obtain by "just meanes a certaine number of the natives Children to be educated by them in true Religion and civile course of life."[26] As noted earlier, the English refused to consider the Native American practice of exchanging children with neighboring tribes. When efforts to recruit Indian children failed, Governor Sir George Yeardley decided to recruit entire Indian families. Those who agreed to move from their villages to live among the English would receive a house, land for crops, and even some livestock. While the parents learned to deal with the English social and economic model, the children could be in school, and perhaps all could be converted to Christianity. Although such efforts looked better on paper than they functioned in practice, the governor did convince Chief Opechancanough to allow a few Indian families from the confederacy villages to move into the English settlements.[27]

While Yeardley strove to incorporate those few villagers into the colonial society, authorities in England urged support for schools and even a college for Indian youth in Virginia. As early as 1617 King James I ordered church officials in England to take special offerings twice each year to support Indian educational and missionary activities, and by 1619 the church had provided fifteen hundred pounds for the project. The Virginia Company designated ten thousand acres of land for the support of a "University and College" and provided some funds as well. Apparently the English expected to begin serious mission work among the nearby Indians.[28] Within a year Virginia authorities began to survey the college land at what came to be called Henrico, and in 1619–20 some one hundred tenants who would work that land arrived in the colony. Also in 1619 the authorities named Patrick Copeland president-elect and Richard Downs to the staff.[29]

Both the Virginia Company and private persons continued to provide support for the would-be school. A wave of optimism about the prospects for "civilizing" the Virginia tribes grew in England as several wealthy individuals donated money for the project. One offered an incentive for recruiting young Indians when he provided £300 to the college if it had enrolled ten native children. Another supporter, this one anonymous, gave £550 to be used for missionary work and vocational training for tribal young people. Other philanthropic English families donated items that varied from books, maps, and communion sets to small amounts of cash for the college.[30] Clearly they thought that the education of young Indians would solve their diplomatic, military, and social problems and at the same time would carry out their obligation to bring salvation to the tribal people. When in operation the Indian college was to train native ministers who would then return to their home villages or tribes and help in the task of religious conversion that the English expected to take place.

Despite the negative Indian responses, the invaders remained convinced of the rightness of their actions and the purity of their motives. For example, George Thorpe, one of the leading proponents of dealing kindly and fairly with Indians, never considered the possibility that the villagers might not welcome English domination or that they might want to preserve their own native way of life. Rather, he complained that the Jamestown settlers all seemed to hate and fear their tribal neighbors, and that most of the English "with their mouthes give them [the Indians] nothing but maledictions and bitter execrations."[31] Certainly the English expected the Indians to do things the European way, and despite some experience in working together, living near each other, and even intermarrying, as in the case of John Rolfe and Pocahontas, they rejected any substantive cultural mixing. Even the supposed missionaries lost patience with the lack of progress in "civilizing" the Indians. By 1621 one of the ministers argued that there was no hope of converting the villagers "till their Priests and Ancients have their throats cut."[32] Clearly under such conditions there was to be little real exchange of ideas, much less of people.

In the Spanish, French, and Dutch settlements in America intermarriage was far more common than in the English-dominated regions of North America. Yet from the start, English reports describe Indian women in positive terms. Arthur Barlowe reported after his 1584 journey to Carolina that the Indian women there were "most gentle, loving, and faithful, voide of all guile and treason, and such as live after the manner of the golden age."[33] The early printed versions of John White's watercolors of the Roanoke people perpetuated this positive view by depicting the women as attractive and, although generally bare-breasted, modest as well. Despite these early favorable ideas about the native people, assumed English cultural superiority and ideas about Christian separation from the heathen limited Indian-white intermarriage sharply during the colonial era.

At first this may have been because of settlers' fears that possible Indian wives might murder them in their sleep. For native women, Englishmen lacked the wilderness survival skills that would have made them attractive marriage partners. Probably more important than either the fear of native treachery or the lack of attractiveness to Indian women, though, was a deeply held aversion to interracial marriage on the part of most colonists. A recent discussion of Anglo-Indian intermarriage that traces English cultural attitudes shows that while informal sexual contacts might occur, English social mores prevented any substantial effort to foster intermarriage. One observer explained that intermarriage with native women would not be "profitable and convenient (they having had no such breeding as our women have)."[34] Undoubtedly this attitude of cultural superiority further strained relations between the villagers and the newcomers.

Despite the modest colonial efforts to establish a biracial but English-dominated society, the Virginia tribes saw little reason to become mere copies of the English. Few parents allowed their children to live among the settlers, and only a handful of families accepted the inducement of homes and farmland offered to the parents of children turned over to the whites. In fact, while the ethnocentric whites congratulated themselves on their philanthropic efforts to "civilize the savages," leaders of the Powhatan Confederacy set out to learn white military skills, acquire weapons and ammunition, and foster a growing resistance to the invaders. Tribal chiefs, headmen, and shamans recognized clearly the threat the Jamestown settlement posed. They could see that the European population was growing and was unlikely to leave. They saw too the alarming loss of population brought by European disease and warfare with the colonists.

Mutual hatred resulted from tension, warfare, and ethnocentrism, yet from the Indian point of view the most significant issue between the races in early colonial Virginia was that of land use and ownership. Until John Rolfe developed an exportable strain of tobacco the invaders were too few and occupied too little land to pose any serious threat to the local villagers' economy. But during the 1614–22 era the English population grew dramatically. When a virtual "tobacco craze" swept through the settlement Englishmen streamed into the woods and, more often, onto cleared land that the tribes had farmed for generations. Waiting until the villagers had gone to the coast to gather seafood or west into the hills as part of their annual cycle of hunting, fishing, and gathering, the whites seized Indian cropland, claiming that it had been abandoned and therefore was now theirs to put to good use. In other cases individual villagers sold or exchanged land for beads, ironware, or even firearms.

The most pressure on tribal leaders to surrender land came shortly after the

1614 peace agreement between Powhatan and colonial leaders. At that point in the settlement process English population and land hunger practically exploded. A paucity of records limits a thorough understanding of the process of land transfer from the tribes to the colonists during these early years, but an example related by John Rolfe provides some insight on this explosive issue. Possibly in need because of military campaigns in previous years or suffering the effects of famine, in 1615 several minor chiefs had agreed to mortgage all of their tribal lands in exchange for grain. Whether the villagers understood the nature of their agreement with the English is unclear, but it seems unlikely. It is also unlikely that the whites took pains to explain the terms thoroughly. In any event, only three years later Governor Samuel Argall described the local Indians as being too poor to pay either their debts or their tribute.[35] Again it must be noted that existing records of the period give no accurate indication of whether the Indians actually lost land or, if they did, how much of it went to the whites, but both Rolfe and Argall described a situation likely to result in major Indian land losses. In fact, a later observer noted that the Virginia tribes lived in "dayly feare" that the whites would seize all of their lands and push them out of the tidewater completely.[36]

THE SECOND ANGLO-POWHATAN WAR

While the English strove to expand their population, landholdings, and control of the situation, the Powhatan Confederacy changed its approaches to the invaders. Despite Powhatan's apparent acceptance of defeat in 1614, the aging leader and his advisers were not yet ready to accept a position subservient to the whites. Shortly after the 1614 defeat Powhatan became more an elder statesman than the actual leader of the Indians. His younger brothers began directing relations with the whites more actively, and between 1615 and 1622 the leadership grew increasingly more militant and anti-English. His brother Itopan took over nominal leadership, but after a short time Opechancanough came to the fore.

As a leader Opechancanough exercised his skills carefully. Repeatedly he professed his peaceful intentions to the Virginia leaders and early in 1622 he protested that the "Skye should soon falle" before he would destroy the uneasy peace between the races.[37] Despite such protestations the chief harbored a deep mistrust of the English and appears to have realized that their continuing advance into the Indians' country represented a deadly menace for the future well-being of the tribes. Stressing that his warriors should acquire firearms and learn to use them to defend against the English military tactics, he began to equip members of the confederacy for eventual conflict with the whites. Apparently hoping to keep peace, in 1616 Governor George Yeardley provided some firearms to the Indians and appointed one of the warriors to lead a column of musketeers in a public parade. As myopic as the colonists appear to have been, even some of them recognized the potential threat posed by well-armed and experienced Indian warriors. Between 1618 and 1620 several individuals complained that lax control of muskets and other weapons had allowed the Powhatans to get many of them and to become skilled in their use. When the Indians became more certain of their skill with European weapons, they strove eagerly to increase their supply. In 1619, after several colonists died under questionable circumstances, their armor and weapons turned up in the possession of the villagers. Even the early Virginia court records identify six specific individual Powhatans and Chickahominys as expert marksmen with English weapons.[38]

By 1618 the English realized the potential danger of allowing their competitors to have guns and the skills to use them. In the spring of that year Governor Samuel Argall prohibited the colonists from teaching any Indian to use a musket, and he proclaimed the death sentence for any whites doing the teaching and for Indians being taught. What effect the governor's efforts had is unknown, but by 1621 the Jamestown authorities recognized that their Indian neighbors posed a serious threat to the colony. In fact, contemporary estimates of Indian capabilities suggested that it would take at least three hundred armed musketeers to successfully attack Opechancanough's Pamunkey villages. This figure said nothing about other tribes in the confederacy, and at that time the English viewed the tidewater tribes as a major challenge to colonial hegemony.[39]

While some leaders of the Indian confederacy fostered a growing military preparedness, others took a different but still anti-English tack. One prominent shaman and war chief, Nemattanew, proved especially adept at generating anti-white feelings among the confederacy members. Known as "Jack of the Feathers" by the colonists, this charismatic leader soon came to be seen as dangerous to the Jamestown settlement. A veteran of the pre-1614 fighting against the English, he had proven ability as a leader as well as considerable skill as a marksman. His threat, however, extended well beyond mere military capabilities because he assumed a religious stance when opposing the whites. He wore a costume of feathers to demonstrate his invulnerability to English musket fire, and he encouraged a growing warrior cult based on cultural pride, belief in the spiritual powers of the tribal deities, and the existing anti-English bitterness among the confederacy villagers. Namattanew functioned as did numerous other leaders of later cultural revitalization movements in the course of North

American Indian-white relations. He convinced the warriors that he was protected from English guns and that they might enjoy the same immunity to danger in battle if they used an ointment he offered. The records provide little more specific data about Jack of the Feathers, but it is clear that he enjoyed widespread influence, that other confederacy chiefs, in particular Opechancanough, welcomed his nativist message, and that prior to 1622 the tidewater tribes experienced a major cultural regeneration.[40]

Clearly during this era the tribal people did not consider themselves inferior to the whites. Rather, they appear to have decided that another test of arms was necessary to reassert their dominance over the invaders, and between 1619 and 1622 the potential battle lines formed between the races. In those three years over thirty-five hundred immigrants arrived. They represented a growing threat to existing landholdings by the coastal peoples, particularly in the region between the York and James Rivers, where the heavy concentration of new settler activities threatened the actual survival of the local Indians. By 1620 the tribes faced the unwelcome alternatives of being driven from their homes, of joining the hated white society, or of fighting against the invaders. Meanwhile the English settlement spread throughout the tidewater region as tiny clumps of settlers scattered widely across the countryside and offered Indian warriors invitingly weak targets nearby. On the other hand, retreat in the face of the expanding white population brought the Powhatans into closer contact with their Siouian enemies the Monacan and Manahoac farther west in the Piedmont.[41]

What Indian leaders felt about these choices is not known, but their actions show that they never gave serious thought to any of them except military resistance. By 1620 Opechancanough led a confederacy of people reasonably well united by feelings of cultural pride, a deep sense of injustice at the hands of the English, and a growing religious assurance of protection from the white's firepower. They even expected broad support and assistance from the nearby Chickahominy tribe, which the Virginians had antagonized through treachery only a few years earlier. In that instance Governor Yeardley had ordered thirty or forty of the Indians killed without apparent provocation, and the rest of the tribe now had no great love for the English.[42] What was necessary to turn the suspicion and hatred into warfare was a spark or incident to galvanize opinion on either side, and that occurred early in 1622 when two white servants shot and killed Jack of the Feathers.

The colonists knew of Nemattanew's reputation among the Indians, so it is not surprising that during a dispute with the Indian leader the whites took the opportunity to kill him. According to John Smith's account, Jack of the Feathers persuaded a man named Morgan to go to an Indian village for trade and killed him on the way. When he returned to Morgan's house without the colonist, two of Morgan's servants tried to apprehend the chief. He resisted, was shot, and soon died. At least one discussion of this event suggests the possibility that the action was a deliberate assassination. Whatever the case, removing an influential and powerful Indian leader cheered the Jamestown settlers. The tribal people responded differently. When Opechancanough learned of the murder he was outraged and called for revenge, but retracted his angry statements when threatened with "such terrible answers" by the English.[43] Nevertheless, Nemattanew's death made him a martyr and gave Opechancanough the incident he needed to mobilize and focus the simmering antiwhite feelings among the tribes of the Powhatan Confederacy.[44]

Secretly rallying his forces, Opechancanough launched a coordinated, well-planned, and devastating attack on the English throughout the colony. On the morning of 22 March 1622 apparently unarmed Indians filtered into settlements and stopped at the scattered farms as well. Without warning they assaulted and killed their hosts wherever possible, seizing guns, ammunition, and any other arms they could get. At least 330 whites died in the first day of violence. This so-called Massacre of 1622 set off an intermittent and vicious war that dragged on for nearly a decade. That conflict, now called the Second Anglo-Powhatan War, eventually brought victory and supremacy to the English, but not before both sides suffered horrendous casualties and repeated atrocities. When the usual English columns marched into Indian country, the Indian warriors used surprise attacks and ambushes as their most successful tactics, repeatedly punishing the colonial militiamen. In September 1622 the warriors ably defended Indian villages by ambushing the attackers. Six months later, in the spring of 1623, the Indians destroyed a company-sized English force under Captain Henry Spelman almost entirely by using colonial weapons. The same warriors then did the unthinkable. In about sixty canoes they attacked the pinnace *Tiger* as it lay at anchor on the Potomac River. Thus even the apparent superiority of English naval forces seemed to offer little defense against the determined Indians.[45]

The ferocity and skill with which the tribesmen defended their homeland and carried out widely separated raids against the astonished English brought a grudging measure of respect for the warriors and their leaders. In fact, because of his daring leadership Opechancanough became known as the "Great General of the Savages" among the whites.[46] More important for long-term relations between the races, the English attributed the Indian victories to their savage nature, and this perceived native savagery allowed or even justified using extraordinary measures against the tribes. For example, after repeated efforts to capture Indian leaders failed, the colonists turned to treachery. During a lull in the fighting they proposed a peace parley; when Opechancanough and more than two hundred Indians gathered for the talks, their hosts poisoned the drinks. The chief survived and escaped, much to the chagrin of colonial officials, but most of his companions succumbed or were slaughtered by the whites. The victorious colonists celebrated by scalping, decapitating, and otherwise mutilating their victims and bringing the grisly trophies back to Jamestown.[47]

A DECADE OF CONFLICT

Colonial leaders' determination to avenge the short-term Indian victory of March 1622 led them to organize a decade-long campaign to destroy or drive coastal tribes out of the area. Official pronouncements about the need to destroy the Indians, to consider them as enemies, and to continue annual or even more frequent attacks on the tribes underscored the English determination to dominate the region completely. In fact, as late as the fall of 1632 the Virginia authorities labeled the Indians "irreconcilable enemies." Campaigns became a part of colonial life. Each year colonists marched into the Indian country to burn crops, kill adults, and seize children for enslavement. As the settlers became inured to the warfare and destruction, the level of violence intensified, and eventually they attacked specified targets every four months rather than just once a year.[48]

The 1622 uprising and resulting decade of conflict destroyed the tentative efforts by some of the English to merge white and Indian societies. The mingling of the two peoples ended or was sharply curtailed, and the English freely expressed their fear of the tribal people as well as their desire to take the good land from the Indians. In late 1622 Edward Waterhouse combined both English outrage and greed when he wrote that "our hands which before were tied with gentleness and fair usage, are now set at liberty by the treacherous violence of the [Indians]. So that we . . . may now by right of Warre . . . invade the Country, and destroy them who sought to destroy us. . . . Now their cleared grounds in all their villages (which are situate in the fruitfullest places of the land) shall be inhabited by us."[49]

Numerous scholars of these events agree that the Indian attack of 1622 spelled the end of any major effort by the invading English to deal with the Virginia tribes as equals or potential friends.[50] That event caused a fundamental shift to occur. The English dropped their halfhearted effort to develop a partially biracial society. In its place they began actively to exclude Indians from their colonial settlements. The annual military campaigns against the nearby tribes that lasted until 1632 constituted the first steps in this process. With the Indians now seen as the enemy, efforts to drive them away characterized Virginia policy. Clearly the ease with which the colonists shifted their priorities from incorporating the tribal people to excluding or even destroying them indicates that many of the English never seriously considered including large numbers of Indians within their Virginia society. Other and later English settlements had similar experiences and in general, along with the Dutch, seemed to be the most unwilling of the European invading groups to consider any real degree of fusion between the two cultures. To a degree the Spanish, and even more so the French, proved to be more accommodating with their native neighbors. English determination to exclude or at best acculturate and marginalize native peoples proved a distinct difference from the French and Spanish North American colonial activities for a time. In addition, it indicated clearly to the Indians that the English despised them and their culture.

Nevertheless, for a time the Virginians continued some of their efforts to incorporate at least a few native people into their society. For example, in 1629 colonial records indicate that Virginia funds supported "a number of Indians" who lived within the region controlled by the whites. In addition, as late as 1640 money bequeathed a generation earlier to support education for Indian boys until Henrico College came into being was still being used each year "to defray the cost of instruction of three infidel children."[51] The record gives no indication of what sort of education these children received, and it is likely that they served as indentured servants while getting some minimal education. That continuing English needs for laborers led to repeated abuses is clear because in 1655 the colonial government passed legislation requiring that Indian parents first give their consent before their children could become indentured servants. This provision also limited the indentures to a specified length and called on their masters to educate the children in "the Christian religion."[52] The next several years saw other laws regulating the use of Indian children and spelling out the conditions under which whites could assume responsibility for them. In each case, the regulations indicated that the whites were to provide some type of education as well as an introduction to Christianity, and the laws specified how long the Indian children might remain as servants.[53]

Colonial authorities made ever-increasing demands upon their Indian neighbors, and as the growing white population spread across the land in search of good tobacco lands, Indian resistance stiffened. Tensions between the races increased steadily between 1632 and 1644 because of continuing English efforts to dominate the Virginia tribes. During the 1630s colonial authorities approved the construction of a log palisade between the James and York Rivers, a sort of Virginia version of the Great Wall of China. This was to help exclude most Indians from the settlements and also to limit cattle rustling by both whites and Indians on the frontier. Of more significance was a series of land grants authorized by John Harvey during the late 1630s, which brought white pioneers into immediate contact with tribal people living in the newly granted areas.

As Indian resentment to the new settlers grew, domestic strife leading to civil war rent English society at home. According to one contemporary account, the Indians claimed that Opechancanough learned of the English Civil War and decided to attack the colonists a second time.[54] He strengthened the Powhatan Confederacy and urged the young warriors into another major war with the English. Although so feeble that he had to be carried to battle on a litter, the chief commanded the respect of his warriors, and they attacked successfully once more. As they had in 1622, the confederacy forces caught the colonists unprepared and inflicted major defeats and serious casualties on the Virginians. The fact that there seems to have been even less warning of the impending attack in 1644 than there had been two decades earlier indicates that the native people still maintained an active and effective alliance, and that most of them shared a deep hatred of the invading whites.[55] Surely none of the warriors who participated in the 1644 attacks was ignorant of the destructive retaliation that followed the earlier war and that had ceased a mere twelve years earlier, and yet they joined in the new round of fighting with determination.

The war proved a disaster for the Powhatan Confederacy. By 1646 the English had won and extracted another one-sided treaty from the tribal people. Opechancanough fell captive to the whites, and one of the guards killed him while he was held in Jamestown. His successor, Necotowance, signed a treaty under which the tribes recognized their tributary status to the English. Furthermore, he accepted the idea that his position as chief depended on the authority of the Crown, and that his successor could be appointed or ratified by the colonial government. This certainly marked a drastic shift in Indian views and a major loss of tribal independence. In return for these concessions, the Virginians agreed to protect the subject tribes from invading Indians. The treaty called for Necotowance or his representative to provide twenty beaver skins each year "at the goeing away of Geese."[56] This agreement forced the tribes living in closest contact with the Virginia settlements into a permanently subservient status. They surrendered land, even agreeing to the death penalty for any Indian found on land between the James and York Rivers unless that person were a messenger for Necotowance. In return, English who trespassed on Indian lands were considered to be guilty of a felony, but the punishment, if any, for their actions remained unspecified.[57]

In the continuing struggle between tribal people and the invaders for control of Virginia, time clearly favored the English. Gradually the legal and power relationship between Indians and whites shifted from the situation that had existed at early Jamestown. By the middle of the seventeenth century the tribes had lost their original position of local superiority and autonomy. In dealing with the English they found themselves in a subservient and dependent relationship. The Virginians classed the tribal people in three general categories: groups who negotiated as equals or at least as independent neighbors, villages and tribes that had fallen into a tributary status, and individuals who worked among the whites as servants, slaves, or even as freemen without any tribal connections.[58] By this time the degree of contact between Indians and whites varied widely, as did the treatment of the tribal people by the now-dominant English.

For example, the legal system and its functioning demonstrates the unequal treatment afforded Indians under English control. After 1662 Indians accused of capital crimes faced trials in the courts of oyer and terminer. At least in theory, the proceedings followed the same prescribed course they would have for white defendants in the same courts. In fact, the situation appears to have been somewhat different for Indians. To speed justice and cut costs, the trials occurred in the counties where the alleged offense took place. This differed from the usual Virginia practice of trying whites accused of major crimes at the colonial capital, and it may have exposed Indian defendants to local passions that might have been avoided in a different venue.[59]

BACON'S REBELLION

The Indian position worsened gradually between 1646 and 1676. During that time a growing white population, continuing spread of colonial settlers, declining availability of fur-bearing animals, and disease combined to reduce sharply the tribes living along Virginia's frontiers. By the eve of Bacon's Rebellion in the mid-1670s tribal populations in Virginia had virtually collapsed. A 1669 Virginia census included only eleven of the twenty-eight tribes mentioned in 1608 by John Smith. While the number of tribes had dropped slowly, overall Indian population suffered an even more dramatic collapse, if the 1669 figures are accurate. The estimated thirty thousand Indians present in 1608 had melted away to a mere two thousand by 1669. Even if the 1608 figures represent an inflated estimate, this drop shows the drastic effect of the European invasion of Virginia. Some of the population decline resulted from the Indians' inability to unite against the whites. The impact of European diseases on the coastal people was another important factor in population loss.[60] Whatever the relative weight each of these factors deserves, by 1675 the Indians of eastern and central Virginia stood on the brink of cultural destruction.

By that year continuing white population growth and territorial expansion, combined with intracolonial squabbles over the control of the fur trade and local government, once more brought war to the tribes along the Indian-white frontier. In 1675 a fur trade disagreement between the Doeg tribe from Maryland and Thomas Mathews, a Stafford County trader, brought new violence. He had purchased goods from the Doegs but then refused to pay the tribesmen. They responded in July 1675 by entering Virginia and trying to steal some of his hogs as repayment. The English stumbled upon them and killed several of the Indians as they fled. This brought a retaliatory raid and the death of one of Mathews's workers. News of the attack persuaded the frontier militia leaders to strike the Indians hard, and soon the Virginians invaded Maryland. There they divided their force and then found two Indian cabins. One contained Doegs, most of whom the Virginians killed. The second, however, housed friendly Susquehannocks. When these people heard the nearby shooting they rushed out of the cabin, only to be shot down by the English. By the time the militia leaders realized they were attacking the wrong people, they had killed fourteen of the Indians.[61]

Despite a formal complaint by the governor of Maryland, the Virginia authorities made no effort to punish the militia commanders. They also took no steps to make an immediate peace with the Susquehannocks or to meet the demands of some frontiersmen that all of the tribes be driven from the region. In late August 1675 Governor William Berkeley called for an investigation. Instead the frontier commanders called out more than seven hundred men and asked the Maryland pioneers for help as well. On 26 September 1675 the combined force of some one thousand men surrounded the Susquehannocks' fort and demanded that the leaders come out to parley. The militiamen first denounced the Indians for raids along the frontier, then murdered the five tribal spokesmen. From inside their fort the warriors defended themselves successfully for some days. They then killed the colonists' sentries, slipped out of the fort, and fled into the forest.[62]

From there they launched hit-and-run attacks, and in January 1676 they killed thirty-six persons near the Potomac and Rappahannock Rivers. The English tried to pursue the warriors, without success. At that point Governor Berkeley called out more troops, but then he countermanded his order. Meanwhile the Susquehannocks sent a complaint to the governor, asking why the Virginians had attacked them and killed their chiefs and calling for peace. They told him that they had killed ten common Englishmen to avenge the death of each of their chiefs and so felt that they had achieve adequate revenge. Berkeley, failing to respond to the Indians' complaint, asked the legislature for money to build forts at the river headwaters to protect the frontier settlers. In this way he hoped to keep any hostile groups at bay while continuing the peaceful trade with the tributary Indians within the colony. In trying to accomplish these goals the governor ignored the raging anti-Indian feelings of many pioneers. His actions seemed to put the interests of a few traders, including some of his immediate associates, above those of the settlers who wanted the Indians destroyed or driven away. This led directly to Bacon's Rebellion.[63]

That conflict swept through Virginia in 1676, causing widespread destruction and almost toppling the government. It resulted from a complex set of issues, with the dispute over Indian affairs providing the spark that set off the violence. One of the war acts the legislature passed prevented existing traders from dealing with the tribes because they were known to have provided weapons and ammunition to the Indians. This brought angry denunciations from western leaders who had participated in the trade. They accused the governor of excluding all but his favorites from the trade. Nathaniel Bacon Jr., one of the frontier spokesmen, led the verbal attacks on the governor. Eventually he came to lead the armed forces that opposed Governor Berkeley in the colony. Bacon used the anger over the governor's Indian policies to try to bring about political and economic changes to the colony. The rebellion ended abruptly in October 1676 when Bacon died of dysentery. For the Virginia tribes it brought yet another treaty, this time signed on 29 May 1677 at Middle Plantation at Williamsburg. There the tribes accepted a position of total dependency and again agreed that they held their land at the pleasure of the king. To indicate their complete subservience, they promised to pay an annual quitrent, or tribute, as well as the three arrows and twenty beaver skins each year that they had agreed to as a part of the 1646 agreement.[64]

The raids and fighting of 1675–76 resulted directly from the Virginia pioneers' continuing anti-Indian violence. By this time they had accepted fully the idea that the tribal people were backward, "uncivilized," and "brutish" folk who stubbornly refused to make way for their betters. The earlier English ideas about the backward and savage Irish, the undeserving poor, and the ever-increasing negative ideas about the black slaves expanded gradually to include Indians. Whether racial, class, or ethnic, some combinations of these antagonisms characterized white-Indian relations in late seventeenth century Virginia. The 1677 treaty, which essentially ended hostilities there for the rest of the colonial era, demonstrates the declining fortunes of the tribes as they contended with the invading whites. Clearly, by then the Indians in Virginia had passed through the stages that characterize most Indian-white relationships in North America. They descended from a position of superiority to equality to subservience and dependence—all within a single lifetime.

3 Indians and English in
New England, 1600–1670s

INDIANS IN NEW ENGLAND experienced relations with the English that were similar to those of the tribes along the Chesapeake. Europeans sailing along the New England coast in the early seventeenth century committed the same kinds of depredations against the tribal people they met there that the Roanoke voyagers had off the Carolina coast. As early as 1605 George Waymouth, leading an expedition on the *Archangel*, kidnapped five Abenakis and took them back to England. Eventually several of these men got back to their home villages, and once there they warned their fellow villagers against trusting the English.[1] A few years later, in 1611, Edward Harlow kidnapped others along the New England coast. At one stop he captured three men, one of whom escaped to lead a retaliatory raid against Harlow's ship. At Martha's Vineyard Harlow grabbed three more Indians, taking these and his first two prisoners back to England. There Sir Fernando Gorges spent three years in an effort to persuade one of the captured Martha's Vineyard sachems, Epenow, to support English settlement and trade in his homeland. This effort failed; when Gorges sent him back in 1614, Epenow escaped, returned to his village, and helped lead resistance to English encroachments on the island. That same year an expedition under Thomas Hunt antagonized the tribes on the mainland as well. Hunt seized twenty-four Indians, sailed to Malaga, and sold them into slavery among the Spanish.[2] Thus before the English tried to establish settlements in New England, their explorers and traders had antagonized many of the local people. By the time actual settlers arrived, the tribes along the coast had come to fear, if not hate, the English.

Despite this disastrous start, the relations between the local tribes and the English settlers proved to be relatively calm. Certainly there was suspicion and violence between Indians and English, but the New England circumstances differed sharply from those farther south along the Chesapeake. Several factors help explain that, but two stand out as of major importance. First, in 1616–18 a plague or a series of diseases swept through the peoples of coastal New England with a virulence seldom recorded in eastern North America. Whether a single catastrophic disease, a series of plagues, or repeated visits of one or more, the result was disaster for the tribes.[3] When Thomas Morton traveled through the region five years later he reported that the "bones and skulls [of the dead] made such a spectacle . . . that, as I travailed in that Forest near the Massachusetts, it seemed to me a new found Golgotha."[4] Scholars differ only on the extent of the devastation, with estimates of the deaths ranging from about 75 percent of the coastal population to as high as 90 percent.[5] Either figure portrays a demographic disaster of gigantic proportion.

The regions most affected lay directly in the path of the first Pilgrim and Puritan settlements. Entire villages simply disappeared, leaving open and readily cultivable lands available to the newcomers. To the colonial English settlers, this validated their struggle. As he had done in Old Testament times, God was punishing his enemies, and now he cleared the promised land for English settlement. What few of the settlers realized was that the demographic collapse that followed 1616–18 shattered existing tribal alliances, strained native economies, and perhaps endangered the mere survival of previously well-established tribes, bands, and villages. What the whites saw as a nudge from the Almighty brought permanent changes in the political, diplomatic, economic, and demographic landscape of New England. The plague weakened those tribes remaining within fifty miles of the coast to such an extent that they had little inclination to contest the English invasion of that region. Certainly violence between the native people and the Europeans occurred, but clearly in early New England whites rarely faced opposition as formidable or well led as the Powhatan Confederacy had been just a decade earlier in Virginia.[6]

Not only did the New England tribes include fewer people than those in the coastal regions of Virginia, but the Algonquian people there competed vigorously with each other. Those most important included the Abenakis in Maine; the Massachusets, who occupied the northern and eastern portions of that region; the Nipmucs, directly to the west of the Massachusets; the Narragansetts and Wampanoags in Rhode Island; and the Pequots in the southern Connecticut Valley.[7] Unlike the Virginia situation, where Powhatan dominated most of the local tribes, in New England open rivalry and occasionally bitter warfare separated the major Indian tribes. This allowed the English to play one native group against another. The Wampanoags and their neighbors to the west, the Narragansetts, offer a clear example of this. The Narragansetts not only fought against the Wampanoags but against most of the other regional groups as well. Farther to the west, the invading Pequots had subdued the smaller tribes of the Connecticut River Valley and maintained uneasy relations with the larger groups to the east.[8]

While the Indians failed to present a unified front to the colonial settlers, the Europeans proved equally ineffective. Competition and violence separated the French, English, and Dutch and occurred even within and among the English communities as well. In New England early settlement often produced small, scattered villages that were unable to support themselves, to maintain effective communications with each other, or to deal with the native people under any coherent plan. At first the local tribes held the upper hand because they had the knowledge and skills to use the local environment successfully, whereas the invading English frequently suffered from hunger and even starvation. After the first half century of settlement, however, the situation in New England closely resembled that in Virginia. In fact, the fighting that ended the major conflict in New England known as King Philip's War (1675–76) took place within a few months of Bacon's Rebellion in the South.

PLYMOUTH

Certainly the individuals, events, and chronology in New England differed from those along the Chesapeake, but the general pattern remained similar. The earlier kidnappings and skirmishes between the English and Indians along the coast and on offshore islands meant that when the first colonists arrived in New England they were afraid of possible retaliation by the local people. The Pilgrims felt this way even before they landed in North America because of what they had read. William Bradford mentioned this several times in his account of early Pilgrim activities at Plymouth. When discussing obstacles to successful settlement facing the group, he mentioned "the savage people, who are cruel, barbarous and most treacherous." He admitted that the Indians' savage nature and actions made "the very bowels of men to grate within them and make the weak to quake and tremble."[9] The fear shows too in Miles Standish's action.

Taking the same approach that John Smith had in Virginia, he tried to use force and intimidation to make the local people "respect" the English.

At the same time, the Indians feared that the whites might repeat earlier offenses. Even before the pilgrims aboard the *Mayflower* had chosen a site for their first settlement, tribal leaders sent scouts to keep the newcomers under surveillance. The English realized that they were being observed, but it took them four days to catch sight of any Indians. Even then they failed to make contact because the tribesmen fled. A few days later the whites located an Indian corn cache and after breaking it open took corn for food and seed.[10] While adding to their meager supplies of food certainly helped some of the colonists to survive the first bitter winter, stealing corn that belonged to the local villagers did little to ensure peace or good relations.

Occasional sightings of Indians in the distance, as well as finding several villages and an occasional temporarily empty lodge, kept the Pilgrims aware of the local population, but personal meetings failed to occur. The villagers wanted to meet only on their own terms, and as in Virginia, violence marked the early contacts. On the night of 7 December 1620 the local Indians came up to the English camp making "a great and strange cry." Although frightened, the whites made no response. The next morning, after the warriors showered the palisaded camp with a rain of arrows, the English responded by firing a few muskets; the attackers withdrew. There were no casualties on either side, but these actions reinforced Pilgrim fears and strengthened Standish's claims that one had to deal forcibly with the native people in order to be safe.[11]

This ominous beginning notwithstanding, no major conflict between the invading English and the local tribesmen occurred. The nearby villagers kept a careful watch on the whites but chose to avoid contact. During the 1620–21 winter the Pilgrims faced sickness, starvation, and death, and by the spring fewer than half of the original inhabitants of Plymouth remained alive. During those months a few Indians took some abandoned tools from one of the fields; another time, several men climbed to the top of a nearby hill and harangued the English. Unable to understand what had been said and suspecting that this was a trick to lure the whites into an ambush, Standish and others at Plymouth mounted their cannons on a hill outside the village.[12]

Despite the near collapse of the settlement, the Indians kept away from the village. In March 1621 this changed, and none too soon for the Pilgrims. Leaders of the Pokanoket or Wampanoag appear to have avoided the English until they felt safe, or perhaps until they realized that the invaders were too weak to harm the tribe. In any event, Samoset, an Abenaki sagamore from Maine, strode into

Plymouth. To the whites' amazement, he spoke some English and proceeded to describe the area tribes to the colonists. When he left the next morning he promised to return with other local chiefs and to bring furs to trade too. Within a couple of weeks relations between the English and nearby villagers changed dramatically as the "stolen" tools were returned and a fur trade began.[13] If the latter succeeded, the colony might be able to sustain itself.

On 22 March 1621 Massasoit, chief of the Wampanoag tribe within the larger Pokanoket Confederacy, arrived at Plymouth along with his brother and sixty warriors. While the pilgrim leaders worried about how to deal with the chief while excluding his warriors and yet not insult anyone, Squanto arrived at the village. A former captive of the English and now living among the Wampanoags, Squanto spoke even more English than did Samoset, and initially he served both Indians and whites well as an interpreter. After some hastily planned pageantry, the Pilgrim leaders met Massasoit and other tribal leaders. These talks resulted in an alliance between the two groups. The Wampanoags needed help against the Narragansetts, their enemies to the west, while the whites wanted to secure peace. The resulting agreement seems to indicate the utmost goodwill on both sides—or perhaps the desperation of each. In any event, Massasoit agreed to enforce peace between Indians and whites, to end the pilfering that had been taking place, and to punish those Indians who either hurt or robbed the English. Governor John Carver and the chief agreed that each would aid the other if either were attacked by a third group. Thus whites and Indians became joined in a mutual defense alliance. The Indian leaders also agreed that they would enforce this agreement on neighboring tribes, turn over Indian offenders to the white authorities, and become allies of the English king.[14]

Clearly at this point the situation in New England differed sharply from that in Virginia. In the North the devastation left by the plague had weakened the tribal people nearest the invading Europeans, whereas in Virginia the best-led and most highly organized group lived in the immediate vicinity of Jamestown. The Wampanoags welcomed European aid and the alliance that they hoped would help them regain lost influence and territory in the face of the still-strong Narragansetts to their west. At the same time in one general sense the situations resembled each other. The Indians recognized the English newcomers as a factor within the local and regional political and diplomatic competition. Certainly for a time Powhatan in Virginia had hoped to strengthen his hand among the coastal peoples through the support of the English as did Massasoit of the Wampanoags near Plymouth. Yet in Virginia the tribal leader looked at the situation from a position of local dominance, while the New England sachem was in a different situation. In fact, Massasoit needed the Pilgrim help against his tribal neighbors just to retain his status.

For him, the whites appeared as valuable allies, and even had he considered them as overlords of a sort, they were preferable to his Narragansett neighbors. At first the colonists demanded little, if any, real tribute, and they gave more gifts in exchange for diplomatic relations than did Indian allies. In addition, English support allowed Massasoit to lead an expansion of Pokanoket power eastward and north along the coast near Plymouth, into areas where the Narragansetts had no influence, and where Massasoit's people may well have exercised some jurisdiction prior to the plagues. For the Indians the alliance with Plymouth must have seemed highly desirable. It is unclear, however, if any tribal leaders understood what the agreement meant to the Pilgrims. However the Indians felt about the alliance, their accord with the English tipped the scale in the Indian-European balance against the local people. By agreeing to enforce terms of the treaty on other nearby tribes and bands, Massasoit became in effect an agent for the colonists. In addition, by tolerating the authority of the English to try and punish Indians who failed to live up to the accord but refusing to let the Indians do the same to white treaty breakers, Massasoit accepted a clearly subordinate status in relation to the English right from the start.[15]

Whether either side considered this inequality as significant at the time is not certain, but the Pilgrim leadership assumed that it had the right to set ground rules for interracial relationships. For example, the Indian custom of unlimited hospitality to visitors and guests frightened the English. They feared a possible sneak attack if they welcomed fifty or sixty Indian warriors into their tiny settlement. If hungry Indians stopped for a meal at any time, the English worried that they might be unable to feed themselves during the winter. European ideas about private property provided another basis for the Pilgrim objection to feeding their tribal visitors. They had no custom of large-scale sharing as did the tribal people of the region. The Plymouth authorities thought that it made little sense to work hard, acquire surplus food or other property, and then squander it through reckless giving, particularly to the Indians. As a result, the whites soon asked Massasoit to limit Indian visitations to Plymouth to his official representatives or to himself and his immediate advisers.[16]

Before leaving, Massasoit invited the whites to his village; soon the Plymouth authorities sent Edward Winslow and Stephen Hawkins to visit. Taking Squanto as a guide and interpreter, the two traveled about forty miles to the Indian town. Along the way they stopped at other small villages, and at each the inhabitants welcomed and feted them. Chief Massasoit greeted the colonists kindly, but much of his hospitality was wasted on the whites. They complained about the "barbarous singing" and grumbled that "we were worse weary of our lodging than of our journey" after spending the night sharing the chief's lodge and bed.[17] Eagerly they returned to Plymouth as soon as they could, having misunderstood much of their treatment. Despite the rigors of the trip, it accomplished several things. Certainly it cemented the relationship between the tribal people and the settlers. Moreover, the Pilgrims claimed to have negotiated another accord with the chief, in which Massasoit had agreed that he was "King James his man."[18] According to the colonists, with this statement the chief had shifted his status voluntarily from that of ally to that of subject. Without a doubt, Massasoit would have rejected this view of his status. Nevertheless, his words served as the basis for further Puritan expansion and as one of the later underpinnings of Plymouth policy toward the Indians.

That same summer, 1621, the newly formed Wampanoag-Pilgrim alliance faced its first real test. Corbitant, sachem of one small Wampanoag band, and several others became jealous of Massasoit's growing power and plotted with the Narragansetts to kill some of the pro-English individuals. Corbitant and several followers seized Squanto and two others, but unfortunately for the plotters, one of the captives escaped, fled to Plymouth, and warned the whites. Miles Standish led a detachment of troops to rescue Squanto and his companion and to subdue the plotters. At the village Standish frightened Corbitant's followers, who then fled while Standish told the sachem to desist or face military retribution.[19] The Narragansetts, meanwhile, had not yet mobilized for their proposed attack against Massasoit and took no action. This prompt English response assured the Indians that they had dependable allies, but it also set a precedent about taking a direct role in Indian disputes. While Massasoit may have welcomed this first intervention on his behalf, he would live long enough to have second thoughts about the wisdom of involving the English in local native affairs.

A year later the alliance faced another severe test. During the summer of 1622 the English established a new village, called Wessagusett, on Massachusetts Bay. Within a few months the new settlement had run short of food and asked the Plymouth authorities for permission to take some from nearby villages if the Indians refused to sell them any. Poor crops that year had limited the yield for everyone, so neither the whites at Plymouth nor most of the nearby Indian settlements had much food to spare. Hoping to avert trouble, the Pilgrim authorities attempted, without success, to buy extra corn for themselves and those at Wessagusett. By winter 1622–23 the Wessagusett men began raiding

Massachuset villages for corn and other foodstuffs. Their actions outraged the villagers, and soon news of another Indian conspiracy swept through the settlements. To make matters worse, Squanto, the best translator, died that winter. Shortly after that the English, learning that Massasoit was sick, sent a delegation to bring medical assistance. Edward Winslow successfully treated the chief, who then told the whites details of a Massachuset plan to destroy the Wessagusett village. The Plymouth leaders dispatched Miles Standish with a few armed men yet one more time. They traveled north and in late March 1623 killed several Massachuset tribal leaders, then dismantled the village. This ended the threat, although it did nothing to improve relations with the Massachuset villagers. In fact, after that incident the Indians called the English "Wotawguenange, which in their language signifieth stabbers or Cutthroates."[20]

THE PEQUOT WAR

By the mid-1620s the patterns of Plymouth-Indian relations appeared firm, and although the two groups continued to encounter minor difficulties with each other, no wars or other major disasters occurred. At the end of that decade, however, as the advanced parties of the vast English Puritan migration reached New England, the situation changed drastically. By 1630 events in the Massachusetts Bay colony began to overshadow the Plymouth settlers as far as Indian affairs were concerned. As the new immigrants surged into eastern Massachusetts they benefited from the Pilgrims' earlier experiences with the local tribes and from the continuing demographic havoc left in the wake of the 1616–18 plagues. Because the Massachuset tribe and related small villages remained weak and saw themselves as threatened by the Abenaki from the north and west, they welcomed the English as allies and protectors from their Indian enemies.[21]

The leaders of the Massachusetts Bay Company assumed that they would have peaceful dealings with the native people. As early as 1629 John Endicott received orders to "have a diligent & watchful eye over our own people, that they . . . demean themselves justly & courteous towards" the Indians.[22] Colonial authorities took their directions seriously; during the first few years of settlement they strove sporadically to protect Indian rights and property from harm at the hands of the English. Individual settlers received such punishments as being whipped, branded, fined, and banished, or even losing the title of Master, for misdeeds among the Indians. The colony even accepted corporate guilt in 1634 when Charleston had to pay damages to nearby Indians because the settlers' swine had damaged the villagers' crops.[23]

Not only were the leaders admonished to limit the contacts their people had with the natives and to avoid trouble with them, but the company expected them to obtain land and settlement rights with care as well. This is clear from the instructions that directed the New England leaders to pay local chiefs for any claims they had for town sites and farmland. This directive came despite English refusal to accept most tribal land claims as valid. To the colonists, people who migrated from spring fishing sites to summer agricultural villages to fall hunting camps and back to their summer villages could not really own all the territory they used each year. Yet because they feared Indian power they moved with care when early obtaining tribal lands. At the same time, their certainty that they were doing God's work led them to assume that their policies and actions were just.

The Pequot War of 1636–37 offers the first graphic example of these attitudes. Often described as a conflict between expanding and aggressive English and Indian societies, this conflict actually proved both complex and decisive. Dutch traders had tended to dominate Long Island, Narragansett Bay, and the lower Connecticut River Valley prior to the Puritan migration to New England. In those regions they allied themselves with the Pequots and the Narragansetts successfully for nearly a decade. By the early 1630s, however, increasing pressure from the English and growing disputes among the Indians changed the situation. When the Mohegans, under the leadership of Uncas, split away from the Pequots, the Narragansetts used this as a means of weakening their erstwhile Pequot trading partners. During the three-way Indian struggle that resulted from this split, the Dutch moved further into the Connecticut Valley and established a sort of seventeenth-century free trade zone, where they welcomed all villagers and tribes to deal directly with them. This undermined the Pequot position as middlemen in the trade system of the region, and soon Pequot raiders attacked the Dutch and those Indians trading with them, including small parties of Narragansetts.[24]

In the middle of this growing collapse of their trading and diplomatic situation Sassacus, the Pequot leader, found himself unable to retain the allegiance of many tribes allied or subordinate to the Pequots. A major smallpox epidemic during 1633–34 further complicated the situation by spreading death through the coastal people, as several thousand Indians died that year. At that point John Stone, a semipiratical English trader, sailed his small vessel up the Connecticut River and while there attempted to kidnap several Pequots for ransom. He failed to post adequate guards, however, and other Indians stormed aboard the craft, killing Stone and eight companions. This gave the colonials an excuse for demanding that the Pequots submit to white domination. Discussions of this incident vary widely, one suggesting that it was a party of Western Niantic Indians who killed Stone, while another blames the Pequots or a tribe subservient to them for the incident. Whatever the reasons for Stone's death, the English in Massachusetts, unable to ignore that Indians had killed nine white men, demanded that the Pequots pay reparations and submit themselves to colonial authorities.[25]

Facing a possible war with the Dutch, the Narragansetts, and some of their own subject peoples, the Pequots decided that they could not afford conflict with the English as well. In late 1634 they sent representatives to the Massachusetts Bay colony to ease their relations with the Puritan authorities. On 1 November 1634 the Pequots and the Massachusetts authorities signed an agreement to end their difficulties. Although the Pequots claimed to be innocent of John Stone's death, the treaty called for them to capture and turn in the last of Stone's murderers. More importantly, the tribal leaders accepted English settlement in the Connecticut Valley, where the land would be obtained from local groups then subject to the Pequots.[26] At first glance this might not seem to have weakened the tribe, but actually it allowed the Massachusetts authorities to interpose themselves between the Pequots and their allies and subjects. Thus, from the first official meeting with the tribe the English made clear their determination to control the situation for their own benefit and at the expense of the Indians. Whether either group realized what lay ahead or not, the Pequots rejected their subordinate position quickly, and colonial efforts to dominate tribal affairs soon led to open conflict.

From the 1634 signing of their treaty of friendship until fighting broke out two years later, neither the Pequots nor the English remained peaceful or blameless in the continuing difficulties. The tribal leaders did not or could not capture and turn in those suspected of killing John Stone as they had promised, and they paid only part of the agreed-upon wampum reparation for Stone's death. Meanwhile, English settlement expanded along the coast and up the Connecticut Valley, and aggressive white actions toward the local Indians kept Pequot resentment high. Whatever colonial motivations were in this situation, the Boston officials refused to ignore continuing Pequot rejection of English demands. During the summer of 1636 the Massachusetts Bay authorities ordered John Winthrop Jr. to demand that tribal leaders hand over the men accused of killing John Stone and pay the rest of the wampum tribute. The Indians balked. They had explained the earlier murders, paid what they thought was enough wampum to cover the debt, and now the English had revived the two-year-old demands. To the Pequot leaders this was unwarranted interference in their customs and a clear effort to expand colonial domination over tribal affairs.[27]

When war erupted between the Massachusetts Bay colony and the Pequots, it began for reasons related to intertribal relations as well as the continuing disputes with the Indians. In July 1636 the English learned that Indians had overrun John Oldham's trading vessel on the coast near Block Island. Although the warriors had killed Oldham, most of the raiders themselves were killed during the brief fight. Available evidence pointed to the Narragansetts or the Block Island people, who were subject to them, as responsible for the attack. Hurried efforts by the Narragansett and English leaders ended the threat of war between the two groups, and in fact secured Narragansett neutrality in the continuing dispute between Massachusetts Bay and the Pequots.[28] This allowed the colonists to begin a series of harsh reprisals against Indians suspected of anti-English acts.

The campaign began only a month after the attack on Oldham's boat, when John Endicott led a party of ninety volunteers to Block Island. There the English drove the Indians into the swamps and then spent the next two days destroying their villages and crops. Using the murder of John Oldham as an excuse, Endicott led his force to Fort Saybrook, in Connecticut. Now the colonial authorities ordered him to demand the killers of both John Stone and John Oldham and then force the Pequots to pay a further one thousand fathoms of wampum as punishment for their earlier lack of cooperation. In addition, he was to require the Indians to surrender some of their children, who would be held as hostages. Pequot leaders declined taking any immediate action, claiming that some of the chiefs were on Long Island and were still trying to discover who had killed the whites. Enraged by the Indians' failure to comply, Endicott and his colleagues attacked. In the raid one Pequot man died, while the other warriors fled to the woods, leaving the whites to destroy their villages, crops, and other property. While taking these actions the colonials failed to capture the accused men or to get the reparations they had demanded. Instead, they infuriated the Pequots and then returned to Boston.[29]

This military aggression left the Pequots with few options. Their culture called for vengeance, and their shaky diplomatic situation forced them to retaliate or lose status and influence over the smaller nearby tribes. During the fall and winter of 1636–37, Indian warriors ambushed Englishmen several times. In April 1637 they killed nine settlers and carried off several more as prisoners. At the same time, Pequot diplomats tried to heal their rifts with the Narragansetts, but that effort failed. In fact, the Narragansetts promised to either kill or capture and deliver to Massachusetts Bay any Indians thought guilty of killing whites and to stay away from the English communities unless they gave notice of their intentions or came in the company of whites.[30] This meant that in the final campaign the Pequots had few Indian allies to help them oppose the flow of Puritan expansion.

The Massachusetts Bay leaders entered the conflict fearing that their control over the region faced collapse. Settlers in the Connecticut Valley had challenged their leadership, while the Pequots had killed nine colonists. Within the eastern settlements themselves some people had begun to oppose the religious and political leaders for a variety of reasons. These occurrences seemed to indicate a fragmentation of the tightly knit religious commonwealth the Massachusetts Bay leaders sought to maintain. In response they explained the difficulties in largely religious terms as the result of slipping piety among the general populace. They saw the crisis as a test of their faith and came to depict the Pequots as servants of Satan, who sought to block the expanding Christian settlements. Once they labeled the Indians as representing Satan it became easy for the colonists to excuse the resulting savagery. After all, they had used such tactics against other Europeans—even against other Englishmen—in the religious wars of the not-too-distant past. In fact, they likened this conflict to those of Old Testament times when God had commanded the Israelites to destroy their heathen enemies.[31]

The campaign itself was swift, brutal, and decisive. Despite some minor intercolonial bickering, all of the major English settlements joined forces against the Pequots. On the Indians' side, the Mohegans under Chief Uncas, the Narragansetts, and some of the Connecticut Valley tribes all encouraged or aided the whites, leaving the Pequots standing virtually alone. On 26 May 1637 John Mason led English troops in a surprise dawn attack on a major Pequot village at the Mystic River while most of the men were absent. The attackers stormed the palisaded town, set the village afire, and withdrew quickly. Then they surrounded the palisade and shot the women and children as they tried to flee. Indian allies of the whites killed the few Pequots who broke through the colonists' lines. A large part of the Pequot tribe perished within an hour that morning. The slaughter overwhelmed the villagers and even appalled the victors. William Bradford, the longtime colonial governor, wrote that "it was a fearful sight to see them thus frying in the fire and the streams of blood quenching the same, and horrible was the stink and scent thereof."[32]

A second English force followed the scattered remnants of the Mystic River villagers, and by mid-July 1637 much of that portion of the Pequot tribe had been destroyed. Even the most conservative figures for Indian fatalities and captives stand at more than seven hundred men, women, and children.[33] Jubilant colonial authorities handed over the surviving women and children to the tribes that had helped them fight the war, while killing most of the captured men. Then in August 1637 the Mohawk tribe of New York sent word that they had killed the Pequot leader Sassacus and forty of his men who had fled there. They sent a scalp to support their claim. Before the year ended the remaining sachems and their scattered followers all sued for peace. In late 1638 the victorious colonists held a conference to end the hostilities. The settlers, the Mohegans, and the Narragansetts all demanded that the tribe be abolished to avoid having to deal with this once-powerful enemy sometime in the future. As a result, on 21 September 1638 the officials forced the Pequot survivors to sign the Treaty of Hartford. Under the terms of that agreement the Pequots disappeared at least temporarily as an independent tribe. The treaty excluded them from their former territory, while it assigned the survivors almost equally to live in villages under Uncas of the Mohegans, Miantonomo of the Narragansetts, and a few captives to Chief Ninigret of the Eastern Niantics. These groups were to adopt all of the surviving Pequots, a long-established Indian tradition.[34]

Because it reduced the independence of other tribes in the region, the Treaty of Hartford not only obliterated the Pequot tribe but also allowed the English to seize control of most of southern and eastern New England. For example, the Indian leaders who accepted captives for incorporation into their villages had to pay an annual tribute for the right to supervise their defeated Indian enemies.[35] The brutal destruction of the Pequots also sent an obvious warning to other tribes in the area—cooperate or be destroyed. One of the participants later remarked that the colonists had enjoyed supernatural help in defeating their tribal enemies because the Lord had "put a fear and dread of us into the hearts of the Indians round about us; and many of them did voluntarily put themselves under the government of the English."[36] Having seen the whites crush one of their most powerful neighbors easily, the remaining New England tribes tried not to antagonize the settlers. Consequently, relations between the races for the next several decades remained peaceful as English numbers grew and those of the tribal people diminished.

THE PURITAN MISSION IN NEW ENGLAND

The destruction of the Pequots in 1637 did not end Indian-white friction, suspicion, or hatred. It was, however, the last major fighting between colonists and their tribal neighbors for nearly forty years. Hoping to maintain peace, the English authorities attempted to prevent warfare between competing tribes, even among bitter enemies. To their dismay, colonial leaders found that they could not enforce peace and calm immediately after their 1638 treaty. With the Pequots effectively removed from the New England scene, the Narragansetts and the Mohegans renewed their long-standing quarrels. The two chiefs, Uncas of the Mohegans and Miantonomo of the Narragansetts, each at the head of large tribes and enjoying the apparent support of numerous allies, continued practices that brought about five years of violence against each other. While the Indians sought to weaken their tribal enemies, the expansion of English settlement, competition over land titles, and colonial efforts to dominate the regional tribes all complicated matters. Massachusetts, Rhode Island, Connecticut, and New Haven all sought their own best interests when dealing with tribal leaders, so it is difficult to imagine a circumstance in which peace and goodwill could have emerged.[37]

In the contest between Miantonomo and Uncas the former proved less successful. Determined to maintain traditional Narragansett interests, and a lukewarm ally of the Massachusetts Bay authorities, he seems to have been no match for the devious Uncas. When rumors of an anti-English Indian conspiracy surfaced by 1640, the Narragansetts appeared as the villains to the colonial authorities. News of a plot to assassinate Uncas, supposedly instigated by Miantonomo, led to renewed fears of colonial war; in response, the authorities summoned the Narragansett leader to Boston. The chief's testimony quieted some fears, but on his way home he killed the other Indian who had supported his story. That act convinced the English that he had lied and was organizing a conspiracy against them. At that point Uncas persuaded the whites that his alliance with them was endangered by the Narragansett chief's actions. Hearing that, the English seized Miantonomo and turned him over to his Mohegan enemy, who promptly killed him. This murder enraged the Narragansetts, but deprived of their most widely recognized leader, they took no aggressive action.[38]

Frequently during the next several decades Indian conspiracy scares swept through the colonial settlements, but as time passed the whites' strength grew while that of the tribes declined. There seems to have been little basis for fears of another major war, but friction and suspicion continued because of English determination to dominate all phases of tribal life, while Indian leaders strove to retain tribal independence. From the start the Puritan leaders in the region had viewed their meetings with the tribes as part of a major spiritual contest between the forces of good and evil, always assuming their English culture and Protestant Christianity to be on the side of good. With that general idea as their intellectual basis they strove to replace all elements of Indian life and culture, including the village "Powwows" or shamans, with those of white society. At the same time, committed religious leaders wanted to maintain doctrinal and community purity by excluding all who deviated from their accepted standards of belief and action.[39]

No sooner had the Puritans used Uncas to rid them of their perceived enemy, Miantonomo, than they turned their energies to fundamental alterations in the New England ethnic landscape. While the Indians continued to live in their villages following traditional leaders and social practices the English had difficulty imposing their control over the tribes. If, however, the local people could be induced to accept European cultural values and practices, the continuing friction and threats of violence between the races might be eliminated. To achieve this general goal of Indian cultural transformation, in 1644 the Massachusetts legislature or General Court ordered the shire or county courts to take the lead in what they called "civilizing" the tribal people. The Puritan leaders strove to control Indian diplomatic and military actions while seeking to provide schools and religious instruction for them.[40]

Given the repeated English statements about converting the heathen, it is surprising that the New England authorities waited so long and made so little effort to destroy and replace the Indian religious practices. Their modest commitment of manpower and funds suggests an unwillingness or inability to give full support to efforts that might make Indians resemble white settlers. Yet both company officials in England and Massachusetts Bay colonial leaders talked about the need to carry out a missionary program. Company directives and correspondence from both sides of the Atlantic make this abundantly clear. For example, during the winter of 1629 Matthew Cradock reminded John Endicott not to forget the "main end of our Plantation . . . to bring the Indians to the knowledge of the Gospel."[41] Similar messages dot the communications of the settlement era.

Despite this rhetoric, and in contrast to Spanish and French proselytization, the English mission efforts never became wholehearted. In fact, no more than a dozen New England missionaries worked among the tribes during the entire seventeenth century. Yet Calvinism, which underlay the central beliefs of the Puritan clergy, did not preclude the possibility that some Indians might accept the missionaries' teachings. Nor did it exclude any effort to avoid evangelism. In fact, it included the idea that humankind could never know God's will or understand why the Almighty granted salvation to some people and not to others. Conversion depended entirely on God's initiative and resulted in a complete change in the convert's subsequent life and actions. These fundamental tenets might have been used to support an aggressive program of mission work, but that did not happen.[42]

A variety of reasons explain the New Englanders' lack of zeal. Clearly they shared the general European ethnocentrism of that day, but the Puritans carried other cultural baggage as well. Recent English experiences with the Irish had prepared them to consider their tribal neighbors as backward and savage. More central was the fact that the Puritans had left their homeland rather than compromise their basic religious convictions. Under those circumstances it was not likely that they would have accepted deviations from their Christian beliefs or practices to accommodate the Indians. One other basic factor inhibited New England clergymen form working among the local tribes. That was the idea that one had to have a specific congregation in order to practice the ministry. Working among the Indians was deemed an unfit occupation for the highly trained Puritan divines.[43]

Although they responded only halfheartedly, Puritan missionaries of the seventeenth century laid the foundations for subsequent religious work among the tribes. Their method and approach included a heavy emphasis on preaching, with the sermon topics based mostly on Old Testament ideas. The preachers sought to encourage a personal acceptance of Christianity and a simultaneous rejection of tribal religious beliefs and practices. If all went as hoped, once individual Indians accepted the missionary teachings the clerics would begin local church congregations among the villagers resembling those among the whites. To accomplish this, the authorities expected that they would have to teach the Indians how to read. Then, they assumed, the villagers would accept other facets of English culture such as clothing, food, work habits, and a cash economy. Once the native people came to look and act like the colonists, the whites expected to train Indian pastors and teachers, who would then continue the mission work among their own people.[44]

Despite these plans the English moved slowly in bringing Christianity to their Indian neighbors. That was surprising because the missionary activities "presupposed their domination of the prospective converts and the latter's isolation from outside influences, [and they] fit into English plans for regional control."[45] For much of the seventeenth century most of the Indians ignored Christianity, and the New England authorities provided little overt support for religious work among the tribes unless support came from outside the colonies. In fact, colonial missionaries did so little that in 1649 Parliament authorized the organization of the Corporation for the Propagation of the Gospel in New England. The funds, however, went to the Commissioners of the United Colonies of New England, a group organized to manage the diplomatic and military relations with the tribes, not a body much interested in Indian religious well-being.[46]

Indian missions in seventeenth-century New England followed a general pattern with only a few minor variations. Rarely did the English ever bother to learn more than a few basic Algonquian words or phrases, so efforts to spread Protestant Christianity among the tribes proceeded slowly. One exception, the Thomas Mayhews, a father-and-son team, worked conscientiously on Martha's Vineyard following their 1641 purchase of the island. During that decade they learned several local Algonquian dialects and preached among the tribes on that and nearby islands; by 1650 they reported some twenty-two converts. Their efforts enjoyed more success than some of other missionaries because of the limited area on the islands—the tribesmen had nowhere to go to escape them. Apparently the local situation made the inhabitants receptive to the Mayhews' preaching, but there as elsewhere the English had trouble accepting the results of their efforts. In fact, it took the English nearly another ten years to accept the Indians' professions of faith as genuine and for the whites to allow their Indian converts to establish a congregation of their own.[47]

In Massachusetts Bay, John Eliot soon became the person most involved in efforts to spread Christianity to the nearby tribes. During the early 1640s he began his study of Algonquian, and by 1646 he felt confident enough to discuss religious matters with a few of the nearby Indians. In late October 1646 Eliot conducted his first service in Algonquian at the village of the sachem Waban. Weekly visits to the village continued for some months as word of Eliot's efforts spread, and other sachems either came to hear the missionary for themselves or invited him and some of his followers to their villages. By the summer of 1647 he led a group of his converts to Cambridge, where he conducted a service and catechism exercise for the clergymen and colonial lay leaders. It is uncertain what the gathering of Puritan divines and English officials thought of his demonstration, but they continued to encourage and support his efforts in eastern New England.[48]

Colonists in Rhode Island and Plymouth also financed modest efforts to spread Christianity to the Indians, but with less response than in either Massachusetts or on the coastal islands. This variety of efforts brought only modest results when compared to rhetoric about the need to carry their beliefs to the heathen. Clearly the difficulty in learning Indian languages well enough to express complex theological ideas and themes inhibited the missionaries. Perhaps more important in explaining the limited support for and results of the missionary activity was the ingrained English ethnocentrism on the one hand and Indian desires to retain their culture and beliefs on the other. In fact, prior to the 1650s all the major New England tribes such as the Wampanoags, Narragansetts, Niantics, and Mohegans had avoided or rejected the English efforts to change their beliefs.[49]

Puritan Indian missions had little overall effect for another reason. The English could not bring themselves to accept Indian converts as religious or social equals. For the colonists personal salvation came only after years of study, reflection, and self-examination. They assumed that conversion to Christianity transformed the individual completely, and also that one had to adopt the broad attributes of European culture before that process could occur. These ideas slowed the missionaries' efforts to gain public recognition of their converts, but they defended their work forcibly. Comparing English missionary tactics with those used by the Spanish and French, one of them wrote that "if wee would force them to baptisme . . . or if wee would hire them to it by giving them coates and shirts, to allure them to it as some others have done, wee could have gathered many hundreds, yea thousands it may bee by this time, into the name of Churches."[50]

In this situation it is not surprising that the New England religious authorities hesitated to accept evidence that Indian converts under the tutelage of Eliot, Mayhew, or Richard Bourne actually understood what they were saying or doing. For the Puritans admission to full church fellowship resembled initiation into a club that came only after a thorough screening and careful training. Once membership was offered, full equality followed.[51] The actions of the missionaries themselves reflected Puritan ambivalence about Indian conversions. Eliot dragged his feet in organizing independent Indian congregations until he and all other colonial religious leaders could find no fault with the converts. In fact, at Natick in Massachusetts it took from 1646, the year of his first conversions, until 1660 before he agreed to organize a congregation. On Martha's Vineyard the Mayhews, facing similar doubts, established a "church fellowship" rather than a congregation of full standing.[52] This gave converts a chance to increase their knowledge of the new faith while it gave the missionaries time to observe their charges' behavior to see whether Indians understood what they professed.

Acceptance or rejection of Puritan missions varied in direct proportion to the size and independence of the tribe as well as its distance from English centers of population. Remnants of the Massachusets and other small coastal groups proved most willing to accept English teaching and practices. John Eliot knew this, and by the time he began working among a tribe "it had been devastated by epidemics, it had sold or otherwise lost much of its land . . . it had become economically dependent on the English, and it had submitted to the political authority of the colonial government."[53] The career of the Massachuset sachem Cutshamekin illustrates this. He allied his village with the English during the 1630s and then lost most of their land that same decade. By the mid-1640s his people had become politically dependent upon the English, although he remained sachem for a time. When the missionaries challenged his authority in 1650 he became an early convert, and when they established Natick as the first "praying town" he was among its early leaders. Whatever the reasons for Indian acceptance of Christianity, by the 1670s the colonial authorities reported a total of about twenty-five hundred converts, perhaps a fifth of the remaining Indian population. Almost all of those lived in Massachusetts or on offshore islands, however, leaving Connecticut, Rhode Island, New Hampshire, and Maine virtually without recorded converts.[54]

In trying to break down Indian cultural differences and to remake the villagers into acceptable neighbors, the English used education as well as religion. Their theology took for granted the ability of Christians to read and write. If people were to hear and understand biblically based sermons, they had to be able to read the scriptures for themselves. To make this possible, a few of the missionaries learned local Algonquian languages and then translated the Bible, the catechism, hymns, and other religious materials into the tribal dialects. Eliot and the Mayhews had the most notable early successes, but even they produced only a few things for Indians to read. It proved far easier to teach the Indians English than to learn their languages, but it also helped efforts to destroy tribal cultures. As soon as villages and small tribes accepted English dominance, a few children or even adults would receive some language instruction. Indian children were placed in English homes where the boys would learn trades and the girls household skills. However, continued objections by Indian parents to having their children separated from them slowed this particular effort.[55]

As early as 1645 Massachusetts established free common schools, which were open, at least in theory, to whites and Indians alike. A few native children attended these institutions. By the mid-1660s the authorities had paid for "a score or more" of Indian boys to attend schools in Cambridge and Roxbury in the hope that they could be prepared for entrance into Harvard. The authorities wanted the adult Indians to learn to read too, and as early as 1649 John Eliot proposed that they receive daily reading instructions. Clearly some Indians became literate because by 1651 Eliot employed Indian teachers and a year later Thomas Mayhew reported conducting a school for about thirty Indian children on Martha's Vineyard.[56]

When the Massachusetts authorities founded Harvard College they followed the example set by the Virginians in their earlier effort to establish Henrico College. The school's 1650 charter opened it to both whites and Indians, and the first president stated his hope "to make Harvard the Indian Oxford as well as the New England Cambridge."[57] School authorities organized an Indian College in 1654 and within two years had built a separate building expected to hold twenty students. Apparently no more than six or eight Indians got into Harvard during the seventeenth century, and for most of that handful the experience was a disaster. The curriculum made no allowances for whatever educational deficiencies they might have, and few of the young tribesmen seemed able or interested in attending. Several of the students died while there or contracted diseases that killed them soon after they returned home. One was murdered and another dropped out of school. Discouraged by the lack of response, college authorities used some of the space in the Indian College for the new Cambridge Press. By 1692, when the press shut down, the authorities razed the building.[58]

While striving to use religion and education to "civilize" their tribal neighbors, the New Englanders combined these efforts with the idea of creating new villages for those Indians who wanted to participate in white society. This effort came chiefly from the efforts of John Eliot of Massachusetts, but Plymouth used similar towns too. Actually, the towns grew because of religious conversion, educational plans to acculturate the villagers, and colonial efforts to reduce the amount of land individual villages claimed to own. Colonial leaders hoped that by segregating the converts to new towns they could negate tribal influences and protect them from lawless whites. Living in a community with other Christians would help the residents to strengthen their faith while making it easier for the English to impose their cultural standards. So for a variety reasons, often religious as well as racial, the missionaries supported a system of segregated Christian Indian communities, much as the Jesuits had tried briefly in Canada.[59]

Creation of the so-called praying towns for the newly converted Indian believers brought the missionaries and their supporters immediate and continuing objections from Indians and whites alike. By moving converts out of their native communities the whites disrupted tribal life. Sachems protested because they lost followers and could no longer collect tribute from tribal members who left for the new settlements. That left the chiefs unable to supply food and other items to villagers in need or for ceremonial uses. The Powwows, or medicine men, objected too because acceptance of a new religion disrupted the traditional local ceremonies and reduced their stature among the remaining villagers. Relatives of the converts became angry because the departure of the "praying Indians" disrupted clan and family obligations within the villages. White objections centered on two issues. Some people begrudged having to set aside land for the praying Indians, while others feared having towns populated by potentially untrustworthy Indians within the settled bounds of the colony.[60] Under the circumstances, the missionaries and their charges faced an uncertain and difficult future.

That failed to discourage the effort. When John Eliot organized the first of these settlements in 1651 at Natick, Massachusetts, he set the pattern for the new communities. Often over the open objections of the sachem, the missionary persuaded the residents of one village to move and create a new one. In establishing this and other praying towns, Puritan clergymen strove consciously to replace native practices and institutions with English or at least non-Indian ones. Eliot modeled the local town organization on Old Testament principles. He divided the people into groups of hundreds, fifties, and tens within the town. Then he helped the leaders to adopt local regulations for personal and social life to ensure Christian behavior in the village. These rules proscribed polygamy, drunkenness, sexual misconduct, and Sabbath breaking, as well as a host of lesser actions, and included a set of fines and other punishments for lawbreaking.[61]

Residents of the praying towns lived in a circumstance somewhere between those who remained members of active tribes and individual Indians who dwelt among or near the English settlements. In 1656 the Massachusetts authorities appointed Daniel Gookin as superintendent of those Indians who "acknowledged the authority of the colony." In that capacity he acted as sort of a superior court judge or a high-level local magistrate, overseeing the work of the quarterly Indian courts, swearing in town officers, giving orders about local matters, and in general serving as an overseer for the praying towns and their inhabitants. Under his supervision each village chose constables, marshals, and wardens for local duties. By 1658 these leaders, working with Gookin, heard local civil and criminal cases. Despite the appearance of Indian autonomy, however, the English retained careful control. For example, although Indian magistrates exercised the same authority as the English town courts, when they constituted a county court one English magistrate had to preside. The colonial judge also chose the location and date of the proceedings, and any decisions the Indians reached had to meet his approval. Clearly the Europeans wanted their client people to use English forms but proved unwilling to give the residents of the praying towns actual equality.[62]

In their efforts to subvert local tribal culture and authority, colonial New Englanders employed one other tool. They enforced English legal ideas, practices, and laws whenever possible; as the number of invading whites grew, so did the pervasiveness of their legal system. In the long-term relations between the two groups, English rejection of tribal customs was a major element in the invaders' cultural onslaught. For the Europeans, an impersonal legal system represented the collective force of the state. They expected the government to settle disputes between individuals and among groups. The colonists' strong religious beliefs insisted that through the legal system humankind strove to attain God's desires for society. Such ideas were totally foreign to the Algonquian tribal people of New England. They recognized no formal state but depended on their village, clan, and family to provide the framework for their lives. Justice resulted from personal relationships and family obligations rather than a set of laws, and they settled disputes either by paying compensation for damage or injury to others or through retribution when compensation was inadequate or unsatisfactory. In the Indian view, law depended on individual actions rather than the imposition of an impersonal set of laws or government officers. Clearly for Indians to understand and come to accept the European approach to law and government demanded a complete cultural transformation, something few of the native people were either willing or able to make.[63]

From the start, the English sought to extend their mastery over the tribes through treaties. In Plymouth, for example, as early as 1621 colonial treaties called for village sachems to surrender Indians accused of crimes against the invaders to the English for trial and punishment.[64] At the same time, at least in Plymouth, where the Europeans were few in number, they treated the Indians as equally as possible. In 1638 Arthur Peach and several of his servants murdered a young Narragansett man, but before the victim died he identified his attackers. On the basis of his testimony Peach and two of the other three men were arrested, tried, found guilty, and hanged, despite the murmurings of "some of the rude and ignorant sort" about punishing Englishmen for crimes committed against the Indians.[65] This resulted from a Pilgrim effort to deal fairly and equally with their tribal neighbors, and from terror because the outnumbered residents of Plymouth feared their Indian neighbors.

That incident was a clear exception, as the New England courts rarely treated Indians and whites alike. Rather, colonial officials used treaty agreements and the legal system repeatedly to extend their authority over the tribes. As early as 1629 the Massachusetts Bay leaders assumed that their charter rights granted them sovereignty over the local people. At first they adopted the Indian system of working through the village or tribal sachems to obtain the return of stolen property or learn the identity of Indian lawbreakers. This gave the appearance of tribal autonomy, but gradually Indian leaders found themselves being held responsible for crimes or suspected misdeeds of their followers or even neighbors, a concept totally foreign to them.[66]

As settlement increased, English strength grew and that of the tribal people decreased. For example, in Plymouth by 1640 the authorities assumed the right to protect Indian groups by limiting who might purchase tribal lands and under what circumstances such transactions might take place. They also sought to protect themselves by regulating Indians' right to trade freely with the traders and settlers, particularly when the purchase of firearms and alcohol was concerned. In both cases the colonials strove to prevent violence between the races. While doing that their laws set a precedent for other limitations of Indian rights and proved an effective part of efforts to subjugate the tribes by reducing their economic rights when dealing with the English.[67]

From the start, the English treated their tribal neighbors unequally through the developing legal system. In disputes between Indians a few of the villagers might serve on the jury, but this was rare. Not only did tribal people not participate fully, but usually if convicted of a crime they received harsher punishment than did whites for the same action. Indians, but not Europeans, might be seized for the use or possession of alcohol, and by the late 1650s at least Plymouth had begun to develop a separate legal code for use in controlling the actions of the local Indians. If colonial laws gave a temporary advantage to the tribesmen, authorities soon amended or altered them to the detriment of the Indians. Throughout the colonial era, even when courts ruled fairly for both Indians and Europeans, the latter often received lighter or less harsh sentences. Frequently judges fined whites for a particular crime while Indians received corporal punishment. It is possible that the sentence merely reflected the different level of participation of the two groups in the colonial cash economy, but undoubtedly many Indians would have preferred to pay a fine rather than receive a public whipping.[68]

By the 1670s some Indians had become familiar with English legal practices, and individual colonial governments began to allow tribal members to serve on juries. Rhode Island and Plymouth both impaneled mixed juries on several major cases. Plymouth included Indian jurors as adjuncts or observers in the trial of the Indians accused of murdering John Sassamon, a Christian Indian. It also made provision for accepting the testimony of those Indians who could not or would not take an oath on the Bible to tell the truth. This was particularly significant in cases between tribal members and colonists because the colonial authorities concluded that "the Indians would be greatly disadvantaged if noe Testimony should in such case be accepted but on oath."[69] Clearly by the eve of King Philip's War in the mid-1670s individual Indians, members of subject tribes, residents of praying towns, and even native people not fully subjugated by the English had come under the powerful influence of the colonial legal system.

KING PHILIP'S WAR

Having expanded their authority in matters of diplomacy, economics, law, education, and religion, the New Englanders assumed that they would prevail in their relations with the nearby tribes. Yet frequently Indian sachems objected to and resented English policies and actions. In fact, a major conflict, King Philip's War, developed as a direct response to colonial high-handedness and tribal resentments. As the colonists assumed ever-widening control of the regional situation, Indian leaders felt their independence and honor slipping away. Eventually this led to open conflict. King Philip's War, or the Second Puritan Conquest, as one scholar calls it, was much more than a simple white-Indian fight. It resulted from continuing English expansion and aggression; intercolonial competition over land and control of Indian affairs between Plymouth, Connecticut, and Massachusetts; ongoing tribal rivalries between the Narragansetts, Wampanoags, and Mohegans; stresses between Christian Indians and their tribal relatives; and the ambitions and personal influence of individual sachems.[70]

Metacom, or King Philip, as the English called him, and his older brother came to prominence as Wampanoag sachems during the 1660s when their father, a longtime friend of the English, died. Wamsutta, the elder of the brothers, assumed tribal leadership but after a 1662 interrogation by colonial leaders sickened and died, leaving Metacom to become the new sachem. Following his brother's lead, he reaffirmed his father's treaty of peace and friendship with the Plymouth authorities. At the same time he took a more openly independent stance toward the whites. An astute leader, he recognized the threat colonial expansion posed for the tribe and sought to strengthen Indian abilities to resist

English encroachment. While trying to accomplish this he strove to discredit his traditional Indian rivals such as the Narragansetts and the Mohegans by informing the whites of Indian plots against them. In particular he warned the Plymouth officials about the efforts of Ninigret, sachem of the Niantics, as that leader sought to extend his influence over lesser tribes.[71] Clearly Metacom hoped to gain favor with the English and then use his good standing with them to deflect activities that might reduce his power or damage Wampanoag interests.

By 1667, however, the chief stood accused of plotting to cooperate with the French and Dutch against the English. Plymouth officials demanded that he appear and explain his actions, and it seems likely that this experience was the basis for his later hatred of the English. Two years later rumors that the Wampanoags again threatened war brought yet another colonial investigation. In April 1671 Metacom and his advisers appeared before Plymouth officials to explain their actions. Nervous about continuing rumors of plots and possible war, the colonial leaders took a hard line in dealing with the Wampanoag sachems. Although the authorities thought that Philip had not encouraged Indian belligerence, they said that he had not done enough to defuse hostile acts either. The English forced the chief to admit some guilt, but even more damaging to his leadership and tribal welfare was the Plymouth demand that his followers surrender their guns. This left them vulnerable to enemy attack and limited their hunting effectiveness. Forced to sign a new treaty with the colony, he and his followers were disarmed and sent home. This outraged the chief. In fact, it may well have convinced him that English authority extended into too many aspects of Indian life and actions.[72]

From this point on the Plymouth authorities' hard line toward the Wampanoag leader did not waver as white actions continually antagonized Philip without giving him any effective way to maintain his stature within the tribal society. By 1675 Indian resentment over real and imagined slights, anger over English land grabbing, and colonial fears of an Indian conspiracy had created a volatile situation. In January of that year several Plymouth Indians discovered the body of John Sassamon, a Christian Indian who, just a few days earlier, had warned colonial authorities that the Wampanoags were organizing for a broad multitribal war. When they found Sassamon's body under suspicious circumstances, the officials decided that he had been murdered. Eventually a single Indian testified that three Wampanoags had killed the victim, and in June 1675 the accused men faced trial in Plymouth. The jury convicted them and eventually all three were executed, but not before the last of the trio had confessed to the crime. Because one of the murderers was an adviser to Metacom, the Plymouth officials assumed that the sachem had ordered the killing to cover his conspiratorial actions. From there it was only a matter of weeks before violence broke out, quickly leading to all-out war.[73]

Although the conflict has come down to the present as King Philip's War, that name paints too simplified a picture. The causes were varied and complex. Some Indian groups had suffered from English abuse, while others managed to avoid most difficulties. Groups as varied as the Abenakis in Maine, the Nipmucs and Pocumtucks in Connecticut, and the Narragansetts in Rhode Island all joined the Wampanoags against the colonists. Often English aggression led directly to their participation. The Narragansetts, for example, had maintained a strained neutrality until December 1675, when a large force of colonial troops attacked them in the Great Swamp Fight, which resulted in several hundred Indian deaths. That event brought the Narragansett sachem Canonchet to leadership in the war. In fact, it should more rightly carry his name than that of Philip. Canonchet led far more warriors than any other tribal leader, and his participation gave the hostile groups renewed strength and enthusiasm. Among the major New England tribes only the Mohegans under Uncas and the Niantics led by Ninigret supported the English with any substantial number of warriors.[74]

The fighting, some of the bloodiest and most destructive in American history, destroyed the Indians' ability to resist further English expansion. During the conflict tribal forces attacked more than half of the ninety towns in New England. Of those, they destroyed seventeen settlements and inflicted heavy damage on another twenty-five. About 11 percent—nine thousand out of perhaps eighty thousand—of the total population on both sides perished in the fighting. Thousands of others fled, and many Indians were enslaved by the victorious whites. While the tribes suffered most of the casualties, the New England settlements experienced severe economic and social stresses that affected the region for generations.[75] As a result, the war changed the face of the countryside and the multiracial societies there never returned to their preconflict conditions.

The war resulted from many causes, but most of them were the fault of the expanding colonial societies. Except for the Pequot War in the 1630s, relative peace had characterized relations between the Indians and their English neighbors for nearly two generations. By the 1670s leaders like the aging Roger Williams, who had worked for peace in earlier decades, had been nearly all pushed aside or replaced by younger, more impatient men. Overlapping land claims put forward by the various colonies brought friction too. Initial titles and questionable land cessions negotiated with numerous sachems clouded the issue of who controlled which land in an area with more would-be farmers than good farmland. Indian leaders accused each other of conspiring against the colonists in the years before the war. In short, by 1670 the circumstances of intracolonial and intercolonial relations were unstable at best.

When Plymouth authorities planted the new settlement of Swansea in 1667, their action brought settlers into almost immediate contact with the Pokanoket villagers, who lived at what had been Massasoit's old principle town. Friction over land use, hunting, and the destruction of Indian crops by colonists' livestock brought difficulties and bad feelings on both sides. After repeated incidents in 1675 the colonists reported that Indians who encountered settlers there had begun to pilfer, bully, and then threaten the whites as hysteria swept across the colony. Rumors of tribal alliances abounded, and by mid-June roving bands of warriors began to strip and burn abandoned farms and other buildings. Within weeks the other colonies learned of the difficulties, and Massachusetts dispatched troops almost immediately. As the whites combined forces, most of the tribes moved against the colonists. Once fighting began, Indian war parties swept through outlying settlements, destroying many of them and sending terrified families fleeing east to the larger settlements. Despite their repeated victories, by August 1676 the undermanned tribes went down to defeat.[76]

The war brought immense destruction and population loss to both colonists and tribes. Whole towns and villages disappeared, while the population on both sides of the conflict dropped sharply. Nevertheless, the conflict proved more crucial to Indian survival than to that of the colonists. The whites had crushed the Wampanoag, Narragansett, Nipmuc, and Pocumtuck tribes, while they already dominated the much-reduced Pequots and Mohegans. Most of the individual survivors from each of the defeated tribes surrendered to colonial forces, but some fled out of the region, seeking homes among related groups in New York and even eastern Canada. Those villages and individuals who remained found themselves at the mercy and under the domination of the New England colonial governments. Even the praying Indians who had sought to serve as allies suffered greatly from this conflict. After the war they were allowed to return to their towns, but of the fourteen that existed in 1675 only four remained. There, broken in health, spirit, and numbers, the remnant of John Eliot's converts lived out their days. In the years immediately after the fighting, the English used their political-legal system to control all the New England tribes socially and to reduce their rights. The whites, too, lost heavily, as they had to abandon numerous towns completely, but they had the population and economic power to rebuild. King Philip's war proved a disaster for the New England tribes, but it was merely the last step in a half-century process. When it ended, the English controlled the situation. As in Virginia their laws, legal system, economy, and religion had triumphed.

4 Trade, Diplomacy, Warfare, and Acculturation, 1670s–1750s

 BY THE END of the seventeenth century the Indians in both Virginia and New England had been conquered as their English neighbors expanded their population and control in each region. In New France by 1701 the Iroquois challenge receded as those tribes accepted a general peace. Meanwhile in New Mexico the Pueblo Revolt of 1680 had driven the Spanish from the region temporarily, but by the end of the 1690s the invaders had regained control over much of the Rio Grande Valley and the village dwellers there. During those conflicts many tribes experienced dramatic shifts in their circumstances. Many lost their initial position of superiority over the Europeans. Some had their economies and societies gravely threatened, while others experienced disease, warfare, or dislocations. Not only did the growing populations of the colonial settlements impinge on the aboriginal people, but the French, English, and to a lesser degree the Spanish clashed with each other. This kept the eastern and central portions of the continent in frequent turmoil and was one element in the long-term evolution of interracial relations.

Indian initiatives and responses to the dramatic changes then sweeping across North America provide another significant part of the story. Scattered remnants of eastern groups accepted other refugees as they regrouped and transformed their isolated villages into multitribal settlements. Some chose to welcome one or more groups of European traders. Others used the turmoil brought about by international rivalries, diseases, and warfare to play one group of colonials against another, sometimes with great success. Often tribes sought alliances with the whites to protect themselves from their Indian enemies. Occasionally native people tried to get the colonial powers to punish their traditional rivals for them. In the century that followed the founding of successful European colonies, the tribes struggled to retain their independence and traditional cultures. They used trade, diplomacy, and warfare with other Indians as well as the intruding whites to accomplish their goals. While they strove to avoid European domination, they welcomed some white technology and household items, incorporating them easily into their local customs. This brought gradual change and some slight acculturation to colonial ways, but whenever possible they retained their cultural identity.

In the far north the English gained a toehold at Hudson's Bay on one flank of New France, while the Quebec-based traders from the Saint Lawrence spread west into the Mississippi Valley and north to Lake Winnipeg. Gradually the French extended their trading posts and territorial claims south of the Great Lakes into the Ohio Valley, while by the 1750s English colonial traders based in Pennsylvania and Virginia breached the Appalachian barrier, bringing them into direct competition with the French in present-day Ohio. This continuing emphasis on the fur trade as an aspect of imperial domination had a major impact on Indian-white relations. Frequently Canadian men living in the wilderness took Indian wives and fathered large numbers of mixed-race children. While both French and English traders participated, the attitudes toward and treatment of Indian spouses and children varied widely between the competing Europeans and laid the foundations for the differing treatment of racially mixed people down to the present.

During the first half of the eighteenth century Indian relations with the colonial powers shifted gradually so that the fur trade became the tribes' best means of retaining economic strength and political independence. By this time repeated Iroquois raiding and warfare had disrupted and even destroyed some village societies. For the many refugee groups who had fled into Wisconsin and Illinois the French appeared as almost their only possible allies. At the same time, the basis for good relations between the tribes and the French shifted gradually from economics to diplomacy and military assistance when the Europeans demanded more help against the English traders and settlers. Except for the Hudson's Bay Company employees in the north, the English usually represented groups of settler-dominated colonies. Because they wanted to have the land and its resources, they viewed the Indians as minimally useful at best or dangerous enemies at worst. While each of the colonizing powers in the north sought tribal allies, both continued their efforts to provide Christian teaching as well as European culture and technology to those who cooperated with them, but with less effort than they had provided a few decades earlier. Their reduced missionary presence resulted from the continuing disputes and wars that racked North America and, more importantly, from most Indians' rejection of European religion and society.

In the far north the English landed on the rocky shores of Hudson's Bay, while they renewed their colony founding farther to the south. During the 1660s New York had fallen into their hands, and in the next two decades they began settlements in Pennsylvania and Carolina. As they pushed west from these eastern enclaves the French countered by establishing themselves at Mobile and then New Orleans. The Spanish presence in Florida and along the Gulf Coast west to Pensacola as well as their claims to the Atlantic Coast north into Carolina certainly complicated the lives of the southern Indians and produced a three-sided competition in the region. Nevertheless, much of the time the basic contest occurred between the tribes and their English allies on one side and the French and their Indian trading partners on the other. Through that rivalry, by 1750 the precarious balance between Indians and whites had tipped sharply and permanently in favor of the invaders.

At the turn of the century the French sought to strengthen their colonial holdings in North America. As part of this effort Pierre Le Moyne d'Iberville received orders to establish a new settlement at the mouth of the Mississippi River. Arriving just before competing English and Spanish expeditions in 1699, the French built a small settlement on the lower Mississippi. Moving eastward, Iberville ordered the construction of forts at Biloxi and Mobile Bay, anchoring a national presence on the lower Mississippi Valley and the Gulf Coast. With this move the French claimed to control the waterways of eastern North America from the Saint Lawrence west and south down the Ohio, Great Lakes, and Mississippi to the Gulf of Mexico. This action screened the growing English Atlantic settlements and the Spanish gulf holdings from the interior of the continent and would bring these colonial powers and their trading partners into repeated clashes for dominance.[1]

BRITISH EXPANSION NORTH AND SOUTH

Meanwhile, the English had not remained idle. Moving from Hudson's Bay in the far north, New York, Pennsylvania, and Virginia in the center, and Carolina and Georgia to the south, they extended their population and trade with the Indians in direct competition. Actually, French authorities inadvertently brought the English to Hudson's Bay when in 1659–61 two *coureurs de bois,* or woods rangers—Médard Chouart, sieur des Groseilliers, and Pierre Esprit Radisson, unlicensed French traders—slipped out of Saint Louis lacking permission for their upcoming trade. They spent the winter trading in Wisconsin and on the shores of Lake Superior, but when they returned to Montreal with prime furs, the governor confiscated most of the furs and levied a fine as well. The two traders angrily left New France to seek other financing in London.[2]

There they interested wealthy men in and out of the government in the possibilities open to those who would penetrate North America through Hudson's Bay. After some confusion about who would support the venture, the two Canadians sailed west during the summer of 1668 on English vessels. Apparently the English hoped to find copper and other usable minerals in the Canadian north, but that was not to be. Rather, for the next century and a half the Governor and Company of Adventurers of England Trading into Hudson's Bay, or the Hudson's Bay Company, focused its efforts and attention almost exclusively on the fur trade, competing with French traders from the Saint Lawrence Valley. In 1672 the company had sent men to build a year-round trading post. The European presence was not a colony but rather a small permanent settlement or factory similar to those already operating in Africa and Asia. Such a trading entrepôt provided the northern Indians an alternative to the French along the Saint Lawrence and introduced tiny, isolated groups of Englishmen to the nomadic tribes of the north. Because there would be no formal colonial settlement developing out of the factories, the lack of European women brought the company employees into competition with local Indian men for the companionship of Indian women, and eventually resulted in substantial interracial marriage and the growth of a group that came to be known as the country-born among the English and their trade partners of the north.[3]

While the Europeans sought to extend their imperial claims through exploration, settlement, and trade, the Indians adapted the invaders' activities to their own benefit. In Canada the Hudson's Bay Company trading posts brought new groups into contact with the expanding European commercial system. From the 1670s on into the next century the Plains Cree and Assiniboine tribes moved into a central position within the growing trade network that stretched southwest from Hudson's Bay. These people lived and hunted along the lakes and rivers of Manitoba and Saskatchewan. At first they took their surplus skins and pelts down the Nelson River to York Factory, on Hudson's Bay. Within a generation they became middlemen in the trade and began taking European goods to the isolated tribes of the interior and exchanging those items for more furs.

As their trade became firmly established their way of life changed to accommodate the new circumstances. These people had always hunted and traded with their tribal neighbors, but now the men took an ever-larger part of each year for travel and trade. In late spring each year the young men loaded several hundred canoes with pelts and set off down the rivers to the English outposts. By midsummer they returned home and went back to their food gathering and hunting. After using the manufactured items for a while, they traded them to people more distant from the English, taking the furs obtained in that barter to the Hudson's Bay centers the next year. Because the Crees and Assiniboines occupied the region through which the trade routes passed, they tended to dominate the process as the Ottawas and Hurons had done earlier and farther to the east.[4]

Some of the people the English called the Swampy Crees settled near the larger trading posts and gradually came to be known as the Home Guard Indians. They worked sporadically by hunting, fishing, guiding, and occasionally hauling material for the Europeans. Living in close proximity to the English, and having forgone most of their annual migration cycle to remain there, these people suffered more drastic social changes than the hunting and trading bands did. When English traders took Indian wives the women usually came from the Home Guard groups, and that practice disrupted the sex ratio within the native communities. Despite Hudson's Bay Company directives limiting intermarriage with the Indians, the practice grew, as did a mixed-race population centered at the trading posts. The tribal people here, then, had sharply different relations with the English than did tribes in the settler-dominated colonies to the south. In many ways their experience more closely resembled the situation in parts of New France than in the other English colonies.[5]

Both Indians and individual traders benefited from the interracial marriages. The European men brought with them access to desirable trade goods, while their native partners assured them of acceptance in the village or band society. Among some groups particular individuals or families dominated trade with outsiders, so often women from such families willingly married the whites. Over the years the introduction of European men into the village societies brought cultural, economic, and genetic changes to the frontier. French traders too acquired native mates and fathered people now known as Métis in Canada. In most cases, the children of these unions remained in their home villages, growing to adulthood as Indians. Yet some became bilingual, even bicultural, and often came to play a major role in directing relations with outsiders for their village relatives. In the long run such unions led to fundamental changes that

Richard White describes as "the Middle Ground." At that point the village peoples combined elements of both Indian and European societies.[6]

Far to the south a different set of relationships developed after the English founded the colony of Carolina during the late seventeenth century. Initial settlement in South Carolina began in 1670 when the proprietors sent colonists up the Ashley River to begin Charles Towne (Charleston). Settlement at the first site failed, and ten years later the colonial center moved to the junction of the Ashley and Cooper Rivers at the coast. There the pioneer colonists erected a village of some thirty houses and several government buildings, all surrounded by a log palisade. Established at the northern fringe of Spanish influence in eastern North America, the tiny settlement clung precariously to the coast, while its residents hoped to avoid Spanish attacks. Although the colonial proprietors granted land to many settlers, the colonists failed to develop any profitable agriculture and turned instead to the fur trade. Soon they competed directly with both the French and, to a lesser degree, the Spanish in the Southeast. Having access to traders from more than one nation allowed the Indians to direct and shape some of the interracial dealings for the next three-quarters of a century. Often the relations between the tribes and the Carolina settlers proved more similar to the situation in early New France than in the other English colonies or at Hudson's Bay.

The proprietary government controlled English dealings with the tribes, and it ordered that "no person whatever, shall hold or claim any land in Carolina, by purchase or gift, or otherwise from the natives."[7] From the start colonial developers strove to keep peace by separating the pioneers and the Indians. For example, in July 1669 they directed the whites to maintain a buffer between their land and that of the tribes. In addition, the regulations prohibited any settlement or land use within two and a half miles of any Indian town unless it was across a river from the villagers. They also authorized gifts for each tribal or village leader and ordered the colonial storekeeper to provide manufactured goods to the nearby Indians in exchange for furs and hides.

These gifts brought the English into existing patterns of exchange with the Carolina tribes almost immediately. Local Indians had engaged in gift exchange, trade, and raiding long before the Europeans arrived, and those practices continued. At first, as with the French along the Saint Lawrence and the English at Hudson's Bay, the tribal people forced the newcomers to accept their patterns of meeting, exchange, and trade. Their ceremonies and ritual gift giving continued, although after a few years the English presence altered them gradually. Some traders married into leading families among the villagers. After the whites arrived, the Indians learned that the English would pay well for captives, a practice that encouraged intertribal raiding and warfare and led to the growth of a well-organized slave trade. At first these developments only modified existing native practices, rather than causing distinctly new ones among the tribal peoples in the Southeast.[8]

The coastal tribes saw the English settlers as potential allies against their enemies, in particular the Westos, a small but aggressive group of newcomers who threatened the earlier residents. As early as March 1670 a nearby cacique or chief urged the English to settle near his village on the Ashley River and to join him against the Westos. The latter, armed with firearms gotten from Virginia traders, posed a problem for the Carolinians too. They had the choice of either uniting with the small coastal tribes against the Westos or coming to terms with that tribe as protection against the others. Employing Henry Woodward, a trader who had lived among the Indians during the late 1660s, as their spokesman, the proprietors decided to open trade with the Westos. Following Woodward's successful trip and his trading with them, the Westos became allied with the Carolina pioneers and from 1674 to 1680 cooperated with the English in both trade and defense.[9]

Like officials in New France who tried to ignore or subvert directives about how to deal with the Indians, Carolina leaders objected to the English proprietors' efforts to control their local affairs. The London-based company expected to dominate the fur and hide trade with the major tribes of the interior, leaving only the small coastal groups to trade with the colonists. As a result, disputes over who could deal with particular Indians continued, and representatives of the proprietors and local elite clashed repeatedly. Thefts, murders, and general confusion marked Indian-white relations in the settlement during the 1670s, and following two murders by Westo men, the whites prohibited their entry into the settlement. Then in 1680 Westo attacks on another tribe allied to the English led to war. The Carolinians joined forces with a group of Shawnees known as the Savannahs, and by late 1683 they defeated the Westos. The survivors either fled or were captured and sold into slavery by the triumphant whites.[10]

Flushed with their victory and anticipating large profits to be made selling captives as slaves during the early 1680s, the colonists encouraged Indian raids into northern Florida. Soon hundreds of Cherokees, Creeks, and men from smaller coastal tribes raided the Spanish mission tribes in northern Florida.

Before the decade ended, their campaigns hastened the collapse of the Spanish missions among the tribes there and set into motion tribal migrations that would last for the next several generations. When the Spanish proved unable to protect their Indian allies and converts and instead tried to force them to move south out of the reach of the marauding bands from Carolina, many of the people revolted. Fleeing from the Spanish, these Indians migrated north and east, and by the mid-1680s several thousand Yamasees began moving into the lower Savannah area. When the English pushed their trading interests south and west they encouraged groups of Creeks to move east from what is now Alabama into Georgia. In retaliation the Spanish tried to attack the settlements at Port Royal and Stuart's Town. Their fleet of three tiny vessels headed north to attack Charleston in 1686, but a hurricane destroyed two of the ships and frustrated the Spanish campaign. This military foray proved to be the high point of Spanish efforts to rebuff English settlement along the coast of Carolina.[11]

The English-led attacks on the Spanish mission tribes spread disaster through northern Florida quickly and exposed the inherent weakness of Spain's American claims there. Long-simmering tribal anger over Franciscan mistreatment now burst forth as hundreds of mission neophytes fled or revolted and joined one of the invading war parties. Tribes not then subject to the clerics launched raids of their own. When Queen Anne's War broke out in 1701, that European conflict spread quickly to America. The next year Carolina forces moved south to attack Saint Augustine, but they failed to capture that fortress. In 1704 former Carolina governor James Moore organized two large slave-gathering expeditions that marched into Apalachee, burning settlements, killing Spanish and Indians, and seizing several thousand captives destined for slavery in the West Indies. Only two years later, in 1706, other raids crushed the rest of the Franciscan missions, reducing the Spanish to little more than the region adjacent to Saint Augustine. At that point, while a few clerics, officials, and traders remained, Spain lost its position as a major competitor in the Southeast. Its role became clearly secondary to that of either France or Britain.[12]

FRENCH AND ENGLISH RIVALRIES IN THE SOUTHEAST

When the Carolina traders and their Indian allies defeated the Spanish, the French moved into the region too. The presence of competing groups of Europeans provided the southeastern Indians with both opportunity and danger. For all, the whites' activities in the region brought long-term changes. By the time the French explored the region around the mouth of the Mississippi River, Carolina traders had already worked their way west from Charleston and had initiated dealings with all of the major tribes of the region. As a result, British traders enjoyed strong relationships with the Cherokees, Creeks, and Chickasaws before the French made any alliances. Among the major tribes in the region only the Choctaws of Mississippi and the Alabamas usually sided with the French throughout that era,[13] although all of the tribes there shifted trading partners occasionally.

The renewed contacts between the tribal people and the intruding Europeans in the late seventeenth century brought epidemic diseases to the region as had happened elsewhere. Smallpox, influenza, measles, and a host of other pathogens carried away thousands of villagers, disrupting the normal social and economic patterns of life throughout the region. Once again the Indians contended with a partial collapse of their societies while they confronted the newcomers. Population estimates for the precontact era remain vague and unreliable, but figures for the eighteenth century show clearly the devastating impact the Europeans had on Native American societies. Recent scholarship concludes that Indian population in the Southeast dropped from about two hundred thousand in 1685 to only fifty-six thousand by 1790. Within that area the rate and speed of decline varied widely, but all of the tribes lost substantial numbers of people.[14]

These population losses reduced aboriginal self-sufficiency and persuaded Indian leaders to increase trade with the Europeans. As had been the case elsewhere, the growing trade meant many things, often different, to the tribal people and the Europeans. At least at first the village leaders sought to bring the strange visitors within diplomatic and social bounds that the Indians took for granted. They assumed that gift exchange meant peace between the two groups as well as a possible future alliance against mutual enemies. The white traders and diplomats saw no such thing. While they might hope that a village or tribe would cooperate and remain loyal to their side in the international disputes that swept across eastern North America, more often they sought only short-term economic gain. They failed to understand Indian motivations in property exchange and as a result often brought further misery to the villages they visited during the eighteenth century.[15]

While the Europeans misunderstood the situation, both the French and the English encountered tribal people facing increasingly difficult circumstances. French arrival in the region at the beginning of the eighteenth century brought them into immediate contact with the Chickasaws and the Choctaws, the largest tribes in the immediate area. These two peoples had been fierce competitors, even enemies, for generations, and the Europeans' presence allowed them to continue their bitter rivalry indefinitely. English traders from Charleston provided arms and other commercial goods to the Chickasaw, so when Choctaw emissaries arrived, Governor Pierre Le Moyne d'Iberville sent them home loaded with presents. In part he did this because he knew Indian customs, but he also realized that unless he provided the Choctaws with a reliable supply of weapons, powder, and lead they would be forced to slip away to join the British. If that happened, the French would face a solid front of tribes allied to their enemies.[16]

The presence of the two European powers in such close proximity should have given the southeastern Indians an opportunity to play one group of white traders off against the other for better goods and lower prices. Unfortunately, for most of the next five or six decades one side or the other clearly dominated the region, greatly reducing the Indians' real bargaining power. As they had in New France, officials in Louisiana slipped into existing intertribal rivalries and wars all too easily, keeping ongoing competition alive for several generations. Because the Choctaw and Chickasaw had been rivals for years, each now tried to maintain good relations with the whites in order to get arms and trade goods for use against the other. At times the Indians insisted that the Europeans assist in their raids too. Hoping to avoid that expense and danger, the whites had to negotiate continuously just to keep an uneasy peace in the region. For the Choctaws, then, the French represented not only potential allies and a source for trade goods but also, and at least as important, a screen between themselves and their tribal enemies, who were assisted by the advancing Carolina and later Georgia traders.

For the Europeans, on the other hand, whether in the back reaches of the Hudson's Bay country or the Gulf Coast region, the nearby tribes represented a significant market for trade goods first, and then allies and a buffer behind which imperial expansion could progress. The basic trade in the south focused primarily on the hides of white-tailed deer rather than beaver and other fur bearers because the mild southern winters did not encourage the growth of heavy furs as in the north. The traders preferred dressed or worked hides that had been scraped clear of hair and stretched and smoked. In this state the hides were more pliable than the raw skins. The Indian men hunted deer for meat and hides regularly each year, and the women prepared hides for their own use. So at first gathering and preparing a surplus of deer skins for exchange with the traders brought no fundamental changes in village economic practices, merely more work for the tribal people.[17]

ENGLISH ENCOUNTERS WITH THE SOUTHEASTERN INDIANS

Each year after the 1680s pack trains loaded with English goods headed south and west from Charleston to all of the major tribes of the Southeast except the Alabamas and Choctaws. At times the Carolina traders even risked visiting those two tribes in hope of finding a receptive chief or two and a ready market. Although the English offered more and better-quality goods and charged less then their French competitors, the Indians objected to European practices repeatedly. Unscrupulous traders who cheated or introduced alcohol caused much dissatisfaction. One tactic of the most greedy traders was to extend nearly unlimited credit and, when the Indians could no longer pay their debts, to seize the women and children of a village and take them back to Charleston to be sold into slavery. A second trick guaranteed to cause anger was to hire Indians to serve as bearers when returning to the settlements heavily laden with hides but to refuse to pay them what had been promised or even to enslave them once they reached Charleston.[18]

While the more dishonest traders angered their partners with those tactics, James Moore chose more direct action. His 1704 attacks against the Apalache Indians in northern Florida led thirteen hundred of those people to settle near Charleston. Campaigns against the Spanish brought Carolina Indians and whites to the gates of Pensacola in 1707 in response to a failed French-Spanish seaborne attack on Charleston. The English objective, however, lay farther west, at Mobile, and that same summer Captain Thomas Nairne proposed raising another white-Indian force to attack the French there by land and water. This never took place, but in 1707–8 news of it kept the population there in turmoil and brought increasing presents to tribes allied with the French.[19]

Meanwhile the Carolina Indians experienced increasing trouble with the English. The Tuscaroras, an Iroquoian people living in the Piedmont of North Carolina, exemplified this. A large and active tribe, they dominated the smaller Algonquian groups along the Atlantic Coast and also had played a major role in trade with the interior for several generations. By 1700 the Carolina Tuscarora villages had coalesced into two broad divisions. The northern villages followed the nominal leadership of Chief Tom Blount, while those to the south looked to Chief Hancock for general direction. Lacking any real unity, the villagers had tolerated the tiny English settlements in North Carolina because they assumed that the colonists posed little threat to them. However, the efforts of colonial officials to disrupt Tuscarora domination over the smaller coastal tribes angered the Indians and brought some minor violence.

Still, it took until the first decade of the eighteenth century for the situation to become dangerous. In 1708 smallpox, blamed on the colonists, swept through the Carolina villages, disrupting society and leadership. That same year Indians from the northern Tuscarora villages killed Simon Kilcrease, an Englishman from Virginia. That brought a major diplomatic crisis when Indian leaders refused English demands that they surrender the accused for trial. Eventually the colonists captured some men, but most escaped and one was released. Just a year later, in 1710, Carolina settlement increased unexpectedly when the Baron Christoph von Graffenried and several English partners founded New Bern, a community of Swiss and Palatine Germans, in territory claimed by the southern Tuscarora villagers.[20]

Apparently hoping to force the new colonists to leave tribal lands, Chief Hancock led warriors from the southern Tuscarora towns into what became a major war. In 1711 the Indians captured a group of explorers led by the well-known trader John Lawson and Baron von Graffenried. After torturing and burning Lawson to death, they extracted a promise of neutrality from the baron and then began raiding nearby farms and small villages. In their first attacks they killed at least 120 of the colonists while gathering booty and captives. Other raids followed quickly as the warriors cleared the whites from their country. The conflict spread quickly to involve colonists in both North and South Carolina as well as groups of Indians who fought alongside the Tuscaroras or against them.[21] Long-existing quarrels motivated some tribes to oppose the Tuscaroras, while others joined the fray to acquire promised rewards of European trade goods, captured material, livestock, and slaves.

The Charleston traders led the attackers during the conflict. John Barnwell, who came to be called "Tuscarora Jack," led a force of more than five hundred whites and Indians from South Carolina north to burn crops, destroy villages, and seize captives. At the Neuse River his army failed to capture the fort defended by Chief Hancock. In fact, during the assault on the Indians some of Barnwell's men fled when the defenders opened fire, and several were "deservedly shot . . . in their arses."[22] Despite this setback, the Carolina force returned home, leading large numbers of captives headed for slavery. The next year, 1712, another group trekked north to continue the war. This army of thirty whites and nearly a thousand Indians proved more able, and after heavy fighting and many casualties on each side, the invaders broke Tuscarora resistance. The defeat forced Tom Blount, the leading chief, to sign a one-sided treaty accepting a tributary status to the English. The end of this war saw hundreds of Tuscaroras killed, hundreds more enslaved, and the survivors forced onto a small reservation from which many of them fled to join Iroquois relatives in New York.[23]

No sooner had the hard-won peace begun after the Tuscarora War when another and more dangerous conflict, the Yamasee War, broke out. It resulted from the repeated English abuses of the Indians. Settled in the Port Royal area south of Charleston, the Yamasees had seen their landholdings shrink steadily between 1698 and 1711 as thousands of acres of land were granted to white settlers. Also, as they had in New England prior to King Philip's War, the whites' livestock foraged in Indian fields, destroying crops and angering the villagers. In 1707 the colonial authorities tried to protect tribal lands, but pioneer encroachments continued. Hungry colonists would frequently seize Indian livestock, poultry, and crops and then refuse to pay a fair price for those things. Some traders forced Indian men to carry heavy packs as much as five hundred miles for almost no pay "and when they had sent the men away . . . [the traders bragged] of Debauching their wives."[24] When hunters fell into debt to the traders the whites demanded that the Indians surrender members of their families to be sold into slavery to settle the debt.

These issues might not have been enough to trigger a major Indian war against the South Carolina settlements had not many of the tribes there not just participated as allies to the whites in the Tuscarora War. During that conflict Virginia traders had continued to supply arms and munitions even to the tribes fighting against the Carolina forces. The Indians thus came to see the existing divisions and repeated lack of cooperation among the English. More important, in the two years of multitribal campaigning against the Tuscaroras, warriors from coastal and inland tribes met and lived together for months on end as they came to share their concerns about the invading whites. As a result, when Yamasee messengers calling for an all-out war against the English arrived, village leaders often proved receptive. By early 1715 many coastal groups joined the Yamasees, and even the distant Cherokees sent a contingent of seventy men as allies.[25]

Like the 1711 campaign against North Carolina, the attack that set off the Yamasee War was well coordinated, and at least the early phases of the conflict demonstrated a rare unity among the coastal and upcountry tribes. By this time it appears that some of them realized that their continual debts to the Carolina traders, and the growing difficulty in gaining captives from the smaller tribes then being destroyed, might mean eventual slavery for themselves. Under these circumstances, rumors of growing Indian anger and plots to attack the settlements led the Carolina authorities to send three experienced Indian traders to negotiate with the Yamasees. The three, Thomas Nairne, John Wright, and John Cochran, met with tribal leaders in April 1715 and after an apparently satisfactory council stayed overnight at the Indian village. The next morning the whites awakened to a scene none would survive. Warriors painted red and black for death surprised them and their companions, killing Wright and Cochran immediately and burning Nairne slowly for three days until he too died.[26]

At dawn that same day, 15 April 1715, other Indians attacked English farms, homes, and outlying settlements around Port Royal, where they killed sixty of the English. Another war party, slightly farther north, killed over one hundred more. At Port Royal some four hundred white survivors fled as reports of Indian attacks swept through the colony. An early counterstroke failed miserably when on 15 May a mounted force of a hundred colonists, Indians, and blacks under Captain Thomas Barker rode out of the Goose Creek settlement searching for hostile warriors. The Yamasees ambushed the colonial troops successfully, killing Captain Barker and routing his command. At the same time a group of Catawbas and other tribes marched south of the Santee River, attacking plantations and small settlements there. It was one thing to deal with the angry Yamasees, but facing a combination of the tribes from both north and west of the settlements terrified colonial leaders. The Reverend Francis Le Jau reported that hostile Indians "Surround us on Every Side but the Sea Side . . . from the Borders of St. Augustin to Cape Fear. [W]e have not one [Indian] nation for us."[27] During late April and early May 1715 triumphant warriors swept everything before them as their attacks cleared the settlers from all but a few strongly fortified cabins in the region between the Santee River and Charleston.

As had happened so often before in other Indian-white conflicts, surprise had helped the tribes to get the upper hand at the beginning of the Yamasee War, but in the long run the colonists had too much military strength for the Indians. Once the severity of the situation was brought home to colonial leaders, Governor Charles Craven proclaimed martial law and called out the militia. In June 1715 he led those troops and Indian auxiliaries in an attack on the Yamasees, who fled south into Florida. When that campaign succeeded, legislative leaders supported building a circle of frontier forts about thirty miles out from Charleston. The tide began to turn in the north when, on 13 June, Captain George Chicken led a force into a camp of warriors who were still celebrating their earlier victories. More unusual, the tribe's women and children had joined the men there, so the whites caught the Indians totally unprepared. Fighting a stand-up battle in the open rather than their usual hit-and-run raids cost the warriors dearly, and when they fled during the night they abandoned all of their booty from earlier raids and sixty dead comrades. This major defeat apparently caused some of the northern Piedmont tribes to sue for peace with Virginia authorities.

In July 1715 Governor Craven led another militia army against the tribes from North Carolina, but the troops had marched only a few miles from Charleston when they were recalled hastily by news of a successful attack from the south by the Apalaches, who had broken through the ring of defensive posts and come within ten or fifteen miles of Charleston. With both the Creeks and the Cherokees considered hostile, prospects appeared bleak, but at that point circumstances changed. Negotiations with the Cherokees persuaded that tribe to withdraw from the conflict. At the same time, raids by Iroquois war parties encouraged by New York officials forced some of the Piedmont tribes to defend themselves from their traditional enemies and to abandon the fight with South Carolina. When English traders from the neighboring colonies refused to provide more arms or ammunition, the Indians realized that their situation was hopeless, and by 1716 most of the fighting had ended. Occasional raids disrupted the peace until 1720, but the Yamasee uprising had been crushed; the English in Carolina never again faced an Indian conflict with the same potential seriousness.[28]

This conflict had a profound effect on Indian-white relations in the Southeast. Some tribes moved for safety or to avoid retribution. The Yamasees abandoned their lands near Port Royal and fled southward into Spanish Florida, where they settled near Saint Augustine. Villages of Lower Creeks that had migrated east to the Ocmulgee River in present-day Georgia to be nearer to the Charleston traders now returned west to the Chattahoochee River. Some joined with the Upper Creeks along the Alabama River. Their movements helped the developing Creek Confederacy to present the Europeans a more united front than in the past. Under the leadership of Old Brims the Creeks remained determinedly neutral in the English-French-Spanish controversies during much of the eighteenth century. The defection of the Cherokees during the war reopened their traditional quarrels with the Creeks, who had joined the Indian confederacy against the English.[29]

FRENCH ENCOUNTERS IN THE SOUTH AND WEST

Yamasee defeat brought striking changes to European relations with each other and the southeastern tribes. The Spanish moved quickly to welcome the defeated Yamasees and strove to increase their influence among the remnants of the Apalaches near Pensacola. In 1717 they built a new presidio of San Marcos, but their efforts paled by comparison with those of the French. While the English had fought for their very survival, French traders strengthened their influence and trade alliances with the Mississippi Choctaws and nearby smaller tribes. In 1717 the French built Fort Toulouse or the Alabama Fort on the Tallapoosa River. From there they challenged the influence of the Carolina traders directly.[30]

Even before the Yamasee War the French had increased their trade and diplomatic efforts in the lower Mississippi Valley. The Natchez tribe, living along the east shore of the Mississippi, offered an opportunity for French action. Not yet enmeshed in the trade network that stretched west from Charleston, these people lived in a fertile region. In 1714 Antoine de La Mothe, sieur de Cadillac, the new French governor, sent men to open trade. Cadillac hoped to build a fort in the Natchez country to oppose possible English penetration of the region, but lacked both the men and supplies for such a venture at first. The governor himself managed to offend tribal sensibilities in 1715 when he traveled up the Mississippi without bothering to stop at the villages. Then on his downstream journey he halted among the Natchez only long enough to reprovision his party, neglecting either to smoke the calumet, a customary ceremonial pipe, or to pay respects to Great Sun, the Natchez chief.[31]

Several Mississippi Valley tribes complained about the French snub of tribal leaders, but in early 1716 some of the Natchez went beyond words, attacking and killing a small party of French boatmen passing down the river near their villages. News of the killings reached the governor, who ordered Jean-Baptiste Bienville, long experienced in Indian affairs, to retaliate and to build a fort in Natchez territory. Bienville led a small force north from Mobile in early 1716, halting in the territory of the Tunicas, a tribe friendly to the French. From there he began negotiations with the Natchez, who outnumbered him by about eight hundred to only fifty men. In early May the Indians visited his palisaded camp, and while talking to Great Sun, Tattooed Serpent, and Little Sun, he tried to smooth over the difficulties while demanding satisfaction for the murders. Bienville reminded his visitors that the French had surrendered whites guilty of crimes against the Indians and told them that he expected them to respond the same way. After some hesitation, the chiefs told the Frenchmen that internal divisions within the tribe made that impossible. Eventually they brought in the heads of two of the murderers and of a third person killed to pacify the Europeans. Not satisfied, the French leader eventually killed two chiefs he had held as hostages because they spoke for a pro-English faction within the tribe. Then he sent a work party to the Natchez country to build what became Fort Rosalie.[32]

Surprisingly, Bienville's actions calmed relations between the tribe and the French for a time. During the next several years colonial authorities encouraged increasing numbers of French settlers to move into Natchez country. The region stood high above the flood danger that many Louisiana settlements experienced, and soon French farmers trekked north to the new settlement. Although the Natchez had invited French pioneers to settle nearby at the end of the 1716 conflict, that tribe remained badly divided by pro-French and pro-English elements. Both Great Sun and Tattooed Serpent sided with the French, but they did not control all of the Natchez villages. This led to continuing tension and eventual violence and warfare.

By 1722 over one hundred French colonists had settled among the Natchez, hoping to profit from tobacco production there. The Europeans' presence brought the almost inevitable smallpox epidemic to the villagers, while frequent personal trade also generated misunderstandings and violent incidents. When soldiers and settlers gave Indians manufactured goods they expected things in return, but often the villagers accepted the items as gifts and saw no need to repay the whites. In October 1722 a trading dispute between two Indians and a sergeant led the Frenchman to kill both villagers. The dead men belonged to the Apple Village, which housed the anti-French minority of the tribe, and Ancient Hair, the current chief, ordered an attack on the French. The warriors shot or stole livestock and killed or wounded a dozen of the French and their slaves. By November that year the pro-French leadership in the tribe had stopped the violence, and Tattooed Serpent led several warriors to New Orleans to explain the situation. Bienville, not wanting to antagonize this tribe further, sent small presents back with them rather than demanding more deaths in retaliation for the attacks.[33]

The anti-French Natchez, apparently persuaded by Bienville's moderate response that they had little to fear, continued to raid for another year. When Bienville chose to respond more strongly, in late 1723, he led six hundred troopers to Fort Rosalie. There he found most of the Natchez willing to assist him in the destruction of the anti-French villages, and tribal members did much of the fighting. The violence resulted from many elements common in frontier Indianwhite relations, such as trade disputes between pro-English and French groups, indebted Indians being unable or unwilling to pay what they owed, tribal resentment over European incursions into their home territory, and in this case, ineffective military leadership among the colonists. It is also possible that one of the French settlements had been laid out on a worn-down former temple mound, possibly still held to be sacred ground by some in the tribe. It may well have been considered that by the Apple Village people, who seem to have been an outside group in the process of being assimilated into the tribe. If so, that would explain why the clearly recognized tribal leaders Great Sun and Tattooed Serpent felt no compunctions about letting the French farm on that particular land. Whatever the specific basis for the internal disputes among the Natchez, Bienville succeeded in temporarily ending the hostilities.[34]

In 1725 Tattooed Serpent, the most pro-French of the Natchez leaders, died, and only four years later the Natchez went on an anti-French rampage. Again, French agricultural incursions into tribal territory and stupid actions by the local commanding officer at Fort Rosalie helped cause the violent Indian response. During the Natchez celebration of the Great Corn Feast, the most sacred ceremony of their year, Captain de Chepart told the assembled tribesmen that they would have to move their villages so the French could use their cleared fields. Angry, but unwilling to resist at the moment, the villagers moved a short distance away, but this high-handed action brought simmering anti-French feelings to a boil. Borrowing muskets and ammunition from their white neighbors on the pretext of going hunting, in November 1729 the warriors went to the fort and asked the captain to smoke the calumet with them to seal their exchange of land. When the French officer foolishly ordered the Indians away from his quarters, the Natchez warriors opened fire, killing him and many other settlers at the fort and in nearby settlements. By the end of the day they had killed 237 whites. That evening the victors displayed the heads of murdered French on the Fort Rosalie palisade, and they took the survivors to their villages as slaves.[35]

This set off a bitter three-year war of extermination against the Natchez. Clearly once the French had shifted some of their economic focus from trade to agriculture new tensions resulted. As the settlers moved onto Indian land their desires mirrored those of their English competitors. They wanted land and safety from Indian attacks. At the same time, however, colonial officials still pursued trade and diplomatic goals that further complicated interracial dynamics. Once the French and their allies had destroyed the Natchez they turned against the pro-English Chickasaws for nearly two decades. That tribe, assisted by English traders and supplied by the Carolina leaders, fought the French to a standstill. Complicated maneuvering between pro-English and pro-French factions within the tribes of the Southeast had continued since the beginning of the eighteenth century, and as the Europeans tried to use the tribes as allies against their imperial competitors, the issue of trade became ever less significant. The English dominated the region most of the time because they had more, better-quality, and often cheaper trade goods. Traders and officials from both countries, however, dealt with the tribes in a similar manner. Whether the English encroaching on the land of the Yamasees at Port Royal or the French ordering the Natchez off their ancestral lands near Fort Rosalie, European expansion brought resistance and war. When trade threatened to disrupt village life, endangered the environmental base, or increased intertribal competition, war resulted as well. Clearly by the middle of the eighteenth century the southeastern Indians and their French, Spanish, and English neighbors and trading partners were locked in an unhappy embrace from which none of the groups could extricate itself short of retreat from the region. For the intruding Europeans this was unthinkable; for the tribes, impossible.[36]

In the region south of the Great Lakes, Indians, French, and English dealt with each other in a shifting, confusing situation that rarely seems to have satisfied any of the three for any long period of time. During the decades before peace between the French and the Iroquois Five Nations in 1701, the many tribes from central and western Pennsylvania and the Ohio country migrated westward, away from the conflicts to the east. Groups of Senecas and other Iroquois shifted gradually into Ohio and there became known as Mingos. Algonquian peoples including Delawares, Shawnees, Ottawas, and Miamis also moved about in present-day Ohio and Indiana. The latter peoples maintained diplomatic relations with the French in Canada, but the alliances proved difficult as frequent shifts in French policy and intertribal wars wrecked peaceful relations. Multi-tribal villages resulted from the population mobility as the Indians strove to reconstitute their societies under trying conditions.[37]

The Fox Wars, which stretched from 1710 until 1783, provide a clear example of these issues. This complex series of actions lasted nearly thirty years and showed the French at their worst. In 1701 Cadillac founded a new trading center at Detroit, encouraging Great Lakes region tribes to move nearby. A large number of Fox or Mesquakies, sometime allies of the Senecas and hoping to expand their contacts with British traders, accepted the invitation. Once there they caused and experienced continued friction and violent incidents with other tribes. Eventually this led to open fighting as both the local French officials and Indian leaders called for extermination of the troublesome Mesquakies. In 1712 they destroyed over one thousand of these people in events that included bitter fighting and repeated betrayals of the Mesquakies. From then until 1738 frequent campaigns against this tribe reduced its numbers to a few hundred fugitives hiding in the villages of other tribes. By 1738, when the last of the fighting ended, the tribe had ceased to be a significant factor in regional affairs.[38]

In this case the French succeeded in their genocidal war because they had adopted Indian campaign tactics and focused the anti-Fox hatred of the other regional tribes, whose warriors did most of the killing. Their actions in this conflict and the Natchez and Chickasaw Wars in the south at about the same time demonstrated an anti-Indian fury or hatred seldom exhibited by the English colonists outside of Carolina. While the English might well have wanted to destroy their tribal enemies, usually they lacked the willpower to do so. Even when they virtually destroyed the Pequots in 1637, their overwhelming success seems to have surprised, even embarrassed, them. The South Carolina leaders, on the other hand, practiced their own version of genocide and enslavement that rivaled anything the French did at the time.

By the 1740s more of the New York Iroquois began migrating into the upper Ohio region. During that and the next decades tribal people there again became closely involved in diplomatic and trade disputes with both the British and French traders. At Detroit, French leaders worried when Chief Orontony led his Wyandot followers close to the new Iroquois settlements and opened trade with Pennsylvania traders there. When King George's War broke out in Europe the strains from that conflict spilled over into North America. The successful British blockade of French ports cut off supplies from Europe and disrupted French and Indian trading patterns. To strengthen their position when dealing with the Europeans the Ohio region tribes created an alliance that included the Iroquois, Wyandots, Shawnees, Delawares, and Piankashaws. In the summer of 1749 the French in Canada responded to the growing influence of Virginia and Pennsylvania traders among the Ohio tribes. They sent Captain Pierre-Joseph Céloron de Blainvulle with a force of militia and traders to visit the tribes. Although the Indians received the French force correctly, their visitors feared an attack at any time. When Blainvulle asked his hosts to continue their trade and alliance with the French, the Indians asked him if he could provide the needed trade goods. Because he could not promise to do so his effort failed. By the 1750s tribes in the region found themselves pulled back and forth by their loyalties and needs as well as by intertribal competition. Traders from both the British colonies and New France challenged each other along the Ohio and set the stage for the mid-1750s warfare that followed.[39]

During the decades from 1670 to 1750 the English colonies outstripped the populations of New France and Louisiana by one million to perhaps sixty thousand people, while in 1745 Spanish Florida could muster a mere twenty-one hundred people. As the colonial populations grew, many transplanted Europeans became increasingly less tolerant of their Indian neighbors. Still government officials in Britain, France, and Spain continued their modest efforts to convert the Indians to Christianity and to provide education for them, while some local authorities worked sporadically to implement those goals. In New France and Louisiana the Jesuit missionaries continued to spread their faith among the tribes. At times they had the active support of the civil authorities; at others, such backing proved only passive. In Florida the Spanish Franciscans clung to their residual work. Missionary and educational enterprises within the English colonies varied more than did those of their competitors, but in the long run none seem to have proved itself particularly successful.

The repeated failures of missionaries, teachers, and other "civilizers" resulted from many causes. The fur trade and settled village life needed for educational and missionary activities proved incompatible. Of equal importance, the colonists could not agree on how to achieve their goals. At times they saw segregating Indians from white society as the best approach, while at others they stressed physical integration of the two peoples. Some wanted to proceed with conversion to Christianity immediately, while others demanded that the tribal people first be acculturated to French, Spanish, or English culture and learning before religious teaching began. The Europeans' assumptions of cultural superiority affected relations too. Only the most isolated villagers missed the fact that many whites throughout the North American colonies rejected the idea of having Indian neighbors or of having to treat tribal people as equals.

Indian ethnocentrism easily matched that of the invaders, however, as missionaries soon learned. The Jesuits in particular decided that they would be more likely to succeed in converting Indians if the priests lived among the villagers, but in doing so they exposed themselves to much derision and abuse. The most serious obstacle they had to overcome was the absolute Indian belief that their culture was superior to that of the "Black Robes" in every aspect. The tribesmen saw the missionaries' clothing as effeminate and a major hindrance in the wild countryside. The Indians gloried in long hair, and the clerics' closely cropped hair alienated them. To have a beard invited ridicule, as the Indians described facial hair as "very ugly," "deformed," "a monstrosity," and "the greatest disfigurement that a face can have."[40]

The celibacy of the Jesuits and Franciscans puzzled their Indian hosts, who enjoyed liberal and open sex lives, but at least the priests were no danger to the Indian women. On the other hand, clerical vows of poverty proved a major liability in village societies that demanded reciprocity of gift giving and hospitality among their members. To the Indians priests appeared to be selfish men who reneged on their obligations to share and exchange food as well as gifts. The French clerics also had to stay out of the way during raids and attacks, thus failing to act as brave men should. With this many deficiencies, in addition to their inability to speak the Algonquian, Iroquoian, Muskogean, or other local languages, it was not surprising that the villagers viewed their unwelcome guests as men of little sense or worth. Until the priests learned how to get past that native judgment, their work made little progress.

Their willingness to live and travel with the Indians set the French clerics apart from nearly all English missionaries during the late seventeenth and eighteenth centuries. Assuming the need to follow the Indians "to their homes and adapt ourselves to their ways, however ridiculous they may appear, in order to draw them to ours," the Jesuits did just that. Through much trial and error and repeated bitter failures the missionaries gradually came to understand that their success depended upon their being able to get a few adults in the village to accept them and their ideas as rational from the Indians' point of view. This meant that they had to master the languages, though good teachers were few. Gradually some of them learned tribal customs such as sharing, got adopted by a local family, and often even received an Indian name. Because of their obvious honesty, their avoidance of liquor, their courage in the face of danger, and their good health during the periodic epidemics that swept through the Indian camps, the Jesuits achieved enough acceptance to be able to begin their campaign of conversion.[41]

More than the other clerics in New France, the Jesuits appear to have been divided over how much of Indian culture could be accepted and modified for Christian uses and how much had to be destroyed. Whichever they tried, it soon became clear that "you cannot all at once eradicate the deep-rooted customs and habits of any people," and the priests reconciled themselves to working among the villagers for generations. To get around this obstacle they tried to modify or incorporate certain Indian practices into their religious work. For example, the Indian custom of smoking the calumet and using the smoke to send prayers to the spirit world could be incorporated in having an acolyte carry a censer whose incense smoke was supposed to represent the ascent of prayers to heaven.[42]

At the other extreme, both the Jesuits and Franciscans used open confrontation and ridicule as a means to get attention and to disrupt village practices, particularly those of the native shamans. This shocked and angered their listeners because usually the village societies avoided open criticism, relying on more indirect social pressure. Writing in 1710 one chronicler noted that "to jest in the victim's presence, or to make a verbal attack, face to face, is not acceptable to the Indians."[43] Recognizing this, later missionaries turned to their modest knowledge of disease and their acquired immunities that helped them remain healthy during epidemics when they nursed many villagers back to health. They also played upon their knowledge of coming eclipses of the sun and moon to show that their power exceeded that of the village shamans. Nevertheless, village culture remained central to the Indians' existence and usually the best the missionaries could achieve was to split a single village or to secede with their followers to start a new community of believers.

While most of the Canadian missionary work focused on sending the clerics to live and work among the tribes, the priests did establish some modest-sized reserves or missionary-dominated villages almost entirely for refugees. As early as 1650 Jesuits helped some three hundred Huron fugitives by starting the village of Lorette, near Quebec. This settlement moved several times and by the end of the century it stood on the Saint Charles River and is still called the Village des Hurons. The present community at the Iroquois settlement of Caughnawaga began in the 1660s near Montreal. Sokokis, retreating from war with New England, arrived in 1670, and a decade later Abenaki refugees settled at the village of Saint Francis. By 1708 they had received the seigneury of Bécancour, opposite Trois-Rivières. Indians continued to flee from the border areas between French and English colonies, and as late as the 1750s some Iroquois from New York migrated to Canada, where they settled on the Saint Regis River.[44]

The French missionary and educational efforts begun during the seventeenth century continued with only minor variations. Differing orders of clerics tried their particular approaches, and the government and church vacillated between programs aimed at cultural transformation and religious conversion. Earlier reserves continued, although at times the particular group of clerics working with a tribe or settlement did change. By 1682 the Intendant De Meulles described Indian education in New France briefly by listing the religious orders then in the colony and their particular approach to the native people. The Sulpicians, he reported, taught their charges French and Latin, along with some handicrafts and agriculture. The Sisters of the Congregation, on the other hand, gave practical training in domestic subjects to the Indian girls they saw. As usual, the Jesuits stressed the Indians' tribal languages rather than teaching them either French or Latin, while the Ursulines taught the girls only "to say prayers and to speak French."[45] When this report reached Versailles, officials there ordered that no more Indian girls be sent to the Ursulines. Rather, they dispatched women to teach the Indian girls to knit, spin, and make lace "in order to introduce these manufactures which will be advantageous to the colony."[46] Despite these efforts, in 1700 the church abandoned the earlier policy of "Francization"—it had failed—and shifted its efforts to gathering Indians into villages, something akin to the praying towns of New England or the Spanish missions of Florida and New Mexico.[47]

In the English colonies similar issues arose. Unlike the French and Spanish, who worked through a single church even if the various missionary orders did compete with each other, the English had no such unity. In the southern colonies the established Anglican Church competed with dissenting groups such as the Moravians, Quakers, and Presbyterians. Farther north, missionary societies founded in England urged conversion of the tribes but had only limited funds and received only modest support from the colonial populations. As in New France, the Indians who had any choice paid little attention to the missionaries other than being hospitable, as they were to all their visitors. Thus the tribes that remained independent and relatively self-sufficient economically retained their cultures effectively by avoiding the disruptions caused by having clerics among them.

English failure among the tribes resulted from more than Indian resistance to the clerics, however. The colonists' continuing ignorance of Indian customs hurt colonial missionaries more than the French because the latter spent much time among the villagers and therefore learned the languages and social customs. As the population in the English colonies grew to more than one million people, of necessity they pushed against the regulations supposed to separate them from the Indians. Land encroachment remained a continuing difficulty, an issue of little significance most of the time in New France, Louisiana, or Florida. With a settler-based society, the settlers in English colonies expressed more fear of Indian raids because they viewed the tribes as enemies and competitors for resources rather than partners.[48]

Typical ethnocentrism played a major part as well. While the colonists expected their tribal neighbors to learn English, few of them bothered to learn an

Indian tongue. As late as the 1740s even some of the missionaries rejected the need or even the possibility of learning tribal languages. In recruiting a young missionary to work among the Dutch settlers at Albany, New York, and the Mohawks living nearby, the Rev. Henry Barclay nominated one John Ogilvie. His qualifications, beyond his willingness to accept the assignment, included an ability to speak Dutch and his training from Yale. According to Barclay, anyone who spoke Dutch could learn Mohawk because no English speaker could "utter those Barbarous Sounds unless Accustom'd to them from their infancy."[49] Whether viewing language or other aspects of native culture, the colonists found much to criticize. In Carolina one missionary suggested that the society would gain more from having the black slaves converted than from having "to run up in the woods after miserable creatures [Indians] who breath nothing but blood and slaughter."[50]

Even when missionaries thought that Indians could understand Christianity, the continuing trade and intertribal wars that racked many regions limited success. Usually the tribal people most willing to accept Christianity or the white man's education belonged to those groups that had most nearly lost their aboriginal culture and identity. For example, in 1683 the "King" of the Pamunkeys and his leading warriors asked to become Christians. These men represented the survivors of the Powhatan Confederacy, which had confronted the Virginians for the entire century. Having lost two devastating wars and suffered disease, forced removal, and drastic population reduction, the remnant moved to join at least the fringe of white society. Despite this particular event, just a little more than a decade later, when asked about actions that had been taken to convert the Indians, Virginia governor Edmund Andros replied "none ever heard of."[51]

By the 1680s, when the frontier calmed after Bacon's Rebellion, educators in Virginia returned to schemes for educating nearby Indians. The 1693 charter for William and Mary College called for the education and conversion of tribal people. In fact, two years earlier a bequest offered money to Virginia authorities so they might support Indian boys in the still-hoped-for school. Few Indian families wanted to risk their children's lives by sending them to live among the whites, however, so the colony bought children taken captive during frontier and intertribal wars and placed them in school. In 1711 Governor Alexander Spotswood promised to remit the annual payment the tributary tribes had been forced to make to Virginia since the 1677 treaty at Middle Plantation if each Indian town would send two sons from leading families to attend school and to act as hostages "for the fidelity of their Nations."[52] By late 1711 all of the tributary tribes had accepted the governor's "offer," and a few of their boys lived among the English.

Although the number of young Indians attending William and Mary College fluctuated widely, in 1712 Spotswood reported twenty boys at the school. Because the tributary tribes sent more children than could be supported by available funds, the governor had to look elsewhere for money. Soon he created the Virginian Indian Company, organized to regulate the fur trade and provide for educating native children. By 1715 Spotswood had funded a new school at Fort Christanna. By late that year he reported seventy Indian children there under instruction by the Rev. Charles Griffin, a Quaker with experience in Carolina. Exactly what Griffin taught the children is not entirely clear, but by late 1715 the governor wrote that many of the children could "say the belief, the Lord's prayer, & ten Commds perfectly well."[53] Whether their instruction included more than religious teaching and basic literacy is not known, but clearly whatever the boys learned was of little use to them when they returned to their home villages except for occasional duties as translators.

By 1717 the governor's efforts had failed, as the school at Fort Christanna had to be closed and the one hundred students scattered. The next year Griffin moved to the grammar school at William and Mary. In 1723 the college had enough money to build Brafferton Hall, which it then used to house the young Indians and their teacher. Yet only a few tribal students lived at the college, and they received only basic grammar school instruction from Rev. Griffin. Thus the colonial effort to educate large numbers of boys who might then return home to teach and convert their families and fellow tribesmen failed. Few Indians received more than a limited exposure to education in Virginia, and those who did appear to have "returned to the blanket," if contemporary observers can be trusted. Hugh Jones, writing in 1724, noted that, even after receiving baptism, once the boys left William and Mary they returned to "their own savage Customs and heathenish Rites."[54] William Byrd II echoed this when he complained that after having been educated and receiving Christian instruction the young men failed to try to civilize or convert their fellow villagers. Instead, he claimed, they relapsed into barbarism.[55]

Nearly a generation later missionaries in newly settled Georgia would try to establish a school among the Yamacraws, a people of mixed Creek and Yamasee descent. There in 1736 Benjamin Ingham and a Moravian couple, Peter and Catherine Rose, began their efforts at a village a few miles upriver from Savannah. Ingham studied the Muskogee language from a mixed-race woman, Mary Musgrove, while the Roses tried learning it while living with the villagers. The missionaries persuaded the Georgia leader James Oglethorpe to finance a school for these Indians, and in September 1736 the school had been completed. It opened a month later, but within little more than a year Ingham had returned to England and the Yamacraws had left the area because of a threatened war between England and Spain. Thus the missionaries never had enough time to learn the tribal language thoroughly, and the young villagers had only a modest taste of what their self-proclaimed benefactors had promised them.[56] As long as the major southern tribes maintained their independence from the competing Europeans, they politely turned away most requests to have their children educated, and few chose to adopt English customs or thought unless their own communities and cultures disintegrated.

In New England the extensive missionary and educational activities of John Eliot and the Mayhews that had preceded King Philip's War continued after that conflict, but on a much reduced scale. By the 1680s, for example, Plymouth authorities claimed nearly fifteen hundred Indian converts to Christianity, although few of these people actually belonged to an organized congregation because of Pilgrim beliefs about the need for a personal conversion experience. Nevertheless, the English considered virtually the entire tribal population of Plymouth as thoroughly Christianized. In Massachusetts remnants of the praying towns continued as settled communities, and individual Indians served as teachers, preachers, translators, and even printers. Three or four of the praying villages continued to operate among the Algonquians still living in the colony, and the white leaders supported and encouraged missionary and educational efforts among them.[57]

Few of the tribes welcomed the whites' religious teachings, however, and during the 1700–1730 era they objected to the colonialists' cultural offensive. For example, after a blatant white land grab near the town of Groton in 1714 village leaders refused to meet with the missionary Experience Mayhew. He reported sadly that the land dispute had "produced in the Indians a greater aversion to the English and their Religion than otherwise they would have had."[58] However, tribal objections to Christianity and to colonial English efforts to acculturate the native people went far beyond temporary anger over bad land deals. Indian leaders denounced the whites repeatedly, telling missionaries to work among their own people first to make certain that the whites all lived up to their professed beliefs before trying to change the Indians' way of life. A Narragansett sachem pointed to the competing groups and factionalism among the Christians themselves as a reason for the tribes to retain their traditional beliefs. He declined any Christian teaching, saying the "ye Indians could not tell what religion to be of, if they had a mind to be Christians."[59] Some village leaders refused to accept schools for the children, accusing the English of using their skills in reading and writing to "cheat and hurt other people."

Despite Indian reluctance, white educational efforts continued, spurred on by the effects of the Great Awakening. Beginning during the 1740s, the religious fervor that swept through the colonies had a direct connection to efforts to educate Indians for the next several decades. A new urgency about converting the heathen permeated religious thought from the 1740s on, and schools of many varieties opened or accepted tribal young people as students, often for the first time. Noted missionaries and religious leaders of the era often participated directly in Indian education, hoping to train native leaders who would preach and teach their own people and achieve a complete cultural and religious transformation.[60]

In the eighteenth century, officials in both French and English North America suggested interracial marriage as a way to incorporate the tribes into the emerging colonial societies. Yet their support for this idea remained halfhearted, and only a few Europeans considered intermarriage. Nor did most Indians, who saw the colonists as nearly worthless spouses. Yet some race mixing did occur during the colonial era. Most, although not all, of this took place within the context of the fur trade as the French coureurs de bois, the English Hudson's Bay Company employees, and traders heading into Indian country from Carolina, Virginia, or Pennsylvania acquired "country wives" from among the villages they visited or the tribes they met. For the Indians, having a trader marry into the village assured them a steady stream of goods as well as presents. For the whites such an arrangement meant a safe place to live while in the Indian country, a steady supply of furs, a way to learn the language quickly, and the physical comforts that came from village life.[61]

In New France and Louisiana, often such fur trade unions occurred over the objections of the church authorities, and frequently priests living among the Indians denounced the traders for debauching the villagers. Nevertheless, despite the lack of enthusiasm shown toward interracial unions, parish records did record a small but continuing number of such marriages. Usually French men married native women, sometimes merely living with them until pressured to marry or get rid of their companions. Occasionally priests married a couple without following the prescribed steps required by the church and the government, and that brought trouble for the errant clerics. During the early 1670s a priest warned another at Tadoussac not to "marry with the rites of the

Church any Frenchman to a Savage woman without the consent of parents, and without Monseigneur's [the bishop's] approval."[62] Clearly formal church marriages of this sort were unusual, and to avoid trouble with the tribes care had to be taken to make certain the whites did not breach Indian customs. On the few occasions when Indian males married French women a formal notice of the ceremony appeared in church records. Often the men were captives, referred to as Panis or Pawnees, who had lived in the settlements for years.[63]

The English settlers proved no more comfortable with interracial mixing than did their French competitors. Their traders and Indian women often lived together for years, but the English colonial frontier consisted of settlers and their families, and that left little need or room for biracial unions outside the fur trade. English ethnocentrism and the cultural imperative of retaining their civilization amid the forests and squalor of colonial society inhibited intermarriage. On the other hand, the colonial governments rarely outlawed such unions. In fact, marriage laws ignored Indians, and only in North Carolina and for a short time in Virginia could whites and Indians not marry if they so chose. When the Massachusetts General Court discussed a bill calling for the enslavement of interracial children in 1705, Samuel Sewell got Indians dropped from the legislation. Several colonies even encouraged race mixing as a means of ending the "Indian problem," and prior to independence Patrick Henry supported a bill in the Virginia House of Burgesses to offer bounties for children of white-Indian marriages.[64]

Interest in the subject continued throughout the eighteenth century. Writing in the 1720s, William Byrd of Virginia denounced English colonists of the preceding century for not marrying the Indians when they first reached North America. He thought that the tribes would never consider the colonists as their friends because the whites avoided intermarriage. He even suggested that Indian complaints about white land grabbing would have been muted because some of them would have come to own land by inheritance.[65] Farther north the British government decided to encourage miscegenation between the settlers and the tribes in Nova Scotia, a region of long-term competition between England and France. In 1719 the official instructions to the colonial governor included the promise that any white of either sex who chose to marry an Indian would get a fifty-acre land grant free from any quit rent for twenty years and a cash gift of ten pounds. How many people chose this route to land and cash is unclear, but the records fail to show any flood of applicants for the promised rewards.[66]

While the Europeans shared mixed views about intermarriage with the Indians, they took different approaches toward the land the tribes claimed. From the start the English and Spanish chose to assert their eventual sovereignty over their tribal neighbors, while in New France the officials moved with great care. Badly outnumbered until the eighteenth century, the French accepted Indian ownership of the land and sought to share its use with them as allies. Except in the vacant Saint Lawrence Valley, few Frenchmen actually settled in North America for generations, and one of the few places where they had disputes over land occupation and use was among the Natchez of Louisiana. Otherwise they avoided claiming landownership and accepted the tribes as fur trade partners and as diplomatic and military allies against the English and, to a lesser extent, the Spanish.[67]

When the Treaty of Utrecht ended Queen Anne's War in 1713, the British insisted that much of the region occupied by the Micmacs in Acadia now belonged to England. The Indians objected, saying that they had never been subjects of France and therefore the French king could not cede what he had never owned. The New York Iroquois made a similar claim, pointing out that the French had asked their permission before building Fort Niagara in the Iroquois country. In 1725 officials at Montreal told visiting New England diplomats that the Abenakis had been French allies, not subjects, for the preceding eighty years. A generation later Indians told visitors from Boston that they were "entirely free; we are allies of the King of France."[68]

The different European ideas about property, tribal rights, and Indian sovereignty continued throughout the colonial era. The Abenakis' difficulties with the English in Nova Scotia illustrate the two approaches clearly. When the victorious English told them that their lands now belonged to the king of England rather than that of France, the Indians refused to believe what they heard. Angrily they demanded how their ally the Great Father, the king of France, could sell their land. Just three years later some English settlers tried to seize Indian lands, claiming that France had ceded the region to England. The Abenakis objected quickly, again stating their position as independent allies of France, not its subjects. They told the would-be landowners that "the French could not have ceded to the English lands that belonged" to them, the Indians.[69]

Because Indians in New France rarely lived among the Canadian settlers, getting an idea of their legal position within the community is difficult at best. In the English colonies, this is less a problem. From Nova Scotia in the north to

Virginia in the south the English colonial authorities considered the Indians as a subject people, and once the white population equaled or exceeded that of the nearby tribes, the Europeans strove to extend their jurisdiction. By the 1670s the colonial courts in New York considered accusations against whites and Indians alike. The severity of the punishments varied, but not necessarily by race. At times the courts set fines or awards to Indians according to tribal standards. For example, in an incident where a settler shot a Mahican woman, the authorities invited tribal leaders to the hearing. The accused claimed that the shooting was accidental, and the chiefs accepted a payment in wampum as a reparation. Sentences or punishments that followed tribal customs in some manner seem to have brought little resentment. When two Indian men killed a soldier they were sentenced to death, while in another instance, in which an inebriated Indian had killed a black slave, the tribe had to pay the owner for his property loss.[70]

In the generation following King Philip's War and Bacon's Rebellion both New England and Virginia came to treat the resident Indian people in similar ways. Each considered the tribes residing outside the immediate limits of the colonial settlements as independent groups to be dealt with through treaties or similar agreements. Tribes near the settlements occupied a tributary position, often living in specified areas or on lands reserved for their use. The other tribal people who may have lived within the English communities as slaves, servants, hired workers, or children attending schools fell under the direct jurisdiction of the local legal officers and courts. In either region the whites strove to dominate their Indian neighbors and whenever possible applied their ideas and legal systems to disputes between the two races.[71]

From the late seventeenth century through the middle of the eighteenth century the legal systems in both Virginia and Massachusetts evolved several means of dealing with Indian people in those colonies. For the tributary tribes and individuals living among the English a surprising degree of at least surface equality existed. For example, it was not until 1705 that the Virginia authorities imposed any limitations on an Indian's right to hold public office or to exercise some leadership within the society. In nearby North Carolina a 1715 law prohibited free Indians from voting for legislators there. Virginia took longer to restrict voting rights for minorities and then did so only after a 1723 scare over a planned black insurrection. The law stated that no Indian or free black "shall hereafter have any vote at the election of burgess, or any other election whatsoever," implying that such people might previously have voted occasionally.[72]

In actual court proceedings the position of Indians varied widely. As early as 1705 Indians, mulattoes, and blacks could testify in courts, particularly if the proceedings involved other minority people. Those who professed some degree of Christianity could appear as witnesses, although whites did not have to profess any faith at the time. In theory members of the tributary tribes had the same rights in the Virginia courts as did the English, but that they received such treatment seems unlikely with whites running the courts and serving on the juries. A 1732 legislative act excluded Indian testimony, but because this weakened evidence in many trials, only two years later the legislators again allowed free Indians to testify against other Indians in criminal trials. They altered proceedings in civil trials a decade later because many Indian debtors could not be forced to pay without the testimony of other Indians against them.[73]

Before the 1670s Indian magistrates had operated minor courts in the praying towns under the supervision of colonial authorities in Massachusetts, but after King Philip's War this system atrophied. In 1694 a new law enabled the governor to appoint justices of the peace, to be assisted by Indian constables and other local officials. A half century later, during the 1740s and 1750s, the legislature altered the system several times, and not always to the Indians' liking. The result was that gradually the white commissioners appointed as guardians assumed ever-increasing authority, and by the end of the colonial era the tribal people had little if any control over their local circumstances.[74]

For Indians not living in the segregated towns the colonial legal system supposedly treated them equally with the rest of the colonial population. They were not sent back to their tribal villages for punishment, but entered the colonial court system with the same charges and defenses available to them. It is difficult to know how fairly the courts treated native people, but it seems likely that anti-Indian feelings played at least some part in the outcome of such cases. In 1691, hoping to save money, the Massachusetts governor set up a special court of oyer and terminer to handle capital crimes, and the records indicate that most of the cases in these courts involved Indians. There was one exception to the similar treatment of whites and Indians, and that had to do with civil debt collection cases. Apparently the good New Englanders cheated their tribal neighbors and got them into debt frequently, because in 1746 and again in 1758 legislative acts protected Indians from suits for debt over a mere ten shillings. These laws called for an investigation by the local court before any suit for more than that amount might proceed.[75] From this it seems clear that the English authorities assumed that Indians within the colony would be considered a part of the regular legal system and be treated accordingly. In New France and Louisiana so few tribal people lived in the French settlements that this never became a major issue.

The period from the 1670s to the 1750s proved to be one of rapid growth of European settlements, population, and influence. The fur trade stretched from the Gulf Coast north to Hudson's Bay and from the Atlantic west across much of North America. It joined tribes, traders, diplomats, and soldiers in both an economic enterprise and a giant scramble for empire across the continent. The resulting wars, physical dislocations, environmental alterations, and dwindling Indian populations meant that by the end of this era the Indians rarely could dictate the course of events. Throughout much of this century tribal people had controlled the fur and hide trade through their means of gathering the skins and their willingness to work with the Europeans. In the ever-changing diplomacy of the time tribal leaders extracted concessions from the English, the French, and even the Spanish at times. In the long run, however, this merely bought time for the Indians as the settler-dominated English colonies outdistanced their European rivals to gain control of the regions.

5   Striving for Independence, 1750–1790s

 ON 21 JUNE 1752 Charles Langlade, a mixed-race Ottawa, led a French-sponsored attack by Ottawa and Potawatomi warriors on the Miami village of Pickawillany, in west central Ohio. Many of the local men had left for their summer hunt when the raiders surprised the village. The French Indians captured the women and children and disarmed some of the Pickawillany men; fewer than twenty of the latter fled to the nearby British trading post. From there, aided by a handful of British traders, they tried to defend themselves, but the more than ten-to-one odds persuaded them to parley. Langlade promised to return his prisoners and leave if the Pickawillany chief La Demoiselle, sometimes called Old Briton, would surrender and turn the British over to him. As soon as the defenders left the stockade Langlade's men killed Old Briton, cut out his heart, and ate it. Next they dismembered his body, boiled it, and ate it in front of the remaining villagers.[1]

This incident illustrates how central interethnic dealings had become for both the Europeans and many Indian groups. As the population of transplanted Europeans in North America grew, that of the native peoples continued to decline. Recurrent epidemics, intertribal and Indian-white warfare, physical removals, the ever-growing reliance on manufactured goods, and the impact of alcohol all brought havoc to tribal societies. Because their long-term methods for dealing with the Europeans all proved ineffective, some of the tribal people strove to distance themselves from the invaders. In doing so they sought to regain their native independence, strengthen their village cultures, and regain their lost power to make connections with the spirit world. Their efforts to achieve these goals brought them into direct conflict with each other and with the expanding Euro-American societies.

ORGANIZED RESISTANCE TO EUROPEAN LAND GRABBING

By the end of the 1740s, following King George's War, refugees from villages that had been overrun by British, French, or colonial forces had fled beyond the frontier settlements. There they joined polyglot communities where the survivors of earlier migrations had established new villages. Some of these represented what the French had described as "Indian Republics" earlier in the century. Others consisted of new waves of migrants. In almost every village, Delawares, Shawnees, Mingos, Miamis, and others came together as they struggled to reestablish their customs or to find ways to combine native practices with new ones from the other tribes and the Europeans. In these efforts the Indians had several options, but most often they chose one of two: either to develop stronger village or tribal leadership such as the so-called treaty chiefs, or to look beyond their borders to pan-Indian ideas and groupings. Their efforts to choose one of these approaches or to combine them proved central in their actions during the second half of the eighteenth century, at least within the United States.

By 1750 continued British and French efforts to penetrate and control the upper Ohio Valley had brought the Europeans and the native peoples of that region into repeated contact. For those Indians who had migrated west to escape such meetings, the Europeans' efforts stirred feelings of dismay and animosity. These, in turn, made many of the villagers receptive to new teachings from their shamans and prophets, as those individuals offered ideas for refocusing Indian life and for dealing effectively with the invaders. Individual prophets appeared and disappeared, as did many of their pronouncements. Nevertheless, the prophets sparked repeated efforts to cleanse Indian villages of perceived contamination introduced by witches or the whites. Some of them urged pantribal cooperation as a way to reacquire their spiritual powers. Regardless of their specific teachings, the prophets symbolized and focused Indian discontent. Their efforts encouraged significant tribal efforts to retain native cultures and independence.

As early as the late 1730s reports of Delaware prophets or seers filtered back from the frontier. Those mentioned called for an end to killing animals for the fur trade and demanded that alcohol use be stopped. By 1750 anti-British ideas had entered the rhetoric too, as the visions and subsequent teachings came to focus more on ritual cleansing and rejuvenating village life. Repeatedly the prophets related stories of traveling to the spirit world while in a trance, and upon their return they offered their listeners messages from the Master of Life. The specifics of their teachings varied, but most included a call for returning to some aboriginal spiritual practices as well as promises of a better life when they broke off their relations with the whites. Although some taught a virulent anti-British message, others urged peaceful relations with all peoples.[2]

By 1760 the Delaware prophet Neolin came to the fore, preaching a set of nativistic, anti-British ideas to eager audiences. Beset by the related difficulties caused by a shortage of available game animals, the continuing flow of pioneers into the Indian country, and the obvious British dislike of the Indians, many of the prophets' listeners accepted his ideas readily. In addition to calling for an end of trade with the British, he urged village leaders to reinstitute training the young men and boys in the use of traditional methods and weapons of war. To achieve a complete break with Europeans he asked his followers to take the "black drink," an emetic then in use among some tribes of the Southeast. His teachings combined traditional Indian practices with elements taken from Christian missionaries then active among the tribes. Central to his ideas was the prediction that the tribes could not escape a war with the British in the near future. Neolin and other prophets all sought to have their listeners turn away from contact with the whites and urged them to practice tribal rituals in order to reopen their contacts with the native spiritual world.[3] Their teachings set the stage for an active resistance to further Anglo-American advances into the upper Ohio Valley.

While Indians sought ways for dealing with their changed situation, the Seven Years War ended with an English victory over France. For some tribes it took only a few months to recognize their greatly reduced power and independence. For others that realization had come earlier. For example, during the war the English had encouraged Cherokee warriors to march north to fight against the French, and some six hundred of them did so. With these men away serving as allies with the Virginia forces, in 1757 colonial authorities had built two military posts in Cherokee country—Fort Prince George among the Lower Cherokees and Fort Loudoun among the Overhill villagers. This led to almost immediate disputes and ill feelings. Continuing abuse of the Indians by dishonest traders further strained relations. The presence of the two English forts in the Indian country encouraged pioneers to encroach on tribal lands, and the colonial governments used the distractions caused by the war as an excuse for not removing the ambitious settlers.

Meanwhile, British delays in campaigning against the French discouraged those Cherokees who had traveled north to fight, and during 1758 Virginia pioneers and Cherokee warriors quarreled repeatedly over charges of horse theft and murder. Apparently, while lying around for months waiting for the British commanders to gather their forces, the Indians had killed some horses belonging to the whites. In retaliation, the frontiersmen attacked and killed some of the Cherokees. With clan retribution still a strong social force within the tribal society, friends and relatives of the slain men felt it necessary to retaliate against the English for the murders of their kinsmen. One other factor caused trouble as well. When Governor William Lyttelton of South Carolina met with a large Cherokee delegation in 1760 to settle the continuing disputes and bad feelings, he erred grievously. Chief Oconostota came to Charleston seeking ammunition and improved trade relations, but instead of trying to satisfy the Indians, Governor Lyttelton seized him and some of the delegation as hostages until the other village leaders would turn over those charged with the murder of white pioneers. Then he dispatched a military force into Cherokee country to resupply the existing forts there.[4]

Tensions mounted when the Cherokees protested that they could not capture or surrender the accused murderers to the whites, and the Carolina authorities refused to release the hostages, including Chief Oconostota, until they had turned over the accused. Eventually the whites relented and sent the chief back to his village. Angry at having been held captive, he lured a force led by the commander of Fort Prince George into a fatal ambush; in response, the troopers still at the garrison killed the remaining hostages there. The colonial authorities raised several military forces but proved unable to campaign effectively that year. Lacking supplies or enough men, the small garrison at Fort Loudoun surrendered after being promised safe conduct back to the settlements. As the whites moved out of the fort, Indians attacked, killing or capturing almost all of the prisoners. Hearing of the Indian capture of Fort Loudoun, the British commander General Jeffrey Amherst ordered another expedition into Cherokee country to punish the tribe and bring peace there. During the summer of 1761 colonial troops smashed into the region, destroying villages and burning crops. Although the warriors attacked the invaders repeatedly, their numbers and weapons were no match for the colonial forces, so at the end of the summer peace talks began. By late September 1761 tribal leaders and British officials concluded a treaty that called for the return of all prisoners, a reopening of trade, the reoccupation of English forts within Cherokee territory, and a major land cession by the tribe.[5] What had started as a cooperative venture with the English shifted to a tribal move toward more independence but ended with just the opposite taking place.

In the north, particularly around the Great Lakes, tribal responses to the French surrender followed a similar path. Realizing that they needed to meet with the tribal leaders of that region, British authorities sent Sir William Johnson and the trader George Croghan to Detroit for a grand council. General Amherst in the meantime readied his forces to send detachments to garrison the former French posts on the frontier. By September 1761 the English officials had reached Detroit, where they held meetings they hoped would pacify the western tribes. As a skilled, experienced negotiator, Johnson avoided telling his Indian listeners all facets of General Amherst's policies for interracial peace and trade. Amherst considered the tribal people to be backward savages and at times acted as if they were a conquered, subject people. He rejected the need of "purchasing the good behavior of the Indians by presents" and recommended that it would be wise to keep them "scarce of ammunition."[6] This played right into the hands of French traders living among the tribes, still angry at their loss to the British. Long-standing French, colonial, and Indian council etiquette called for generous gifts to Indian leaders for distribution to their companions. Now the English chose to disrupt that pattern.

Equally difficult for the tribal leaders to accept was Amherst's determination to provide them as little ammunition as possible. Most of their supplies had been used during the preceding war and for hunting they sought powder and lead, as well as the repair of their weapons. Closely related to their shortage of ammunition for hunting and fur gathering was the sharp increase in prices the English traders charged. To make matters worse, the English sought to reduce violence and cheating long associated with the trade by refusing to make alcohol available to the Indians. Although some village leaders welcomed this move, many of the hunters resented it bitterly and longed for the return of their generous and fun-loving French friends with whom the trade had been so much more pleasant and profitable than it was with the British.

The Ohio Valley tribes, then, had major and legitimate complaints against the victorious English as well as strong cultural reasons to resent the whites. The promised low prices for trade goods had failed to materialize, and the whites' refusal to give presents to the chiefs or enough ammunition to satisfy the hunters both proved major sore points. In addition, General Amherst insisted that the Indians return all the white captives then living among them whether those people wanted to return to colonial society or not. Because many of the captives had been integrated thoroughly into the Indian societies, the general's demand upset family stability in villages all along the frontier. English frontier commanders recognized these issues as crucial but hesitated to ignore General Amherst's specific orders, or even to try to persuade him that his approach would bring conflict. Despite that reluctance, at the end of Pontiac's Rebellion (see below) Colonel Henry Bouquet, the commanding officer at Fort Pitt, wrote to his superior officer, General Thomas Gage, that English policies had "visibly brought upon us this Indian War by being too saving of a few presents to the savages which properly distributed would certainly have prevented it."[7] Perhaps as important in pushing tribes into a new war was their perception that, unlike the French, who often genuinely liked their Indian partners, the English despised them.

Basic differences between British and French actions certainly helped cause some of the continuing unrest. In New France—present-day eastern Canada and the Great Lakes region—the officials applied the same standard to themselves and the Indians. Basically the French said that vacant land could be claimed by anyone who moved onto it. As a result, they occupied a modest-sized area along the Saint Lawrence River where Indians had no permanent settlements while recognizing Indian land title in what they called the *pays d'en haut*. That term described everything beyond the French settlements. In that region they recognized Indian self-rule, possessory and territorial rights, and the usufructuary rights of hunting, fishing, and gathering. Essentially they saw New France as being divided in half—one part French and the other Indian.[8] Clearly these ideas did not apply in Louisiana, where large-scale agriculture and slavery came to distinguish the economic base of the region.

Like that southern French region, the English colonies also rejected most tribal land claims. They had no scruples about seizing Indian lands. In fact, they needed the land for agricultural success. The Indians saw English priorities clearly when the colonial authorities reneged on their promises to help the Delawares and Iroquois resettle some of their land once the French had been defeated. Rather than helping the tribes, colonial officers stepped aside when pioneer settlers swarmed into Indian-claimed regions, and the British army proved unable or unwilling to push the squatters off those lands.

Even worse from the Indians' perspective was the British approach toward tribal land claims. Unlike the French, the English claimed sovereignty over the tribes and most of their land, based on long-held practice. In addition, in 1758 Emer de Vattell, a prominent Swiss jurist, had provided a clear statement of European land theory. Having no idea that most eastern Indians were successful farmers, he wrote that the actions of the tribes of North America "cannot be held as real and lawful taking possession," and therefore when the Europeans needed new lands "they may lawfully take possession of them [territories claimed by the tribes] and establish colonies in them."⁹ Whenever they heard of such ideas the Indians objected loudly, saying that the Creator had given the land to them and that no European ruler had any claim to their territories. In fact, there is considerable evidence to suggest that tribal bitterness over white incursions into the west helped trigger what became known as Pontiac's Rebellion.¹⁰

By 1762, then, English high-handedness, Indian dissatisfaction over trade and sovereignty, a severe shortage of powder and lead, possible French intrigue and encouragement, and the teachings of the Delaware prophet Neolin led to talk of hostilities. The Ottawa war chief Pontiac moved to the fore that year, but had he not, it seems likely that the volatile situation might have encouraged another Indian spokesmen to serve as leader of the disaffected tribes. At first Pontiac called for secret councils that included leaders from the Ottawas, Ojibwas, Hurons, and Potawatomis, and those took place near Detroit. At about the same time the Senecas in western New York tried to instigate a rebellion of tribes allied to them. During late 1762 they sent a wampum belt calling for war to the Delawares, Shawnees, and Miamis, but they got no immediate response. Still, growing Indian discontent with British actions and news of the Senecas' war plans seem to have persuaded the band leaders near Detroit to heed Pontiac's repeated calls for war. Although at one time considered to have coordinated the widespread attacks during 1763, Pontiac clearly lacked the experience and diplomatic contacts to lead such an effort. Nevertheless, he did direct an Indian force of nearly one thousand warriors at Detroit that summer.

In May 1763 Pontiac led his followers against the palisaded British outpost at Detroit. The defenders, having been warned of his plans, beat off the attack, and the Indians began a siege that lasted well into the summer. Elsewhere the English garrisons fell to either ruse or attack so that by June 1763 the tribes had captured or destroyed all of the British army posts in the west except Fort Pitt, Fort Niagara, and Detroit. Some bands of Delawares and Mingos smashed into the small settlements along the Monongahela River as they closed on Fort Pitt. Shawnee war parties struck deep into Virginia, sweeping the pioneers from their precarious frontier holdings. Nevertheless, the warriors' inability to keep up their siege at Detroit and British counterattacks discouraged many of them, and the attacking force slipped away gradually. By late summer Pontiac accepted a temporary truce at Detroit and traveled to Illinois, where, it seems, he hoped to gather French support and more Indian warriors for renewed fighting. Continued British campaigning in the Indian country frustrated his hopes, and by October 1765 Pontiac's Rebellion had ended. The British learned a bitter and expensive lesson, one that they would not repeat. They could ignore the tribes only at the risk of violence and warfare.

BRITISH IMPERIAL EFFORTS TO SUPERVISE INDIAN AFFAIRS

While warriors led by Pontiac and other tribal leaders struck across the frontier, English bureaucrats struggled over what policies to apply to their new possessions in North America. With news of Pontiac's uprising ringing in their ears, the British drafted a temporary policy for the immediate regulation of frontier and Indian affairs. The resulting Royal Proclamation of October 1763 set forth several important ideas and provided some of the foundation for both American and Canadian Indian policies that extend to the present. The document called for a separation of crown lands open for white settlement from those reserved for the Indians, if only temporarily. The divide ran along the watershed of the Appalachian chain from Maine southwest to Georgia. Beyond the proclamation line the Indians retained their use of the land, and the regulations prohibited settlers from moving beyond it. Thus with a single stroke the British established a formally recognized Indian country west of the mountains and in much of eastern Canada, all of it under the supervision of the crown.

This seems to show that in their haste the British had stumbled onto the same approach that the French had used in dealing with the Indian title to the lands beyond their dividing line at the crest of the mountains. Yet this was not the case. Clearly, from the start the crown assumed that it held ultimate title to that region and that the Indians used and occupied the territory only as long as the government allowed them to remain there. Non-Indians could not enter the Indian country to settle, and traders needed a license to deal with the tribes. Neither pioneers, who could not settle in the West, nor groups of land speculators could purchase land from Indian groups or individuals. Only crown representatives could do that, and the title went to the British government, not to any colony, corporation, or settler. Within existing colonies the appointed governor supervised land purchases, but only at public meetings attended by the recognized Indian leaders.[11] This started the process through which Indian policies in both the United States and Canada gradually came to resemble each other.

From these provisions it is clear that while British authorities looked at the regulation of Indian affairs differently than North American colonial leaders did, the two shared some basic views on these issues too. Both saw the proclamation line as merely a temporary, stopgap measure to help end the costly fighting then taking place along much of the frontier. Second, and more significant, while the document established a clearly identified Indian country, distinct and separate from the existing colonies, leaders on both shores of the Atlantic assumed that the area protected for Indian use would shrink as Euro-American settlements expanded. Even some colonists admitted that by limiting land sales to imperial officials or their colonial representatives, they would regularize the process of land transfer from the tribes to the whites, thus reducing the potential for chicanery, misunderstanding, or violence.[12]

The Proclamation of 1763 may be seen as the culmination of 150 years of colonial British experience in dealing with the tribes. Certainly its first objective centered in shifting the direction and control from colonial officials to imperial ones. Thus they expected to take full charge of the management of diplomacy with the tribes, of land transfers from Indians to whites, and of the control of the fur trade by a system of licensing. A second goal the document sought to achieve was to gain at least a short-term guarantee of Indian land claims, resources, and rights to valuable hunting territories and fishing locations. Third, and most significant in long-term North American history, the proclamation recognized and protected tribal autonomy as well as political separateness from the expanding colonial societies.[13] Last, it became the basis for central control of Indian affairs in both the United States and Canada.

This followed from the general practice of the colonizing powers. To the Europeans, the regulation of Indian affairs often meant establishing imperial relations with the tribes, but not trying to govern their internal activities. Whenever possible the New England colonial authorities had tried to replace the authority of traditional tribal or village leaders and to incorporate the Indians into the English legal system, but they succeeded only among those people whose tribal cohesion had been destroyed or become so battered that their internal leadership had collapsed. Usually English management limited itself to trying to regulate relations between the whites and the Indians. So when British imperial authorities stressed their sovereignty over the tribes and the ownership of the land, their claims must be understood as being made in competition with the French or the Spanish in the race for North America. While the British claimed sovereignty over the Iroquois Confederacy in New York, and the French made similar claims about the Abenakis earlier, neither government considered trying to govern the internal workings of their tribal allies or neighbors.[14]

In fact, just the opposite occurred. After 1763 the British imperial Indian Department served as diplomats in dealing with the tribes. Working under the supervision of the military authorities, Indian agents had to resort to the time-honored methods of lengthy councils, lavish gifts, persuasion, bribery, or coercion to achieve their goals. Tribal leaders and village councils retained their local, internal structure and authority as they decided whether or not to sell land and to accept or reject the work of missionaries or teachers, as well as determining the amount and style of agriculture they would practice. Clearly the Indians retained their independence until late in the nineteenth century through their unchallenged control of tribal resources, population, and social customs.[15]

In 1764 British authorities moved beyond the temporary Proclamation of 1763 to issue a plan for the administration of Indian affairs. Based in part on recommendations from Sir William Johnson of New York and George Croghan from Pennsylvania, the Board of Trade set forth a system for imperial control. Recognizing that much of the friction between Indians and whites resulted from trade disputes or land grabbing, the authorities strove to exclude colonial officials from dealing with the tribes. The Plan of 1764 divided British possessions into two departments, separated by the Ohio River. It retained William Johnson and John Stuart as superintendents in the north and south respectively, positions they had held for nearly a decade. Each of them was to supervise deputies responsible for a single subdistrict or for individual tribes. To encourage the Indians to remain sedentary, the plan called for stationing blacksmiths, commissaries, and interpreters at each trading post. The traders needed licenses from the colonial governors, and each had to post a performance bond before being allowed to enter the Indian country. On paper this scheme certainly strengthened imperial control over trade and diplomatic relations with the tribes, but the British government had little money to pay for its implementation, so the plan operated only sporadically and in isolated areas.[16]

Not only did British authorities lack funds to fully implement their ideas, but the Indians refused to cooperate. They had enjoyed the luxury of having traders visit their villages to gather their furs and had no intention of traveling many days to meet with English traders far from their home villages. Also, the lack of credit and modest supply of alcohol angered them. Their continuing dissatisfaction with the English persuaded many to sell their pelts to the French, who took the furs south to Saint Louis or New Orleans. Would-be land speculators, represented by such groups as the Military Associates, the Suffering Traders, and the Indiana Company, pressured colonial and imperial officials to open some Indian lands for sale and settlement. With the trade sharply reduced, leading groups of colonists complaining, pioneers ignoring orders to stay out of Indian country, and Parliament unable or unwilling to raise the funds to pay the cost of Indian administration, it was clear that the time had come for changes in the system.

In 1768 the Cabinet revised the British system of imperial regulations. Their new plan retained the Indian superintendents but restricted their duties to supervision of land cessions, adjustments in the eastern boundary of the Indian country, and diplomatic meetings. Control over the fur traders went back to the colonial governors, and, responding to demands from would-be settlers, the British moved the proclamation line west. While pioneers surged into the newly opened regions and traders moved quickly to reopen their business, the British army abandoned nearly all of its posts in the West, and by 1772 only Detroit, Mackinac, and Niagara still had garrisons. Elsewhere empty forts crumbled or virtually disappeared as pioneers stripped their abandoned buildings for usable items.[17]

At the same time the superintendents, Johnson and Stuart, began negotiations to ensure the surrender of tribal claims so the eastern border of the Indian country could be pushed farther to the west. After months of strenuous negotiations Johnson and Stuart concluded the treaties of Lochaber, Hard Labor, and Fort Stanwix, which opened large parts of Pennsylvania and Virginia for speculators and pioneers.[18] The Fort Stanwix Treaty allowed the Iroquois Confederacy to deflect American pioneer settlement southward into West Virginia and Kentucky, shifting the burden of dealing with the onrushing whites from themselves to the Shawnees and their allies. It also gave the Indians a British pledge that the Ohio River would remain as a permanent boundary between themselves and the settlers. As such it promised something that British authorities could not ensure and led to confusion, anger, and continuing violence on the frontier.[19]

By the early 1770s these boundary adjustments brought whites and Indians into more frequent contact and conflict. The pioneers' greed for land and hatred of Indians because of generations of bloodshed led them to commit repeated depredations and murders. From South Carolina north into Pennsylvania, settlers killed Indians repeatedly without an effective response from the colonial governments. In fact, those who committed such acts were deemed, if not heroes, certainly innocent of any crime, and mob actions forced their release from custody. In Pennsylvania after a particularly bloody fray in which Frederick Stump and his servant John Ironcutter murdered ten peaceful Indians, including women, children, and even an infant, a mob removed the two frontiersmen from jail at Carlisle. When the Cumberland County sheriff and his posse located the fugitives, the pioneers refused to let the two men be arrested unless they remained in the county. Physical threats forced the militia captain who had arrested Stump in the first place to flee the county and move to the relative safety of Philadelphia.[20]

Repeated incursions on Indian lands and incidents of this sort caused much anti-American feeling among the border tribes, while the repeated visions and concerted anti-English preaching of tribal prophets also helped lead to hostilities. The Assinsink prophet Wangoment proved one of the most influential shamans after the Indian defeat in Pontiac's Rebellion. He echoed earlier ideas and stressed that the races needed to follow different paths through life. Urging his listeners to avoid the frontiersmen and to follow more traditional Indian practices, he and other prophets blamed the loss of game animals on the corruption of tribal society through the fur trade. These calls to become disassociated from the expanding Anglo-American economy divided the villagers' ranks. Some continued to support their traditional village leaders, while others opposed them and supported the prophets. This strengthened Indian cultural awareness but also weakened their societies when they had to face the onrushing tide of white settlement.[21]

Given these stresses on their social cohesion and the many real grievances of the villagers, it is not surprising that renewed fighting broke out. The Delawares, Mingos, Shawnees, and Cherokees all objected to the pioneers' presence in Kentucky. When the Cherokees attacked an Ohio River trader in early 1774, Virginians under the bellicose John Connolly began wholesale retaliations against the innocent and guilty alike. The most infamous incident took place on 30 April when a group of pioneers lured a band of Mingos into camp, got them drunk, and murdered all of them except for a single baby. This set off a general Indian scare on the frontier, although the Mingos claimed to be satisfied after only a single retaliatory raid. Nevertheless, the whites responded as if the Indians had begun a major war, and by that summer Governor Dunmore dispatched three columns of troops into the Indian Country. Having nearly isolated the Shawnees and Mingos diplomatically, the Virginia militia units fought several battles with them, invaded their Ohio homeland, and forced the tribes to accept peace.[22]

After these experiences with the colonial pioneers, it is not surprising that when the American colonies declared their independence from the British, few tribes supported them. Most remained sullenly neutral or openly joined the British against the colonists. For the embittered tribal leaders, however, the fighting between the colonists and the British authorities offered another chance to strike the hated pioneers. Late in the spring of 1776 anti-American

Mohawks, Ottawas, and Shawnees traveled south seeking an alliance with the Cherokees against the Americans. They visited many villages, presenting their red wampum belt and calling for a war to ensure Indian survival. Anticipating assistance from the British, they insisted that a failure to cooperate would mean destruction for all the tribes. The message split many villages sharply, with some leaders wanting to join the northerners while others hoped to avoid yet another defeat by the Americans.

Among the Cherokees, warriors from villages led by Dragging Canoe struck at frontier settlements and outposts from Georgia to Virginia. Despite the earlier wampum, the southern Indian leaders failed to recruit the Creeks, Shawnees, and other Indians to join their attacks. Consequently, when several large colonial militia armies invaded the Cherokee country and destroyed villages and crops, the Cherokees, lacking enough guns and ammunition, accepted an imposed peace. After the victorious whites extracted a large land cession from the Cherokees in eastern Tennessee, Dragging Canoe led his militant followers west to the Chickamauga River. There they built new villages, adopted the name Chickamauga, and continued their raids along the southern frontier.[23]

In the north the situation proved more dangerous, as nearly ten thousand warriors of the Ottawa, Ojibwa, Miami, Shawnee, Delaware, Seneca, and Mohawk tribes threatened the backcountry settlements throughout the war. Rarely did more than a small portion of this force actually take part in the fighting at any one time, but their pantribal cooperation and hostility kept frontier settlers terrified and American military leaders uncertain about how much attention they should receive. From New York south and west into the Ohio Valley and central Kentucky these Indians and frontiersmen clashed repeatedly in small engagements that destroyed outlying settlements and Indian villages, ruined crops, scattered livestock, and sent noncombatants on both sides fleeing for safety. In New York and Pennsylvania in particular, large bands of Tories and Indians swept across the frontier, leaving hundreds dead or impoverished, taking many others prisoner, and driving much of the population out of the region. By the end of the war few people on any American frontier saw anything positive about their Indian neighbors, and postwar American and British policies reflected those attitudes.[24]

The emergence of the United States as an independent power with the English to the north in Canada and the Spanish to the south in Florida once again allowed the Indians to seek protection and assistance from competing nations. At first glance the situation resembled that prior to the defeat and withdrawal of the French in 1763, when the French and British had vied for Indian trade and alliances. By the 1780s, however, the circumstances had changed drastically. To the south the Spanish had neither much power nor much desire to assist the tribes in that region. American leaders, boasting of their victory over the British, proved in no mood to conciliate their Indian enemies. As a rapidly expanding settler-dominated society, the United States would provide the most immediate and dangerous threat to the tribes.

In Canada the British strove to retain their economic ties with the peoples of the Great Lakes region and the Ohio Valley while waiting for the new republic to collapse. While doing this they kept troops on American soil and encouraged the Indians to continue or reopen their trade with Canadian merchants. For the next generation the English-American competition in the north and west afforded some of the tribes there a chance to extract concessions from both governments, but in the long run repeated violence and warfare would culminate in the War of 1812, which would spell the end of effective diplomatic or military power for the tribes then living east of the Mississippi River.

BORDER DISPUTES WITH THE NEW U.S. GOVERNMENT

Just prior to American independence, pioneer settlers began drifting west from North Carolina into what is now eastern Tennessee. There, beyond the existing bounds of government, they squatted illegally on Cherokee lands. To protect their shaky claims they organized the ill-fated state of Franklin and by the mid-1780s negotiated the Treaty of Dumplin Creek with some Cherokee leaders. Because the state of North Carolina, the struggling U.S. government, and many Cherokees objected to the pioneers' actions, before the end of 1785 the Congress moved to exercise its exclusive control over Indian affairs. U.S. negotiators concluded the Treaty of Hopewell, which repudiated the Franklinites' earlier agreement in an effort to retain peace with the tribes of that region. By June of the following year negotiators from Franklin concluded another agreement, but their cause failed as the U.S. government took control of the region. Its objective was to avoid open warfare with the Indians because negotiations and modest presents proved far less expensive than continued fighting.

The United States won this uneven tug-of-war with the pioneers in Franklin in 1790 when it created the Southwest Territory, an area south of the Ohio River that included present-day Tennessee. Having established its control over relations with the tribes of the Southeast, the government acted to reduce tensions in eastern Tennessee. First it negotiated yet another agreement with the resident Cherokees, the Treaty of Holston, in 1791, clearing the Indians out of lands south and east of the Clinch River. At the same time federal troops moved against pioneers illegally squatting on Indian lands, demonstrating to the tribes that the government meant to keep its promises and to the frontier population that they had to accept and obey federal regulations concerning tribal lands.[25]

With the United States beginning to assert control beyond the Appalachians, the tribes there turned to other governments for advice, trade, and diplomatic assistance. South of Tennessee, the Muskogees or Creeks looked to the Spanish for aid. Directly in the path of an aggressive Georgia population that paid little attention to Indian claims, they faced the pioneers as a divided people. In the years immediately after American independence when the Confederation struggled to hold the nation together, determined Georgia leaders extracted several land cessions from chiefs representing only a few Creek villages, and the rest of the tribe repudiated the agreements angrily. Led, at least in their negotiations, by the mixed-race leader Alexander McGillivray, they used the possibility of Spanish support and their own determination to retain their homeland. The Chickasaws and Choctaws joined the Creeks in 1784 when the three concluded treaties placing themselves under Spanish protection and ensuring a steady supply of goods from the traders then operating out of Florida. Thus, at least briefly, some of the Indians of the Southeast used American weakness and Spanish diplomatic pretensions to their advantage in holding back the flood of pioneers.[26]

Having signed the Treaty of Pensacola with the Spanish in 1784, tribal leaders split sharply over the issue of further negotiations with Georgia officials. One group, led by Eneah Miko and Hopoithle Miko, sought to reopen talks with the Georgians. They signed agreements in both 1785 and 1786 that surrendered much of the tribal land along the Georgia border. This induced the other faction, led by Alexander McGillivray, to assert its control over relations with the Americans. McGillivray moved to strengthen his position of leadership in Creek affairs by using unofficial "constables" to suppress opposition to his leadership. Then he launched a series of raids through the Georgia frontier regions, as Creek warriors forced the pioneers living in the disputed area to flee east. By 1787 the Creeks had succeeded in pushing the settlers east and off Creek tribal lands. The Spanish authorities, fearing American retaliation, pressured McGillivray to stop his aggressive tactics. When he ignored them they cut back the ammunition and trade goods available to the tribe.[27]

Despite their success in clearing their eastern territory of American pioneers, the Creeks had to bow to Spanish and American pressures because of their economic dependence on trade goods coming from Florida and Alabama. When the new U.S. government began operating in 1789, American peace commissioners visited the Creeks to demand the acceptance of the Georgia treaties concerning the disputed territory. At that point McGillivray broke off the talks, exclaiming, "By God I would not have such a Treaty cram'd down my throat."[28] President Washington then invited the Creek leaders to New York City for renewed negotiations. In August 1790 McGillivray and Hopoithle Miko joined forces and traveled north, where they concluded the Treaty of New York.

In that treaty, the United States accepted the tribal position on the disputed territory, while the Creeks recognized that their land lay within the borders of the United States. That provision appeared to offer the Creeks protection against the Georgia expansionists because, under the newly ratified Constitution, the federal government held sole responsibility for Indian relations and the individual states lacked any authority to negotiate treaties or buy tribal land. In addition, the treaty allowed the Creeks to expel squatters from their lands. Because the leadership had surrendered about two-thirds of the disputed territory to get these provisions, the agreement perpetuated bitter splits among tribal leaders. Nevertheless, the situation in the Southeast stabilized following this treaty, and in 1795 the Spanish signed the Treaty of San Lorenzo with the United States, clarifying the border and promising to maintain peace in the region.[29]

In the north the situation remained confusing and violent. There the bitterness accompanying Anglo-American settlement in West Virginia and Kentucky continued during the Revolution and into the era of uneasy peace that followed. As the Confederation Congress strengthened its hold on the territory west of the Appalachians during the 1780s, it came to realize that continuing difficulties with the Indians there could not be avoided. The Treaty of Paris recognizing American independence had ignored Indian claims altogether, apparently through British oversight. Thus the tribes found themselves living within a nation that acted as if they were its mortal enemies. In October 1783 the Congress decided to send commissioners west to make peace with the tribes. The commissioners would tell tribal leaders that the British had ceded their lands to the United States, and that because they had fought as British allies the United States considered them to be defeated enemies. To show its goodwill, however, the new government would forgive the Indians. All they had to do was to cede most of what is now Ohio, something they had no intention of doing.[30]

During the era from 1775 until the Constitution went into effect in 1789, the U.S. government operated under the Articles of Confederation. That document established a Congress to conduct the war and gain independence from Britain. It recognized the near independence of each state but retained sole authority over war, diplomacy, and Indian affairs. In 1786 the Congress restated its right to direct Indian affairs in the Indian Ordinance of that year, which announced U.S. authority over Indian matters and outlined the first American plan for dealing with them. Actually, the system it established resembled the previous British system, with northern and southern superintendents and the licensing of traders by placing the operation under the direction of the central government.[31]

While the bureaucrats discussed how to deal with the Indians, American negotiators extracted a series of harsh treaties, including the 1784 Fort Stanwix Treaty with the Six Nations Iroquois, the 1785 Treaty of Fort McIntosh with the Delawares, Wyandots, and Ojibwas, and the 1786 Treaty of Fort Finney with the Shawnees. One-sided and land-grabbing, these agreements infuriated the Indians, who had not been defeated and who rejected the American claim that the English could cede their homeland without the consent of the tribes. Ignoring these clear tribal objections, and bowing to pressures from land speculators and some of its own members, the Congress passed the 1785 Land Ordinance, designed to establish a system for the survey and sale of western lands, particularly those claimed by the tribes just mentioned. Two years later, in 1787, Congress passed the companion Northwest Ordinance, a plan to create new territories and to provide government in the west. This legislation encouraged pioneers to move west onto Indian lands and increased the levels of tension and the possibilities for violence there.

While the U.S. government acted in this undisciplined manner, British authorities also did things that undermined peace. Recognizing the depth of Indian anger at having been ignored and in the peace settlement, the British in Canada, following orders from Governor Frederick Haldimand, refused to negotiate the surrender of the garrisons, then still occupied by their troops, that now lay within the United States. Haldimand's excuse was that he had not yet received instructions from the Crown about how and when to abandon the posts. His stated reason for refusal to negotiate, however, beyond giving the English and Canadian fur traders time to strengthen their ties with the tribes, was to give his Indian office personnel a chance to calm the angry tribesmen over what they saw as a British betrayal.[32] Thus the British officials in North America tried to recover from their counterparts' blunder in Europe when they overlooked Indian matters entirely in the peace negotiations. The retention of the so-called Northwest Posts set the tone for early British-Indian-American dealings south of the Great Lakes. Having once encouraged the tribes to retain their economic and diplomatic ties, it proved easy for officials in Canada to continue that policy for the next several decades.

Once the Indians learned that the British had abandoned them to the tender mercies of the avaricious Americans, efforts to renew intertribal ties began anew. Ohio Valley Shawnees and representatives of the New York Six Nations Iroquois exchanged messages and speeches. Northern and southern peoples such as the Shawnees, Muskogees, Cherokees, and Chickamaugas worked together too. Those Indian leaders and villages trying to remain at peace with the Americans suffered the most through attacks by frontier militia units. Because of the harsh treaties, British encouragement to resist the advancing Americans in the upper Ohio Valley, and continuing attacks by the pioneers there, tribes reopened their raiding, attacking settlers on their tiny farms and travelers on the Ohio River and fighting repeatedly with settlers in Pennsylvania and Kentucky.

Under President Washington the new government responded by mobilizing militia troops under General Josiah Harmer. Indian actions against U.S. troops during the 1790s showed how effective their cooperative efforts had become. In 1790 Harmer directed several forces in a move north from the Ohio River toward northeastern Indiana, and he led an army of some fifteen hundred regulars and militiamen north from Cincinnati. Burning villages and crops as they slowly marched northward, his troops lost their skirmishes with the Indians. The warriors, led by the Miami chief Little Turtle, tried repeatedly to lure the undisciplined troops into an ambush. This succeeded in late October at the banks of the Eel River, when a part of the militia stumbled into an Indian attack, panicked, and fled, leaving a company of regular troops alone to fight and be nearly destroyed. On 22 October a larger fight occurred, and again the Indians surprised and defeated the invading force. With that loss Harmer marched his troops south. The campaign ended with a perceived Indian victory, but the tribes suffered that winter because of the damage to their homes and crops.[33]

The following spring, 1791, the War Department gathered another force, and in October that year the governor of the Northwest Territory, Arthur St. Clair, led the mostly militia army north from Fort Washington, near Cincinnati, along the same route Harmer had taken a year earlier. At first this invasion fared better than its predecessor. Capturing large numbers of women and children, scattering the men, and burning the villages and crops of groups in central Indiana, the troops moved northward. Unfortunately, St. Clair's army moved so slowly that Indians for miles around knew its whereabouts, and the warriors prepared to defeat the whites as they had done the previous year. Despite St. Clair's careful posting of his troops and accurate assessment of the terrain at the battle site, he fared no better than Harmar had because warriors from several tribes united under Little Turtle. On 4 November 1791 this combined force struck. In the attack they concentrated their early fire on the artillerymen, who manned the weapons most feared by the Indians, and the clearly marked officers. By midmorning, when St. Clair called for a retreat, his men needed no further orders. They fled, abandoning the artillery, much of their supplies and other equipment, and many of the wounded as well. Only the late arrival of Major John Hamtramck and his regular troops prevented the disordered retreat from turning into a complete disaster. Nevertheless, the Indians had repulsed a second U.S. army in two years at what the Miami called "The Battle of a Thousand Slain," and their morale was high.[34]

The same could not be said for either the American pioneers in the region or for Washington's new government. Unable to dislodge the British from the Northwest posts, and having difficulties with the Spanish and the Indians to the south, the administration needed to pacify the northern frontier to achieve some appearance of success. The Indians, on the other hand, thought themselves in a position of strength because of their two recent victories over the Americans. British diplomatic initiatives and encouragement stiffened their resolve too, as Canadian authorities exceeded their orders by urging the tribes to reject any new American diplomatic efforts and to retain all of their lands.[35]

Tribal leaders needed no such advice, and continuing American efforts to settle the dispute failed. In 1792 the Indians killed two American negotiators sent to persuade them to talk rather than fight. Some villages did accept an invitation to meet the next year, however, but at the discussions with American representatives the Indian leaders insisted that the Ohio River was the border and demanded that pioneers then living north of that river be evacuated immediately. This was not what the U.S. commissioners had expected to hear. There was more bad news, too. Claiming that they sought peace rather than war, the Indian spokesmen announced that "our only demand is the peaceable possession of a small part of our once great country. . . . We can retreat no farther, because the country behind hardly affords food for its present inhabitants; and we have therefore resolved to leave our bones in this small place to which we are confined."[36] With this rejection, partly the result of pan-Indian and nativist ideas, U.S. leaders dropped their effort to acquire the territory through negotiation and turned to the newly reorganized army for success.[37]

Having pushed legislation to reconstitute the army, President Washington called his friend and former colleague General Anthony Wayne out of retirement to lead another expedition against the Northwest tribes. Wayne began recruiting and training his force during 1793; by the time he had learned that the negotiations had broken down it was far too late to enter the Indian country any more that year. He moved his little army into western Ohio and spent the winter of 1793–94 completing its training. Then in the summer of 1794 Wayne marched the troops north. This group was well trained and skillfully led, and when Indian warriors tried a surprise attack in June it failed. On 30 June–1 July the two sides clashed at Fort Recovery, where heavier-than-expected Indian casualties persuaded some of Little Turtle's allies to withdraw. As their force began to shrink, Indian leaders struggled to retain enough men and unity to repulse the Americans one more time, but they failed. On 20 August 1794 Wayne's troops met the tribes in the Battle of Fallen Timbers at the rapids of the Maumee River, where a divided and scattered Indian force proved unable to repeat the earlier one-sided victories and had to flee. Hoping to get help from British troops at Fort Miami, the outnumbered warriors retreated there, but the British officers, with orders to stay out of any fighting between the Indians and the Americans, could offer neither help nor shelter.[38]

The Indian defeat at Fallen Timbers came on the heels of the 1794 British-American agreement known as Jay's Treaty or the Treaty of London. That accord included a British promise to abandon the Northwest posts they still occupied, and their troops left two years later. Having apparently solved the dispute with Britain, the United States turned its attention to extracting a satisfactory treaty from the Ohio and Indiana tribes. Anthony Wayne issued a call for negotiations during the summer of 1795, and the defeated chiefs gathered at Greenville to learn their fate. The discussions that followed included no real negotiations, as Wayne dictated the terms of what became the Treaty of Greenville. Concluded that summer, the document called for the Indians to cede all of southern and eastern Ohio and a strip of eastern Indiana. The chiefs accepted U.S. demands for sixteen more small land cessions for military or other governmental uses in what was left of their territory in Ohio and Indiana.[39] Clearly the multitribal confederacy that had sought to retain the border between itself and the advancing Americans at the Ohio River had failed, but similar efforts to unite and resist the onrushing pioneers in that region continued for another two decades.

THE CANADIAN FRONTIER IN THE LATE EIGHTEENTH CENTURY

While American authorities treated the tribes as defeated enemies and strove to punish them by taking land, the British in Canada used different approaches. First they strove to persuade the Indians that the king had not abandoned them in 1783 by recognizing American independence and that the English still considered them friends and essential allies. This action resulted from the local officials' fear that angry and dissatisfied Indians might attack the Canadian settlements. Reporting from Fort Niagara in May 1783, Alan Maclean told Governor Haldimand that the tribesmen had denounced the treaty ending the war as "treacherous and cruel" and rejected any negotiations that gave away their lands. Stating their position as allies rather than subjects of the British, they promised "to defend their just rights or perish in the attempt."[40]

As the negotiations to conclude the war ended in 1783, officials in Canada worked to persuade the tribes that they needed to come to terms with the Americans. Lord Dorchester, Guy Carleton, fearing that ongoing warfare between the tribes and the expanding U.S. settlements would endanger Canada, urged his superiors to continue their generous support for the Indians. Whether his request had any direct impact is not clear, but during the mid-1780s the British government spent more than twenty thousand pounds on presents for the tribes.[41]

When the Americans and the Indians of the Ohio Valley returned to war with each other in the early 1790s, the British government worked to avoid its involvement and urged Carleton to use every means available "for healing the differences which at present exist [between the Indians and the United States], and for effecting, if possible, a speedy termination of the war."[42] This resulted from England's desire to keep the tribes in Canada and along its border with the United States at peace, thus ensuring the continued safety of the colony. It seems clear that British objectives remained chiefly political and diplomatic rather than economic and continued to focus on the safe retention of the northern territories from possible American aggression.

Under the 1791 Constitutional Act Britain divided its eastern North American territories into two provinces—Upper Canada (present-day Ontario), and Lower Canada (Quebec). In part this action stemmed from the differences between the two regions: Lower Canada included much of the former French territory, whereas Upper Canada consisted of mostly new settlements founded after 1783 and of Indian lands. As the new lieutenant governor for Upper Canada, John Graves Simcoe acted as if invasion and conquest by the United States remained a distinct possibility, and he shaped his policies toward the Indians on that assumption. His biggest fear seems to have been of an American victory in the Ohio Valley region. If that happened, he worried, the tribes would turn their rage toward the British for not having helped them enough in their fight with the pioneers. Even should the warfare in Ohio and Indiana cease, Simcoe worried that the Americans might persuade the tribes there to attack the nearby defenseless new colony of Upper Canada. For the new lieutenant governor the situation appeared perilous. Through active diplomacy and military assistance to the Great Lakes tribes, long after such support had lost favor in London, Simcoe sought to defend his colony by encouraging the tribal leaders to demand the Ohio River as the border between themselves and the United States.[43]

While they strove to retain Indian goodwill during the era of the American Revolution, Canadian leaders faced a related and potentially dangerous issue—that of finding places where they could settle American Loyalists who fled the new United States and of getting lands to give their Indian allies who chose to move north at the same time. At first glance the problem appears minor because only about fifty-five hundred tribal people lived in southern Ontario or along the Saint Lawrence River, the most likely region for refugee resettlement. Not only was the resident population small, but the newcomers included only about five thousand Loyalists and another two thousand Indian people who would be settled somewhere in Upper Canada. Yet having to get land for this many people within a single decade frightened the authorities, who moved cautiously in following the guidelines laid down by the Proclamation of 1763. Thus from 1783 Canada and the United States took different paths in dealing with Indian land cessions. The British colonial authorities based their policy and actions on the theory of tribal title stated in the Proclamation of 1763, whereas the Americans often acted as though earlier British policies and legislation concerning Indian affairs could be disregarded because of national independence.

The Mississaugas, an Algonquian-speaking Ojibwa people, were the most important tribe in early efforts by officials of Upper Canada to get land for refugees from the United States. During the late seventeenth and early eighteenth centuries these people migrated south and east into the region at the western end of Lake Ontario. Primarily a fishing and hunting people who traveled from place to place during their annual migrations, they agreed, apparently willingly, to numerous cessions of land before 1800. Like other tribes, the Mississaugas had no concept of formal personal ownership of land and used no fences, but did recognize claims to control or use specific areas or even plots of ground. Gradually as they watched the spread of the whites and learned about European ideas of landownership, they grew less willing to agree to further land cessions.[44]

Early land acquisitions by British authorities in present-day Ontario began even before the American Revolution ended. Increasing numbers of loyalists and Indian refugees at Fort Niagara forced the government to act, and in 1781 Governor Frederick Haldiman negotiated cession agreements with the Six Nations and with the Mississaugas for a strip of land on the west side of the Niagara

River. As the Revolutionary War ended Governor Haldimand had to reopen negotiations with the Mississaugas for more land to accommodate Indian refugees from the United States. Two groups of Iroquois, a band of some two hundred Mohawks under Chief John Deseronto, and a larger group of some eighteen hundred people from the Six Nations under the Mohawk leader Joseph Brant chose to accept lands in Canada rather than accept the terms of the 1784 Treaty of Fort Stanwix, which stripped them of much of their territory in New York.[45] Hoping to use Indians as a buffer between Canada and the United States, Haldimand expected to locate both groups at the Bay of Quinte, on the northeastern part of the lake. Although Deseronto accepted that site, Joseph Brant decided that it was too isolated and asked for lands closer to the Seneca holdings in New York. This forced the British authorities to make two purchases. While they struggled to do that, growing numbers of Loyalists moved north from the United States. These people rejected Haldimand's efforts to keep them out of Indian country and within the older, more settled parts of Quebec, so the governor had to purchase more Indian lands for them. Thus by 1785 the British had talked the tribes living on the northern and western shores of Lake Ontario into making five separate land cessions.[46]

Rather than settling the issue, these purchases brought more trouble to the white-Indian frontier in Canada. The government had tried to follow a policy of land acquisition for whites and Indians new to the region, something clearly distinct from what the United States did at the same time, but its early dealings with the tribes proved only slightly more successful at maintaining peace and stability than those of its neighbor to the south. While the Americans fought bitterly contested campaigns against the Cherokees in the south and the Delawares, Shawnees, and their allies just south of the Great Lakes, in Canada no such open wars occurred. Nevertheless, the entry of "foreign" Indians such as the Mohawks and of white Loyalists into southern Ontario brought discord and violence there too.

Bad feelings and friction between the pioneers and the Indians grew slowly at first, but within a decade the situation on the Lake Ontario frontier resembled that south of the Great Lakes in all but its particulars. At first the Indians felt satisfied that they had received a fair payment for their land, but apparently they thought that the land had been rented, not sold. For the British, on the other hand, the agreements extinguished Mississauga title to the area. Because the treaties of the 1780s all included vague terms and questionable boundaries, by the following decade the Indians had come to regret their openhanded dealings with the English. In a personal history written decades later, an educated Mississauga recalled hearing of this discontent from tribal elders who told how the whites had asked for "a small piece of land on which they might pitch their tents; the request was cheerfully granted." Later, however, the whites "continued to ask, or have obtained by force or fraud, the fairest portions of our territory."[47]

When the land purchases took place, at least according to Indian memories, the British promised that the white settlers who would come to live nearby would be of great help to the tribe. When this proved false, Mississauga leaders complained that "Colonel [John] Butler told us the Farmers would help us, but instead of doing so when we encamp on the shore they drive us off & shoot our Dogs and never give us any assistance as was promised to our old Chiefs."[48] The discontent erupted into violence in August 1796 when a soldier named Charles McEwan and two other white men killed Chief Wabakinine, the recognized leader of the Mississaugas, when he tried to prevent them from having a sexual liaison with his sister. After beating the chief senseless, they attacked his wife as well; when other Indians heard the noise, the whites fled. The chief died from his beating the same night, and his wife died several days later.

These brutal killings sent a chill of panic through the nearby frontier settlements; the tribal people vastly outnumbered the whites and certainly had reason to seek retaliation. The accused murderer stood trial as the authorities tried to calm the situation, but when no Indians appeared to testify against him the court set him free. During the weeks before the trial Canadian officials strove to forestall a possible war. Joseph Brant, the Mohawk leader, declined to send the four hundred warriors the Mississaugas requested. Instead he cautioned them against an attack on the English. At the same time, the tribe was reeling from heavy population losses through recent epidemics of smallpox and measles; the fabric of their society seemed to be coming apart. While the Indians considered what actions to take, British negotiators strove desperately to isolate them, and that diplomacy, combined with the weakened conditions of other tribes who otherwise might have joined in a new war against the whites, discouraged them. Although anti-Indian incidents failed to stop, and tribal anger remained high, the Mississaugas found themselves isolated and virtually powerless in the face of the continuing white aggression.[49]

The second difficulty arising out of the early British land acquisitions centered on the Grand River lands granted to the Mohawk leader Joseph Brant. The tract given to Brant and his followers was six miles wide on each side of the river and extended from its mouth on Lake Ontario to its source some miles inland. By 1785, a year after the land cession, 1,843 Iroquois, some from each of the Six

Nations, had moved to the area. Despite the British generosity in providing land for these people, their leaders' actions created both confusion over land titles and fear that they might reunite with their relatives in the United States to strike against Canada. Particularly during the 1790s Canadian officials kept a wary eye on Joseph Brant as he met with some of the Ohio Valley tribes, but no overt anti-British actions resulted from his actions at the time.[50]

Of more long-term consequences, Brant's actions in attracting whites to the Grand River lands and his actual sales of tribal land to some whites brought confusion over land titles for another two generations. Claiming that the British grant of land to the Six Nations meant that the whites recognized the Indians as a nation, equal to either the United States or Britain, Brant acted on that assumption for some years. Not only did the chief claim Iroquois independence and sovereignty, he acted as if the land grant had been given to him personally to do with it as he pleased. With little government presence in Upper Canada to challenge his actions, the Mohawk leader invited white farmers, millers, and others who he thought would provide good examples for the Indians onto Iroquois lands. Gradually he gave actual land titles to them, having sold substantial amounts of the grant during the first ten to fifteen years after acquiring it.

These actions brought him into direct conflict with Governor Simcoe when the latter issued a patent for the Haldimand Grant to Brant that failed to mention any Indian right to sell or lease any part of the land grant. In taking this stand Simcoe merely followed official British doctrine in terms of Indian land claims stemming from the 1763 Royal Proclamation. The nearly three-decades-old policy was that the Indians held a right to use the land, but that it could not be sold or leased to anyone except at a public meeting with tribal leaders present and in agreement, and then only to crown representatives. Brant objected to what he saw as this limitation on tribal sovereignty and his right to do what he wished with the lands, and the issue remained unresolved for another several decades.[51]

During the 1780s and 1790s, Canadian officials continued to buy land from the tribes along the north shore of Lake Ontario. During that era the Indians agreed to cessions for which they received a payment in goods at first and later a lump sum of cash at the time they signed the transfer documents. These agreements gave the English desirable lands on the north shore of the Saint Lawrence from the Ottawa River to Lake Ontario, the north shore of that lake, and the north shore of Lake Erie as far west as the Detroit River, with little objection from the Indians. Because of the modest white population in the region, few incidents occurred and little pressure on the Indians to move existed. The tribes of the area had little tradition of working together, and some, such as the Mississaugas and the Iroquois, actively disliked each other. By working to keep the tribes apart, Canadian officials employed the same policy Americans used at the same time.[52]

U.S. EXPANSION IN THE OLD NORTHWEST

Although appearing similar, the process of land acquisition in Upper Canada differed markedly from that in the United States. Certainly both governments negotiated with tribal and band leaders for the cessions, and both paid the Indians in goods, cash, or both. Yet in Canada, at least until later, tribal spokesmen did not have to be tricked or threatened to sign the land surrenders. Necessary or not, such tactics characterized American dealings with the tribes during the late eighteenth century. The ideas of George Washington, along with his secretary of war, Henry Knox, and his fellow Virginian Thomas Jefferson, provide an insight into the approaches the United States tried during this era. The nascent government gave little consideration to dealing with the tribes except to keep peace and to acquire land titles.

In 1789 Henry Knox pointed out to Washington that conciliation was unlikely to cost more than fifteen thousand dollars a year for possibly half a century. Not only would "coercion and oppression pursued for the same period . . . probably amount to a much greater sum of money," he commented, "but the blood and injustice which would stain the character of the nation, would be beyond all pecuniary calculation."[53] Knox offered only two alternatives for dealing with the tribes—extirpation or peace, and he favored the latter. Washington's immediate response to Knox is unclear, but within a year American forces under General Harmar had suffered ignominious defeat in the Ohio Country.

By 1791, while Arthur St. Clair was readying another frontier army for his disastrous invasion of Ohio and Indiana, Thomas Jefferson offered another scenario for dealing with the tribes. "I hope we shall drub the Indians well this summer," he wrote, "and then change our plan from war to bribery." Once the fighting ended he thought it best to follow the British and Spanish example of using "liberal and constant presents." Like Knox, Jefferson saw clearly that peace was far cheaper and less dangerous than the continuing warfare on the frontier. In fact, he suggested that "the expense of this summer expedition [1791] would have served for presents for a half a century."[54] Such statements demonstrate at least a surface level of understanding of the causes for tribal dissatisfaction and frontier violence, but few American leaders had much firsthand knowledge of Indian societies. For instance, they seem to have been ignorant, or willfully dismissive, of the eastern tribes' successful methods of mixed-crop agriculture. This becomes ironically clear in a 1791 letter that Henry Knox wrote to the Seneca chiefs Cornplanter and Big Tree in which he offers to send men to teach the Iroquois how to farm.[55]

The government had hoped to keep peace with the tribes and to persuade them to cede parts of their land. During the 1780s and 1790s the constant pressure from land speculators and pioneer settlers kept leaders on the defensive, reacting to Indian complaints, frontier violence, and bitter recriminations from all sides. By his second term as president, Washington repeatedly warned the Indian chiefs that it was virtually impossible to keep the races apart, and he urged them to adopt intensive agriculture and livestock production, to make use of the whites' plow, and to welcome schools and teachers for their children.[56] As his second term drew to a close, the president grumbled that "scarcely any thing short of a Chinese wall, or a line of troops, will restrain . . . the encroachment of settlers upon the Indian territory."[57] By the time he made these comments the Indians had weakened dramatically. Whereas at one time he had addressed the tribal leaders as brothers, in a 1796 letter he crossed out that word and inserted "Children" in its place. Clearly American leaders thought that the balance between the Indians and the aggressive pioneers had tipped in favor of the latter.

While American officials proposed modest funds to help Indians improve their agriculture or learn how to care for livestock, Canadian authorities did little more for their tribal neighbors. During the 1780s government officers gave a few location tickets for farmland to individual Indians in Nova Scotia, and in 1786 the British made their first direct grant of land to tribes in that province. Using a sort of carrot-and-stick approach a few years later, the government there gave seeds and hand tools to Micmac people, and even promised a gift of two blankets each fall to all families that had raised enough food that year to support themselves through the winter.[58] When war broke out between Britain and France in 1793 people in the Maritime regions feared that the local Indians might side with the French as they had done thirty years earlier. George Monk, the provincial superintendent of Indian affairs, investigated and found little reason for the fears. Nevertheless, he urged his superiors to provide regular supplies of food for the Indian communities so they would have no major reasons for complaint. In addition, he provided the men with ammunition for hunting and cloth and household goods for the women.

As in the United States, Canadian leaders faced the problems of separating or incorporating the tribal people into their society. Their attempts to deal with the issue appear similar, although to their credit they did manage to avoid most of the repeated violence that marred the American experience. That is not to say that the Canadian actions were any more enlightened or less self-centered and ethnocentric, however. For example, in the Maritime regions of Canada the populace despised the Micmac and Maliseet people who lived near them, and they did everything possible to deprive them of their long-accustomed fishing sites and croplands. Then when destitute Indians became a problem during the late 1790s, an investigating committee recommended against providing the poor with any direct charity. Instead, they offered relief only to those who abandoned their native pattern of seasonal migration and chose to settle down as farmers.[59]

At the same time, local leaders looked beyond the borders of their province, hoping to attract outside help for meeting the costs of dealing with the tribal people. As early as 1787 an English philanthropic organization, the New England Company, began work among the Maritime tribes. Through local representatives it chose potential sites for Indian schools and actually began some. There was little chance of success, however, because few of the Micmac bands would agree to cease their seasonal migrations, and even fewer proved willing to surrender their children to the whites. By 1791 the company operated three small schools, and several years later it consolidated its entire educational effort in one institution located at Sussex Vale. There the company hoped to convince the parents to settle on a small plot of land it owned and to send the children to school. The young children would receive primary school training, and the older children were to be apprenticed to local tradesmen.[60] Indian reluctance to part with their children defeated this effort, however. Not a single child received an adequate education, and none completed any apprenticeship. The efforts of the New England Company were hampered mostly by its shortage of money, but at least in part by the open hostility of English settlers who lived near these tribes.[61]

The period from 1750 to 1795 provided enormous changes in eastern North America. The British drove the French off the continent, only to lose many of their colonies to the independence movement. With the French gone the Indians lost their long-available counterweight to the British, but that situation resurfaced briefly with the eastern part of the continent divided among Britain, the United States, and Spain. As the American population burgeoned and pioneer settlers poured into the frontier regions tribal leaders sought to retain their land, independence, and culture. Most of their efforts succeeded at the time despite the one-sidedness of the contest. More significant in the long run, their cultures took such a battering that what remained often lacked the unity necessary to hold the village peoples together. Religious ideas, economic practices, the sexual divisions within the villages, and the ideas about clan or family loyalty and sharing within individual villages all lost some vitality and applicability because of the continuing white onslaught.

In Canada during these decades, relations between Indians and others remained calmer than in the United States. Nevertheless, stresses did occur. Officials sought to satisfy Indian demands for fur trade markets, to placate tribal unhappiness about a diminished supply of presents, and to treat them as valuable partners and allies. At the same time they strove for good relations, British colonial officials had to make room for refugees—white and Indian alike—from the newly independent United States. To do this they began to negotiate land cessions similar to those south of the border. For the most part they avoided the anger and violence that characterized Indian relations in the United States at the time. Two basic differences explain this. In Canada only small numbers of whites moved into tribal areas. In addition, most of the tribes there were not sedentary agriculturalists. Rather they depended on hunting, gathering, fishing, and trade. As a result, there was little reason to quarrel about the land, at least at first.

In the United States, by contrast, the advancing pioneers wanted to enter areas most densely populated by the tribal people or into the territories of the larger and more organized tribes who had no desire to surrender their homelands. This led to repeated efforts to bribe or cheat Indian leaders, and frequent promises that the cession under discussion would be the last one. Trying to retain their lands, tribal leaders refused to negotiate, organized diplomatic combinations to block the American advance, worked to strengthen their tribal cultures and religious foundations, and finally resorted to warfare.

For the native peoples in both countries the era had brought fundamental changes in politics, economics, diplomacy, and society. The continuing growth of both Anglo-American societies meant more pressure on the tribes in the East to cooperate with their white and Indian neighbors. In the United States this situation produced repeated nativist movements helped along by the visions and teachings of shamans and prophets. Continuing efforts to link tribes south of the Great Lakes with those in the South succeeded repeatedly in blocking or slowing American expansion and land grabbing. Nevertheless, demands that Indians surrender their territory continued, and the turmoil that produced would extend until after the War of 1812.

6 Old Threats, New Resolve, 1795–1820s

 WHEN THE OHIO AND INDIANA tribes ignored the Miami leader Little Turtle's urging to accept peace with the United States in 1794, they went on to fight and lose the Battle of Fallen Timbers. That defeat and the 1795 Treaty of Greenville destroyed Indian efforts to unify and block pioneer expansion in the Ohio Valley for over a decade. At the same time, the British and Spanish importance in North American Indian affairs shrank drastically. In Jay's Treaty of 1794 the British accepted American demands that they withdraw their troops from army posts along the northeastern border. Two years later, in 1796, the Union Jack came down and the troops left. Just a year earlier, Spain and the United States concluded Pinckney's Treaty, related to American use of the Mississippi River and also to Spanish-Indian relations along the nation's southern border. As a result of these actions, by the late 1790s tribal leaders faced an expansive, confident, and still hostile United States with few resources and options.

Having defeated the tribes of the old Northwest and settled the disputes with their European competitors, American authorities turned their attention to dealing with the Indians through economic expansion and the fur trade. As early as 1783 George Washington had suggested that some kind of government-sponsored effort would "engross their Trade, and fix them strongly in our Interest."[1] Just over a decade later he proposed that Congress establish trading houses on the frontier to wean Indian traders away from their British and Spanish partners. Supporters suggested that government-subsidized trade was far cheaper than war and that when used in conjunction with diplomatic efforts, such a trading system would help ensure peace. Congress authorized an experimental beginning in 1795 and subsequently renewed and enlarged what came to be called the factory system or the trading houses. The factors, government-appointed traders, provided the Indians with what were supposed to be quality foods at fair prices, and in each year until its demise in 1822 the system earned a modest profit. Yet forcing the Indians to travel to the trading post, limiting credit, and prohibiting alcohol all hindered long-term success.[2]

Almost every year opponents questioned having the government involved actively in the fur trade, but until the War of 1812 the opposition remained ineffective. At the same time many officials saw the trading houses as a useful part of government policy, particularly when it came to persuading tribes to sell more of their land. Thomas Jefferson's often-quoted comments to William Henry Harrison provide a good example. He hoped to encourage the Indians to turn away from hunting so they would need less land to support themselves. Then they could be persuaded to cede it to the government. If that failed, he suggested using trade in ways that would cause "the good and influential individuals among them [to] run into debt, because we observe that when these debts get beyond what the individuals can pay, they become willing to lop them off by a cession of lands."[3] Such arguments by high officials helped retain support for the trade.

While the federal government encouraged frontier settlement and worked to clear the tribes from vast areas, Indians continued to use ideas and methods that had divided their villages for a generation. In Canada, despite the fears of British officials there, tribal people and Europeans managed to cooperate. Certainly disputes and difficulties arose, but the large area and small population kept relations calm most of the time. Clearly that was not often the case south of the border, as the government responded to the demands made by hordes of avaricious land seekers that the tribes be pushed aside. As a result, the era from the 1790s until just after the War of 1812 saw repeated disputes, conflict, and tribal divisions within the United States.

Village and band leaders divided sharply over how to deal with the Americans. The Miami Little Turtle and the Shawnee Black Hoof spoke for those who accepted the idea of accommodation rather than open military resistance. Apparently the repeated invasions of their Ohio and Indiana lands, destruction of crops and stored food, and the burning of many villages persuaded all but the most determined nativists that they had little choice but to cooperate with the Americans. That left Indians with the idea that they could not avoid gradual acceptance of some white practices. Not all of the militant anti-American clamor ended during the 1790s, but government acceptance of the pioneers' demands and goals masked the continued Indian rejection of the whites' plans for tribal people. In many villages nativists continued to nourish dreams of pantribal confederacies and of calling upon the spirit world for renewed power to destroy or expel the hated pioneers.[4]

THE EARLY PANTRIBAL REVITALIZATION MOVEMENTS

By the end of the eighteenth century leaders in both Canada and the United States had expanded earlier efforts to impose education, Christianity, and capitalistic economic practices on the Indians. While those actions disrupted local village societies and customs, they failed to bring much acculturation to the tribal communities. Instead, they hastened the ongoing cultural destruction then taking place. Acutely aware of their collapsing village world, many Indians, particularly those in the United States, turned inward one more time seeking spiritual strength and a renewal of their power. As a result several movements of cultural revitalization and religious fervor swept through the tribes south of the Great Lakes and the Iroquois of New York and Upper Canada. Stemming largely from the near destruction of village economies, continuing land losses, epidemic disease, endemic alcoholism, and fears that their village societies stood on the verge of destruction, such movements offered hope for both the present and the future. Based on a combination of native religious ideas and elements of Christianity, these nativistic revival movements grew out of a yearning for stability, a means for dealing with the unending problems caused by the invading whites, and a hope of finding a way to direct their own affairs. None of these movements succeeded in achieving more than a part of its goals for more than a few years, but their very existence indicates the level of social crisis the Indians perceived.

As had happened a generation earlier, some prophesies came from unknown villages, in several locations about the same time. Christian missionaries reported accounts of a child's visions among some displaced Delawares then living in Ontario. These dreams called upon the Indians to return to their traditional rituals in order to strengthen their spiritual powers. Just a few years later a Seneca girl urged her people to reject the teachings of the Quakers then working among the villagers. Other shamans repeated her ideas and continued efforts to reshape tribal ceremonial practices in order to reject the whites' cultural onslaught. Among the Mohawks in Ontario came a call to reinstitute the whitedog sacrifice and to reject the uses of alcohol. All of these seem to have grown out of genuine desires of the Indians to retain their battered customs and to live without having to accept the European demands pressing in on their lives.[5]

Two more widespread revitalization movements occurred. The earliest and most long-lasting of these came under the tutelage of Ganeodiyo or Handsome Lake, a Seneca shaman of only modest repute. The brother of Chief Corn-planter, he experienced a series of visions beginning in 1799 that continued for several years and formed the basis of his later teachings. Certainly influenced by Quaker missionaries who had worked among the tribes of Pennsylvania and New York, the new prophet highlighted the forces then tearing village society to pieces. Depressed about the near collapse of Seneca customs and worried about the impact of alcohol and the repeated witchcraft disputes within the tribe, Handsome Lake fell into despondency and was thought to be dying by his family and friends. In mid-June his daughter thought he had died and called Corn-planter and others into the cabin to prepare the corpse for burial, but the supposedly dead man was only in a trance. When he recovered he related his vision, in which supernatural beings sent by the Creator had brought him instructions for his own cure and for a general Seneca recovery. The heavenly visitors gave Handsome Lake what he called four words—alcohol, witchcraft, love magic, and abortion and sterility—that encompassed the evil things that had to be removed from among the Indians to ensure their survival.[6]

Other visions followed, and soon the shaman's preaching included apocalyptic descriptions of world destruction, denunciations of personal and corporate sin, and exhortations to follow the road to salvation. To these essentially Christian ideas he added traditional Iroquoian ideas and called for the strict observance of tribal ceremonies, tending to identify the personages in his visions with the Four Winds of Seneca beliefs. Handsome Lake, then, called for his people to accept some new ideas taken from Christian teachings as well as for a revival of cultural practices that had bound the Iroquoian villages together. His teachings added some major cultural changes, too. He called for the secret medicine societies to meet openly and refrain from including alcohol in their ceremonies. Believing that people needed to repent from sin, he emphasized personal confession of misdeeds. Fearing that the Seneca focused too much attention on death, he tried to limit mourning to the usual ten days after a person died. These practices, he hoped, would improve village life and social cohesion. Eventually his followers organized Handsome Lake's teachings and orally passed them from generation to generation as the Long House Religion or the Code of Handsome Lake.[7]

Of shorter-term but considerably more immediate significance, the teachings of the Shawnee prophet Tenskwatawa led to a renewed effort to revive the Northwest Indian confederation under his religious leadership. While he preached anti-American ideas, his half brother Tecumseh sought to organize a diplomatic and military intertribal movement against the United States. Like Handsome Lake, the Shawnee prophet had been a tribal shaman of little repute. A village drunk sarcastically known as the "Rattle" or the Noise Maker, he too experienced a series of visions during which he traveled to the spirit land to receive teachings to bring back his people. Again, as with the Seneca religious teacher, Tenskwatawa focused his suggestions on the fundamental problems bothering the Indiana, Illinois, and Michigan tribes. Excessive use of alcohol, dependence on white trade goods, the collapse of village and clan obligations and ceremonies, difficulties caused by witchcraft, and continuing land cessions to the United States all received his attention.

In 1805 he fell into a trance and, again like Handsome Lake, his wife thought that he had died. When he revived he related his vision to the skeptical villagers. Changing his name to Tenskwatawa, or the Open Door, he stopped using alcohol and began preaching in his new role as a holy man commissioned to lead the Indians to paradise. Urging his listeners to avoid the whites and their products, he spoke in favor of peace and harmony. To achieve this goal the Shawnees had to start with their own families and in their villages; to that end he denounced brawling, wife beating, and drinking. On the one hand, he condemned the Americans and white trade goods, urging the Indians to reinstitute their own traditional crafts and practices; on the other, he denounced some tribal practices as well. The ancient medicine bundles, he claimed, had lost their power, and those chiefs and shamans who rejected his teachings he labeled as fools or even witches. In sum, his teachings told the villagers that their only hope for survival lay in rejecting all dealings with the Americans. If they did that, peace and contentment would follow.[8]

A persuasive teacher, Tenskwatawa met delegations from other tribes and villages, filling their ears with his new ideas and more often than not gaining at least some adherents. During 1806 he visited several Delaware villages in Indiana, where recent converts to his teachings began searching for witches; he participated in the ceremonial burnings of several of the accused witches. Often nativist leaders focused their witch-hunts on villagers who accepted or supported American cultural penetration of tribal society, as long-standing quarrels rent the Indian societies. When news of these actions reached the American settlements, William Henry Harrison, the governor of Indiana Territory, denounced the Shawnee prophet and his adherents and issued his famous challenge: "If he is really a prophet, ask of him to cause the sun to stand still—the moon to alter its course—the rivers to cease to flow—or the dead to rise from their graves. If he does these things, you may then believe that he has been sent from God!"[9] Harrison's effort, ironically, increased Tenskwatawa's credibility among the villagers, because the shaman had learned of an upcoming eclipse of the sun from some survey crews in the area. Telling his followers that the Master of Life would blot out the sun in order to show them that his disciple spoke the truth, the prophet accepted and surmounted Harrison's challenge when on 16 June 1806 the eclipse occurred.[10]

After living at Greenville, Ohio, for several years, in early 1808 Tenskwatawa and a small band of his followers accepted the invitation of Main Poc, a Potawatomi leader who lived near the junction of the Wabash River and Tippecanoe Creek in northwestern Indiana. When the Miami chief Little Turtle opposed his passage to the Wabash, the prophet replied that the Master of Life had ordered the move and that mere humans could not prevent it. He continued that all Indians were to join his settlement on Tippecanoe and from there they would be able to prevent the whites from crossing the boundary line between themselves and the Indians. This appears to have marked a shift away from his religious and cultural teachings to a diplomatic pronouncement, and from 1808 on he devoted more effort to dealing with the whites than previously.[11]

As increasing numbers of converts flocked to his settlement, Prophetstown, the shaman realized that he needed help just to feed the new arrivals, and although he taught that the Indians needed to avoid contact with the whites, he turned to the British for aid. William Claus, the deputy superintendent of Indian affairs at Amherstburg, had been uncertain about the prophet's motives, but when Tenskwatawa said that he wanted to visit British officials in Canada, Claus welcomed the chance to learn more about the tribal situation south of the Great Lakes. By early summer of 1808 so many western Indians had flooded into Prophetstown that the shaman decided to send Tecumseh, his half brother, instead of traveling to Canada himself. Later, Claus reported that Tecumseh had told him that the Indians had no interest in the quarrels between the whites, but that if the Americans continued to encroach on tribal lands, then the Indians at Prophetstown intended to attack them. The warrior also told his British hosts that if a war between them and the Americans broke out, once the Red Coats marched into the region the Indians would join them. As a result of this visit, Canadian officials begged for an enlargement of the Indian Department, claiming—Tecumseh's message aside—that through inaction the British government had encouraged the Indians to side with the Americans. Expressing an often-stated fear, the governor general urged his superiors to authorize policies that would prevent the tribes from becoming enemies of the British.[12]

While strengthening long-standing ties with Canada, Tenskwatawa boldly sent a delegation to visit General Harrison at Vincennes. There the Indian spokesmen duped Harrison with professions of peace while they begged for corn and other supplies to feed the hundreds of new arrivals at Prophetstown. Next, lacking enough food, the prophet led many of his followers to Vincennes, where Harrison had to feed them for several weeks. Although successful in getting promises of British aid and actual food and supplies from the Americans, the Indians still lacked enough food to get them through the rest of that year, and during the 1808-9 winter they nearly starved. Then disease struck, killing several hundred people among the camps of the tribes from Michigan and Wisconsin. Some Ottawas and Ojibwas claimed that the prophet had poisoned their people or that he was a witch, and the continuing intertribal tensions split the Indians.[13]

While the prophet dealt with this latest challenge to his leadership, Tecumseh began traveling from one village to another fanning Indian resentment over army posts or new pioneer settlements nearby. Using Tenskwatawa's reputation and his own considerable oratorical skills, the war chief called for a larger intertribal confederacy to protect remaining Indian lands. With the two Shawnee leaders working toward related goals, Governor Harrison decided that the pressure of increased settlement demanded another series of land cessions. So in September 1809 he met Miami, Delaware, and Potawatomi leaders at Fort Wayne. Convincing them to sell another three million acres of tribal lands for a pittance, Harrison sharpened the inter- and intratribal disputes among the northwestern tribes. Men such as Little Turtle, Five Medals, and Beaver had little respect among the militant followers of the Shawnee brothers by this time, and their acceptance of the Fort Wayne treaty infuriated both Tenskwatawa and Tecumseh. In fact, the Shawnee leaders threatened to kill all of the chiefs who signed that or any subsequent treaties, and Tenskwatawa urged Harrison to keep white pioneers away from the Indians' villages. By this time, then, the lines of future conflict appear clearly set. Western tribes from Illinois and Wisconsin sent delegations to settle among the people already living in Prophetstown, while the British followed through on their promises to send food and supplies to the northern Indians.[14]

That year and into 1811, increasing numbers of Indian delegations crossed Michigan regularly to visit British Indian Office officials at Fort Malden. There Matthew Elliot treated them well, torn between the need to keep the tribesmen on friendly terms and having to restrain them from attacking pioneer settlements. Despite this, a Miami chief reported to Governor Harrison that Elliot had told him, "My son, keep your eyes fixed on me; my tomahawk is now up; be you ready, but do not strike until I give the signal."[15]

The Indians, the British at least in Canada, and the Americans along the frontier all seemed to expect, and perhaps even welcome, war by then. Tecumseh crisscrossed much of the United States to enlist recruits for the Indian confederacy headquartered at Prophetstown. In places he proved highly successful, while in others caution and long memories of past defeats by the Americans chilled the enthusiasm of many would-be followers. Nevertheless, as the United States and Great Britain drifted toward war, tensions remained high in the northwest, and it took little to spark a frontier conflict. During the summer of 1811 Tecumseh traveled south to address leaders of the major tribes there, and while he courted Creek, Cherokee, and Choctaw help, Harrison decided to destroy Prophetstown and disperse the Indians there. Before marching his troops north for that purpose, he gave diplomacy one last chance and sent several Miamis to tell Tenskwatawa that if he would send the non-Shawnees from the camp, return the stolen horses, and promise to surrender those guilty of depredations against the pioneers, Harrison would not attack. The prophet appears to have sent no response and seems to have been uncertain what to do about Harrison's troops then marching northward.[16]

On 6 November 1811 Harrison's army approached within several miles of the Indian camp. Halted by Tenskwatawa's call for a parley, the whites camped nearby, and on the next morning the Indians attacked. In a bitter predawn battle both sides suffered many casualties, but the Indians proved unable to break the soldiers' lines and fled. Later that day Harrison's force destroyed Prophetstown and then marched south back toward Vincennes.[17] This action began the fighting that continued on the frontier through 1815. The prophet's unsuccessful attack on Harrison's army left the Indians scattered and destroyed any chance Tecumseh had of gathering the warriors of that region for renewed fighting against the Americans for a time. Once the British and the Americans went to war with each other, however, most tribes in the Northwest either joined the British or remained neutral. They had tried religious and cultural revitalization, accepting American demands for more land cessions, and intertribal diplomacy and confederation, but all had failed. The onrushing tide of pioneers and the U.S.

government's unwillingness or inability to restrain the western population led inevitably to conflict.

INDIAN PARTICIPATION IN THE WAR OF 1812

Although the basic causes for the War of 1812 stemmed primarily from diplomatic disputes between the United States and Britain, Indian relations played a significant role in the trans-Appalachian region. There the near constant demands for opening more tribal lands for speculation and settlement fueled continuing antagonism between the races. In the old Northwest British efforts to encourage and supply the tribes so they could defend their homeland infuriated the American pioneers. Certain that every minor incident resulted from British agitation of the Indians, and rejecting any suggestion that American actions helped cause even some of the tension and violence between the races, the settlers complained bitterly to the federal government. It is true that beginning in 1807 British Indian Office personnel invited the Great Lakes and Ohio Valley tribes to visit Fort Malden at Amherstburg in Canada each year. As tribal delegations traveled north into Canada to receive presents, medals, and listen to often anti-American speeches, the frontier population grew increasingly worried about the possibilities for war.[18]

For British officials on the Canadian frontier, the situation appeared strikingly different. They had clear orders to avoid actions that might lead to conflict, although they were to retain good relations with the tribes from within the United States should they be needed to help defend Canada at some time in the future. The Indians had their own objectives as they worked for their best interests while the two white governments moved toward war. For example, Tenskwatawa's requests for supplies from the British enabled him to help feed the hundreds of his followers who converged on Prophetstown in 1808 and 1809, when the Indian farmers proved unable to raise enough surplus for the sudden demand. Clearly this was an immediate need and no long-range alliance. Nevertheless, the residue of bitterness and suspicion between Americans and the Indians of Indiana and Ohio magnified the tribal need for food into a sinister British plot aimed at igniting an anti-American war. On the other hand, Tecumseh clearly desired British assistance for a diplomatic solution to the problem of continuing American aggression against the tribes of the northern United States. If that failed he sought a military alliance to crush the pioneers as the Indians struggled to retain what was left of their homelands.

The war itself brought short-term victories for tribes in both the northern and southern United States, but when it ended the United States stood more firmly in control than ever, and Indian power lay shattered, along with their hopes for help from Britain and Spain. At first everything went in favor of the Indians and the British. During the summer of 1812 Captain Charles Roberts led a force of some seven hundred to eight hundred Canadians and Indians west to capture Fort Mackinac at the northern tip of Michigan, assuring the British domination in that region. Soon after that post fell, General William Hull ordered Fort Dearborn at Chicago abandoned, and when the garrison began its march east in August 1812 hostile bands from the nearby tribes killed or captured the entire force. During that July and August General Hull had invaded Canada via Detroit, but his opponent General Isaac Brock refused to surrender and then began advancing against Hull's army. Hearing rumors that Brock had large numbers of Indian auxiliaries, the timid commander surrendered both the town of Detroit and his entire army, giving the British control over the entire west that year.[19]

While American tribes flocked to join the British west of Lake Erie, native people living in Canada reacted less enthusiastically when the call went out asking for troops. General Brock's urgings brought only a token response from the Six Nations at either the Grand River or Caughnawaga. Groups there saw little danger from American attacks farther west and, at least at the start of the war, sent only a few dozen men to aid the British. Still, in the Battle of Queenstown Heights in mid-October 1812 the timely arrival of the Iroquois force helped the British to turn back the threat to Queenstown and apparently played a role in the American militia units' refusal to cross the border to assist the regulars on Canadian soil. Six Nations warriors actually won an important victory by defeating and capturing an American force led by Colonel Charles Boerstler at the June 1813 Battle of Beaver Dam on the Niagara peninsula. Despite their initial neutrality, then, the Iroquois and other small groups of tribal warriors aided the British defense of Canada serving as scouts, auxiliaries, spies, and messengers, and in assuming these duties they helped turn back American efforts to conquer Canada.[20]

Of more significance to British strategy, the Mississippi Valley tribes such as the Winnebagos, Sauks, Mesquakies, and Kickapoos, with Tecumeseh's urging and their own self-interest at stake, assumed a strongly anti-American stand. During 1813 British and Indian forces moved south from Detroit along the Maumee River to attack Fort Meigs. Although the American forces turned back the attack, they lost heavily in the fighting. During late 1813 William Henry Harrison led American forces against the British across the river from Detroit. Having gained naval control of Lake Erie, Harrison invaded Canada, and his opponent, Henry Proctor, abandoned Fort Malden. With the American army at his heels and his Indian allies melting away because he chose not to fight, Proctor made a stand at Moraviantown on the Thames River. There, with Tecumseh leading a large force from the United States, the small British force broke and ran, leaving the Indians to face Harrison's army alone. Although they resisted fiercely, the warriors were outmanned and outgunned, and after suffering heavy casualties, they fled too. Tecumseh died directing the Indian defense in this battle, and his death took the heart out of continuing Indian resistance in the Northwest. When the war ended the tribes there faced an angry United States with a much reduced land base and greatly smaller population than a single generation earlier. The American victory in the War of 1812 completely broke Indian power south of the Great Lakes and any further major efforts to oppose the government demands or the advancing pioneers.[21]

In the South the Spanish replaced the British as the Indians' hope for help against the aggressive American advance. Continuing demands for removal and land surrenders by Georgia kept the Creeks and Cherokees discontented in the decade preceding the war. Tecumseh's visits to the Creeks in 1811 and 1812 encouraged some of the more anti-American warriors to form a faction known as the Red Sticks and to prepare for war. One delegation even traveled to Canada and participated in the River Raisin massacre on their return trip. In 1813 frontiersmen attacked a delegation of Red Sticks on its way home, apparently without provocation. The Indians suffered few casualties, but, their anger aroused, they gathered others and under the command of Red Feather (William Weatherford) and Peter McQueen attacked and destroyed Fort Mims, north of Mobile. This so-called massacre brought a retaliatory campaign that led to the defeat and destruction of the Red Sticks.

While several frontier armies marched against the Indians, the force under Andrew Jackson eventually had the most success. He led his militia army south into Creek territory during the fall and winter of 1813–14, attacking the Indians whenever he could locate them. On 27 March 1814 Jackson's army met the main Creek force at Horseshoe Bend. The militia outnumbered the Creeks, but they defended themselves bravely until being overrun and destroyed. Most of the Red Sticks died or surrendered in this battle, and Jackson promptly built Fort Jackson in the heart of Creek country. Then in August 1814 the crusty general extracted the Treaty of Fort Jackson from the peaceful elements of the tribe. This agreement surrendered most of the Creek lands in Alabama and marked the end of their active resistance to American expansion in the Southeast.[22]

As the War of 1812 drew to a close, victorious American officials moved quickly to punish the Indians for trying to defend themselves. Strangely, the very actions most people would have recognized and even lauded as showing bravery and patriotism, when carried out by the tribal people, brought only denunciations from the American public. Apparently few citizens could believe that Indians felt a sense of ownership toward their land or of betrayal by the United States when it promised to stop asking for more cessions or to keep avaricious pioneers away from the villagers. Perhaps their greed for land simply blinded them from any honest assessment of the situation. Whatever the reasons, once the sounds of war ceased the governments in both nations worked to extend their control over the tribes residing in each country.

THE WAR'S AFTERMATH

With the signing of the Treaty of Ghent in 1815, officials in Canada and the United States began their dealings with the Indians from a different perspective. American leaders, expressing anger at the tribes that joined the British during the war just ended, immediately strove to impose peace on them. To accomplish that, President James Madison appointed three peace commissioners, and in July 1815 they met with some two thousand Indians representing many of the midwestern tribes that had been at war with the United States. Meeting on the west bank of the Mississippi River at Portage des Sioux, the U.S. peace commissioners heard the chiefs' speeches and complaints, and by late October that year they had signed thirteen treaties with the groups represented there. In these agreements each side forgave the other for past acts of aggression; both promised to keep perpetual peace, agreed to exchange any prisoners still being held, and accepted the validity of earlier treaties between them. The Indians agreed to consider themselves as under the protection of the United States and to forgo relations with any other nation. Tribes that failed to participate in the 1815 negotiations signed similar agreements during the next several years. The government even sent negotiators to groups that had remained neutral in order to explain the provisions of the Treaty of Ghent and to discount rumors apparently circulating among some Indians that as a result of the recent war they now enjoyed a more independent position in their relations with the United States.[23]

These negotiations produced signed treaties between the two sides, but to ensure that peace continued in the frontier regions the American leaders decided to strengthen or extend their military presence in the region between Detroit and the Missouri River. Working hurriedly, the War Department rebuilt or strengthened forts in Michigan, Indiana, and Illinois and began construction of new outposts as well. Soon a line of forts stretched south and west from Green Bay, Wisconsin, to Rock Island, on the Mississippi, separating the strong and still disgruntled tribes of the Northwest from the areas being opened for settlement. By 1822 the army extended its presence north to Fort Sault Sainte Marie in Michigan, west to Fort Snelling at present-day Minneapolis–Saint Paul, southwest to Fort Atkinson (north of present-day Omaha), and south to Fort Smith, Arkansas. In each case army planners hoped that these military installations would restrain tribal aggressions, help prevent pioneer excursions into Indian territory, and most significant of all, enable American officials to inhibit contacts between Indians and Canadian and English fur traders. Given their experience with British Indian Office personnel along the frontier preceding the War of 1812, American officials' fears of foreign agents and their influence among the tribes of the northern and western United States were neither surprising nor irrational. To retain Indian allegiance and trade it seemed absolutely necessary to exclude the British from the region.[24]

Although it had been nearly dismantled during the War of 1812, the government revived its factory system of trading houses immediately after the conflict ended. Its goal of keeping Indian hunters away from British traders or officials made it appear as central to American interests at the time. Led by Thomas L. McKenney, who supervised the trade, some officials hoped to use the trading houses to offer religious and educational programs, but despite their strenuous efforts little acculturation took place through the trading posts. At the same time, commercial traders such as John Jacob Astor led an effort to abolish the system because they saw it as unfair government competition. Astor actually kept Ramsay Crooks in Washington as a paid lobbyist, where by 1821 he worked with Thomas Hart Benton, the newly elected senator from Missouri, to end the government trade. Governors from Illinois and Michigan joined the attack, and even the Reverend Jedediah Morse, who investigated Indian affairs for the secretary of war, agreed. As a result in 1822 Congress voted to close the trading houses.[25]

Throughout the early decades of independence American officials strove to keep peace with the eastern Indians through a schizophrenic program of trying to acculturate tribal people while urging them to move west. Some migrated without being asked. For example, as early as 1788 bands from the Ohio Valley began moving across the Mississippi River. By the 1790s traders among the Osages in present-day Missouri and Arkansas reported that Miamis, Delawares, Shawnees, and Ottawas had immigrated into Osage territory there. Just over a decade later hundreds of members of the Chickamauga band of the Cherokees had crossed the Mississippi, and once the War of 1812 ended the migrations increased. In 1816 reports indicated that thirteen hundred Shawnees, five thousand Cherokees, six hundred Delawares, and smaller numbers of other eastern Indians inhabited land along the lower Arkansas River. These migrations began the shift of most tribal people west beyond the Mississippi and opened land for speculation and sale.[26]

Canadian officials focused their fears on possible American invasion or Yankee agents trying to lure the northern tribes southward into their economic and diplomatic orbit. Nevertheless, they too saw Indian affairs from a diplomatic and military perspective for a time. Many tribes had been allied to the British, and a few had played important roles in the campaigning just concluded. Yet the policy of encouraging Indian resistance to the advancing American pioneers in the region south of the Great Lakes had failed. Earlier the English diplomats had pushed for the area south of the lakes as a permanent Indian reserve, but the Americans rejected that idea. British efforts during the negotiations leading to the Treaty of Ghent had gained nothing for the tribes. In fact, reporting on the talks leading to the treaty, one British negotiator wrote with some astonishment that "I had till I came here no idea of the fixed determinism which prevails in the breast of every American to extirpate the Indians and appropriate their territory."[27] Given this view, the British failure to effect changes in the Great Lakes frontier settlement process, and the Rush-Bagot Agreement of 1817 between the United States and Britain demilitarizing the Lake of the Woods to the Rocky Mountains at the forty-ninth parallel, made it clear that earlier Indian policies needed modification, if not outright change.

Like the United States, Upper Canada experienced an influx of new settlers in the era immediately following the War of 1812. In fact, between 1812 and 1851 the estimated population of the province increased tenfold, from 95,000 to 952,000 people. During those same decades Indian numbers shrank because of disease and dislocation, but even if they had not diminished, the significance of the tribes in Canadian society in the province would have. Their numbers in 1812 constituted a mere eight thousand, or less than 10 percent of the Upper Canadian population, so that by 1851, the year for which the next figures are available, even a stable population for the Indians would have shown less than ten thousand people, or a mere 1 percent of the general population. This rapid decline in relative tribal strength meant that British officials in the area could acquire more land and resources for the growing white population, and they moved to do so quickly.[28]

Land acquisition in both nations proceeded in a similar fashion, although in

Upper Canada the compensation shifted from a single payment in goods and cash to a system of annuities in perpetuity. In both countries government negotiators met with tribal or band leaders, asked for the lands in question, explained what the government would pay, and listened to Indian questions, complaints, or requests. From existing records of these councils it seems clear that the officials agreed to more than their orders allowed, and the final treaty agreements rarely included everything that the Indians had requested or even thought that they had been promised. For example, in cessions begun on the eve of the War of 1812 and not completed until 1815–16 this proved particularly true. The Indians complained about pioneers' incursions into their territory and about whites cutting timber on tribal lands without permission or offering to pay compensation, and they asked repeatedly for officials to deal with these issues. They also requested that they be given axes for clearing land, hoes for working their crops, and spears for hunting and fishing, as well as having blacksmiths sent to their villages to repair their metal goods. Under the completed treaties, the Indians received some of the items some of the time, but the blacksmiths they needed never appeared.[29]

Clearly the British thought that they had little choice but to promise native leaders what they sought in order to get the land. However, they had little real fear that the tribes would begin a war against them if the promises went unfulfilled. Rather, the pressure for getting the land came from continuing nervousness about future attacks from the United States. Seen from the present this worry seems groundless, but in 1815 leaders in Canada had experienced two generations of conflict with the United States. After all, in both the War for Independence and the War of 1812 American leaders had threatened to conquer the northern British colonies. As a result, English officials planned a series of new settlements along the border, where discharged War of 1812 veterans received land in strategic locations to forestall future invasion. With the local Indians living in small bands that moved over large areas throughout the year it is easy to see why the British thought that the tribal people would agree to modest cessions of land along the Saint Lawrence River and along the northern shore of Lake Ontario. Their assumption proved correct, but by the decade following the end of the War of 1812 tribes in that area, now realizing what the land cessions meant for their future, became increasingly restive and less cooperative about deeding away more of their holdings.

As a result, British authorities altered their approach and changed the method and amount of payment for new lands being acquired. This occurred in 1818 when continuing efforts to cut costs brought orders from London to change the system for dealing with the Indians. Strangely, throughout the preceding war, at least in Upper Canada, civilian officials directed dealings with the tribes, but in 1815 supervision of Indian affairs went back to the military authorities. Then three years later a second change occurred. Previously, payments for ceded lands consisted of lump sum payments of cash or gifts at the time the two sides agreed to the terms. Beginning in 1818 the bureaucrats devised a means to cut the costs to the British government, get the land, and satisfy the Indians all at the same time. The Lords of the Treasury decided that the government of Upper Canada rather than Britain would have to fund future purchases, a major problem for the thinly settled province. With what he must have thought a stroke of near genius, the lieutenant governor decided to auction off portions of ceded Indian land, asking the purchasers for only 10 percent down and annual interest payments. These annual funds might then be paid to the tribes as annuities, thus avoiding the need for high taxes to raise cash for large single-time payments to the Indians. For the tribes, long used to annual presents, the annuities represented a tie with the past and what they saw as a sign of continuing English friendship and support.[30] This approach characterized Canadian Indian land cessions for the rest of the nineteenth century.

Despite the modest expenditures for land purchases, the cry to cut government spending continued, so the tribes got only modest prices for the territories they vacated. Yet some Indians considered the benefits they would receive as equal to the land they sold. Clearly, some recognized that traditional hunting and fishing would no longer support them, and by this time, at least for the Mississauga peoples of Ontario, the focus of the fur trade had shifted to the far north and west beyond their range. Others felt trapped and on the verge of despair because of previous white incursions, the loss of their hunting, and the impact of disease. Some may have simply resorted to age-old Indian phrases that had brought generous gifts in the past. Whatever the reasons, council minutes record instances of band and village leaders pleading for assistance and claiming poverty while asking for the whites to be generous.[31] Others tied their requests for axes and farm hand tools to a recognition that their survival depended on the skills of the few Indians who did try farming. As the tribal population dropped while that of the whites grew steadily, the native people had few other options.

Canada, then, by the decade following the War of 1812, followed no long-range policy toward the Indians. When necessary its officials negotiated for land from the tribes, thus compressing their territory. Some people began to discuss what they called amalgamation, that is, persuading the native people to adopt a sedentary, agricultural life and to live near or even among the whites. Few

Indians or whites seemed enthusiastic about this approach, however, and except for the existing small mission reserves in Lower Canada and the Iroquois settlement on the Grand River, few changes occurred. Yet as British and Canadian fear of invasion or other trouble with the United States declined, so did the perceived value of the tribes as allies or a blocking force between the settled regions of the provinces and the expanding republic to the south. That being the case, British and local officials in the Canadas grew increasingly reluctant to spend large sums of money on retaining the Indians' goodwill.

On the East Coast the government received complaints about the Indians and requests from them for some land on which they might live free from the avaricious settlers. In late 1819 the lieutenant governor of Nova Scotia ordered his surveyor general, Charles Morris, to lay out such parcels for the tribal people in each county. Under this directive he divided the province into ten districts with at least one reserved plot in each, and during 1819–20 the survey crews located some reservations at up to one thousand acres each. Others had existed previously, so their size varied, but in every case the authorities granted the land to local magistrates in trust for use by the Indians. Thus the tribal people failed to receive any title to the land, and only in unusual cases did the local officials work to remove intruders from the reserved lands. By the end of 1820 the surveyors had run out of money to continue their work, so although land for the tribes had been identified, in some cases the workers had quit before settling claims to the plots in question.[32]

Several other difficulties disrupted these efforts. The local governments either would not or could not evict squatters from Indian land. The Micmacs and other Maritime Indians had always done some farming, but during their annual cycle of hunting, fishing, and gathering they abandoned the villages at least part of each year. While they were away, whites moved onto their cleared fields, claiming them for their own use. Although the government planned to give each Indian family thirty acres of land on the reserve, those who did not improve the land according to white standards would lose it. Under this plan only those Micmacs who forsook their annual migrations would be able to keep any of the land. Even that plan failed to get far, though, because the legislature refused to pay the costs of surveying a small farm for each family. It did continue to vote for modest relief funds but provided no money for seeds, tools, and equipment, or even to survey and divide the land.[33] Public perceptions of the Maritime people as those who spent their time loitering around the docks in Halifax or who "infest the barber shops," and appear "meager, squalid, dirty in person and habit," certainly did not persuade the general population that the

Indians should be incorporated into their developing society.[34] In fact, most people in Nova Scotia considered the tribal people to be drunken nuisances, fit only for either public ridicule or embarrassment.

While the British shifted their attention away from Indian issues in the north, by 1821 Spain had surrendered its lands in North America. Pioneers from southern states moved onto Spanish lands steadily, and in 1810 those near Baton Rouge revolted, asking for American protection. President James Madison extended U.S. authority only a month later. During the War of 1812 General James Wilkinson seized Mobile, and it never went back to Spanish control. In 1817 fighting between pioneers and Seminole Indians and runaway slaves brought demands that the border region be pacified, so President James Monroe ordered General Andrew Jackson into action. Promptly he led several thousand troops across the border, captured the Spanish post of St. Marks, and ran up the American flag. When the dust settled, Spain decided that it could not afford to keep Florida and surrendered it to the United States as part of the 1819 Adams-Onís Treaty. This left the southeastern tribes wholly under American control. In the West, Mexican independence in 1821 ended three hundred years of Spanish presence in North America.[35]

Meanwhile, many Americans held anti-Indian views, and these came to bear on national actions. In the years after 1815 pioneers flooded many parts of the trans-Appalachian frontier, so much so that the 1820 census indicated at least a million more people in that region than had been there ten years earlier. As wave after wave of settlers swept west, pressures on the tribes there and on the government mounted. From Alabama and Georgia in the south, north through the Great Lakes states and those of the upper Mississippi Valley, whites pushed into areas previously held by tribal people, bringing the usual cycle of mistrust, hatred, and violence. By this time, however, the federal government, more powerful than in decades earlier, moved to deal with the issues of peace and welfare on the frontier. Nearly always hoping to solve the problems peacefully, the authorities called for a transformation in tribal economic activities from hunting, trapping, and seasonal agriculture to settled farming in imitation of the whites.

Efforts on the part of the U.S. government to "civilize" the Indians extended back into the 1790s, but despite congressional appropriations for tools, seeds, and other farming needs, federal officers saw few changes among the frontier tribes. Nevertheless, those dealing with the Indians tried this program repeatedly. Frequently, treaties from the early nineteenth century included provisions for such items, or even of specific grants of land to individuals, but until forced to accept the whites' terms, not many of the tribal people chose to become sedentary farmers. Because few whites seem to have really wanted that result either—it would have meant that Indian farmers would use land sought by eager pioneers—frontier support for such a program remained weak. If given their choice, it seems likely that most frontier whites would have preferred a government effort to move the tribes west beyond the Mississippi River, and by the end of the 1820s the removal policy doing just that had gone into effect.

Earlier, however, the government sought to gain the objective of a sedentary population of Indian farmers by encouraging private philanthropy through churches and missionary societies to sponsor missions and schools among the tribes. Many Protestant denominations sent missionaries, schoolteachers, and others to operate model farms near the native villages even before the War of 1812. In 1810 the Presbyterians and Congregationalists joined forces to form the American Board of Commissioners for Foreign Missions, one of the most aggressive and well organized of the mission groups to work among the Indians in the nineteenth century. These people saw their goal as one of "civilizing" or acculturating the tribal people they worked with; to their thinking, they set out to reclaim their charges from barbarism. Using what became the central institutions—school, church, and farm—they poured money and personnel into the effort once the war ended. Other groups, including the Methodists, Baptists, Moravians, and Quakers, all joined the grand venture.[36] Rarely did any of them question their goals or objectives. Even more infrequently did they consider the Indians' desires in any of their actions. Apparently the religious groups thought that right-thinking and honest Indians would gladly reject their traditional cultures and seize the new teachings of the missionaries with enthusiasm. When that did not occur, it startled and dismayed the civilizers, who had assumed that they had the best interests of the tribal people at heart.

To encourage these efforts at acculturation, in 1819 the federal government established the Indian Civilization Fund and through it provided an annual sum of ten thousand dollars. That amount was in addition to existing agreements to provide some tribes with livestock, tools, and assistance in learning how to use these things profitably. The Indian Civilization Fund demonstrated that some government officials had accepted the idea of helping the Indians transform their ways of life so they could merge into the majority society. Often the money provided by this annual appropriation went to church groups and missionary societies with specific religious goals, but few at the time objected to this obvious union of church and state. In fact, without the cooperation of the religious groups even the modest program of acculturation that developed would have been impossible, as the missionaries, teachers, and other helpers all worked for minimal salaries because they saw their duties as part of God's call to them.

Early nineteenth-century supporters of the acculturation program faced the same dilemmas that teachers and missionaries had since the early days of European settlement in North America. The dispute over whether to transform the native people into copies of the whites first, or to convert them to Christianity and then move them toward "civilization," split their ranks just as much as it had done for the preceding two centuries. Nevertheless, in the decade after 1815 the work went forward. Regardless of which religious group sponsored the mission churches, schools, or demonstration farms, the white participants all seem to have developed a stubborn optimism and a determination to complete their chosen tasks as quickly as possible. Despite their obvious lack of progress, they assumed that they could alter Indian culture, beliefs, and practices within a couple of decades, or certainly during a single lifetime. Ignoring the frequent rebuffs and failures they experienced, their optimism, based on their belief that they were doing God's will, carried them through difficult times and helped them retain a positive attitude toward their challenge.[37]

Responding to frequent Indian requests for economic assistance and vocational training in farming techniques and livestock production, the mission groups developed programs that frequently had a strong emphasis on vocational training rather than conversion to Christianity. In fact, even before the War of 1812 northern would-be missionaries had traveled south to visit the major tribes there, hoping to find leaders receptive to their goals. For example, as early as 1804 the General Assembly of the Presbyterian Church sent Gideon Blackburn into Cherokee country to open a two-building school, with a teacher's house and dormitory spaces for boys and girls as well as a dining hall. The Presbyterians hoped to keep the Cherokee children away from their families and thus reduce what they saw as the negative influence of village culture on the students. During the same decade the New York Missionary Society commissioned Joseph Bullen to work with Chickasaw chiefs in Mississippi who had asked for farmers and mechanics to help the tribal people learn trade skills. Bullen sought to hire more than twenty people, including a blacksmith, a shoemaker, a saddler, a farmer, and a teacher, who along with their families would move south to work with that tribe. Although inadequate funds thwarted this plan, the proposal illustrates a combination of mainline Protestant thinking about how to help the Indians, Jeffersonian ideas about incorporating tribal people who accepted Anglo-American ideas and skills into the general society, and the Indians' desires for economic assistance.[38]

These and other early efforts had limited success, yet by 1807 the Reverend Blackburn reported that the two schools he operated showed that Indian education had moved well beyond the experimental stage. In fact, the enthusiastic missionary proposed raising more funds to support several primary schools that would prepare the students for high school. He envisioned his most successful scholars as being trained for leadership roles within the Cherokee tribe. Others shared his optimism, and in 1823 one of the mission boards stated flatly "that the American Savage is capable of being both civilized and Christianized."[39] As was so often the case, however, the funds necessary for such an effort never materialized. Still, these ideas permeated the thinking of those Americans who hoped that their society would be able to incorporate the individual Indians after having destroyed the tribes.

By no means all Americans shared these attitudes toward the eastern tribes, and in the decade following the War of 1812 the earlier ideas about Indians being successfully transformed into acceptable fellow citizens lost their appeal. In their place ideas about radical differences focusing chiefly on blacks and Indians became heard more frequently. Rather than viewing all people as part of a unified human race, the new ideas suggested a hierarchy of races, with the Anglo-Saxons and their descendants at the top and the Native American, African, and Asian peoples ranked below them. As white Americans came to define their society increasingly in terms of western European norms, they began to reject any possible equality for other races, and that led to a gradual reduction of possibilities for the tribal peoples. If they were, in fact, degraded savages, a patina of primary school education and some exposure to Christian missionaries could hardly overcome their innate nature or improve their social status within the republic.[40]

Because earlier American idealism clashed with the hardening of racial attitudes and the growing demands that the tribes vacate their lands east of the Mississippi River, Secretary of War John C. Calhoun commissioned the Reverend Jedediah Morse to travel through the Indian country and to report on conditions there. Morse visited tribes from Wisconsin to Georgia, and in June 1822 he submitted his findings. He noted that on every frontier white pioneers squatted on tribal lands long before the Indians surrendered them to the government, often despite the tribes' strenuous objections. As a result of increasing agricultural activities, the game fled, leaving the tribal people with neither their best land for crops nor hunting as an alternative. The invading pioneers made their distaste for the Indians clear, insulting and degrading them whenever possible, and as a result the Indians kept backing away from the white intruders.[41]

Because he saw the tribes being destroyed by the continued pioneer advance, Morse called on the government to clarify its goals and policies toward them. He proposed an increased program of acculturation through missions, schools, and model farms, but went beyond those usual efforts. While admitting that civilized people would be revolted by the idea of intermarriage with the Indians, he claimed that it was natural and necessary if the tribal people were to survive. Pointing to the fact that many leaders among the Cherokee, Choctaw, and Chickasaw tribes were themselves mixed-race people, he noted that these individuals and their children made up a large group with "promising talents and appearance."[42] For the intermarriage scheme to work, Morse called for the careful education of Indian women, who then could serve as the primary means through which the entire tribe might be acculturated. When the tribal people had acquired "all branches of knowledge pertaining to civilized man," then intermarriage should become common, and by merging with the rest of the population the Indians would be saved from extinction.[43]

To achieve this utopian state, Morse also proposed establishing a college for young Indians, supported by the profits from federal land sales of tribal lands and staffed by a competent faculty. When the graduates demonstrated the needed skills, they should be appointed to the faculty and administration of the institution. He hoped that the result of such an effort would allow the tribal people to become educated and then to help each other. Once the churches and schools had done their job the tribes would be able to take charge of their own affairs and without government expense would become accepted members of the general society. Morse defended his call for major expenditures on the tribes with the idea that because the United States was in the process of taking all of their lands away from them, it should have no objection to repaying them with something more lasting than cash payments. In fact, he went so far as to write that the Indians deserved just, kind, and paternal treatment from the government.[44] While his ideas represented a wide spectrum of thought on these matters, they did not prevail.

In both countries the situation in the early 1820s differed markedly from the mid-1790s. Indian efforts to develop multitribal confederacies had failed. Prophets came and went, and except for the teachings of Handsome Lake, the traditionalist calls for cultural and spiritual revitalization faded from the forefront of tribal considerations. An expanding and aggressive American population stood poised to push past the Mississippi River, sweeping the Indians before them. The Canadian situation reflected a less intense version of what had occurred south of the border. An expanding white population pushed against resident tribal people, while the Indians sold modest portions of their land to make way for pioneer farmers and developers. Canadian officials still worried about possible danger from disgruntled Native Americans, but in the years following the end of the War of 1812 the increasing costs of ceremonial presents and land purchases seemed unreasonably high. Scattered and modest efforts to provide missionaries and schools for the tribes lacked any central direction and either public or governmental support. As a result, by the early 1820s Canadian officials sought ways to cut their costs when dealing with the Indians and to keep relations between themselves and the tribes peaceful.

7 Cultural Persistence, Physical Retreat, 1820s–1860s

 ON 17 JUNE 1825 Peter Jones (Sacred Feathers), a mixed-race Mississauga, penned a letter to the local Indian agent James Givens. He wrote that about fifty of the Mississaugas had "planted potatoes . . . embraced Christianity, and are attending to the means of education."[1] While this news surprised the agent, it demonstrated one option open to Native Americans in the era after the War of 1812. As a supporter of acculturation, Jones, a recent convert to Methodist Christianity, personified one strain of leadership among the tribal peoples of North America. Other individuals and groups might choose this same path, but for many the white man's way appeared uncertain, even forbidding.

Sacred Feathers' initiative developed because of his intense personal religious feelings. It also grew out of the apparent collapse of the traditional Indian world. Certainly by the 1820s many tribal people in both the eastern United States and Canada lacked the unity, leadership, or cultural strength they had demonstrated earlier. With some exceptions the tribes found themselves being pushed from their homes, forced to surrender large portions of their land, and facing demands that they accept Anglo-American education, religion, technology, and control of their lives. During the middle decades of the nineteenth century the increasing white domination in both countries threatened to overwhelm native societies and left Indian people with an ever-narrowing set of choices for their lives.

Despite that, some groups took or held the initiative when dealing with the onrushing pioneers and the governments. Often fully realizing the weakness of their position, most tribes strove to retain the central elements of their cultures. Certainly Christian missionaries made inroads, but nativist prophets such as Handsome Lake, Kenekuk, and Abishabis all attracted followers. Tribal band and village leaders split repeatedly over how much, if any, acculturation to accept as well as how to answer the repeated demands for surrendering large portions of their lands. Men such as the Sauk Black Hawk and the Ojibwa Wawanosh both rejected white culture and governmental demands for movement or land, but to no avail. Other leaders recognized some need to accommodate. Grudgingly or not they reconciled themselves to less territory, intruding missionaries, and meddlesome government officials as they cooperated with Canadian or American authorities.

The situation in the eastern half of the two countries bore striking similarities as pioneer actions and government programs continued to disrupt tribal life and bring permanent changes to native peoples. At the same time, important differences existed. In the eastern United States the larger populations of both races and the agricultural basis for many tribal economies made the contest for the land and its resources bitter. The forced removal of thousands of Indians to the west did not occur in Canada. In the one instance where officials tried removal, public objections ended the experiment. While violence and warfare against Indians dot the pages of mid-nineteenth-century American history, north of the border that was not usually the case. Mixed-race individuals received different treatment in each country too. In Canada the Métis or country-born people became recognized as a distinct legal group eventually gaining specific rights. No such thing occurred in the United States, where such people generally chose to remain with the tribes. Except for slight mention by a few minor provisions in treaties, no distinct Métis people obtained recognition. In fact, even the term *métis* has had little use in the United States, and historically, mixed-race people there have not sought a separate identity.

By 1820 neither the United States nor Canada saw Indian affairs as particularly important unless violence or a political crisis erupted. Still, dealing with the tribes could not be avoided because the non-Indian population in both countries grew dramatically. In Canada it rose from about half a million people at the end of the War of 1812 to over 2.5 million in 1867, when Confederation occurred. South of the border, Indians faced an even larger disparity between themselves and the whites. The U.S. general population stood at perhaps 7.5 million in 1815, while a half century later it had passed 30 million. During that time the number of tribal people east of the Mississippi River diminished from, at most, perhaps two hundred thousand to only a few thousand people in isolated parts of Florida, North Carolina, Mississippi, New York, Michigan, and Wisconsin.

Both governments tried to acculturate the tribal people, but by the 1820s the Canadian tribes came from a situation that differed markedly from that in the United States. They had served as military allies rather than enemies of the government and pioneers. They had played a central role in the fur trade, still a significant part of the Canadian economy. Yet instead of being seen as an asset, the tribes appeared as a liability—as people who slowed or inhibited development. One traveler expressed the pioneer attitude succinctly when he wrote that "these Indians ought to be altogether kicked out from here," because "they are a lazy race, and hinder the progress of our undertakings." He denounced them as "stupid" and "idle" while grumbling that the "government makes a great deal too much ceremony with these fellows and their rights of property."[2]

Despite such views, tribal people in Canada had cooperated with English efforts to purchase lands north of Lake Ontario for several decades. Just before the War of 1812 the Mississauga leader Quinipeno recalled earlier Indian generosity in giving land to the British. By then, however, native leaders had learned that the agreements they signed meant the physical loss of their lands, and they objected to losing any more territory.[3] Their growing reluctance to additional land surrenders and continuing demands for cost cutting in Canadian government brought a shift in relations between the tribal people and the expanding white society.

As early as 1823 financial pressures from Britain encouraged Canadian bureaucrats to reduce or end presents for the tribes, but objections raised in Canada ended that idea temporarily. In 1827 the new colonial secretary, Frederick John Robinson, Viscount Goderich, called for an examination of the administration of Indian affairs. This led Major General Henry C. Darling to inspect the department. His 1828 report called for making the operation more efficient, not for ending it. He claimed that the tribes had to be protected from possible "plunder and persecution" by the pioneers and that the Indian department stood ready to do this.[4] In his view, the situation for Upper Canada (Ontario) seemed dangerous if the government were to renege on its responsibilities. He warned that the Indians would need full government support to avoid becoming paupers and criminals who might disrupt colonial society. If that assistance disappeared, he feared, the tribal people might "throw themselves, with vengeance in their hearts, into the arms of the Americans."[5]

To prevent that, he proposed a full-fledged acculturation program. Under this initiative the migratory peoples would get village sites where the government

The Indian Fort Sasquesahanok, 1720. An example of a typical Atlantic coastal village perhaps fifty years prior to the date given. Engraving by Herman Moll, National Archives of Canada, c36345.

Nicholas Vincent Isawahonei, principal Christian chief and captain of the Huron Indians, 1825. His cloth coat, Indian leggings, and wampum belt show the ongoing merging of the two cultures. Lithograph by Edward Chatfield, National Archives of Canada, C038948.

Group of dead Crow Indians, 1874. The Piegans killed these people during the winter of 1873–74, in the continual intertribal warfare of the northern Plains. National Library of Canada/Bibliothèque nationale du Canada, PA74646.

Unidentified Sioux young men, 1890. The typed inset on the photo reads, "Three of Uncle Sam's Pets. We get rations every 29 days. Our pulse is good. Expressive medium. We put in 60 minutes each hour in our present attitude," and shows strong Western discontent with U.S. treatment of the Indians. Courtesy of the Library of Congress, 613564.Z62.17759.

Lieutenant Taylor and seven of his Indian scouts, Pine Ridge Agency, 19 January 1891. In the late nineteenth century the army employed Indian scouts such as these unidentified men to police the reservations and help chase runaways. Courtesy of the Library of Congress, 613564.z62.43656.

A chief forbidding the passage of a train through his country (from *Harpers*, 1874). This generic scene depicts Indian objections to the depredations of pioneers moving west. Courtesy of the Library of Congress, 613564.z62.55600.

Seminole family, 1910 (individuals unidentified). Seminoles lived in camps such as this, from which the men hunted and trapped while the women traded with their white neighbors. Courtesy of the Library of Congress, 12763.z62.104529.

File Hills Indian Colony Band, ca. 1915. This Saskatchewan settlement brought together graduates of Canadian boarding and industrial schools from several tribes but failed in its effort to assimilate the young Indians. Robert Borden collection, National Archives of Canada, c33258.

Cree Indian children attending Anglican Church Missionary School, Lac La Ronge, Saskatchewan, March 1945. Bud Glunz, National Archives of Canada, PA134110.

Chief Joseph John from Tofino, Vancouver Island, British Columbia. His ceremonial headdress is characteristic for the coastal peoples of the Pacific Northwest. A. V. Pollard, National Archives of
Canada, c89133.

A trip to Zuñi. The Shalaco cross to the south side of the river to dance and plant plumes, 1917. This depicts the forty-ninth and last day of the major Zuni winter ceremony, during which the masked figures representing the gods leave the village. Courtesy of the Library of Congress, 613584z 62.115456.

Leonard Crow Dog (foreground), Dennis Banks (with chin on hands), Russell Means, unidentified, Ramon Roubideaux, and Kent Frizzell, in a tepee trying to negotiate an end to the AIM-led 1973 Wounded Knee incident. Stanley D. Lyman Photograph Collection, Manuscripts Division, J. Willard Marriott Library, University of Utah Libraries.

would help them build homes and give them tools and seeds for farming. Then the Indian department would recruit missionaries, teachers, and men to operate model farms to help the newly settled villagers fit into the developing Canadian economy. To pay what this effort would cost, the bureaucrats decided to sell Indian land and use the proceeds.[6] If all worked according to plan the local officials expected to avoid violence or strenuous objections from the tribes. These arguments persuaded the British, and from that time on Canada offered tribal people an acculturation program based on the church, school, and farm, usually under provincial or later federal direction.

Darling's proposals resulted from Canadian circumstances that differed from the situation in the United States at the time. Canada was not yet an independent nation, so outside pressures proved highly significant there. Clearly social reform groups then active in Britain, such as the various antislavery societies, the Aborigines Protection Society, and several Protestant missionary organizations, all had some influence on dealings with the Indians. Even the efforts to accomplish similar goals in the United States offered a justification for the new program. Yet the primary motivation of Canadian and British authorities came from the need to cut local costs and, if possible, avoid violence on the frontier. Certainly in the United States none of these factors played a major part in the discussions about policy. The plans and actions of both governments demonstrate white paternalism and a determination to impose cultural dominance on minority groups.[7]

When the potential threat of war with the United States ended by 1815, the scattered Indian bands in the Canadian Maritime regions caused little fear. For some years the governments there had issued food and other supplies to Indians as temporary relief assistance. However, unlike the payments in other parts of Canada, the officials did not view these as gifts or payments to former allies, and certainly not as payment for any lands surrendered to the whites.[8] Because of the strong anti-Indian feelings present in the region, the English-supported New England Company, which had paid for tribal schools in Nova Scotia, questioned its continuing efforts. In 1822 and again in 1825 the company sent investigators to learn what was being done with its money. Their inquiries indicated that all educational activities among the Indians had failed.[9]

Over the years several things had undermined the reformers' efforts. Most important, the Indians refused to let their children attend the small schools regularly because they moved about in seasonal cycles of planting, hunting, fishing, and harvesting, and few parents would leave the children behind. In addition, Micmac leaders complained that the schools failed to teach either tribal culture or language. Some families objected to how the teachers treated the children. The New England Company reports validated these complaints, stating that some of the English had tried to profit economically and sexually from the Indian young people then serving apprenticeships. A local clergyman was among the worst offenders. One of the investigators described his actions while supervising the Sussex Vale School and a local apprenticeship program as more "like a mad dog—after his prey— than a Clergyman in the habit of praying for things requisite and necessary."[10] Under those circumstances it is little wonder that the Maritime Indians fared badly.

THE BEGINNING OF WESTWARD REMOVAL

While acculturation efforts went forward in Canada, American authorities and Indians faced similar questions. The real debate centered on where the tribes should live while becoming acculturated and how long that would take. Almost nobody except the Indians themselves thought that they might retain their tribal cultures. Americans of the early nineteenth century saw them as savages. The possibility of a society that included people identified as Indians found no support within the mainstream culture. Yet this is what most tribal people desired, and the clash between these irreconcilable positions brought endless difficulties to federal officials and misery to the Indians.

After 1815 the growing demands that the federal government move the eastern tribes west across the Mississippi River ran headlong into the ongoing efforts to acculturate the Indians. Missionary societies such as the American Board of Commissioners for Foreign Missions, Protestant church denominations, and some government officials sought to continue using schools, farms, and related efforts to make the tribal people more compatible with the rest of American society. In response the president and secretary of war chose to funnel the money through the missionary societies rather than having the government try a program of acculturation itself. The federal funds brought quick action, and by 1824 they had paid for all but three of the existing twenty-one Indian schools. While the effort to bring English literacy to the villagers had its critics, the schools continued, and a few hundred Indian children acquired some parts of a basic education.[11]

At the same time, pressures on the government to push the tribes west increased steadily. In 1802 Georgia and the United States agreed that if the state would surrender its land claims reaching west to the Mississippi River the federal government would clear the Indian title to lands within Georgia. When this did not happen, Georgia politicians built parts of their careers on attacking the federal leadership over this issue. The Indians reacted to the situation in the opposite way. They complained to Washington that renegade Georgians threatened their peace and security. In 1824 President Monroe defended his administration's inaction when he asserted to Congress that federal authorities had no obligation to force Indians west against their will. He called for voluntary removal because he thought that to force the tribes west would be "revolting to humanity, and utterly unjustifiable."[12]

While state and federal leaders bickered, events among the Cherokees brought matters to a head. The Christian missionaries made rapid inroads among the often-discouraged Indians. Their lessons of personal worth, redemption, and hope for the future found eager listeners. While this helped many Indians, it also threatened to divide the villages over religious matters. At the same time, in 1821–22 Sequoya, or George Guess, developed a new syllabary for writing Cherokee. Apparently easy to learn, by the mid-1820s its use swept "through the [Cherokee] nation like fire among the leaves."[13] Although learning how to read and write helped Cherokee self-confidence, missionaries and some mixed-race tribal leaders worried that it might inhibit the acculturation then taking place. Like Christianity, then, language literacy worked both to revitalize tribal society and to divide it further.

Before leaving office in January 1825 President James Monroe proposed voluntary removal one last time. Four years later, President Andrew Jackson called for a general removal act. His plan produced bitter and widespread debate both inside and out of the government. Yet when the rhetoric faded, it seems clear that a solid majority backed the president's determination to force the tribes west. By the mid-1830s the removal policy went into effect. Tribal efforts to avoid removal or respond to it provide one of the most significant differences between Indian experiences in the two countries. While the United States pushed its native people out of their traditional homelands in the East, Canadian officials merely compacted the tribal holdings for the next generation. Their actions resembled the earlier Jeffersonian approach south of the border before the United States abandoned that policy and carried out its removal plans.

The removal of the major southeastern tribes has received the most attention, but Indians in all parts of the country west to the Mississippi River faced the same dismal treatment. In each region would-be frontier settlers demanded that the tribal people surrender their desirable lands and move west. Frequently they claimed that nearby Indians had committed depredations, stolen their livestock, or hunted on their property. State authorities from Georgia in the southeast to Illinois in the northwest all called upon federal officials to force the tribes west. Their tactics included such things as threats to destroy the Indians themselves, petitions to the federal government to remove the tribes, and legislation asserting state control over the regions occupied by the native people. Through these efforts they asserted their ownership of all territory within individual states and demanded quick federal action.[14]

Facing such attitudes and pressures, tribal leaders used a variety of initiatives and responses. They negotiated with federal commissioners repeatedly, but only rarely did this prove successful. In the 1831 *Cherokee v. Georgia* case and *Worcester v. Georgia* the following year, the Cherokees and their supporters appealed to the U.S. Supreme Court, but in vain. In the first case Chief Justice John Marshall ruled that Indians could not bring suit because they lacked an independent political status. He found them to be a "domestic dependent nation," a designation that has colored Indian-federal relations ever since it was first announced. In their second appeal the court ruled against Georgia, but to no avail.[15]

By 1833 some tribal leaders came to accept the impossibility of staying in Georgia and, led by the acculturated John Ridge, began to call for cession of their lands and removal. Although the majority of the tribe supported Chief John Ross in his refusal to accept such an agreement, in December 1835 the federal negotiators and the Ridge supporters signed a removal treaty. After heated debate the U.S. Senate ratified it by only a single vote, and the removal process began. By 1838 the Indians were to be across the Mississippi; because they refused to go, late that year federal troops marched into the Cherokee country, rounded up the people, and sent them west on the infamous "Trail of Tears."[16] Once beyond the Mississippi the divisions that had prevented a united front against the United States continued, as the followers of John Ross enforced an earlier tribal law that decreed the death penalty for anyone involved in selling tribal lands to the whites. That brought death to John Ridge, Elias Boudinot, and several other pro-removal leaders and set off difficulties within the tribe that lasted for several decades.

Other tribes tried different strategies. The Chickasaws living in Alabama and Mississippi depended on the negotiating skills of their mixed-race leaders. In particular Levi Colbert and his family provided effective resistance to removal demands for a generation. Because of their efforts and strong tribal unity the Chickasaws were the last major southern tribe to accept removal. They signed the Treaty of Doaksville in 1837, but only after years of successful delay. As early as 1826 federal negotiators had begun the last phase of their campaign to persuade tribal leaders to move west. Despite the threats of federal officials Levi Colbert rejected their demands completely. He told the commissioners that the tribe had no intention of selling any more of its territory. What remained of tribal property was its traditional heartland, and all the Chickasaws agreed that this region should not be surrendered. "We never had a thought of exchanging our land for any other . . . it being the land of our forefathers," he reported.[17] He saw removal as offering only a slight delay until the existing pressures would come to bear on the tribe beyond the Mississippi once more.

Outright refusal to accept federal demands provided only one option for dealing with the removal issue. In 1827 Thomas L. McKenney, then the commissioner of Indian affairs, visited the Chickasaws for informal talks. He encouraged the leaders to travel west, inspect the land there, and choose a region that offered similar resources to those they had in Alabama and Mississippi. After a yearlong delay twelve Chickasaws set out for Saint Louis, where they joined smaller delegations of Choctaws and Creeks. They traveled through Missouri, Arkansas, and Oklahoma before heading home. Even after their western tour at government expense, Colbert and the other tribal leaders rejected federal urgings to sell their eastern territory. Instead, in June 1829 they reported that "we cannot consent to remove to a country destitute of a single corresponding feature of the one in which we at present reside."[18]

Continuing Chickasaw resistance ended quickly once Congress passed the 1830 Indian Removal Act and authorities in both Alabama and Mississippi extended state authority over the tribe. Both states threatened heavy fines and imprisonment for Indian leaders who dared to exercise their authority, and they abolished all tribal laws. When Chickasaw leaders protested the destruction of their government to President Andrew Jackson, he offered no help. At that point they accepted renewed negotiations and soon signed a removal treaty. Even then, however, the chiefs delayed the process again. Although they agreed to another western tour, the delegation found no suitable land. Levi Colbert wrote to the president that except for Mexican territory along the Sabine River, "we see no other country which we think would suit us so well."[19] This new delay proved short-lived. In 1834 Colbert died, and without his negotiating skills, tribal leaders soon bowed to the inevitable. Removal in 1837 was well planned and relatively incident free when compared to the experiences of some other tribes.

The Vermillion Kickapoos of eastern Illinois also avoided forced migration for a time. They depended on the negotiating skills of their leader, the prophet Kenekuk. Like many shamans, his teachings combined traditional Indian ideas with some aspects of Christianity. Kenekuk preached against alcohol and violence, hoping that by having peaceful relations with their neighbors the villagers would be allowed to retain their lands. During the 1820s he met repeatedly with William Clark at Saint Louis or his subordinates elsewhere, and despite their constant urgings that the Indians sign away their Illinois lands and move west, the prophet evaded doing either. His claims about having direct revelations from God impressed most of his followers, and they tried to live according to his teachings. When the whites saw how sober and peaceful the villagers were, they found it difficult to claim that the Indians posed any threat to peace. In his discussions with William Clark the prophet insisted that he followed the will of the Great Spirit. "If I do not act agreeably to His will," Kenekuk said, "He will reduce us to nothing and finally destroy our nation."[20] Although temporarily effective at avoiding removal, such talk could not stem the tide of settlement that engulfed the Vermillion Kickapoos. The Black Hawk War of 1832 provided the final push as the government and citizens of Illinois demanded that all Indians be forced from the state that summer. By the spring of 1833 Kenekuk and his followers had crossed the Mississippi.

Not all of the tribes objecting to removal had their resistance end peacefully. In Illinois and Iowa the Sauk and Mesquakie tribal leaders split over surrendering their homeland and moving west. During the 1820s, following the leader recognized by federal officials, Keokuk, a majority of these people moved their villages into eastern Iowa. The remaining third of the villagers returned to western Illinois each spring to plant new crops. Led by the aging warrior Black Hawk, they refused to recognize an 1804 treaty that had ceded their traditional lands to the United States. After years of minor incidents between pioneers and Indians, when the Sauks returned to their major Illinois village in 1831 they found it occupied by squatters. Objecting bitterly to the whites' seizure of their lodges and fields, the leaders drove the pioneers away. In response to cries of an "Indian invasion," the governor of Illinois, John Reynolds, called out the state militia and asked for federal troops to help. Only the direct intervention of General Edmund P. Gaines with regular troops prevented bloodshed. Gaines then forced the unhappy Indians west into Iowa.[21]

After a cold, miserable winter in Iowa, Black Hawk led nearly two thousand men, women, and children back into Illinois the next spring. He hoped to move onto lands owned by other tribes and plant crops for the summer. The aging leader rejected American claims to Sauk lands. He also heeded the assurances of White Cloud, a Sauk-Winnebago prophet who told him that the Americans would not object to the Sauk and Mesquakie return. One of the chiefs reported promises of British help from Canada if the situation became dangerous. Later that summer Black Hawk realized that his advisers had misled him, but by then Illinois militiamen had attacked, and a peaceful return to Iowa became impossible. U.S. regular troops joined the militia force then in the field, and together they chased the Indians across northern Illinois and southern Wisconsin. In early August 1832 they overtook the exhausted fugitives at the Mississippi River and at the Battle of Bad Axe killed most of Black Hawk's followers. Later that year the victors took Black Hawk and the other band leaders off to prison. Then American negotiators extracted a large land cession from the peaceful majority of the Sauks and Mesquakies living in Iowa.[22]

A more serious armed resistance to removal broke out in Florida during the winter of 1835–36 when the Seminoles attacked and destroyed an army unit and killed their agent at the same time. The Second Seminole War, which followed, proved to be one of the most difficult and frustrating of American Indian conflicts for the U.S. Army because of the scattered villages, the environment in central and southern Florida, and the general lack of competence displayed by nearly every senior officer who served in that conflict. While patrols of soldiers failed to locate their elusive foes, the antiremoval movement gained new strength, partly because of the war. Claiming that the Indians were defending themselves and their homeland, a modest peace movement arose. Humanitarians objected bitterly to the use of bloodhounds to track the fugitives through the Everglades, and to the officers' treachery when they seized the Seminole leader Osceola while meeting under a flag of truce. Despite these objections and the army's continuing failure to defeat or capture the bulk of the Seminoles, the war slowed, and in 1842 major campaigning stopped. Gradually small groups of Seminoles surrendered and the government sent them west.[23]

One other response to removal rarely gets much attention from historians. That was flight to Canada. The northward migration that had begun at the end of the American Revolution, when Joseph Brant had led a significant portion of the Six Nations across the border into Canada, continued throughout the midnineteenth century. Many of the Potawatomi of Michigan and Illinois chose to migrate north rather than accept forced removal. Because some of the Potawatomi bands had mixed-race leaders who negotiated skillfully and received more than their share of the benefits from the 1833 treaties, much of the rest of the tribe decided to move into Canada. In 1835 the first groups straggled north, and a second movement occurred in 1837 once forcible removal had begun in the United States. The immigrants moved from northern Illinois, Indiana, and southern Michigan into Ontario. During the next several years, several thousand Potawatomi migrated into Canada, so many that in 1844 the authorities there began to have second thoughts about this influx. In fact, they asked the Indian agents why they had allowed so many American Indians to settle in Canada. In reply, the agents referred to promises of refuge made to the tribes because of their service during the War of 1812, and to specific 1841 instructions to encourage the emigration.[24] While most Indians did not try to escape from the United States, for a few flight offered an option to warfare or forced removal.

THE DEBATE OVER ASSIMILATION

During the 1830s the supporters of removal triumphed, but the proponents of acculturation remained active and once the tribes had been moved west gradually regained dominance over the direction of Indian affairs. Nevertheless, the incorporation of tribal people into the general society remained only a dream. For the people on the frontiers and the Indians themselves, it became more nearly a nightmare. Many national leaders questioned even the possibility of the Indians being taught European thoughts and ways. For example, Henry Clay, the powerful senator from Kentucky, labeled the tribal people as "essentially inferior to the Anglo-Saxon race" and as not "an improvable breed."[25] Lewis Cass, secretary of war during the 1830s and the man who directed much of the federal removal program, noted that the Indians of North America had not been "improved"—he meant acculturated—by their two centuries of contact with the intruding whites and suggested that the fault resulted from the "institutions, character, and condition of the Indians themselves."[26]

Taking these ideas to their logical conclusion, some commentators suggested that the solution lay in intermarriage between the races. The argument claimed that as a barbarous race the Indians could be incorporated into mainstream society only by racial or genetic rather than cultural changes, because the alterations being called for were too profound for anything less than a complete restructuring of the tribal people. Yet while some demanded race mixing, other people, perhaps most, despised the offspring of such unions, and the pejorative terms "half-breed" or "breed" came into widespread use. As the United States and Mexico moved toward conflict in the Southwest during the 1840s, learned American writers suggested that the people of Mexico could not stand up to the strength of the United States because most of the population consisted of Indians or "half-breeds." By this time Americans differed widely over how to bring Indians into the general society or if the tribes would survive at all.[27]

During the 1830s and 1840s Americans demonstrated a degree of confusion about what to do with the tribal people that exceeded the usual mixture of positive and negative ideas about them. The general removal law made little provision for what would happen to the newly transplanted groups in the West. Apparently many people assumed that the mere act of crossing the Mississippi River would solve what they called the "Indian problem," but that proved false even before all of the eastern tribes had completed their migration. Recognizing this, a combination of politicians and social reformers worked for the creation of an Indian territory complete with federal officials west of Arkansas and Missouri. The proposal called for a territorial government with an appointed governor, a territorial secretary, agents for each tribe, a marshal, a prosecuting attorney, and a court system. Within this framework the individual tribes might still regulate their separate internal affairs, but clearly the bill's backers hoped to break down tribal distinctions as one step in the acculturation process. For a time it appeared as if the scheme might be enacted, but Congress rejected it.[28] Canadian officials never seem to have made a similar proposal.

American politicians and reformers shared their racist ideas and confusion with their counterparts in Canada. Although only restrained public debate over Indian policy occurred north of the border, a variety of opinions existed. Continuing pressure from Britain to cut imperial administrative costs, combined with the demands of settlers in both Upper Canada and the Maritime areas to clear those regions of Indians by the 1830s, pushed the authorities toward their so-called civilization policy. Thus, at the very time that American authorities claimed that their efforts to help acculturate the Indians had failed, British bureaucrats decided to try the same tactics in Canada. Instead of removal, they expanded their support of schools, missions, and instruction in white-style farming.

Having decided that the Indians contributed little to the local economy once the fur trade had shifted to the far north and west, and realizing that little further danger from the United States existed, in late 1829 the British settled on a policy of trying to incorporate the remaining tribal people into the majority society. This was a fundamental difference from what was happening south of the border. The British government made no hurried commitment to the proposals, but in November 1829 the Treasury approved an annual grant of twenty thousand pounds to pay the costs.[29] Without thinking the decision through carefully, imperial officials shifted the basic relationship between Indians and whites from that of allies to that of superior and inferior. Unlike the United States, which had the 1831 *Cherokee v. Georgia* Supreme Court decision to mark the formal shift, the Canadian government imposed wardship on the

Indians of Upper Canada merely as a result of cost-cutting efforts begun in Britain. At the time this effort applied only to Upper Canada, but it laid the foundation for later policy and actions throughout all of Canada. Indian relations in Quebec had been quiet for a generation, and no officials there or in Britain sought to alter that situation. In the Maritimes there were so few Indians that the authorities paid little attention to these issues.

Even before the approval of the so-called civilization plan, the personnel involved with Indian affairs in the province had changed. The British placed their revamped administrative structure under civilian control, but many of the men within it had held military positions earlier, and some simply moved from one office to another. In contrast to the sporadic use of individual Indians as interpreters in the United States, from the start the Canadian system included many Indian men as interpreters, clerks, timber rangers, and laborers at the evolving settlements. Basically these men held only lower-level positions in the Indian service, so they rarely had much influence on how the system worked. Nevertheless, employing Indians as part of the bureaucracy, even if only in small numbers, demonstrated a higher degree of sincerity about incorporating the tribal people into the general society than appeared in the United States at that time.[30]

With the new bureaucratic machinery in place by the early 1830s, Indian affairs faded rapidly from public view. The existing "civilization" program appeared successful. Indians and others built schools, and the children attended them. Missionaries and tribal leaders cooperated to erect churches. Using tools and seeds provided by the government, individual Indians began trying to farm. At least at first glance, then, the program seemed to work. At the same time, however, government officials continued to negotiate treaties with the tribes, opening more land for settlement and greatly reducing the Indian land base. Because the land transfers preceded the pace of frontier settlement most of the time, Canadian leaders heard few of the outraged demands to move the tribes out of the way that their American counterparts did. Then too, the political spotlight shifted to other significant issues, including the rebellions of 1837, the Act of Union combining Upper and Lower Canada in 1841, and the ongoing effort to obtain responsible government by the Canadian leaders. At the same time, the current of reform sentiment that had swept across Britain for a decade or more began to ebb, and people there paid less attention to Indian affairs or other areas of social concern than they had just a few years earlier.[31]

Despite the apparent lack of public interest, the program of acculturation and possible eventual incorporation of tribal people into Canadian society moved ahead. For several decades missionaries and others had operated schools and churches among some groups in Upper Canada, and the long-established reserves and missions in Quebec continued the work begun generations earlier. By the 1820s the lieutenant governor of Upper Canada, Sir Peregrine Maitland, assisted the Mississaugas to establish a village near York (present-day Toronto). Within a few years the Indians there had comfortable houses, with furniture and cooking utensils that rivaled those owned by pioneer whites in the area. Authorities had applied an 1824 law establishing primary schools to teach both Indians and whites, so that the curriculum, books, and materials for tribal children, in theory at least, resembled those employed with the English-speaking children at the time. In addition, by 1829 Methodist missionaries already operated seven schools that enrolled 251 Indian children even before the new program formally went into effect. Clearly the 1830 shift from viewing the tribes as economic and military assets to seeing them as people needing help in moving into the regular society was well under way before the government publicly announced its new direction.[32]

The efforts to introduce sedentary agriculture, education, and Christianity to the relatively nomadic peoples of Upper Canada set off a debate over Indian capabilities and the effectiveness of educational and religious work that resembled the discussion taking place in the United States. The Anglican bishop of Quebec characterized the success of his Methodist competitors in Upper Canada in glowing terms. Noting their ability to convert many of the Mississaugas from "ignorance and immoral habits to Christian faith and Practice," he described the changes as so fundamental and so quickly accomplished "that the hand of God seems to be visible in it."[33] The Methodists themselves claimed to have a system of eleven schools, with eleven teachers and some 400 students in attendance, 150 of whom could already read the New Testament. These comments might have overstated the impact of mission schools on tribal children, but they resemble reports coming from teachers at the American Board schools in the United States. Clearly the reformers thought the Indian children and, by inference, all Indians could be educated for a place in Canadian society.

For a time, the proponents of education carried the day, although, like their counterparts in the United States, they often overlooked the minimal influence children and young people had in Indian societies. Nevertheless, government, religious, and even tribal leaders cooperated to establish schools and mission outposts across the Indian country. For example, the Indian Department, the Methodists, the New England Company, and the Anglicans all worked with the Six Nations along the Grand River, building and operating several schools and churches. The Mohawk Institute, founded in 1829, received most attention from these efforts, but only because it stood in an area readily accessible to the whites. Designed to provide vocational training to the students, it taught the boys tailoring and carpentry and the girls spinning and weaving. Organized as a boarding school, it incorporated nearly all of the approaches used in both Canada and the United States during the nineteenth century. By 1841, when the Act of Union combined Upper and Lower Canada to form the United Province of Canada, the former region had twenty-one day and two manual-labor schools serving the Indians there.[34]

At least some of these developed after 1830 when the new group of Indian Department officers focused on opening schools for Indian children. The effort began that year when the new lieutenant governor of Upper Canada, Sir John Colborne, decided to establish schools at Coldwater and the Narrows at Lake Simcoe. Despite having the model of successful Methodist schools to follow, the plan failed. Between 1830 and 1837 the government had land cleared and helped with building shelters, but it took far more than those modest achievements to get wholehearted Indian cooperation. As they had said all along, the local Ojibwa people near the new settlement wanted economic help, but they rejected assimilation. They lived by hunting, fishing, and gathering. While some may have realized that agriculture offered more stability, few agreed to the all-or-nothing approach Canadian officials offered. The Methodists had succeeded in part because of their heavy dependence on Indian missionaries and local leaders. The bureaucrats, on the other hand, ignored or tried to manipulate band leaders with little success. In addition, at both Coldwater and the Narrows sectarian bickering among the Methodists, Anglicans, and Catholics further undermined the program. As a result, by 1837 the government efforts at both sites foundered.[35]

Nevertheless, down into the 1860s work to acculturate and assimilate Indians continued sporadically, but few whites or Indians really wanted to merge their societies. Occasionally incidents of parents being indifferent or even opposed to education for the children occurred, but the missionaries and teachers continued their drumbeat of positive support for the educational efforts. Usually the missionary groups reported that most Indian parents "ardently desire the improvement of their off-spring" and willingly sacrificed to keep the children in school.[36] Students' accomplishments depended on many factors, but when taught in their native language rather than English they learned quickly. While the whites debated the language issue, Indian parents asked for native-speaking instructors, and the Mohawks at the Bay of Quinte even offered to pay the costs of printing textbooks in Mohawk so their children might learn more quickly.[37]

Canadian educational goals and actions resembled those tried in the United States during the middle of the nineteenth century. In neither country did Indian tribal authorities have much control over what the whites offered their children. Often tribal leaders accepted the approaches the teachers and missionaries used because they knew few alternatives. As a result Indian schools put their charges in small desks inside cramped rooms and strove to teach English literacy through reading the Bible and other religious tracts, and writing from copy lines and from dictation. The rigid gender roles within society on both sides of the border existed in the schools too, as they taught the girls domestic skills while the boys' training pointed them toward more active participation in the economy. As they would continue to do for the next century, Canadian officials encouraged both primary day schools and boarding schools that offered a vocationally oriented curriculum.

Whether supported through tribal, mission society, or government funds, none of the schools appears to have been particularly successful. Indian children learned best when taught in their native languages, but the whites preferred English. Given their goal of incorporating the tribal people into the growing white society, that made sense, but it limited educational accomplishments sharply. Throughout the decades before 1860 these institutions had only a modest impact. Certainly the manual-labor schools could not be considered successful. Many Indian parents remained suspicious of the schools, fearing that the Indian young people would lose their tribal culture. Even where parents and schools cooperated, no group in the white society could or would pay the cost of effective education, so the schools limped along with large expectations, small budgets, and inadequate staff and equipment.

Even had the schools graduated well-trained and acculturated Indians, neither U.S. nor Canadian society offered well-paid jobs for them. The whites simply refused to patronize Indian-run businesses or to hire Indian workers except for menial tasks.[38] Equally important, continuing tribal resistance to more than economic acculturation certainly explains why the schools seemed to have achieved so little by midcentury. The Indians valued certain skills and knowledge, and these they encouraged some of the children and young people to acquire. Assimilation into the general society, however, was entirely another matter, and throughout the nineteenth century tribal leaders and individual Indians alike sought to be left alone and to live their lives as they saw fit—usually outside the confines of Canadian society.

Like Kenekuk, White Cloud, or Handsome Lake in the United States, some Canadian Indian shamans and chiefs rejected much of the Anglo-European culture then being offered to them. At Walpole Island and nearby Lake Saint Clair the Ojibwas wanted little to do with visiting missionaries or teachers. Their local chief, Pazhekezhikquashkum, remained firmly opposed to replacing the tribal culture. When Methodist Indian missionaries visited, he rejected all of their arguments. After denouncing the whites for lying, cheating the Indians out of their land, and debauching them with alcohol, he announced that he would never surrender his traditional religion. Other Ojibwas in the same region echoed those sentiments. Wawanosh, leader of a band living on the Saint Clair River, also announced that he had no interest in abandoning the religion of his forefathers.[39] Although these men spoke for only small groups, they expressed the feelings of many native people in both countries.

CANADIAN DEBATES OVER REMOVAL AND LEGAL STATUS

While the local leaders supported the development of schools and missions among the tribes of Upper Canada, some opposition to this program arose at the highest levels of government as it had in the United States. In January 1836 British authorities asked for a detailed report on the social and economic progress of Indians in both Upper and Lower Canada. Responding for the former province, the new lieutenant governor, Sir Francis Bond Head, denounced the civilization program and began to change the policies immediately. Noting that "Whenever and Wherever the Two Races come into contact with each other it is sure to prove fatal to the Red Man," Governor Bond Head criticized the acculturation efforts sharply.[40] All attempts to help the Indians become farmers had failed, he claimed, and gathering the nomadic people into villages near the whites only exposed them to the vices and evil habits of the Europeans. In his view the harm far outweighed any positive benefits the Indians might have gotten from learning new skills. As a result Bond Head decided to launch his own program of removal and segregation for the tribes of Upper Canada. If successful, he assumed, his effort would end the Indian problem and open more good land for Canadian pioneers.[41]

To accomplish this, the lieutenant governor urged the tribes to cede their land and accept new land on the Manitoulin Islands at the north shore of Lake Huron and Georgian Bay. This location offered isolation but little else, as the Indians soon pointed out to him. "Now we raise our own corn, potatoes, wheat," reported Chief Joseph Sawyer. "But if we go to Maneetoolin, we could not live; soon we should be extinct as a people."[42] Despite this and similar objections, Governor Bond Head pushed ahead with his efforts. He rejected Indian complaints and threatened that if the tribes failed to move and land-hungry pioneers overran their title settlements, he could not protect them. In 1836 his listeners, with little hope of blocking the advancing settlers without government help, reluctantly agreed. Bond Head then traveled to Manitoulin Island, where he persuaded Ottawa and Ojibwa leaders to give up some of their land so other tribal groups could settle there. Continuing through the province, he arranged land cessions from the Saugeens and other Ojibwas within his jurisdiction. By the end of the year he had extracted three million acres of land in exchange for the dubious promise of continuing isolation for the tribes at Manitoulin.[43]

Removal, Canadian style, raised angry debate as it had in the United States, although to the north the numbers of people involved in the debate remained small. The lieutenant governor's negative attitudes toward the Indians brought an immediate outcry from the Wesleyan Methodist Conference in Upper Canada, which objected to Bond Head's policies. They claimed that his efforts had brought "circumstances as strange as they were unexpected," because the lieutenant governor had single-handedly disrupted their school and mission activities, efforts that had received the full blessing of the British authorities less than a decade earlier.[44]

By the next year the Methodist Conference reported unrest sweeping the Upper Canada Indian reserves. People at the Saugeen settlement denounced the cession of their lands and circulated wampum belts calling for war. When missionaries warned that resistance would only bring destruction, they agreed. They said that "if we kill a few of the white people . . . they will come and kill us off, and then there will be an end of us."[45] Talk of this sort caused the missionaries to send appeals to London, where groups such as the Aborigines Protection Society added their complaints about the shift in policy. It is unclear how this might have been resolved, but the rebellions in both Canadas forced officials to focus their efforts on other issues. Indian policy slipped into the background quickly, and Sir Francis Bond Head returned to England, apparently leaving little active support for his removal policy in Canada.[46]

While Bond Head had tried to begin a Canadian removal policy, others in the Indian Office continued to work toward acculturation on Manitoulin Island and elsewhere. In 1835 they began a multitribal settlement called Manitowaning on the island. Ignoring a missionary assessment of the area as "23,000 rocks of granite, dignified by the name of Manitoulin Islands," the officers claimed that the main island included over three hundred thousand acres of land "believed to be of good quality and fit for settlement."[47] It took until 1838 for the superintendent to move to the island and only gradually in the following years did two villages, Manitowaning and Wikwemikong, develop. By 1844 the staff at Manitowaning included a carpenter, blacksmith, mason, cooper, charcoal burner, shoemaker, and several laborers, all in residence to help and instruct the Indians, but the community soon disintegrated. Fire swept through the buildings within two years, and although some rebuilding took place, the population dwindled steadily, so that by 1856 investigators found the settlement nearly deserted. The village failed because the area lacked the good soil needed to support the villagers' new way of life. Also, the effort brought together Ottawas, Ojibwas, and Potawatomis, whose clashing tribal customs and political rivalries among competing chiefs kept the village in turmoil. The presence of several Christian denominations also split the villagers. As a result by 1860 only ninety-six people remained there.[48]

During this era, then, both Canada and the United States had tried varied and even conflicting policies toward the tribal people. In the south the government had used military force to defeat and remove those who refused to remain at peace or to migrate west. On the early American frontiers the pioneers outran the efforts of the federal government to control the relations between the races, attacking Indians and seizing their land, mineral, and forest resources while daring the government to do more than recognize their accomplishments. In Canada, while the frontier population grew rapidly, the same pressures and demands for land remained less intense, so usually the government kept the races apart and directed the pace and direction of frontier settlement. In both nations efforts to bring sedentary farming, English-language schools, and missionary establishments resulted in partial acculturation of many Indians. What the acculturators failed or refused to recognize in both countries, however, was that the tribal people accepted only certain elements of the white man's civilization.

By the 1840s the faint outlines of a different legal status for native people began to emerge in Canada. South of the border, the crisis of removal and the resulting appeals to the U.S. Supreme Court had produced the two Cherokee decisions that laid much of the foundation for future U.S.-Indian legal relations. As of 1831 the court had declared the Indians to be "domestic dependent nations," thus legally making them wards of the federal government. In Canada the process took a different turn and, at least during middle of the nineteenth century, led to efforts aimed more at incorporating the tribal people into the society instead of keeping them isolated on reservations in the West. In 1839 Canadian Chief Justice James B. Macaulay reported that the Indians had no claims to any separate nationality that might exempt them from "being amenable to the laws of the land."[49] This was the opposite of what U.S. Chief Justice

Marshall had ruled in the Cherokee cases just a few years earlier. While the American political and legal system moved to isolate the tribes, in Canada Macaulay stated that the courts would enforce Indian contracts and allow them to appeal for redress of personal or property violations. He went on to say that both civil and criminal courts had to be open for Indians, and that if they qualified to vote or to hold local offices they could do so.

An 1840 attorney general's opinion on some of these same questions echoed Macaulay's ideas. Stating that over the age of twenty-one Indians had the same rights as other Canadians, the opinion noted that Indians "are not incapable of making civil contracts" and that they "have legal capacity, either as plaintiffs or defendants."[50] It took much longer for Indians to attain similar rights in the United States, although it is not certain that in Canada they either wanted to or could exercise them without interference. In Canada, on the one hand, it appears that individual Indians were being integrated into the social and legal structure of the society, but at the same time the government continued to treat the tribes in a paternal manner and often ignored their wishes, customs, or even best interests.

This was particularly true when it came to tribal or band claims of land-ownership and local sovereignty, as an 1823 court decision showed the Mohawks. When some of that tribe, led by Joseph Brant, had fled to Canada during the American Revolution, they had received title to land on the Grand River in Ontario for having served as British allies during the war. Brant, acting as if the lands belonged to him personally, leased some of the acreage to Epaphrus Phelps, then married to a Mohawk woman and living among the Indians. Accused of treason during the War of 1812, Phelps fled, but not before putting his lands in trust for his family. Because under British law persons convicted of treason lost their property, the government moved to claim Phelps's land. The Mohawks claimed that the land belonged to them, not to Phelps, and that as British allies they were not subject to the treason laws. In court the crown officials argued that the Indians were not allies as they claimed, but were in fact subjects like the French in Quebec. In fact, the solicitor general told the court that "the supposition that the Indians are not subject to the laws of Canada is absurd."[51] The decision went against the Mohawks, who lost the disputed lands. More important, the court dismissed their assumed sovereignty as an absurdity. That ruling provided the basis for most nineteenth-century Indian litigation and marked the Canadian legal approach to tribal rights as distinctly different from that in the United States at the time.

Shortly after the 1841 Act of Union joined Upper and Lower Canada into a single political body, the United Province of Canada (renaming the two former provinces Canada West and Canada East respectively), the operations of the Indian Department came under renewed scrutiny. In 1844 a two-year investigation produced what is usually known as the Bagot Report. It called for the reorganization of the Indian Office and supported the existing policy of acculturation through the schools. Two years later, the veteran Indian agent Thomas G. Anderson met with Ojibwa band leaders at Orillia to discuss their land claims and to explain government education plans. He urged his listeners to consolidate their villages at a few large settlements so the government could build residential schools for their children. He promised that each band would get legal papers protecting their new landholdings. At the same meeting he and the Reverend Peter Jones persuaded some Ojibwa leaders to contribute up to 25 percent of their annuities to pay for the building and operating of schools on their reserves. Hoping to protect Indian lands from the ever more difficult problems caused by illegal squatters, the commissioners recommended new laws, and by 1850 these came into force. By midcentury the educational program had the full support of local and imperial officials.[52]

Out of these investigations, reports, and laws, a clearer definition of who the whites considered to be a "real" Indian appeared. The 1850 legislation for Canada East, or Quebec, laid down four conditions for classifying individuals as Indians. These four categories included: (1) all people of Indian blood who lived as part of a particular tribe, and their descendants; (2) persons married to Indians and living with tribes, and their descendants; (3) persons living with the tribe whose parents on either side were Indians; and (4) people adopted into the tribe as children who lived on the reserves. With this statute, the government weakened the right of each group to determine its own membership. The motivation for these criteria grew out of the desire to make certain that only legitimate Indians got presents and annuities—again, a decision tied directly to imperial finances, rather than the result of careful thought. The major significance of this action, however, was that it moved the Canadian tribes toward dependency and away from sovereignty or even self-sufficiency.[53]

LAND GRABBING, CANADIAN STYLE

During the late 1840s Canadian Indians complained about the incursions of surveyors and others staking mineral claims on tribal lands along the eastern and northern shores of Lake Superior. Mining companies sent prospectors and others into the region, applying to the Department of Crown Lands for licenses to work any ore bodies they found. The activities of one of the most aggressive firms, the Montreal Mining Company, which bought claims for up to 180 square miles of land, frightened and angered the Indians living near the lake. when one of the chiefs protested to George Ironside, the local agent, the government at first denied the tribal claims and tried to ignore their objections. However, an 1848 investigation showed that the Indians had valid complaints. When the government dithered, Indians and Métis from Sault Sainte Marie raided one of the mining company properties. In response the government sent William Robinson west to conclude land cession treaties that would satisfy the tribes and at the same time secure the region for economic development.[54]

Sent west with a mere seventy-five hundred pounds in currency, Robinson had orders to get all the land possible but at least all the territory on "the north shore of Lake Huron and the mining sites along the eastern shore of Lake Superior."[55] In September 1850 Robinson met with Ojibwa leaders at Sault Sainte Marie. The Indians proved determined negotiators and demanded that they retain their hunting and fishing rights in the ceded areas until the land became private property. Similar provisions in earlier treaties in the United States had caused much difficulty there because the Indians eventually forgot about that particular clause, or settlement occurred so slowly that the next generation of tribal people living in ceded regions had no idea that they would lose their rights to use the land in traditional ways when the pioneers arrived. Indian leaders also secured annuities for their people and retained specific, small reserves for each group. Following established Canadian practice, the government saw no need to push any group out of its homeland, instead allowing the Indians to remain in familiar regions on much-reduced tribal lands. The Robinson-Superior and Robinson-Huron treaties of 1850, then, made few changes in existing Indian-white relations except to obtain far more land at one time than had been exchanged under earlier treaties.[56]

Throughout the nineteenth century regional variations in Indian policies marked the Indian experiences in Canada as more varied than that of tribes in the United States. At first Canada had no central government. Even after Confederation in 1867, the provinces in Canada exercised far more power over these issues than did the individual states to the south. The Maritime Provinces, with their modest numbers of Indians, provide one example of the multiplicity of approaches and policies. In Nova Scotia the colonists despised their tribal neighbors, claiming to see them as unstable people suffering from alcohol abuse and yet posing a potential threat to the local colonial population. When Chief Paussamigh Pemmeenswett appealed for help to Queen Victoria in January 1841, officials there investigated, and a year later the legislature authorized surveys of remaining tribal lands, action against illegal squatters refusing to leave tribal lands, and the admission of native children into the local schools. The program failed quickly because local whites objected. In particular the effort to incorporate Indian children in the public schools collapsed because white parents opposed having their children in school with the Indians. Tribal parents objected, too, however, because they feared losing their language and cultural identity if their children attended white schools.[57]

To make matters worse, Indian farmers no sooner got good-sized crops planted when the first of three consecutive years of potato blight struck, destroying all farming in the province. By 1859 new legislation allowed squatters on Indian lands to purchase the land if the tribe approved. The Indians got the proceeds, but their tiny land base continued to shrink. The squatters wanted the land but refused to pay, so the tribal funds rarely grew to useful size. At the same time the Indians wanted to retain their land in common and rejected efforts to survey and allot it by individual or family, so that by 1866 the whites recognized only ten families of Indians in the entire province as being officially settled on their land. As a result, during the 1850s the whites considered most Micmacs as outcasts from civil society. They might be effective as hunters, guides, or producers of modest native crafts, but they had little chance to fit into the European customs of Maritime society and its market-oriented economy.[58]

In Canada East, or Quebec, Indian relations remained more stable than in most other regions. Six reserves, one dating back to the seventeenth-century Iroquois Wars era, operated prior to the creation of eleven new ones in 1851. The early half dozen included settlements at Caughnawaga, Lorette, Odank, and Saint Regis, where members of the Iroquois, Huron, and Abenaki tribes predominated. The villages included people who tried to adapt to farming as well as those who ignored it and continued their hunting, fishing, and gathering economies. Some of the men worked as laborers in the nearby fishing and timber industries, while the women made handicraft and household items. The early reserves usually dated to the era when various Catholic orders obtained title to the land to be held in trust for the Indians, and some of the settlements had modest churches and schools. Their populations remained fairly static while the villages of the hunting people fluctuated considerably.[59]

Because French-speaking people dominated Canada East, that province did not receive the heavy migration from the British Isles that both the Maritime Provinces and Canada West did. Officials there thus faced much less pressure to clear Indians out of the path of expanding white settlement. Because of long-standing relationships between the tribes and the Catholic Church in what was then called Lower Canada, clerics and government officials had worked closely until the 1830 shift to the acculturation program. At that point competition between Protestants and Catholics and the attempts of long-resident French-speaking priests to disrupt teaching the Indians in English at Protestant or secular schools had brought considerable difficulty. So, unlike the experience of Canada West, that of Quebec prior to 1860 included people with long experience of dealing with the whites, a heavy influence by the Catholic Church, and frequent religious strife over the direction and administration of Indian affairs.[60]

In the Far West, the region that became British Columbia exhibited the most independent approach to Indian affairs of all the eventual Canadian provinces. Authorities there rejected all Indian claims to the land—an action that set them apart from the rest of Canada and the United States as well. That stand also created ongoing friction and ill will between the province and the central government, and between provincial authorities and the Indians. The tribes of the Pacific Northwest differed substantially from those in the rest of North America. Living chiefly along the coast or on the major rivers flowing into the Pacific, they had strong economies and large populations and defended themselves effectively. Yet they did not encounter the same pressures on their land from pioneer settlement that the tribes in Ontario had until the post-1860 era. By that time, however, the basic outlines or relations between them and the intruding Europeans had become clear. Certainly in the long run the British Columbia experience included more misunderstandings, violence, and demands for Indian resources than occurred in most of the rest of Canada. In fact the pioneers' demands that they be allowed to deal with the local tribes without outside interference also placed the far western events outside the usual bounds of Canadian experience.

The Indian peoples of British Columbia had met, traded with, and fought against Europeans for several generations during the late eighteenth century. By the 1770s both the Spanish and Russians had explored parts of the Pacific Coast. The English made contact in 1778 when Captain James Cook reached Nootka Sound. By then European ships stopped frequently to trade for the luxurious sea otter pelts that the coastal people gathered. By the early nineteenth century a land-based trade developed slowly, and once the Hudson's Bay Company and North West Company joined forces in 1821, the newly enlarged Hudson's Bay Company spread into the Northwest gradually. During the mid-1820s Dr. John McLoughlin oversaw company activities from Fort Vancouver, on the north bank of the Columbia River near present-day Portland, Oregon. By 1841 the fur trade became less profitable, and the company moved its far western headquarters north to what became Fort Victoria on Vancouver Island.[61]

The 1846 boundary treaty with the United States brought profound shifts in interracial relations in British Columbia. In 1849 the Hudson's Bay Company and the British government agreed that in exchange for promoting settlement in the new colony of Vancouver the company would receive a trade monopoly there for the next decade. Two years later, chief factor James Douglas became the colonial governor. A veteran trader, he understood Indian practices and dealt carefully and honestly when disputes arose between Indians and settlers. As the latter trickled out to Vancouver Island the governor had to reconcile their demands for land and the extirpation of the Indians with the rights of the tribal people. During the 1850s Douglas sought to protect the native Vancouver islanders from encroachment by the settlers, negotiating fourteen agreements that set aside small reserves for them at their traditional village sites.[62]

The governor based his policies on his long experience with the local people and on existing British views that the Indians had a recognizable title only to land they actually used for farming or for their dwellings. Although that ignored many tribal activities, it did offer some protection from land loss. In laying out specific reserves, Douglas selected areas most central to the Indian economy and rejected calls for removal from the settlers. Douglas offered no payment for the nonreserved lands, however, nor did he provide title for new reserves to the tribes. Fearing that the Indians might lose their lands if they owned them, he retained title to the reserves for the Crown. All of his efforts came amid frequent complaints by the settlers, whose demands he ignored, hoping to avoid the bitter violence then taking place in Washington and Oregon.[63]

As long as Douglas remained as governor, his policies protected the local reserve dwellers. He rejected the concept of tribal sovereignty, stating instead that the Indians "are in point of law regarded as British subjects. [As such they] are fully entitled to the rights and privileges of subjects."[64] Thus, while the coastal people saw their immediate lands protected, they fell into a tributary status without even realizing it. By their treaties with Douglas they avoided further land losses and retained the right to fish, hunt, and gather at their traditional sites. As settlement grew, however, it became increasingly difficult to continue those activities without white interference or objections. Unfortunately for the Indians, Douglas had implemented his policies single-handedly, with no legislative mandate to support them and over the growing opposition of the settler-dominated population. Once he left office in 1864, protection for the local reserves vanished quickly.[65]

While these policies developed in the pre-1860 West, officials in the East took at least one action that had a significant long-range impact on Indian-white relations in all of Canada. In 1857 the Canadian legislature passed "An Act for the Gradual Civilization of the Indian Tribes in the Canadas," which began an open attack on tribalism. For the first time Indian policy rested on legislation that called for tribal acculturation by undermining and eventually destroying the tribes as identifiable units. This approach had begun with missionary activities in the 1820s and gained strength with the Bagot Commission Report in the early 1840s, but no basic changes had occurred since. Now the focus shifted dramatically from group to individual acculturalization. The Gradual Civilization Act called for each Indian person to strive for incorporation into Canadian society and, when ready to take that step, to withdraw from the tribe, taking a plot of land from its holdings and thereby reducing the reservation size.[66] This effort to draw individual Indians into the general society marked the Canadian approach as distinctly different from U.S. policy, which excluded tribal people from citizenship.

The legislation altered existing Indian policy drastically. It aimed at doing away with the self-sustaining tribal communities that previous laws and policies had sought to develop and encourage. If the Gradual Civilization Act succeeded, Indian bands and tribes would cease to exist because the individuals would become freeholders and Canadian citizens. Few Indians welcomed the change, as tribal leaders' comments and council minutes demonstrate. Negative responses to the new legislation appeared immediately, mostly from the chiefs, who saw the law as a direct threat to tribal survival. One objected that the law would "break [the tribes] to pieces" because it clashed with Indian determination to retain their tribal identity and with their customs of group rather than individual control over their land. The chief bureaucrat in the Indian office, R. J. Pennefather, dismissed these objections bluntly by responding that "the Civilization Act is no grievance to you."[67]

His cavalier attitude signified the swift change that overtook Indian-white relations during the 1850s in Canada. Whereas the two groups had previously worked in harmony, or at least had not considered themselves to be adversaries, now the government assumed a threatening stance toward tribal survival. Some chiefs decided that their earlier agreement to contribute 25 percent of their annuities toward building and operating schools needed rethinking if the long-range goal was to destroy their identity as Indians. Those who understood the situation realized that the model farms, churches, and schools represented only the first steps in an aggressive process of acculturation. Band leaders united quickly to protest the changes. They wanted to continue the educational and economic programs then under way, but to improve their administration of tribal affairs, not destroy their traditional groups. At the same time, they rejected the goal of the civilization program, which called for their complete assimilation. By 1860 they had refused to sell any further territory and objected to the shift of responsibility for conducting Indian affairs from the imperial government to that of the United Canadas. They even organized to present their views to the Prince of Wales, then visiting the country.[68]

Despite Indian complaints, no basic changes occurred. In 1858 the British government had ended all payments to Canada for presents to those few tribes still getting them. That same year the Pennefather Commission submitted a lengthy report analyzing the Indian Department and calling for administrative changes for dealing with the tribes. It recognized that American-style removals should be avoided but offered few new ideas. Rather, it echoed the demands of the 1857 Gradual Civilization Act for bringing individual tribal members into the general society. Ignoring the objections coming from band and tribal councils, it called for a system of allotment under which each family head would receive a twenty-five-acre lot for farming once the band had chosen its specific location. In tandem with individual farms, the investigators focused much of their attention on the schools, recommending continued efforts with both day and boarding manual-labor institutions as the best hope for integrating Indians into the local economy.[69] Thus by 1860, when the British government relinquished its control over Indian affairs in Canada to local officials, the basic directions for Indian policy had been set. Assimilation, with its resulting tribal destruction, stood at the center of the program. Only Indian resistance to or subversion of the system would affect its outcome.

U.S. EXPANSION WESTWARD

While officials pushed Indians onto ever-shrinking reserves in Canada West, tribes in the United States faced a momentary lull in their confrontations with the government. By the late 1830s removal, forced or voluntary, was well under way. The flurry of legislative activity in 1834, while rejecting an Indian Territory, did reorganize the Indian Office and lay out new rules for trade and travel in the Indian country. As the eastern tribes migrated west, the government developed the concept of a permanent Indian frontier beyond Iowa, Missouri, and Arkansas and east of the Mexican territory. All of this effort rested on three mistakes or flawed assumptions. First, American planners did not anticipate the dramatic shifts in the West that would extend the national borders to the Pacific during the next decade. In addition, those working with the tribal people failed to recognize the depth of Indian cultural strength and so vastly overestimated the speed of the acculturation process. They also ignored the American pioneers' unwillingness to accept Indians as equals, citizens, and neighbors in a multiracial society. These three miscalculations help to explain the muddled and unsuccessful federal programs for the tribal people during the middle of the nineteenth century.

By the 1840s, with the major removal behind them, officials in the United States once again tried the acculturation program that they and the Canadian Indian office personnel had used earlier. They continued to expect that farms, schools, and churches would solve the Indian problem for the government. As a wave of reform interest swept through the society, federal officials succumbed to it as well. Commissioner of Indian Affairs T. Hartley Crawford voiced this view when he described day schools for Indian children as "indispensable to the civilization of the Indians."[70] Despite his request for increased support, Congress continued to appropriate only $10,000 each year, as it had done since 1819, when it established the Indian Civilization Fund. Nevertheless, missionary societies and some of the tribes themselves donated $150,000 each year to support the fifty-two schools that enrolled a total of about two thousand students The impact of these efforts varied widely, as some parents withdrew their children several times each year for the annual hunt or for tribal cultural or religious festivities, much to the dismay of the teachers, who hoped to wean the children away from those "heathen and savage" practices. Still, some young Indians learned to read and write English, acquired a few basic skills in other academic subjects, and often received some vocational training. The manual-labor school became the capstone of a poorly designed and underfunded system in the American West, just as it was in Canada West.

Other difficulties grew out of the very idea of a general Indian country. The resident Pawnees, Cheyennes, Comanches, and Sioux had little if any contact with the civilizers or government officials. In fact, they resented the presence of the intruded eastern tribes in their country as much as they objected to having whites settle on their lands. Their attacks on the removed tribes forced the eastern Indians to hone their fighting skills, while the lack of federal support and the difficulty of starting new farms pushed them toward a continued heavy dependence on hunting. That brought them into repeated competition and conflict with the tribes already living on the central and southern plains. Thus the move that so many people had assumed would help the Indians become acculturated actually forced them to depend more heavily on hunting than they had done in the East. It also made reestablishing churches and schools difficult because of the renewed costs of buildings, the difficulties of getting committed teachers, and the denominational competition among the Christian groups working on the frontier. Problems surrounding the unchecked whiskey vendors proved just one more complication in an already difficult and painful resettlement process for the tribes and showed up the inadequacies of American efforts to aid the Indians.

American movement into the Pacific coastal regions brought a surprisingly different situation there than developed in the Canadian West at the same time. On Vancouver Island, for example, Hudson's Bay Company officials had a hard time attracting enough pioneer settlers to their domain. In California, Oregon, and Washington, however, just the opposite occurred. Miners, timber cutters, fishermen, and farmers poured into those future states in such numbers that relations with the tribal groups there proved difficult and often violent from the start. In the California interior Mexicans and Anglo-Americans alike had incorporated some Indians into the developing local economy as herders, farm workers, and timber cutters. During 1848 substantial numbers of local Indians worked in the gold mining camps, either mining on their own or as employees mining for others. In fact, by late 1848 more than half of the miners were California Indians.[71]

That changed abruptly the next year when large numbers of forty-niners reached the gold fields. They saw local workers not as an economic asset but rather as competition, even a possible physical threat. Interracial violence erupted quickly, as miners raped Indian women and the warriors responded by killing nearby whites. These early incidents led to bitter and repeated campaigns of extermination against the nearby villagers. By late 1850 companies of California militiamen scoured the valleys looking for Indians to attack. Ironically, by driving the villagers farther into the mountains and away from their regular economic base, these attacks actually increased the Indians' need to raid to feed themselves. As the cycle of raids and retaliatory campaigns continued, the California Indian population plummeted.[72]

The federal government did little to help the situation. Negotiators met with Indian groups and signed treaties to establish reservations throughout central California. Vociferous local opposition and the probable high costs of the agreements persuaded the Senate to ignore the treaties. So while the Indians waited for government action, the murderous warfare against them continued. Several years later, when Edward F. Beale became the superintendent for Indian affairs in California, he struggled to set up five smaller reservations away from the areas most desired by the whites. The new reservations included some good land, but when farming villagers had to share the space with hunters and gatherers from the mountains, trouble came quickly. Many of the Indians fled back to their home areas, and by 1865 the reservations began to close. When the government placed tribal people on land without considering their economic practices it almost ensured that the efforts would fail. So too did the open and bitter hostility of many white Californians.[73]

In nearby Oregon, instead of mining, the new settlers came to farm. Here missionary activities and reports had stimulated interest in the region, and once the 1846 treaty between the United States and Britain fixed the international boundary, migration to the area increased. Joseph Lane, the first territorial governor, spoke for the settlers when he called for extinguishing Indian land title quickly. By 1850 Congress had established a commission to negotiate treaties and clear all Indians from the region west of the Cascade Mountains. Six treaties signed in 1851 failed to get Senate approval, so in 1853 negotiators signed new ones. These extinguished Indian title to most of the desired land and called for the tribes to be moved when and where the government chose. Delays and confusion brought violence, and in 1855 fighting broke out. It took several more years before the government could enforce its will in the area.[74]

In 1853 Washington became a separate territory. Isaac Stevens, its first governor, moved quickly to deal with Indian affairs. Recognizing that the tribes could not be forced from their traditional fishing territories without leading to suffering and probable violence, he tried to place the Indians on greatly reduced lands within their home areas. During 1854 and 1855 he held councils with the major Indian groups in Washington, forcing them to accept much-reduced landholdings. When some groups had to share lands with competitors the chiefs objected, but to no avail. Stevens secured the treaties, and the Senate ratified them. The Indians had signed only to gain time, however, and by mid-1855 they joined those in Oregon in fighting against the United States. The Yakimas and their allies of central Washington led the first resistance, but regular army troops defeated them, forcing the Indians onto the newly created reservations.[75]

Clearly American policy in the Northwest shared little with that of James Douglas in British Columbia. There he managed to preserve small reserves in traditional areas for local people with a minimum of violence. In the United States at the same time, the rapid population influx created pressures on regional officials to get the Indians out of the way quickly. When small tribes did not get safe reservations, as in California, rogue militia bands destroyed many of the native people.

Because of these many difficulties, during the 1850s federal officials began working toward what would evolve into the reservation system during the last half of the century. Despite the talk and political infighting, minor removals from one part of the frontier to another continued east of the Missouri River. Yet the acquisition of Texas, Oregon, California, and the rest of the Southwest during the late 1840s and 1850s forced basic changes in the thinking about what to do with the tribes. As long as they had been on the western border of the country there seemed little reason to disturb them. Now that the United States stretched beyond the plains for another thousand miles, the government could not ignore the issue, particularly once the California gold rush attracted thousands of whites to the Far West. Demands for protection for the immigrants grew. At the same time, interest in transcontinental railroads brought more whites onto the plains and mountains and led to the bitter warfare that swept across the West for the next three decades.

To deal with the tribes of the central plains the government chose Thomas Fitzpatrick, a former mountain man well known to the Indians, as its agent. Between 1846 and the early 1850s Fitzpatrick led the negotiations with many groups living between the Arkansas River and the Canadian border. In 1846 tribes living along the Platte River complained to federal authorities that the immigrants' wagon trains had frightened the buffalo and other game animals away from the river. Picturing themselves as poor, they reminded the government that "it has been customary when our white friends make a road through the Red man's country to remunerate them for the injury caused thereby."[76] When the government made no effort to compensate the tribes, they tried to tax the immigrants by stopping the wagon trains to beg or ask for a small payment. The accosted pioneers' outraged demands for protection from Indian depredations gradually pushed the government toward a new policy regarding the western tribes.

This pressure began in 1848 when agent Fitzpatrick recommended strong military escorts for whites traveling west and building army posts along the central overland trail. Few officials welcomed his ideas because they represented an expensive military measure just as the war with Mexico drew to a close. Army leaders themselves objected to building small isolated forts in the West. Nevertheless, in early 1849 the new president, Zachary Taylor, authorized a troop movement along the Oregon Trail to the West Coast, and in May

1849 the expedition set out from Fort Leavenworth. Along their route the soldiers purchased the fur trading posts that became Fort Laramie in Wyoming and Fort Hall in southern Idaho so troops might be stationed at those places.

During the next two years pioneers brought cholera, which devastated the tribes along the major trails. By 1850 the situation called for making some agreements with the tribes of the central plains, and both Fitzpatrick and his immediate supervisor, David Mitchell, suggested that the government offer some payment to the Indians to compensate for their reduced buffalo herds and other mishaps cause by the pioneers. As a result, Commissioner of Indian Affairs Orlando Brown called for a series of treaty meetings. By early 1851 Congress appropriated one hundred thousand dollars to pay for the talks. The tribes gathered slowly near the end of that summer at Fort Laramie to wait for federal officials and the presents they had been promised. Waiting became both tedious and dangerous as more than ten thousand Indians from many tribes, some of which were traditional enemies, faced fewer than three hundred soldiers at the post. Finally, in early September 1851 Superintendent Mitchell opened the talks. Slowly the officials persuaded tribal and band leaders to draw boundaries marking their home areas, and except for the Sioux, who disputed much of the area claimed by others, the proceedings moved well. The Fort Laramie Treaty signed that September specified tribal lands in the West for the first time.[77]

That agreement set the pattern for American dealings with most of the other western tribal groups, just as the Robinson-Superior and Robinson-Huron treaties with the tribes of the upper Great Lakes had done in Canada only a year earlier. In both instances white officials asked tribal leaders to designate their territorial claims and persuaded them to stay away from the encroaching whites. In neither country did the government have enough authority to actually enforce the terms of the agreement on either the Indians or the pioneers, but in Canada this remained less significant because of the small number of people involved in the interracial encounters. The flood of pioneers pouring across the American West, however, made it imperative that the government keep whites and Indians apart or have the entire region swept into bitter warfare. When the federal government proved unable or unwilling to separate the two groups, the peace collapsed and destructive and bloody clashes occurred. Distracted by its internal divisions over slavery and states' rights, the United States failed to establish any workable policy prior to 1860 other than trying to keep the two sides apart and prevent violence that way. In Canada most political energies focused on issues other than Indian affairs too, but authorities there had the luxuries of more space and time to shield them from most Indian-white violence.

8 Societies under Siege, 1860s–1890

 TALL AND THICK-NECKED, Toohoolhoolzote argued forcefully with the one-armed General Oliver Otis Howard. The soldier, accused of being soft on Indians, strove to disprove that by demanding that the Nez Percé vacate their traditional Wallowa Valley homeland in Oregon. Responding, the older dreamer prophet reminded Howard that this band of Nez Percé had never signed any agreement to move. Rather, he said, the land had come down to them from their fathers and they intended to keep it. Howard interrupted angrily that he had orders from the president and that he wanted to hear no more talk about beliefs, only removal. At that point Toohoolhoolzote answered, "I am telling you I am a chief! Who can tell me what to do in my own country?"[1] Both his tone and words angered the general, who shouted, "I am the man. I stand here for the president. . . . My orders are plain and will be executed."[2] Then he grabbed the Indian by one arm and with an aide walked him across the parade ground to the guardhouse. Following that he issued an ultimatum. The Nez Percé had thirty days to move their property and livestock or the army would drive them to the reservation.

This order set into motion events leading to the tragic 1877 Nez Percé flight toward Canada. It also demonstrated vividly the drastic changes many Indian groups in both nations experienced in their dealings with the rest of society during the last four decades of the nineteenth century. On both sides of the border, railroads stretched across the landscape bringing farmers, miners, and merchants while helping to destroy the plains buffalo herds. Bureaucrats and treaty negotiators followed, greatly reducing tribal landholdings and bringing freedom of movement to an end for most groups. Increasing numbers of teachers, missionaries, model farmers, and government agents brought renewed demands that tribal people cease practicing some of their cultural and religious ceremonies and adopt the invaders' economy and culture. Such urgings were not new in either country, but after 1860 many of the plains and western tribes encountered them for the first time. That led to bitter interracial conflict and crushing defeats for native peoples in both countries.

During the decades that followed, many western Indians in both countries became administered people. That is, government officials told them what they could do, as well as when, where, and how to do it. By the end of the era their loss of autonomy reached into most aspects of their lives. At the same time, substantial differences marked the tribal experiences on each side of the international border. In the United States the army campaigned repeatedly against tribes and bands declared hostile by government policy. Farther north, on the other hand, the North West Mounted Police usually managed to keep peace. Because of the continuing violence and bloodshed in the American West, churchmen, reformers, and other so-called friends of the Indian launched frequent movements to force the U.S. government to end the fighting, reform the operations of the Indian Office, and give them more say in the way tribal people were being treated. No direct parallel existed in Canada at the time. The issue of how to classify mixed-race peoples and then of what to do with them certainly differentiated actions in the two nations. In Canada the two mixed-race groups, the French-Indian Métis and the English-Scots-Indian country born, came to be recognized as a distinct people with some rights akin to those of the Indians. The United States, in contrast, ignored such people unless they chose to live as Indians with the tribe or band to which they were related.

While the differences appear marked in the two societies, frequent similarities continued as well. In fact, during this era the actions of the two countries became more alike than at any previous time. Both nations used education, particularly boarding schools, to wean the children and young people away from their cultures. Church and missionary activity had a large role in both countries; the churches actually operated many Indian schools in Canada. Both governments sought to isolate tribal people while pressuring them to accept churches, schools, and farms as helpers on the white man's path. While American agents demanded that all Indians become small farmers, their Canadian counterparts at least recognized that some of the Plains groups might succeed as stock raisers and small-time ranchers. Yet neither government would accept communal land use patterns so dear to the hearts of Indians, nor would they protect enough land for the tribal people to have a reasonable possibility of success raising livestock. Officials in both countries assumed that Indians had to become integrated into the society and economic system of their particular country. Regardless, few in either nation expected them to survive as identifiable peoples into the twentieth century.

Some tribal people living in the United States resorted to warfare to protect their lands and customs, while in Canada few violent confrontations occurred. Leaders in both countries responded to the continuing demands for more land cessions with delay, rejection, or compromise, but in almost every case they lost territory to the advancing whites. While a few groups such as a part of the Hunkpapa Sioux followed Sitting Bull into Canada briefly, and some Kickapoos fled from Texas into northern Mexico, this was not a popular option for most Indians. As they had done before, shamans and prophets offered guidance. They upheld past beliefs, offered new insights that combined elements of Christianity and tribal practices, or gradually accepted the missionaries' teachings. On reservations or reserves leaders supported education for the children to help the next generation better deal with the ever-increasing numbers of whites. In all of these choices, however, Indians had ever less chance to take the initiative as the century drew to a close.

CANADIAN INDIAN POLICY AT THE TIME OF CONFEDERATION

In Canada Indians complained during 1860 when they learned that the British had turned over the direction of Indian affairs to the local government. From their vantage point, that merely set the stage for worse things to come. The earlier relative goodwill and slight cooperation between Indian Office employees and tribal leaders faded quickly because the tribes considered the leaders of the United Canadas as little more than a pack of land thieves and speculators. During the years immediately preceding Confederation, the tribes of Canada West had made their wishes clear to anyone who paid attention. They wanted education and training, not for acculturation but for economic betterment. They petitioned the government for the repeal of the 1857 Gradual Civilization Act, collectively agreed to refuse further land sales, and rejected the enfranchisement program.[3] To accept it meant cultural suicide; while they might be encountering difficulties, their situation lacked the desperation that might have driven them to accept the Canadian scheme for their future.

Even though their objections to governmental actions seemed to have little impact, Indian unhappiness with national policies continued. The tribal people living on Manitoulin Island had developed two communities there: one at Manitowaning, which had failed by the late 1850s, and a second at Wikwemikong. The latter included nearly five hundred people, who based their economy primarily on traditional hunting, fishing, and gathering practices, and who mostly ignored Canadian efforts to persuade them to become farmers. This settlement of mostly Catholic people wanted no part of the whites' plan to change their society or to encourage pioneer settlement or fishing at the island. In 1860, after white demands that timberlands and fishing sites be made available for development became strident, the government sent several commissioners to obtain Indian cessions. Local village leaders rejected their offers out of hand, refusing to consider any sale of land or fisheries. Because the government had authorized only tiny and clearly inadequate payments, the embarrassed commissioners left without anything to show for their efforts.[4]

Canadian authorities refused to allow Indians to thwart their plan. The government leased several prize sites to commercial fishermen without getting any Indian surrender of tribal rights. That action and continuing demands from would-be settlers and lumbermen that portions of the island be opened for settlement forced the bureaucrats to try again. Once more to their dismay they found that the Indians still had no intention to sell or trade away any part of their land. Yet divisions existed among the islanders, and the whites exploited these quickly. Indian traditionalists who had accepted Catholicism but retained their native economic practices opposed any sale of resources, but the commissioners found a small group at one end of the island that agreed to accept their presents. During 1862 they fashioned a treaty with this group, which all of the islanders had a chance to sign if they so chose. Traditional groups not only refused to sign but rejected the legitimacy of the treaty and in late 1862 moved to expel longtime resident whites from the island. Harassment of white fishermen and of Indians who accepted Canadian demands continued, and when the government sent William Gibbard to pay treaty funds to the islanders, several confrontations ensued. He tried to arrest several village leaders and the priests who lived with the Indians, but their belligerence forced him to flee the island. Shortly after, the government invited the Wikwemikong chiefs to Quebec City to discuss their grievances, and the difficulties soon faded.[5]

While mild by American standards, the incident demonstrates that Canadian officials made their share of mistakes, and that the eastern tribes knew enough about their rights that the government could not push them around as it pleased. It also shows that interethnic violence lay closer to the surface than officials then realized or would admit. This proved true in British Columbia too during and after the 1858 gold rush to the Fraser River. There tribes had little experience with whites other than the Hudson's Bay Company traders, whose best interests lay in keeping the villagers satisfied and at peace. The violent and aggressive miners angered several tribes of the interior. Unlike the fur men, the miners offered the Indian nothing. Instead, they tramped through the country taking what they pleased.

Not surprisingly, the whites' actions brought Indian retaliation. In 1862 British Columbia authorities authorized building a road from the coast to the interior of the province. By summer 1863 some Chilcotin Indians had begun working as laborers and packers for the project. That brought them into close contact with the whites, whose actions and attitudes often angered the Indians. In April 1864 this led to violence. The Chilcotins began a series of attacks on the road workers and other whites nearby. They killed a ferry operator, wrecked the ferry, and while looting a store took large supplies of powder and lead. On 30 April 1864 they killed nine members of a twelve-man work party and later that same day shot four other laborers. The violence stopped briefly, but in late May another group attacked a pack train killing three more whites and wounding several others. Then in June the Indians killed a settler who had seized a favorite camping site and had driven its inhabitants away.[6] When peace returned, eighteen whites had been killed.

These actions angered coastal residents. In Victoria frightened citizens demanded military action. The local newspaper complained that the authorities moved too slowly and called for popular justice. While the whites talked about revenge, six Indian men turned themselves in, bringing gifts to cover the dead following Indian custom. The authorities arrested, tried, and executed five of the men. In early 1865 two more Indian men surrendered. They experienced the same fate as their predecessors. Clearly this uprising demonstrates that when Canadian actions injured tribal self-interest by taking land, camping sites, or other resources, violence might be expected. White aggression brought the same ill will and interracial difficulties in Canada as it did south of the border.[7]

During the late 1860s events that shaped the long-term relations between the races took place in London and the provincial capitals in Canada. Moving to grant more local autonomy to parts of their far-flung empire, the British established the Dominion of Canada in 1867 under the provisions of the British North America Act. The new government had authority over Ontario and Quebec (dropping the earlier names of Canada West and Canada East), as well as Nova Scotia and New Brunswick, and within just a few years it would stretch its control west to British Columbia and north and west to encompass all of Rupert's Land, the vast holdings of the Hudson's Bay Company that lay west of Lake Superior and north into the Arctic. As Canadian leaders organized their new government they looked nervously at the United States, fearing American territorial expansion at their expense, and with good reason. In 1867, the same year as Canadian confederation, William Seward, the American secretary of state, purchased Alaska from Russia. The specter of American territorial growth nearly became an obsession for some Canadian leaders. John A. McDonald, who headed the first government, admitted that "I would be quite willing, personally, to leave that whole country [the West] a wilderness for the next half-century, but I fear if Englishmen do not go there, Yankees will."[8]

For the Indians living beyond Lake Superior this attitude brought mixed results: positive because of governmental determination to keep peace and thus avoid giving the Americans any reason to intervene in the Canadian West; and negative because federal policies encouraged railroad building, settlement, and agricultural development. Despite the growing influx of non-Indians, no army marched west to do combat with the resident tribes. Rather, the North West Mounted Police would serve military, police, and civil governmental functions for the next generation. Their presence in the West showed American authorities that the Canadians could direct western affairs with competence and helped prevent some of the worst difficulties experienced by tribes not too far below the border. At the same time the immense area and the tiny population in western Canada made the Mounties' tasks relatively easy. For example, as late as 1880, when the census of the Dakotas showed 133,147 inhabitants, the 1881 count for the entire Canadian Northwest—excluding Indians, but including Métis and whites—turned up only 6,974 people.[9]

Because the Canadians clearly wanted to avoid trouble with the western tribes, they began their dealings with them using long-standing practices. At least at first, Indian leaders encountered familiar elements such as treaties, land cessions, annuities, reserves, schools, and agents. Yet the new government soon shifted its approach. The long-practiced effort to protect tribal groups and their lands while working gradually to acculturate them gave way to the enfranchisement policy that sought rapid assimilation. This signaled the Canadian officials' desire to dismember the tribes and move the native people into the general society as quickly as possible, exactly the opposite of American policy at the time.

For at least a generation the Indians of eastern Canada had refused to allow previous enfranchisement legislation to function. The traditional chiefs persuaded band members to ignore the program. One angry agent complained that the Six Nations' council had gone so far as to publicly state they were "wholly adverse to their people taking the advantages offered" under the law.[10] Having failed once, the government tried again. According to the deputy superintendent general responsible for Indian affairs, the Enfranchisement Act of 1869 was "designed to lead the Indian people by degrees to mingle with the white race in the ordinary avocations of life."[11] Even the title of the new law signaled its changed intent. Earlier legislation had called for the gradual acculturation of the tribal people. The new act aimed at the rapid assimilation of individual Indians into the majority society. Its framers expected the law to end the tribes' state of wardship by transforming the communally oriented people into individualists.

Because of its goals, the Enfranchisement Act sought to increase governmental interference within native communities sharply. Earlier, Canadian authorities had required proof of some Indian blood for individuals to be recognized as tribal members. Now the legislation excluded anyone with less than one-quarter Indian parentage, adopting a specific blood quantum policy prior to the United States'. In theory this new law limited tribal peoples' ability to define themselves or to grant or withhold band membership. Supposedly it excluded native women who married non-Indians from tribal roles. They and their children now lost any rights to their reserve benefits.[12] Trying to apply European ideas about family membership to the native people created a new minority group that exists to the present. These people are biologically and perhaps even culturally Indians, but they are not classified as Indians. Along with the Métis people of the plains they constitute another group in the ethnic mosaic of modern Canada, one that at least technically does not exist in the United States.

These actions by the new Canadian authorities placed the government in the awkward position of striving for two mutually exclusive goals. On the one hand, they hoped to assimilate their charges rapidly, and on the other hand, they continued to segregate tribal people. Somehow Indians were to learn the best aspects of white society while avoiding getting much experience in dealing with it. While the government worked to disrupt tribal life, at first its efforts had only modest impact. Indians ignored the new law and continued to admit whites and mixed-bloods to their band memberships. For a time the federal authorities had too few employees and too little money to check tribal rolls carefully. Still, the band leaders objected repeatedly to the new level of federal interference in their lives. Complaining about the whites' meddling, they petitioned that "Indian women may have the privilege of marrying when and whom they please without subjecting themselves to exclusion or expulsion from the tribe," which the law mandated.[13]

Federal officials paid little attention to Indian complaints while they took other steps to push the tribal people into the social mainstream of Canada. They tried to attack the power of hereditary chiefs and religious leaders by establishing a system for electing chiefs and tribal councils, at least among the eastern groups. All males aged twenty-one or older could vote, and elected leaders would serve three-year terms. On reserves where life chiefs still governed, the whites accepted their presence and allowed them continuing authority for a time. Not satisfied with changing the governance, however, the legislators gave federal officers authority to remove such leaders for dishonesty, intemperance, or immorality. Clearly the bureaucrats assumed that whatever authority the tribes retained would make little long-term difference because they hoped to control and direct all of the important phases of community life.[14]

MOUNTING CRISES IN THE AMERICAN WEST

While Canadian leaders struggled to get their new broader government in order to keep relative calm, nothing of the sort happened in the United States. Despite nearly a century of experience with tribal people by this time, American officials found themselves experiencing the most difficult times with the tribal people they could remember. The expansion that followed the Mexican War increasingly brought hordes of pioneers into the new territories of New Mexico, Kansas, and Nebraska. With their creation, the only large territory still reserved for the Indians was the present state of Oklahoma, which soon became established as Indian Territory. There and elsewhere in the West, by 1860 the treaties signed at Fort Laramie with the Plains tribes no longer prevented sporadic violence. The advent of the American Civil War drew most of the regular army forces stationed in the West eastward to help put down the rebellion of the Southern states. This meant that at a time of increasing westward migration and a continuous stream of new mineral discoveries, few regular soldiers stood ready to separate whites and Indians in the West.

Both the North and South sought to recruit Indian troops for use in the West, and the Civil War years brought great hardship to the groups in the Indian Territory. There both the Cherokees and Creeks suffered internal divisions, providing troops for both sides of the conflict. For other Indian Territory tribes, the disappearance of the blue coats, as they called the soldiers, ended what little protection they had received from the government. In a few cases, some Plains Indians saw the troop removal as a sign of weakness or distraction and moved to exploit the situation. Before long, however, the government sent volunteer units to the recently abandoned garrisons. Occasionally the volunteers lacked the discipline of the regulars, and their presence in the Indian country only promoted continuing misunderstanding and violence.

With the regulars gone, during the summer of 1862 the eastern Sioux living near Mankato tried to expel the whites from their homeland. Having agreed to land cessions earlier, and feeling closed in by the increasing numbers of pioneers, the Indians struck when their annuities failed to arrive. Actually, the "Great Sioux War," as the settlers called it, began mostly by accident after a minor incident in which several young Sioux men returning from hunting had first been refused water and then offered alcohol. They became drunk and killed a farm family in central Minnesota. Learning of the killings, Chief Little Crow apparently decided that his people had only two choices, flight or battle, so he persuaded his followers to attack. They did so across much of Minnesota, where bitter fighting occurred at the town of New Ulm and several other nearby small communities. Soldiers and militiamen rushed to the scene, tracked the tribe after it fled, and defeated and captured many of the Indians. In December 1862 the army hanged thirty-eight of the captives at Mankato, but some of the warriors had fled, spreading news of their actions among so-called hostile groups on the plains.[15]

By 1864 raiding bands of Sioux, Pawnees, Cheyennes, and Arapahos had cleared many pioneers from the central plains, leading John Evans, the governor of Colorado, to claim that the raiders had virtually isolated Denver and the mining camps in the central Rocky Mountains. That brought retaliation from the Colorado militia, and in November 1864 the Sand Creek Massacre occurred, one of the few incidents so labeled in which the Indians were the victims. The militiamen tore into the Indian village, which flew a large American flag to signal peaceful intentions. When the shouting stopped, the pioneers had killed and mutilated two hundred men, women, and children. This carnage prompted investigations by the army and Congress. Meanwhile, the survivors fled, bringing their story of white treachery to other villagers; thus the war continued, shifting northward where the miners pouring into the northern Rockies had to cross Sioux and Cheyenne territory.[16] Even though the Civil War had ended by 1865, Indians and whites fought a bitter contest for much of the next generation in the West. Along the Bozeman Trail leading north from the Platte River Road to the mining camps of Montana, the Sioux bottled up the troops, at times virtually besieging the isolated army outposts.

Unable to maintain peace as the nation expanded, American leaders hurried to respond to outraged public cries for the fighting to stop. In 1865 Congress dispatched the Doolittle Commission to investigate the situation. While the commissioners toured the West, other federal negotiators concluded treaties with many tribes. Some of these agreements went beyond merely reaffirming peace, assigning particular tribes and bands to their territorial lands; yet the agreements proved transitory because they failed to address what was becoming an increasingly difficult problem—how to keep intruders out of areas reserved for Indians and how to keep the Indians away from the major immigrant trails across the West. In addition, neither side knew what to do about the rapidly diminishing supply of buffalo and other game on which the tribes depended for their basic food supply. As a result, the treaties and commissions failed to halt the sporadic raiding or the movement of miners and others through Indian lands.

The Sioux, particularly the bands under Red Cloud, warned frontier officials that the Boseman Trail to the Montana mining camps ran through the heart of their best hunting grounds. They threatened to attack civilians or soldiers alike along the trail, and on 21 December 1866 they struck. Warriors following High Back Bone lured Captain William J. Fetterman and eighty of his men into an ambush near Fort Kearney, killing the entire command. News of the attack angered national leaders, but they had no good way to respond. As Congress debated how to deal with this new crisis, the long-awaited Doolittle Committee Report appeared. Its authors found that the Indians had experienced severe hardship because of the loss of buffalo and other game and concluded that most hostilities resulted from white encroachments or provocations. The report startled people at the time, as it called for enlarging the reservation system and for increased efforts to acculturate the tribal people.[17]

As citizens called for protection and army leaders proposed crushing the Sioux, humanitarian groups in the East focused public attention on the Indian problem. Looking for a peaceful solution, the Johnson administration agreed to abandon the forts along the Boseman Trail and established a general peace commission to end the conflict soon. That group, including General William T. Sherman and three other generals as well as three civilians, headed west. In October 1867 they held a treaty council with the tribes of the southern plains at Medicine Lodge Creek in Kansas. Five thousand Indians came together to feast at the commission's expense and to hear what the Great Father's representatives had to say. The negotiators reminded their listeners that the buffalo would disappear soon and that they needed to learn the white man's way if they wanted their children to survive.[18]

At first Indian leaders tried to ignore the commissioners' warnings. Silver Brooch, a Comanche band leader, reminded the negotiators that his people had been ill treated for years and that past promises made to them had gone unmet. Because of white mistreatment many Comanches had died. This time he was openly skeptical about getting any of the benefits promised for signing yet another treaty. "I shall wait until next spring to see if these things shall be given us," he said. If not, he continued, "I and my young men will return with our wild brothers to live on the prairie."[19] This apparent threat caused little stir among the commissioners, but other Indian spokesmen echoed Silver Brooch's unhappiness. Ten Bears, speaking for another Comanche group, stated that his people wanted no part of farming or a sedentary existence. "I wish you would not keep insisting on putting us on reservations," he complained.[20] With considerable feeling, Satanta, the aging Kiowa leader, rejected the commissioners' proposals too. He asked them to tell the president that "when the buffalo leave the country, we will let him know. By that time we will be ready to live in houses."[21]

Despite their reluctance, many Indian leaders on the southern plains realized that each year fewer buffalo appeared and that the number of intruding Americans increased. Clearly the commissioners spoke the truth when they told the tribal people that they had to change their way of life or be destroyed. So, despite their misgivings, on 21 October 1867 leaders of the Kiowas, Kiowa-Apaches, Arapahos, Cheyennes, and Comanches signed the Treaty of Medicine Lodge. They agreed to remain at peace, to surrender vast portions of their hunting territories, to live on assigned reservations, and to accept the white man's instruction in farming. In return for their signatures, the government negotiators promised them annuities for the next thirty years and immediate access to the piles of presents displayed prominently throughout the talks.[22]

Finishing its work in the south, the Peace Commission turned its attention to the tribes of the northern plains the next spring. They sent messengers to encourage leaders of hostile bands to negotiate at Fort Laramie, but Red Cloud refused. His price for peace had not changed. "We are on the mountains looking down on the soldiers and the forts," he replied. "When we see the soldiers moving away and the forts abandoned, then I will come down and talk."[23] Leaders of other Sioux groups replied in similar terms. When Red Cloud's followers saw the troops march out of the Boseman Trail forts, headed south toward Fort Laramie, they burned the abandoned structures to the ground, then moved slowly to the council site. During the summer and autumn of 1868 the bands and tribes of the northern plains signed the Treaty of Fort Laramie. In that agreement the government accepted Sioux demands that Americans stay out of tribal hunting grounds and that no forts or new roads would be built along the Powder River. For their part, the northern plains Indians agreed to stay on fixed reservations in Dakota, Montana, and Wyoming, to remain at peace, and to refrain from harassing railroad survey and construction crews as they moved through Indian country.[24]

No sooner had the ink dried on this latest round of treaty negotiations than violence flared once again. Southern Cheyenne raids in Kansas provided plenty of incidents for headlines in the East. With some of the plains-area people back at war, the peace initiative appeared dead. Meeting in Chicago in October 1868, the peace commissioners wrangled bitterly, but the four generals consistently outvoted their civilian counterparts and declared that the time to consider Indian tribes as domestic dependent nations had passed. They wanted to dismember the tribes, end the treaty system, rescind the article of the Treaty of Medicine Lodge giving Indians permission to hunt off their reservations, and bring in more troops to keep the peace. Ironically, only a few weeks after the commissioners had denounced the Indians and the entire peace process bitterly, the last of the significant Sioux leaders, Red Cloud and Man Afraid of His Horse, rode into Fort Laramie to sign the treaty. Despite negotiations such as these, however, fighting raged sporadically for much of the next decade.[25]

Continuing public denunciations of the conduct of Indian relations persuaded incoming president Ulysses S. Grant that he needed competent and honest people in the Indian Office. Even before his inauguration in March 1869 religious leaders asked him to nominate men suggested by the Christian denominations to serve as agents on the new western reservations. Because the first delegation to suggest this plan to Grant happened to be Quakers, his subsequent approach came to be known as the Quaker policy. While hoping for peace, Grant had few illusions about achieving it completely. In fact, he threatened that "those who do not accept this policy will find the new administration ready for a sharp and severe war policy."[26] At that point, unlike their Canadian counterparts, U.S. leaders anticipated needing troops to keep the peace or to punish those who broke it. During the early 1870s the government did appoint individuals to agency and other jobs in the Indian service, drawing them at least in part from lists submitted by various religious groups. Still, some of the denominations got responsibility for tribes or reservations for which they had no nominees, while Protestant-Catholic competition brought continuing arguing and discord, as it did in Canada.

Another basic part of the peace policy as it emerged called for the appointment of a nonpartisan board of volunteers—the Board of Indian Commissioners—to supervise the administration of Indian affairs, serving as sort of inspector general. The reformers hoped that reports by this group would focus enough public attention on the bureaucratic functions to keep them honest. Leading wealthy philanthropists served on the board for the next several generations. They traveled across the country visiting reservations, inspecting the records, talking with Indians and whites alike, and issuing an annual report as well as a stream of comments, suggestions, and newspaper columns through the last decades of the nineteenth century. In historical perspective it is clear that the reformers never had much chance of making long-term changes in the system. They could only recommend actions to the secretary of the interior, the commissioner of Indian affairs, and the various congressional committees charged with the operation of Indian affairs.

As a result, membership on the board changed rapidly, and soon even the most dedicated reformers despaired of bringing any real changes to the system. Still, Grant appointed his friend and aide General Ely S. Parker, a Seneca, as the first Indian to serve as the commissioner of Indian affairs, and during Grant's first term in office he approved the assigning of more than seventy of the agencies to the various church groups asking for a chance to clean up the mess in the Indian Office. The peace policy included one other basic change—that of ending the treaty system. The Peace Commission had recommended the move, and in 1871, when the two houses of Congress became hopelessly deadlocked over Indian appropriations, the debate ended with an agreement to halt all treaty negotiations. From 1871 agreements between the tribes and the government continued, but now as executive agreements rather than treaties that superseded regular legislation.[27]

As its name indicated, Grant's policy aimed at peaceful relations between the races, but obstacles large and small prevented it from achieving that goal. While the secretary of the Board of Indian Commissioners, Vincent Colyer—dubbed "Vincent the Good" by his detractors—traveled throughout the West negotiating agreements and laying out reservations, neither the Indians nor the local frontier citizens understood or supported his efforts. Worse, agents living among the tribal people had the difficult task of explaining why supplies or annuities promised by previous agents or federal negotiators arrived late or failed to arrive at all. Tribal leaders faced rumblings among their followers, particularly from the young warriors who grew restive while waiting for the Great Father's men to keep their promises. On the plains the large tribes that traditionally followed the buffalo herds found their hunting less successful as each year passed. Correctly blaming the encroaching whites for their troubles, they became restive, and violence often followed. During the years under the peace policy and for another decade into the mid-1880s scattered warfare continued. Sporadic fighting with the Sioux and Cheyennes on the northern plains proved only one part of the story. The Modoc War of 1872–73, the Red River War of 1874–75, the flight of the Nez Percé in 1877, the Ute War of 1879, and the Apache wars of the 1870–80s all punctuated the western story with violence and death.

Most attention, however, fell on the wars with the Sioux on the northern plains. Although technically at peace since the Treaty of Fort Laramie in 1868, the Plains tribes kept up a pattern of minor raids throughout the period. Then, Colonel George A. Custer led a column of soldiers, miners, and reporters into the Black Hills during the summer of 1874, setting the stage for a final showdown in that region. Claiming the Black Hills as a sacred part of their heritage, the Sioux appealed to the agents to remove the illegal miners, but to no avail. When the authorities took no action, the Indians began raiding mining camps and supply trains moving toward the area. Their actions brought a quick response and the most famous military action in American western history. In June 1876 Colonel Custer led a large part of the Seventh Cavalry Regiment to its destruction on the banks of the Little Bighorn—or the Greasy Grass River, as the Indians called it. Mistakenly thinking that Crazy Horse and Sitting Bull led only perhaps 150 lodges of Indians there, Custer charged the camp. Instead of the modest numbers of Sioux he anticipated, the impetuous colonel met the full force of the northern tribes that day. Gall, Hump, and many other war leaders joined with Crazy Horse and Sitting Bull to destroy most of Custer's immediate command. News of the defeat electrified the nation, and soon columns of troops chased the offending Sioux in all directions. The war ended the following summer, but only after Sitting Bull and hundreds of his followers had fled north across the "medicine line" into Canada for refuge.[28]

American violence and warfare with the tribal people resulted from a combination of factors, few of which could have been avoided. The native societies in the West were well led and had strong attachments to their homelands, and some had strong warrior traditions. Moreover, they lived atop land seen as desirable for agriculture or athwart roads and trails over which thousands of pioneers trudged. Some of the tribal lands encompassed valuable mineral bodies or timber stands, and westerners had little patience for the idea that those valuable resources should be monopolized by the Indians. Few accepted the Indians' right to continue living a traditional lifestyle. Although only a small proportion openly called for destroying the tribes, many western Americans wanted the government to push the tribal people out of their way. On that issue they shared values with the Canadians. In both nations the people living nearest the tribes wanted them moved. They gave little thought to where Indians should live, and even those who supported the various acculturation programs failed to accept them as equals or to welcome acculturated Indians as their neighbors with much enthusiasm. By the late nineteenth century this left few options for the western tribes.

While the United States and its tribal people fought bloody wars in the decades after 1860, Canada usually avoided major confrontation and bloodshed. More often than not, this resulted from the vast area and small populations north of the border rather than to any superior policy or more careful handling of Indian-related issues by Canadian officials. In fact, in many ways leaders in Ottawa knew less about their western regions and peoples than did their counterparts in the United States. Nevertheless, the fact is that Canada had only two major crises in its west, and these came primarily from the mixed-race population, the Métis, rather than from the Indian tribes there. In both cases, the so-called Red River War in 1869–70 and the Riel-led Métis uprising of 1885–86, the confrontations resulted from government inattention, high-handedness, and parsimony with the Métis and Indians alike. In many ways, the grievances of the groups in Manitoba and later in Saskatchewan paralleled the fears of the Indians there and in the American West during the same decades. New people moved into long-occupied regions, the governments threatened their land base and economic survival, and social prejudice against their customs, language, and sense of independence all combined to produce explosive situations on the frontiers of both nations.

The continued slaughter of buffalo in the United States and their disappearance north of the border brought the Indians to their knees eventually, but in Canada other factors combined to cause trouble between the tribes and the government. At Confederation the new nation included only four provinces, but in 1869 Rupert's Land, the vast holdings of the Hudson's Bay Company, became part of Canada. The next year, 1870, the government established the new western province of Manitoba, while in 1871 British Columbia joined the country, and two years later Prince Edward Island did the same. In their rush to make Canada a continental power, the Ottawa leaders faced daunting obstacles and at times ignored basic problems. Still, by 1869 they had passed the Enfranchisement Act, which incorporated existing rules about tribal membership and protection for Indian lands. It also created a new system that in theory could sidestep the traditional tribal leaders whenever the bureaucrats decided that was necessary.

Assuming that they had settled Indian matters with that legislation, the leadership turned its attention to the west, present-day Manitoba. There a substantial group of Métis and country-born people had lived for years, mostly south of Lake Winnipeg near the forks of the Red and Assiniboine Rivers, just north of Minnesota. As did the Plains tribes, these people depended heavily on their annual buffalo hunt to provide a large part of their annual food and trade supply. In addition to their hunting, however, they maintained homes and small farms along the Red and Assiniboine Rivers; their landholding practices followed the Quebec–Saint Lawrence Valley practice of having narrow but deep lots fronting on the rivers and extending back from the water. As long as they lived within the domain of the Hudson's Bay Company, nobody bothered the Métis settlements, and to the villagers it was clear which family owned what land. Once Canada assumed control of the area, however, the peculiar landholdings and the lack of any careful recording of local claims put the westerners and their new and largely unwelcome government on a collision course.

In their fear of possible American intervention and land seizures in the West, Ottawa officials neglected to consult in any way with the Métis people of Manitoba. In 1869, immediately after getting title to the region, the government sent out survey crews to bring landholdings in the West into line with those in Ontario. Following closely on the heels of the surveyors, William McDougall, the newly appointed governor for Rupert's Land, arrived. Although Ottawa had sent a governor, it neglected to provide for any local participation in governing the region, to the dismay of many living there. Fearing that Canadian officials might ignore their customary landholding patterns, angry at having virtually no say in their own government, and deeply suspicious of Canadian motives for moving in on them, the mixed-race peoples of the West organized under the leadership of Louis Riel Jr., a Montreal-educated Métis, to proclaim their own local government, establish courts, and block Canadian penetration of the region until the disputes could be settled. Riel proclaimed a provisional government in December 1869, and the next year Manitoba joined the confederation as a province, if only a small one.[29]

In trying to settle the confusing land claims in the West, the Manitoba Act reserved 1.4 million acres of land for the next generation of Métis. Placing this group with tribal people in the province, the law called for land to be set aside so the government would be able to extinguish the Indian title to lands in the province. As far as Ottawa was concerned, at least here, Métis and Indians got the same treatment. Unlike the mixed-race people in the United States, however, in Canada the Métis experienced a different relationship to the government. The Métis had at least a claim to aboriginal title to their land, but they remained a separate element within the Canadian ethnic mosaic. Although part Indian, they had different rights, and generally the government classed them as a distinct people. By 1870, then, in Canada the classification of native peoples included what would come down to the present as four distinct groups—status Indians, non-status Indians (people who might be Indian by blood or culture but not by legal definition), Métis, and Inuit, the people called Eskimos in the United States.

Some decades earlier, American authorities had recognized the existence of a mixed-race population, but with few exceptions the government made no specific provisions for them. By the 1820s federal negotiators had begun recognizing these people by allowing them to claim individual allotments of land. During that same era leaders in a few tribes sought special treatment for their mixed-race relatives; yet they also asked that similar provisions be made for whites who had befriended them or offered them special favors or help. Still, up to 1830 American treaties made no specific gifts to mixed-race people. This changed temporarily in that year when several treaties concluded at Prairie du Chien called for establishing two of what they called half-breed reservations, one in Minnesota and the second in eastern Nebraska. These both lasted several decades but represent an anomaly in American policy toward people who occasionally got land or cash, but who more often stayed with their tribal relatives.[30]

Despite the differing experiences of mixed-race people in the two countries, Indians on each side of the border faced similar governmental policies toward land acquisition and pioneer settlement. For example, both nations used treaties or other agreements to extinguish tribal land claims. Ironically, in the same year that the U.S. Congress ended its treaty process, 1871, Canadian officials began negotiations for the first of the numbered treaties (1–11) there. Each of these agreements varied somewhat because Indian spokesmen insisted on particular provisions such as hunting rights, annuities, schools, tools, farm equipment, and even a medicine chest for each agency. Compared to such accords in the United States, these gave the tribal people smaller land reserves, tiny annuities, and fewer other benefits. Yet the treaties resulted from real and even tense negotiations. Although they came as prepared documents, Indian demands forced Canadian officials to make changes and additions. U.S. officials, in contrast, even after they stopped negotiating treaties, tried to dictate executive agreements in their accustomed unilateral manner.[31]

While the Indians and the Canadian government remained at peace during the nation's first decade in existence, by the mid-1880s this broke down. Without an army, Canada turned to a uniquely British institution for its peacekeeping force. Based on the model of the Royal Irish Constabulary, in 1873 the government created the North West Mounted Police. Hoping to keep peace, regulate the introduction of alcohol, and discourage American freebooters from crossing the Montana border, the first units marched west a year later. Distinctly Canadian, the NWMP provided an administrative framework that differed substantially from American frontier institutions for government and law enforcement. In place of the divided civil-military authority in the American West, the Mounties combined both functions. An individual Mountie could investigate a crime, pursue, capture, arrest, and incarcerate the accused, gather the evidence, try the defendant, pass sentence, and even escort the criminal to prison. His duties varied widely from serving as a local justice of the police to participating in military actions.[32] In the United States the Indian Office dealt with civil affairs while the army handled military ones. Generally speaking, by combining functions in a single force, the Canadian government avoided some of the worst difficulties that occurred south of the border.

Yet try as they might, the tribes and Canadian officials could not avoid all of the troubles endemic to a large geographical region with few people, inadequate communication facilities, and rapidly diminishing buffalo herds. Although fewer military conflicts occurred than in the United States, the basic issues remained similar. By the mid-1880s most of the vast buffalo herds had disappeared, and some of the Indians began asking for help to change their economy and way of life. While U.S. troops to the south crisscrossed the plains trying to keep the tribes on their assigned reservation land, Canada used no troops because the Indians chose not to flee. With the hunting peoples exhausting their game supply, their economic patterns needed to change rapidly, and neither the government that would have to pay for that change nor the Indians themselves who would have to adapt to a radically different style of life wanted to face the effort needed to do the job.

The Cree and Blackfoot peoples of the plains bore the brunt of the drastic changes sweeping across the west. Because some groups had complained about their benefits under earlier treaties, during the 1875 talks the Cree leader Big Bear voiced suspicions about dealing with the whites. When a government spokesman offered presents to the Indians, Big Bear warned other leaders that by accepting the gifts they might be agreeing to things not spoken there. He urged the other band chiefs to reject the presents, likening them to the bait trappers used to catch foxes. "We want none of the Queen's presents," he told the government spokesman George McDougall. "Let your Chiefs come like men to talk to us."[33] Clearly he saw the threat to Indian welfare posed by increasing white penetration of the plains and by surrendering tribal lands.

Yet neither Big Bear nor other chiefs opposed talking with government officers or considering treaty signing if they saw that as being in the best interests of their people. His contemporary Crowfoot, a Blackfoot leader, admitted that the Canadian Indians could not expect to depend on buffalo hunting for long. In an 1876 meeting with a visiting NWMP inspector, he said that "we shall all see the day is coming when the buffalo will all be killed, and we shall have nothing to live on."[34] He hoped that when that happened, the whites would treat the tribes fairly. He also calmed the inspector's fears that the Canadian tribes would move south and join forces with Sitting Bull and his Sioux followers in their war against the United States.

Three years later Crowfoot confronted Canadian officials again. By then the near-disappearance of the buffalo herds had forced many Plains people to sell their horses in exchange for flour as well as resorting to eating antelope, gophers, and even mice. In July 1879 Crowfoot told the visiting Edgar Dewdney that "if you will drive away the Sioux and make a hole for the buffalo to come in we won't bother you about grub, but if you don't you must feed us for we are starving."[35] Despite this obvious need, Ottawa officials failed to help. Instead, they ignored or broke several provisions of the 1876 treaty, refused to mark off the lands the Indians wanted, denied some of the bands food vitally necessary for survival, and forced them to move away from the U.S. border to get their treaty payments. Although the Crees accepted reserves out of the region they had requested, by 1884 leaders of a dozen bands met to protest inadequacies of government actions and to negotiate better reserve locations and more assistance from the government. Viewing these Indian actions as dangerous, Lieutenant Governor Edgar Dewdney did all he could to disrupt intertribal cooperation and to force compliance with existing treaties.[36]

While violence erupted on the Plains in 1885, growing Indian militancy did not start the rebellion that year. Rather, the fears and dissatisfactions of the Métis people and their recruitment of the erratic Louis Riel from his home in the United States brought matters on the Plains to a head. The administration of John A. MacDonald knew little of western issues and seems to have cared even less. After the 1869 Red River crisis, when some Métis leaders had called for payments to surrender their land, the government had recognized their land claims in Manitoba. Now, however, MacDonald wanted no part of further expenses in the West. The earlier handling of Métis land claims and the quick sale of their land scrip persuaded him that the 1869 solution had been a mistake. Thus, when the federal government refused to consider their complaints, Saskatchewan Métis leaders sent for Riel, hoping that his experiences in negotiating with Ottawa might prove beneficial. Instead, through what might be described as a comedy of errors, the government, the Métis, and the Indians came to blows on the Plains. When the fighting ended the government won, hanged Riel, and sentenced Poundmaker and Big Bear to long prison terms despite the efforts of both men to avoid the fighting. After the massive invasion that the Riel Rebellion called forth, neither the Métis nor the Indians of the Plains raised much public objection to government policies in the West.[37]

EDUCATING FOR ENFRANCHISEMENT

With their military defeats in both countries mainly completed during the 1880s, the tribes awaited further government actions anxiously. Soon they encountered government agents, missionaries, schoolteachers, and demands that they become sedentary farmers. Ironically, bureaucrats decided that the tribal people should live and work in isolation to speed their absorption into the Canadian and American societies. Somehow they thought that Indians would learn personal discipline, the responsibilities of citizenship, and how to function in a capitalist economy in a foreign culture when they had few successful examples on which to model their actions. At the same time, the whites tried to control all decision making within tribal communities. Teachers, government agents, and missionaries told the Indians what to do, when, where, and how they should be doing their tasks, and gave them little to say about how their economy, social life, or even religion was to function. Nevertheless, tribal people continued to choose which parts of the white man's culture they would adopt.

Except for negotiating the numbered treaties and creating the Northwest Mounted Police, Canadian authorities had taken little notice of Indian affairs in the era immediately following Confederation. Then in 1876, while the United States celebrated its centennial, the parliament passed the first Indian Act, which codified earlier laws and indicated the direction of future policy. Planned to achieve the goals of the Enfranchisement Act of 1869, the Indian Act established federal machinery for an all-out attack on tribal and band government. At first officials applied it sporadically to the eastern tribes, but before long they tried to use it with all Indian groups. The Indian Department hoped to break up reserves, assign land to individuals, begin and operate schools, and literally force enfranchisement on the unwilling people. This full-scale acculturative program differed sharply from U.S. programs at the same time. While both nations wanted to end the Indian problem by making the tribal people disappear as distinct and recognizable ethnic groups, the U.S. government failed to offer citizenship as an incentive. It continued to negotiate treaties and other agreements with the tribes. In fact, in its 1884 *Elk v. Wilkins* decision the U.S. Supreme Court ruled that Indians were not eligible for citizenship. Thus at the time Indians could not enjoy full legal rights within American society, while in Canada the government invited them to do just that.[38]

In the East, efforts to control virtually every aspect of Indian life followed the 1876 call for enfranchisement. The authorities assumed that they had the right to do as they pleased with the tribal people. They issued location tickets giving individuals the right to use a particular plot within the reserve. When Indians became enfranchised, these were similar to the individual landholdings that the Dawes Act brought to reservation dwellers in the United States. Canadian authorities hoped that after young Indians finished the reservation or boarding schools they would go to the universities and colleges to become lawyers, medical doctors, or ministers and priests. Then they would automatically be enfranchised. The system rarely worked as planned because the officials who devised this scheme had never asked the tribal people what they thought about it, and some band councils objected while others ignored it.[39]

The planners decided that education offered the best chance for merging Indians into the general Canadian society. Schools for Indians dated to the earliest colonial decades, but missionary groups or tribal funds paid operational costs. In 1875 the Dominion government provided a grant of two thousand dollars for Indian education, its first one. Over the next two decades the number of day schools gradually increased, reaching 177. In Ontario, Indian schools had existed for several generations, particularly those on the Grand River lands of the Six Nations Iroquois people. Even there, however, as late as 1875 they received little or no government money and suffered from poor attendance. Although 14 day schools and the Mohawk Institute at Brantford all offered classes that year, only 608 of the 1,583 children and young people attended any of them. Nearly all support for the education came from philanthropic groups, with the New England Company of London operating the Mohawk Institute and 9 of the day schools, while the Wesleyan Conference paid for 2 more, the Mississaugas funded 2, and the Iroquois themselves only 1 small one. Most surprising, and certainly ahead of any such move in the United States, eleven of the sixteen teachers then working were Indians.[40]

Too few students attended regularly to satisfy the bureaucrats, and the sporadic attendance frustrated the teachers as well. To remedy this, officials offered several schemes, including a suggestion to provide "suitable books, maps, and other apparatus" to each school. The same official who voiced that idea also called for prizes for good attendance and strong academic achievement. The Indian Department, he recommended, should set an acceptable average attendance figure for each new school and demand that the teacher keep attendance up to or above that level in order to receive his or her salary. On a more positive note, he called for bonuses for each student above the average that any teachers could keep in school on a regular basis. How this was to be done remained unclear.[41]

The continuing attendance problems had several causes. Rather than provide public support for reservation schools, the Indian Department contracted with various church groups to operate the schools. This system reflected attitudes in Quebec and Manitoba, but elsewhere in Canada the church affiliations brought considerable bickering, with the result that many schools had government rather than church support. Getting good teachers continually proved a major obstacle as well. In his annual report one of the inspectors noted that many of the teachers in the Indian schools lacked the qualifications to serve in the ordinary county public schools near the reservations. Often the most experienced teachers avoided tribal schools because they paid only about half as much as the public schools.[42]

Frequently the Indians' actions determined school success. The annual cycle of migration to fish, hunt, or gather took children away for months at a time. Even when seasonal migrations ended, village or band matters directly affected attendance. By the early 1880s some tribal groups ceased cooperating. Some bands refused to pay for schools. Others interpreted their treaties' promises to provide teachers to mean that the government should also provide any buildings or equipment that the teachers might need. One group even suggested that the teachers build their own schools. It is unclear whether this argument reflected Indian understanding of the situation, masked their basic suspicion of the whites and their institutions, or demonstrated efforts to slow acculturation. Clearly, while many traditional leaders wanted education to help their people deal successfully with the encroaching whites, they objected to the curriculum and the methods in use. For example, the Plains tribes objected that they wanted no religion taught to their children. They undermined the missionary efforts so much that the churchmen complained that the "heathen-priests or medicine men do their utmost to prejudice the minds" of the Indian children against what was being taught.[43]

Despite these disruptions, Canadian officials operated an ambitious program of schools for the tribal people. Yet their expectations proved wildly unrealistic, as the whites had no idea how long it might take to replace traditional ideas and practices. For example, as early as 1879 seventeen new agricultural instructors began their work, bringing implements, tools, and seeds to their charges. Within a year the local Indian commissioner stated that he expected that by the next year some of the instructors would have done their job so well that they would be able to move on to other reserves to begin all over again. He was mistaken. In fact, writing a full generation later, an early twentieth-century official remarked, "It is quite within the mark to say that no instructors have been dispensed with" yet.[44]

When they realized that the bureaucrats wanted to replace tribal cultures, the Indians resisted openly and covertly. They saw the boarding schools as a means of disrupting their family and village life. If the children remained at those institutions they could not participate in annual hunting or migratory activities. The corporal punishment of the children ran counter to their family practices. Even the job skills each boy or girl got often resulted from forced labor for the schools, which the teachers described as vocational instruction. Because of these objections many of the Plains bands used the sun dance and other annual rituals as a sort of alternative education. At these ceremonies tribal elders, chiefs, shamans, and other adults helped instruct the children in traditional customs and gave a kind of parallel education that included the initiation of young men for marriage, social activities, politics, and band practices and beliefs.[45]

This resistance succeeded so well that in 1884 the government began requiring school attendance for all Indian children between the ages of seven and fifteen. On the Plains the new policy made little impact on Indian habits or views toward the white man's education. Many western bands rejected farming in favor of hunting, trapping, fishing, and gathering economies that kept their children out of school for months at a time. To help the agents and teachers more easily round up their charges, Parliament amended the Indian Act in 1890 to empower the governor in council to apply the hunting and fishing laws of Manitoba and the Northwest Territories to tribal people in those provinces. In theory, if the Indians could only hunt for part of the year they would not object to their children's being in school for the rest of it. The possibility that the new limits on their hunting and fishing might destroy Indian efforts to feed them-selves and bring disaster never seems to have occurred to the legislators.[46] On the other hand, enforcement remained sporadic for decades.

Regardless of the government efforts many tribal groups continued to ignore the schools. In the mid-1890s one official reported that "only thirteen schools, indifferently patronized, are in operation among the thirty bands occupying this vast district. Two thirds of the Indians are uncompromising heathens, who have for generations successfully resisted all the combined efforts of missionaries to Christianize them."[47] Specific data support this charge, as an 1892 report showed. That year, of the 15,385 school-aged Indian children, only 6,350 even appeared on any school roster, and of those only about half, or 3,630, children showed up in the average daily attendance figures. When asked why they failed to support the schools effectively, one band leader responded that his people did not want to accept many of the whites' customs and ideas at the same time. Rather, they hoped the schools would help the children learn how to earn their living while keeping many of their customs. Also, like some Indian leaders in the United States, they expected the schools to give their young people the skills they needed for dealing with the rest of society.[48]

Although Indians accepted education grudgingly, the system grew. Small boarding schools for some of the children prepared them for the larger industrial schools, at which they learned trades skills. By the 1890s some fourteen industrial schools operated atop the Indian school system. In theory the students attended these schools for five years. During the first two they spent most of their time in class; in the third year they began vocational training half of each day, and for the last two years they worked as full-time apprentices. The Shing-wauk Industrial School, which opened in 1873 near Sault Sainte Marie, offered a typical program. The students got training in such trades as printing, tinsmith-ing, carpentry, bootmaking, tailoring, and the ever-present farming. A few of the students who impressed their teachers with their intellectual skills might be-come teachers or doctors, but this number remained small. While the Indian boys attended the industrial school, the girls had an institution of their own not far away. There they learned homemaking skills, laundry work, and sewing.[49]

To wean the Indian children from their tribal heritage, educators used English to replace their native languages, cut their hair, gave them European-style cloth-ing, and even changed their recreation. Some teachers in the boarding schools hoped that their graduates would move into the general population. As in the United States, however, most Canadians wanted little if anything to do with their Indian neighbors; accordingly, most of the former students returned to the reserves, where they had few chances to use their new skills. Reports by Indian Department officials reflected this difficulty. By 1890 several of the industrial schools had adopted the American putting-out system begun by Richard Pratt at the Carlisle Indian School. One bureaucrat commented that hiring Indian young people appeared at first "to be of a philanthropic character, but will ere long pass beyond that stage, and the schools will be applied to for help because it is wanted."[50] That hoped-for acceptance of Indian school graduates by the rest of society came slowly, if at all, in much of Canada.

In the United States, education in the Cherokee Nation illustrates the one vivid difference between educational efforts in the two countries. Within a few years after the Cherokee's forced removal to the West, the Cherokee National Council began operating schools, and by 1851 twenty-one tribal schools held classes. Students in many of the primary grades went to day schools near their homes. That year the tribe opened two boarding schools, the Cherokee Female Seminary and the Cherokee Male Seminary, to provide a highly structured academic education for the children of its mixed-race leaders. Children from more traditional families often attended class for a couple of years and received instruction in their own language. By 1868 these Indians operated sixty-four schools, and these differed widely from most others in either country. The Indians themselves hired the teachers and supervised course content. Despite strong religious influences, none of the institutions was contracted to church or missionary groups. By the 1880s graduates of both the seminaries began to serve as teachers, and some of them taught in their own language, at least in the lower grades. Despite the clear needs of many Cherokees for some technical skills, the schools gave no manual training classes. All of their instruction in the upper grades and at the seminaries was academic.[51]

Except for the Cherokee experience, the systems in both nations came to resemble each other. Each agency or reserve had at least one school, but on large reservations where many of the people lived far from the agency headquarters, boarding schools seemed to make good sense. As a result, by 1884 the U.S. government ran seventy-six day schools, eighty-one boarding schools, and six manual-labor or industrial schools. While religious groups operated others on a contract basis, they played a smaller role in Indian education in the United States than they did in the Canadian system.[52]

As in Canada, American authorities saw the schools as a tool that would help erase Indian cultural identity. When they heard suggestions that teaching materials be prepared in the tribal languages, officials objected immediately. Secretary of the Interior Carl Schurz, himself an immigrant from Germany who had to learn English after he arrived in the United States, responded to such suggestions, saying, "If Indian children are to be civilized they must learn the language of civilization. They will become far more accessible to civilized ideas and ways of thinking when they are enabled to receive those ideas and ways of thinking through the most direct channel of expression."[53] His subordinates in the Office of Indian Affairs shared that idea. In fact, several years earlier the commissioner of Indian affairs had prohibited all instruction except in English, prompting loud objections from some of the churches that operated schools on western reservations. They complained that Indian children learned faster in their tribal languages than they did in English, and to ban the use of the former would only slow the acculturation process.

While few officials in either country quarreled with the idea that all Indians needed to learn English, usually they kept the tribes segregated. One of the most outspoken opponents of this approach was Richard A. Pratt, the founder and director of the Carlisle Indian School. An army officer with considerable experience with Indians, in 1878 he persuaded his military superiors to allow him to begin teaching Indian prisoners how to survive in the white man's world. At first he moved the captives into a wing of a building at the Hampton Institute, a school for young blacks in Virginia. Then in November 1879 he opened the Carlisle Indian School, with students from the Dakota and Indian Territories. Pratt insisted that Indian young people had to be integrated into American society right from the start. To accomplish this he placed the students in white homes and businesses for several years, hoping to get them enough education and vocational training that they would not have to or want to return to the reservations. In this he failed, but other schools soon followed his example. At the time this plan had little chance for success because the white population in both countries refused to accept Indians as neighbors, co-workers, or employees.[54]

Along with the Carlisle Indian School, Hampton Institute in Virginia educated a steady stream of Indian young people. While many of the later boarding schools got their students through coercion during the 1880s, Hampton recruiters often found more volunteers than they could accommodate. The Sioux, Omahas, and Winnebagos provided most of the students. Both Hampton and Carlisle took the lead in trying to acculturate their pupils, but often they failed to overcome the students' cultural strength. Certainly the returning students lost part of their Indian identity, but they often used their newfound skills to help their communities retain tribal customs and property. The Shawnee leader Thomas Wildcat Alford remembered this clearly. He went to school to learn how "to use the club of white man's wisdom against him in defense of our customs and our Mee-saw-mi as given us by the Great Spirit."[55]

Frequently discussions of the boarding school operations describe how these institutions stripped Indian children of their language, culture, and self-identity, and then sent them home as misfits. Certainly this happened frequently, but that is only part of the story. Many tribal young people returned home determined to remain Indians. The Hampton returnees often used their training well back on the reservation. By 1882 some 122 of these former students toiled as farmers or stock raisers. Thirty-two more taught in reservation schools, while others worked as skilled laborers, merchants, or even professionals. Only 24 held unskilled positions.[56]

Government service soon came to provide many jobs for boarding school graduates. By the 1880s, when the reservation system was well developed and growing, tribal leaders began suggesting that the jobs go to young people returning from school. In fact, on the Lower Brule Reservation chiefs Big Mane, Bull Head, Iron Nation, and Little Pheasant reported "that there were ten boys who should be given employment by the government."[57] Some federal officials supported this idea, seeing jobs as just another part of the acculturation process. Gradually during the 1880s and 1890s the number of young Indians with federal jobs rose dramatically. By 1899 the commissioner of Indian affairs reported that tribal people held 88 percent or "1160 of our 1308 Indian School Service positions." Their jobs ranged widely from teachers to laundresses and from farmers to bakers, but in each case they tended to tie the job holders to the national cash economy. In a similar way the Field Matron Service came to employ a small number of Indian women as reservation workers. There they tried to teach Indian women how to run a middle-class household. At the same time they helped with family matters such as health, diet and clothing.[58]

MISSIONARIES AND REFORMERS

In addition to schools, religious groups and missionary societies worked to spread Christianity and acculturate the tribal people. The work of William Duncan, an Anglican Church Missionary Society missionary to British Columbia, has received the most attention. Arriving there in 1857, he quickly began work among the Tsimshian people along the coast. Within five years he had a modest-sized congregation of converts and in 1862 led some fifty Tsimshians away from Fort Simpson to found a new community. Hoping to build an industrial cooperative that would serve as a refuge for the Indians far from white interference, Duncan promptly began an ambitious plan of constructing public buildings in the new community. By the early 1870s the town—named Metlakatla—had two hundred houses laid out along straight streets that ran perpendicular to the shoreline. Streetlights lined the roads, and the Indians planted poplar trees between the lamps. In addition, impressive public buildings dominated the community. As might be expected in a religiously oriented town, the church stood at the center of the public square. Other buildings included a courthouse, jail, school, town hall, public reading room, and even a museum.[59]

Throughout the 1870s and 1880s Duncan dominated the community, but his ego grew so large that eventually the missionary society split with him, and the Indian community shattered. Some Indians objected to his militant Christianity; others lost their enthusiasm for working as industrial laborers in the sawmill, cannery, soap factory, or the smaller businesses that dominated the local economy. In the end, a nativist movement split Duncan's followers, and he led the hard-core converts out of British Columbia north into Alaska, where they built a second community with the same name.[60]

Other groups, particularly the Oblates of the Roman Catholic Church and the Methodists, staffed schools throughout the Canadian West. All of these missionaries and teachers found acculturation slow work, so by the 1880s they joined bureaucrats in asking that coercion of the Indians be used to achieve their particular goals. This happened when amendments to the Indian Act of 1884 allowed specific attacks on some tribal beliefs and practices in the West. The legislation outlawed spirit dancing and the potlatch ceremony in British Columbia. However, it proved easier for Canadian authorities to legislate against those ceremonies than it was for them to enforce the new prohibition. Indians simply held them at a distance from the agency headquarters, slipped away from their reserve to meet with like-minded friends, or traveled to other reserves, where they continued their rites. To the frustration of the bureaucrats, only one conviction under the anti-potlatch law occurred, and a judge quickly overruled that, finding the law too vague to be enforced.[61]

By 1892 officials predicted optimistically that while the sun dance had been held that year, they thought that it would not be done again. Their guess proved wrong. Repeatedly Indian Department personnel tried to prevent tribal people from leaving the reserves, using a pass system developed during the rebellion of 1885. Indians ignored the passes, and the Mounted Police chose not to try to enforce the system. Once the tribal people met relatives and friends at the reserve boundary and held the ceremonies there. Obviously neither side wanted to back down on this issue. Because of their repeated failure to end tribal cultural ceremonies, white officials went beyond the limits placed by the law and tried to carry out what one described as an "extensive effort to stamp out Indian ceremonialism," but their efforts largely failed.[62]

While Canadians tried and failed to destroy tribal ceremonies, missionary groups and other so-called friends of the Indian in the United States came to realize that acculturation might take generations. As their counterparts north of the border had done, they stepped up their calls on the government, hoping to influence the creation of new policies that might speed acculturation and assimilation. New groups of reformers entered the fray during the 1880s, determined to uplift what they saw as heathen savages so they would be able to join the rest of American society. Such groups as the Women's National Indian Association and the Indian Rights Association worked with the Board of Indian Commissioners, then operating as a sort of watchdog group to oversee federal treatment of the Indians. In 1883 Alfred K. Smiley, a Quaker philanthropist, organized the first Lake Mohonk Conference in upstate New York. This became an annual meeting that brought together government officials and reformers of many stripes for days of discussion focusing on the Indians and what should be done with them.

The presence of large, well-organized, and effective reform groups that watched government actions closely set U.S.-Indian relations apart from the Canadian experience during the late nineteenth century. Although Canadian officials debated policy and how it should be implemented, there seems to have been little of the public outcry that accompanied most federal actions in the United States. The Canadian Indian Research and Aid Society, which combined missionaries and ethnologists, provided the only exception to this. Begun in 1890 but lasting less than two years, this group published the *Canadian Indian*, a journal intended to bring Indian issues to "the ear and heart of the Canadian public."[63] Despite this lofty goal it had little impact on either public opinion or national policy. In fact, almost no discussion or critical dissent marked Canadian Indian affairs during this era.

As early as the 1870s the forced removal of the Nebraska Poncas had raised a storm of protest, and throughout the 1880s American reformers who considered themselves "friends of the Indian" publicized federal mishandling of Indian issues by circulating thousands of pamphlets, gathering signatures, presenting petitions, and applying intense political pressure on many government officials. Added to the glare of attention these groups focused on the issue, individuals such as Helen Hunt Jackson helped publicize the government's difficulties with the tribal people. A popular speaker and the author of numerous articles detailing American faults and dishonesty in dealing with the tribes, in 1881 she published her book *A Century of Dishonor*. In it she presented a series of case studies purporting to demonstrate government wrongdoing. Although one-sided and only partially correct, her book did raise public and political awareness of the issues after she sent a copy of it to each member of Congress.[64]

A desire to help Indians by bringing them into American society as quickly as possible united almost all of the reformers. The major organizations each represented the currents of late-nineteenth-century Protestantism, and they strove to end tribalism, segregation as represented by the reservations, and limits on full legal and political rights for the Indians. Nearly all of the "friends of the Indian" supported the idea of allotment or dividing reservation land and assigning it to individual families. They based this view on the old idea that if only each Indian had some property, he or she would understand white society more clearly and through self-interest would come to adopt white attitudes about work and property. Having supported allotment, they could not object when the government sold the unassigned land on reservations to individuals or corporations. Once white Americans moved to farm next door, the argument went, the Indians would learn from them as well, and within a generation or two the tribes would disappear as individuals on each reservation, blended into the general society.

Canadian officials had been striving toward the same objective since the 1860s through their unsuccessful enfranchisement program. For years it had remained voluntary; to gain status as an enfranchised person, the individual reserve dweller had to pass muster at a hearing conducted by public officials. In the United States the reformers and the government looked to allotment to do what removal, military defeat, schools, churches, and model farms had failed to accomplish—the acculturation and assimilation of tribal people. The process began in 1887, when Senator Henry L. Dawes of Massachusetts guided the General Allotment Act, or Dawes Severalty Act, through Congress. The new law gave the president authority to allot reservations, giving individual Indians title to the land after twenty-five years and immediate citizenship when they accepted an allotment. During the next generation many Indians became citizens. Once all eligible tribal members got their allotments, the surplus land, or what remained after allotment, could be placed on the market. Once the program began, tribal landholdings shrank drastically. They dropped from 155 million acres in 1881 to just under 78 million in 1900 and continued to decline until 1934, when allotment stopped and the Indians retained only 52 million acres.[65]

In addition to allotment and citizenship, the government had moved to bring about acculturation through several other programs. During the 1870s agents on some of the new reservations organized units of Indian police to help enforce peace. These groups allowed members of existing soldier societies among the Plains communities a chance to serve their people in accepted ways. In 1883 the secretary of the interior had established a series of "courts of Indian offenses" to suppress such customs as plural marriages and men wearing their hair long and to help repress some Indian ceremonials or religious festivals. Gradually, re-spected village leaders accepted positions as judges on these courts, thus lend-ing their support to the acculturative push being made by the government. On some reservations local army garrison commanders organized units of scouts; the most famous units included the Nebraska Pawnees under Frank and Luther North and the Apache scouts recruited by General George Crook to guide his forces in their pursuit of Geronimo. In each of these cases, the goal was not only to encourage nontraditional activities to help the government but also, and more importantly, to break up tribal or band solidarity and encourage the ac-culturation of individuals.[66]

These American efforts to acquaint Indians with the white man's approach to law enforcement and socially acceptable habits of dress, language, and fam-ily matters had their counterparts on Canadian reserves. From the start, post-Confederacy policy tried to bring about the rapid acculturation and assimilation of tribal people. As in the United States, Canadian officials assumed that indi-vidualism, personal property, religion, and education would accomplish that goal quickly. For example, in 1874 Minister of the Interior David Laird wrote that the government should enfranchise eastern Indians, give them an allot-ment of land taken from the tribal reserves with its title within four or five years, and a few years later divide tribal funds among the members. Laird saw this as doing two important things. First, it would promote individual skills the Indians needed to develop. Second, it would reduce the tribal holdings and weaken Indian attachment to the tribe as an entity.[67]

Laird's proposal got some consideration, but the 1876 Indian Act took a dif-ferent approach. Rather than assigning land to individual Indians immediately, it demanded that tribal people prove that they had the skills needed to deal with the white society. Before gaining enfranchisement and some land, each Indian had to be able to read and write in either English or French. They had to be free of debt and needed documentation supporting their good moral character. Having passed this first "test," the reserve dweller then got a location ticket for a par-ticular plot of land on the reserve. After a three-year probationary period during which the Indian had to show competence in using and managing the land, he could apply for enfranchisement. This scheme shows the government's basic plan to bring the tribal people into the general society one person at a time. Interestingly enough, these portions of the 1876 law applied only to the eastern tribes. The whites assumed that they might make rapid progress in their acculturation because they had decades or even generations of experience in dealing with Europeans. At this point Canadian leaders saw little future for the Indians other than small-scale agriculture, and the eastern tribes rejected the government's plans for them because they remained determined to cling to parts of their traditional culture.[68]

During the late 1870s and 1880s the officials saw little to cause them to alter their ideas. David Laird complained about policies that retained the tribal system and that granted reserve lands to Indians in large blocks so they could still use them communally. For western bands he suggested that family plots be granted near or in the middle of white settlements. This would disrupt tribal identity and give the Indians plenty of examples of how to live and work. In 1880 the Indian Act focused on the question of acculturation and established the Department of Indian Affairs to supervise and direct the demise of the tribes. Four years later another law expanded the powers of the band or reserve councils, but at the same time, it added to the authority of the government to direct or even overrule what Indians had decided or to replace uncooperative chiefs.[69]

In spite of these elaborate efforts to legislate acculturation, the Indians themselves directed the pace of activity. Frequently the white officials proved wildly overoptimistic or simply ill informed when they assessed events in the West. Certainly David Laird did those things. He claimed to see Indians accepting the principle of individual property because they cleared small patches of ground for raising vegetables. What he overlooked, however, was the fact that many Indian groups included some rudimentary agriculture in their economy, and few if any of the people who tilled small fields ever thought about owning that particular piece of the landscape. By 1879, when facing the imminent collapse of the buffalo hunters' livelihood, authorities suggested that the western tribes might prefer cattle raising to farming, a distinct change in thinking and one that would be rejected in the United States for another decade. Still the focus remained on getting each Indian family to farm. At least one chief taught his own children that any "work at farming, cattle keeping or schools" was not good for Indians.[70] Regardless of what the leaders said, many of the young men refused to farm, preferring to hunt. Even chiefs who realized that hunting was ending complained that "they were told to cultivate the soil, and [then] forbidden to sell" their crops by Indian Department officials.[71] As a result, their people wanted no part of farming.

Despite getting off to a good start as farmers, many Indian groups had little chance for long-range economic success. They broke ground and asked for help with seed, equipment, and livestock, but rarely got much help from the government. Some tried new crops, and others won prizes at agricultural fairs, but they remained dependent on the government for credit and materials. Much of their early labors went for nothing by the late 1880s, when the new superintendent, Hayter Reed, put his ideas into practice. To him Indians had little potential as farmers, and he introduced forty-acre plots on reserves in the West. According to Reed, "a single acre of wheat, part of another in root crops and vegetables, a cow or two could provide for the farmer and his family."[72] If that view of Indians as peasant farmers failed to discourage some reserve dwellers, the permit system that emerged during the 1890s certainly did. Under it no Indian farmer could sell his crops or buy either animals or tools without a written permit. As a result, by the mid-1890s many reserve dwellers gave up the uneven battle for economic progress.[73]

Livestock raising on the Great Plains proved a more innovative approach to the need for incorporating Indians into the economy. By 1880 several bands of the Blackfoot Confederacy had begun cattle raising in southern Alberta. The inspector for the western area reported in 1882 that the Piegans' herd seemed to be growing. In June that year the nearby Stoney tribe held a successful cattle roundup. The Indians asked for livestock repeatedly, and by 1888 many bands had herds of cattle, sheep, and swine. Triumphant officials pointed to the care Indians lavished on their livestock, and one reported that at least one tribe had helped to kill their own dogs because the animals attacked their sheep. Certainly not all of them wanted to become herders, but ranching seems to have been more acceptable than farming to most of the Plains groups. In fact, between 1885 and 1895 the tribes in the Northwest Territories increased their cattle herds from 1,230 cattle to 15,378 animals. Clearly these Indians had more success in influencing policy and the direction of their own economic development than had their counterparts south of the border at the same time.[74]

In the United States the issue of livestock raising or farming proved more difficult. The American obsession with the 160-acre farm that resulted in the passage of the 1862 Homestead Act colored all discussions of this topic. In fact, hoping to encourage tribal people to adapt to family farm–sized plots, in 1875 Congress passed an Indian Homestead law that opened land to reservation dwellers on terms rather similar to those offered to the rest of society. Still some discussion of whether the government should encourage livestock raising occurred. As early as 1869 one writer noted that stock raising was possible for all of the western tribes, but only a few might succeed as farmers. By the end of his term as secretary of the interior in 1881, Carl Schurz remarked that the transition from "the savage state to the pastoral is less violent than that from the savage state directly to the agricultural." Nevertheless, he supported farming over livestock production for the tribes because in order to have enough grazing land for large-scale ranching the government would have to maintain vast Indian reservations, something it was committed to ending as quickly as possible.[75]

Whether by policy or by accident, at least through the 1870s and 1880s, actions by various officials placed cattle in the hands of some tribal groups in the Great Plains and in the mountains of the West. As early as 1875 General Ranald Mackenzie purchased several thousand cattle and sheep for the Comanche and Kiowa people when they surrendered to the army at Fort Sill, Oklahoma. As part of their surrender the Indians had agreed to give all of their horses to the army, and the general sold those animals to get funds for the domestic livestock. With no experience in caring for livestock, and no horses to use in herding the cattle, the Indians lost or killed many of these animals. In 1882, because of food shortages on the reservation, the Kiowa Comanche agent P. B. Hunt asked nearby cattlemen for some 340 head of cattle to help feed his charges. Later, when Congress authorized enough food to prevent violence, Hunt asked for permission to give the animals to the Indians as breeding stock. A few individual tribal leaders, such as the Comanche Quannah Parker, acquired sizable herds, but for most reservation dwellers, raising cattle or sheep was not an option.[76]

Administration of the Indian office varied widely between the two countries during the late nineteenth century. In Canada, at least at the top, stability reigned. Between 1862 and 1900 only three men directed the policies of the Department of Indian Affairs. These were William Spragge from 1862 to 1873, Lawrence Vankoughnet from 1874 to 1895, and Clifford Sifton from 1896 into the twentieth century. At the same time in the United States, sixteen men held the office of commissioner of Indian affairs. Their average tenure was only about three or four years, with several serving even shorter terms. Obviously that much turnover meant frequent shifts in administrative practices. Even the subordinates within the Canadian bureaucracy tended to serve longer than their American counterparts. Yet many agents labored only a short time in both countries. The longevity of high-ranking officials in the Canadian Indian service was positive in terms of administrative continuity, but having the same individuals hold office for decades tended to make them self-satisfied, perhaps even stultified, and in the long run not particularly more effective. In fact, one recent assessment of Canada's dealings with the tribal people during this era found "Ottawa and most of its agents unequal to the task."[77] The same could have been said about U.S. officials.

While both governments worked diligently to remake the tribal people, Indians had other ideas. Many villagers turned inward, seeking renewed strength through their religious ideas and cultural practices. Despite efforts to stamp out the potlatch ceremony in British Columbia, Indian people there continued this traditional practice, ignoring repeated demands that they stop. Missionaries, educators, and agents denounced the sun dance on both sides of the border as a heathen and barbaric practice, but tribes on the northern plains continued it as well. Other cultural practices such as vision quests, wearing blankets or long hair, and retaining their tribal languages allowed Indian people to assert their cultural pride and retain at least a part of their traditional identity. Obviously some of the practices related to the annual buffalo hunt ended once that event ceased, and young men found it increasingly hard to gain admittance to the warrior societies. Still, in the United States at least, some of the young men served as scouts in the army, while in both countries others traveled with circuses and entertainment groups such as Buffalo Bill's Wild West show or even with the medicine shows that crisscrossed the continent during the last decades of the nineteenth century.

In addition to retaining some mobility and cultural pride in these ways, tribal people turned to new or modified religious beliefs offered by shamans responding to the pressures of drastic change in the same manner as Handsome Lake and the Shawnee prophet Tenskwatawa at the beginning of the century. As early as the 1850s Smohalla, a Shahaptian Indian from the Oregon country, experienced a series of visions that he developed into a set of teachings known as the Dreamer religion. His followers spent long periods in meditation and so were called dreamers. Smohalla foretold the return to earth of all Indians, who would then destroy the white intruders. After the Civil War Smohalla added a strong note of resistance to white economic practices and reservation life to his teachings. Urging a complete rejection of the acculturation program, he railed at Indians who took up farming. These militant teachings brought repeated jailings, but he refused to stop opposing the reservation programs, and descendants of his followers continue to practice the Dreamer religion to the present.[78]

By 1881 the Puget Sound region gave rise to another prophet, Squsachtun, or John Slocum, who founded the Indian Shaker religion. He too experienced a series of visions during which he reported visiting heaven. There he received a divine assignment to teach Indians how to overcome the difficulties of reservation life. Combining tribal religious practices with Christian teachings he learned from the missionaries, his ideas included such Christian elements as heaven, hell, God, and Christ, but the rest of the sacred teachings came from his visions. Limiting the faith to Indians, Slocum taught his followers to meditate and fast, and frequently these produced nervous twitchings, a sign that their bodies were casting off evil thoughts and acts. Like Smohalla, Squsachtun opposed the acculturation programs being implemented on the reservations, urging his followers to resist them whenever possible. Federal agents arrested him and tried to disrupt the gatherings of his followers, as they did among the Dreamer people, but without success. Groups on both sides of the border accepted his teachings, and adherents of the Indian Shaker religion continue their practices today.[79]

Few Indian groups in the mountains or on the plains ever heard of either the Dreamer religion or the Indian Shaker religion, but by the 1880s nearly all of them came to learn about the Ghost Dance religion. Originating in the visions of a Nevada Paiute named Tavibo, this set of beliefs taught that the invading whites were to be destroyed in a massive earthquake. Before gaining many followers Tavibo died, but his son Wovoka, or Jack Wilson, continued the preaching. Adding some of his own ideas to his father's teachings, Wovoka developed the Ghost Dance religion. He taught a return to Indian practices including frequent bathing, living plainly, and avoiding alcohol, and prohibited mourning because all dead Indians were to return once the whites had been destroyed. The worshipers meditated, prayed, and danced for up to five days at a time, and the ceremonies produced a mild group hypnosis.

The teachings spread among the disheartened people on the northern plains reservations, and medicine men among the Sioux turned it from a pacific set of beliefs into a militant antiwhite platform. Worried authorities saw danger in the Ghost Dance's development into a secret society with holy clothes reputed to keep the warriors safe from the soldiers' bullets. In late 1890 agents among the Sioux bands called for soldiers to keep peace, but before the situation calmed, reservation police had killed Sitting Bull. Soon after his death soldiers attacked and destroyed many of Big Foot's followers at Wounded Knee. Thus, while the various religious responses to the unwelcome reservation experience brought some solace to the disheartened Indians, others faced loss of their rations, possible jail terms, and even death at the hands of police or soldiers. After Wounded Knee the Ghost Dance disappeared almost as quickly as it had appeared, but it and the other Indian religious movements of the late nineteenth century show clearly the level of Indian unhappiness and the failure of the acculturative programs to help the tribal people in any substantial way.[80]

By the end of the nineteenth century the earlier differences that marked the Indian policies of Canada and the United States had receded, as the two governments moved toward similar goals and methods. Education, religion, agriculture, segregated reservations, and individual landholdings characterized the broad approach of each. In the United States the army continued to man scattered outposts throughout the West, while in Canada the Mounties carried out their work in smaller numbers, but with a presence just as obvious to the Indians. White settlement proceeded on a faster pace in the United States, but small towns, farms, railroads, timber cutting, and mining enterprises appeared on both sides of the border. Indians in each country did begin farming; some acquired herds of cattle, while others learned English and acquired work skills that proved useful on or near the reservations. Still, because government policies sought to destroy Indian identity, a continuing tension existed between bureaucrats and the determination of tribal people to retain their cultural independence. That tension continued into the twentieth century and, in fact, lingers to embitter Indian-white relations down to the present day.

9 Surviving Marginalization, 1890s–1920

 WRITING ABOUT AMERICAN mistreatment of Indians in the early twentieth century, the Lakota author Luther Standing Bear described reservations as places where "people were herded under every possible disadvantage and obstruction to progress until the race should pass out from sheer physical depletion."[1] In many ways this was true in both Canada and the United States as practices became more alike on both sides of the border. Certainly by the early twentieth century native peoples often came to be seen by whites as insignificant in each country. Indians themselves seemed to have ever fewer avenues for initiatives open to them.

Reserves and reservations segregated the tribal people. Boarding schools disrupted family relations, damaged culture and language, trained Indian students for nonexistent jobs, and mixed young people from various tribes together. Many groups ignored or resisted white efforts to destroy their culture or to prohibit important social or religious practices. Yet while facing these government pressures, reservation communities often turned inward for strength and found increased cultural awareness. Some adopted white practices. In western Canada, for example, Indians joined trade unions to gain a larger say in their own economic life. By the 1920s regional and provincial organizations of native people had developed there, while in the United States the Society of American Indians functioned as a pantribal group at the same time.

Continuing pressures on Indians to surrender more of their tribal lands and resources occurred in both nations. Although World War I brought some opportunities, Indians in both countries experienced few positive changes in their circumstances. Often things got worse. Bitter prejudice against reservation dwellers permeated both societies. At the time despair, alcohol abuse, and apathy sapped energies among some groups. Throughout the first decades of the twentieth century the situation deteriorated from what it had been earlier. Difficulties increased while programs failed, and little apparent progress toward acculturation occurred in either country.

Yet this picture ignores several important developments. Some tribal people became ever more discontented. Young, educated leaders learned how to manipulate the legal and economic systems. The Navajos, for example, hurried to adopt some white practices. Their ultraconservative neighbors the Hopis, on the other hand, retained traditional cultural practices despite white efforts to outlaw or destroy them. Reform groups in the United States continued to denounce the federal bureaucracy for incompetence and bungling while corruption at both the local and federal levels continued. This would persuade a growing number of scholars and publicists to call for yet another series of reforms in how the nation treated the Indians. At the same time, developments growing out of World War I rocked all of the major nations of the world. Existing empires unraveled, colonial peoples demanded independence or significantly better treatment, and individuals who served in the armies expected full equality once they returned home.

Gradually these events changed the Indian-white relationships in both countries dramatically, but in 1900 the tribes faced ongoing efforts to acculturate them. When Indians rejected the majority culture their action raised questions about the programs and the commitment of either government. It also brought a sharp increase in anti-Indian sentiment. Politicians in both countries complained of the seemingly endless expenditures for Indian programs and grumbled that education brought little change. In Canada during an 1897 parliamentary debate an Alberta spokesman argued against educating Indian young people in residential industrial schools; if they became competitive with the whites, he argued, they disrupted the economy, and if their training left them unable to compete effectively, it wasted the taxpayers' money. Only two years later Minister of the Interior Clifford Sifton noted that the western tribes were the most difficult to persuade to settle down or to educate. Before leaving office Sifton admitted his doubts about the benefits Indian children got from formal school training. "The Indian cannot go out from school, making his own way and compete with the white man," he observed. "He has not the physical, mental or moral get-up to enable him to compete."[2]

This perceived inability to compete, officials thought, stemmed from many causes, but it appeared certain that tribal customs lay at the heart of the problem. Editors of western Canadian newspapers denounced the Ottawa government and frequently gave advice on how to solve the "Indian question." In 1896 the *Manitoba Free Press* called for the government to teach the "Northwest Indians to live like human beings," although the writer admitted that nobody had any idea of how to accomplish this.[3] Nearly a decade and a half later Duncan Campbell Scott, the top Indian affairs administrator in Canada, bragged about his efforts to suppress the potlatch ceremony in the Pacific Northwest. At the same time he admitted his failure to eradicate what he called "degrading customs" and "other wasteful feasts."[4] Shortly after the end of World War I, when evaluating a suggestion that a recent Indian school graduate be appointed as an instructor for other young tribal members, a western bureaucrat advised against the proposed move. Despite the young man's strong record, he would not do for the position because the students needed "to have the 'Indian' educated out of them, which only a white teacher can do." Although he admitted that the children seemed "capable of improvement," the proposed Indian appointee had "not the social, moral, and intellectual standing required to elevate these children," precisely because he was an Indian himself.[5]

The critics saw even those tribal people who could and did pass through the government or church schools as falling far short of being independent or competitive within Canadian society. They pointed to their tendency to spend their cash on fancy clothes and large amounts of alcohol and to their failure to make the best of their economic opportunities. One agent suggested that this resulted from their lack of personal thrift and their unwillingness to make and follow long-range plans. These comments show the whites' inability to understand what they reported. In many groups Indian customs demanded that they share wealth and goods with their family and neighbors, a practice that dictated at least some communal actions and one the whites hoped to destroy. The Indian "is not indolent," one agent reported. "He is rather spasmodic; he will work well for a while, then become careless." Because the bureaucrats saw these actions as basic cultural practices, one of them noted that "we may improve the type; we shall never make him a white man."[6]

Similar ideas abound in the comments of U.S. bureaucrats, politicians, and editors as well as among the reformers active on the tribes' behalf. Discussing a visit to Santo Domingo Pueblo in New Mexico during 1912, a journalist reported that the village appeared crudely built and filthy. The Great Corn Festival pageant he witnessed reminded him of something a person might see among the people of the South Seas, "but not a mile from the right of way of a transcontinental railroad."[7] He went on to describe the pueblo dwellers as a conservative lot shaped by a "stubborn and abiding faith" in their customs. According to some commentators this very intensity or conservatism limited the Indians' chances for acculturation and assimilation. In fact, one not only labeled the Indians as backward but remarked that they "are dull of mind and slow to adopt new ideas."[8] He went on to question how much effect missionaries, teachers, farmers, and agents really had on tribal people, claiming that the Indians had made few changes in the preceding four hundred years. Clearly one could not expect any rapid acceptance of American social or economic practices from them.

Despite such ideas about the futility of trying to acculturate the Indians, bureaucrats, teachers, and missionaries continued their assault on tribal people in both nations. Determined to incorporate their charges into the general society, they recognized the challenges offered by the native cultures. By the late 1890s some Canadian bureaucrats decided that their so-called industrial schools, often offering little more than farming instruction, had failed to achieve their goals. One official feared that too much or the wrong type of education would educate Indian children "above the possibilities of their station," and might well give them "a distaste for what is certain to be their environment" within western Canada.[9] Nevertheless, during the 1890s the government amended the Indian Act to authorize Indian Department personnel to use force, as occurred in the United States, when sending children from the reserves to boarding and industrial schools.

In Canada the evolving Indian school system included 221 day schools, 40 boarding schools, and 22 industrial schools at the beginning of the twentieth century. Working in close cooperation with the major church denominations within the country, the government had contracts to operate schools with the Roman Catholics, Anglicans, Methodists, Presbyterians, and several nondenominational groups. Both the government and the church groups actively supported residential institutions rather than day schools because the parents and other Indians had less chance to undermine the children's education if the schools kept them away from their homes and tribal associations. Missionaries and bureaucrats alike made no apology for changing day schools into boarding schools whenever they got a chance to do so. Reasoning that life in the village or camp undid whatever progress the teachers made in school, the civilizers strove to control all aspects of Indian children's lives. School operators competed vigorously for students, and according to a 1900 report their "zeal to get recruits" outran their discretion, leading some to ignore or subvert the medical restrictions meant to exclude children with serious infectious diseases. This willful disregard of medical requirements helped spread sickness and death among the students that year.[10]

Although some Indian band councils objected to church-run schools, many groups in central and western Canada preferred them. Even the government wanted to have the denominations operate the education system, if only because the churches paid part of the cost. By 1910, despite repeated Indian efforts to have the schools become secular, 80 percent of them retained some denominational connection. In fact, at least one writer claims that it was "not unknown for band council resolutions requesting secular schools to be buried in Indian Affairs files if their implementation was opposed by respective churches."[11] Nearly all Canadian educators working with the tribes favored keeping the children at boarding schools. Instead, most young Indians learned whatever was being taught at day schools on their home reserves. By 1924, for example, the government and the churches operated 242 day schools but only 73 boarding schools. While the latter usually enrolled more students at each site, most young Indians attended day schools.[12]

Several reasons existed for this. First, the industrial schools cost more than the government wanted to spend. In addition, one bureaucrat complained that when young Indians returned to their reserves they had little chance to use their training and soon quit trying to work. The same official complained that some of the best students "were found to have retrograded and to have become leaders in the pagan life of the reserves, instead of contributing to the improvement of their surroundings."[13] That being the case, he suggested that the most expensive schools be closed. Indian parents joined the penny-pinching officials to oppose boarding schools because those institutions disrupted family life and tribal cohesion. Even the administrators understood their objections. One admitted that the schools offered an efficient way to educate Indian children, but he disliked having to "sacrifice the spirits and souls of these people, to say nothing of the joy of home and children, upon the altar of efficiency."[14] As a result, day schools stood at the center of the Canadian system.

In the United States at the same time, Indians faced similar issues. Since the late 1870s Hampton Institute in Virginia and the Carlisle Indian School in Pennsylvania had offered off-reservation secondary schooling to young Indians. At Carlisle, Richard Pratt's so-called outing system, under which students lived with white families, often did little more than provide cheap labor for communities and businesses near the Indian schools. Nevertheless, the boarding school system operated under a full head of steam at the turn of the century.[15] Of course, day schools functioned on many reservations too, but as in Canada the bureaucrats saw the residential institutions as the best means for breaking down tribal identity, customs, and language.

Despite the experience of having run boarding and off-reservation schools for at least a full generation, by early in the twentieth century bureaucrats and educators alike sought other ways of providing young Indians education. For example, G. Stanley Hall, the founder of educational psychology in the United States, noted that all teaching of elementary-age Indian children should be in their tribal languages. He condemned complaints that the tribal people spoke too many languages as just "an argument of laziness at the expense of the best interests of the child." Teachers should learn and use Indian languages as the missionaries did. He also questioned the vocational skills offered to Indian young people, likening American education as "slow, ethnic death for them." Hall offered plenty of advice for properly educating Indians and how they might be helped to join the rest of society. He denounced schools and teachers for teaching the child to abhor their parents and customs. Seeing those actions as "monstrous and unchristian," he called on the schools to help the tribal people retain their cultural symbols, religious ideals, and group crafts.[16]

Few agents or teachers working on the reservations or in the schools accepted the idea that Indian cultures had any value of that sort. However, when Francis E. Leupp became commissioner of Indian affairs under President Theodore Roosevelt, that attitude changed. Viewing the tribal people as ultraconservatives with a strong communal orientation, Leupp urged moving slowly when trying to acculturate them. He suggested that classes for the children should be held outside rather than in drafty buildings whenever possible. He proposed ramadalike structures with as much screening as possible to relieve the children's dread of remaining inside, at least for the Southwest. Going beyond the children's objections to being enclosed, Leupp examined health issues carefully. He noted that tuberculosis remained a dangerous killer among the tribes and that by giving the children as much fresh air as possible, fewer might contract this disease.[17] As long as he remained commissioner of Indian affairs, Leupp worked to dismantle the boarding school system and return the children to their homes, where they might attend day schools. Nevertheless, he had only a modest effect on the established system, and boarding schools remained in use for several more generations.

Leupp's ideas differed somewhat from those expressed by imperialists, racists, and reformers at the turn of the century, as whites of many persuasions became increasingly frustrated by the high cost and slow progress of Indian acculturation. Many prominent individuals accepted a variety of racial hierarchy theories, often based on social Darwinian concepts and notions about the white man's burden. These currents came together during the 1890–1920 era to disillusion people involved in Indian affairs. Repeated indications that Indians either rejected the education being offered them or, having accepted it, "returned to the blanket" once they got home undermined continuing support for large expenditures on the boarding schools. By early in the twentieth century reformers accepted the idea that Indians lacked the intellectual capabilities of the whites. For example, in 1900 the principal of Hampton Institute described the tribal people as belonging to one of the childlike races. "I believe we should teach them to labor in order that they may be brought to manhood," he remarked.[18]

The bureaucrats soon put these ideas into practice. Estelle Reel, U.S. superintendent of Indian education, thought that Indian children could not compete intellectually with white children and so shaped a curriculum devoted almost exclusively to vocational training. Even there, however, she gave tribal children little credit for being able to learn much. As a result her program focused sharply on a few basic skills, and by 1901 vocational training became central in the education available to Indian children. The Indian Office's Course of Study for the Indian Schools, issued that year, stressed that the students learn by doing and should focus on practical skills. In 1904 Reel issued a circular that took three pages of instructions to teach Indian girls how to make a bed. During this same era she proposed a five-year curriculum in agriculture for the boys that never went beyond simple plowing and insisted that they plant only local crops.[19]

Following the vocational emphasis then in vogue, Commissioner of Indian Affairs Francis Leupp worked to end the boarding schools and return the students to their reservation day schools. In 1905 he established an Indian employment office to secure jobs for the school children. The next year the sugar beet growers in Colorado began to hire these children for stoop labor. Within a few years many became migrant laborers during their summer vacations, working in places as widely separated as Wisconsin and California, at tasks as varied as sheepherding and harvesting sugar beets, and as laborers on government jobs in the West. Leupp saw this work at unskilled, manual-labor jobs as necessary to help incorporate young people from the reservations into the national economy. Citing the well-known Indian "lack of initiative [and] his hereditary lack of competition," the commissioner claimed that the employment service was all that "wooed him into the labor mart."[20]

After 1909 Leupp's two immediate successors, Robert Valentine and Cato Sells, continued his approach of training young Indians for low-skilled work in

American fields and factories. "Our aim at our schools is not the perfect farmer or the perfect housewife," Commissioner Sells noted, "but the development of character and industrial efficiency."[21] He hoped that each boarding school would train students for a particular trade. In his plan, Carlisle, the flagship school in the system, would teach its male students industrial skills and get the graduates apprenticed to the Ford Motor Company. By 1916 Sells introduced a new course of study and organized a three-tiered system of primary, prevocational, and vocational schools. These schools sought employment as unskilled migrant farm laborers for their male students. The only exception to this occurred during World War I, when some Carlisle students actually worked in eastern automobile factories. The girls continued learning household chores, with their employment limited to domestic service as a part of the decades-old outing system. Even there, their employers were supposed to help educate the Indian girls, but few looked at them as anything more than cheap domestic workers.[22]

The effort to reduce the size of the Indian school system and to get the reservation children into local public institutions provided one of the few positive developments during this era. As early as 1891 Commissioner Thomas Jefferson Morgan had worked to integrate public schools near Indian communities, and at one point he convinced some forty-five districts to participate. He demanded equal treatment for the Indian children, however, and by 1908 only four of the districts remained in the program. Beginning in 1906 Francis Leupp called for the public schools to accept tribal children in their vocational programs. He abandoned the earlier demands that the young Indians have the same curriculum as the whites, hoping to get industrial and commercial training for the Indians while cutting the costs of the education portion in his budget. His successors worked with western districts near reservations but with only limited success. They too hoped to get their educational objectives met through the public schools, but apparently neither Commissioners Valentine nor Sells had any deep-seated feelings on these matters. They strove for efficiency and cost cutting, frequently overlooking the human elements of their duties. In that way they resembled the Canadian bureaucrats, in particular Duncan C. Scott, then administering the Department of Indian Affairs.[23]

INSTITUTIONALIZED PATERNALISM

Not only did the U.S. and Canadian systems for Indian education come to resemble each other more closely as the early decades of the twentieth century passed, but so did other governmental policies. Agents' paternalism on the reservations and reserves increased steadily by the turn of the century. Issues large and small found their way to the bureaucrats' desks, and as the white officials made their decisions they chipped away steadily at Indian self-sufficiency and feelings of competence. Indian Department officers in Canada had the authority to depose and replace chiefs who worked to retard the process of acculturation, and they did this whenever they found other local leaders willing to serve in those positions. At the same time, the Canadian government rarely did much more about reserve difficulties than talk about them, and this too undercut the Indians' willingness to make adjustments or take actions the whites expected of them. For example, discussing a band living at Parry Sound, Ontario, the local inspector reported that the local villagers had refused to clear land for farming because the government had not reserved specific lands for them, and "they do not care to clear up land which might afterwards be placed outside the bounds of their reserve."[24]

In some cases, local agents tried to control nearly all facets of reserve life. Literate Indians who recorded their feelings complained about what they saw as white usurpation of control. "After a few years on our reserve," one recalled, "the representatives of the government began to remind us that we were only wards, that the agent was the chief ruler of our lives."[25] More significant, at least in long-term economic development, was the effort to reduce the tribal land base in both countries. Canadians amended the Indian Act frequently, usually at the expense of the tribes. Having struggled to extend the transcontinental railroad to the West Coast, the Ottawa government saw no reason to slow its acquisition and distribution of Indian lands on the prairies. With the federal government's program of enfranchising individual tribal members and assigning them land on the reserves came other efforts to persuade desperate band leaders to sell parts of their land to pay current expenses.

Farther west, in British Columbia, the situation differed sharply from that in the rest of Canada. There officials rejected the ideas and practices resulting from the Proclamation of 1763 that underlay most Canadian Indian policies. As early as 1870 Joseph Trutch, the British Columbia commissioner of land and works, rejected Indian land claims in the province. "The title of the Indians . . . has never been acknowledged by the government, but, on the contrary, is distinctly denied" he wrote to the governor.[26] Speaking for many whites there, he claimed that the region essentially lay vacant when the Anglo-Canadians arrived. According to Trutch and other provincial leaders, the tribes lacked any legal rights to the land. Local officials went so far as to prohibit reserve dwellers from acquiring other land through the preemption system then in operation. Provincial leaders refused to budge from their anti-Indian ideas on this issue, and down into the early twentieth century they deflected most discussion of such matters to an argument over the size of Indian reserves rather than considering the possibility of land title belonging to the tribes.[27]

When the province joined the new Dominion of Canada in 1871, British Columbia officials tricked the Ottawa government into accepting wording that limited future land grants for tribal reserves to no more than ten acres per family, far short of what other tribes had gotten or continued to get in the rest of the country. This issue has continued to sour federal-provincial relations for generations. In 1887 Indian anger over the unjust British Columbia policies surfaced. That year Nishga and Tsimshian chiefs visited government leaders in Victoria. They asked for more land and for access to documents published a decade earlier that would have supported their case, but without success. The politicians diverted the discussion to the issue of local self-government, but not until the officials promised to visit the coastal reserves later that summer. Meeting with Indian leaders, the visitors heard the same refrain repeatedly. Tribal spokesmen claimed that the land was still theirs, that they had never ceded it nor signed treaties doing that. Despite the heated Indian rhetoric, the visitors from Victoria refused to accept any of the tribal land claims.[28] The dispute over land title and arguments over Indian policy between the province and the federal government laid the basis for continuing discontent and political agitation by individual tribes and multitribal organizations in British Columbia throughout the twentieth century.

Meanwhile, in the rest of Canada after 1900 bureaucrats sought to reduce the Indian land base whenever possible in order to open what easterners thought of as potentially productive lands in southern Saskatchewan and Alberta. To get tribal acceptance of the land sales, the negotiators promised immediate cash payments to the adult males. This certainly encouraged many band members to accept the land cessions but failed to convince all of the tribal people, or at times enough of them, to ease the land transfer procedures. For example, on two reserves in 1902 the Indians objected to selling any of their land. They reminded the Indian Department officials that the lands in question constituted the most valuable part of their reserve. More important, they saw the reserve as a homeland, an area to be kept for use by their descendants. They reported that "when our chief died he left us instruction to look after the reserve . . . we cannot consent to part with any of it."[29]

In the United States at the same time, the General Allotment or Dawes Act allowed federal bureaucrats to separate Indians from much of their land base. Competency hearings, collusion between judges and local land speculators or ranchers, and a general demand to reduce the size of tribal holdings in much of the West brought similar disputes over landholdings. As federal officials gradually surveyed and allotted Indian reservations, they found much "surplus" land, that is, land not allotted to any individual Indian. Because such acreage could legally be sold to whites desiring it, the tribal land base shrank dramatically between 1890 and 1910. Although tribal leaders objected strenuously, the result appears remarkably similar to what happened in Canada at the same time. In particular, once the Supreme Court handed down its 1903 *Lone Wolf v. Hitchcock* decision, the government could move ahead rapidly. Because that ruling held that the court had the authority to void or change existing treaties, land sale agreements no longer needed the consent of the tribal people. If Congress chose to reduce the size of any reservation it had the authority to do so, and western politicians stepped up their efforts to shrink or abolish reservations in their states or districts.[30]

Tribal numbers continued to shrink in both countries, and by the turn of the century some officials began to express concern about Indian survival for more than another generation or two. Certainly the era from the 1880s to World War I witnessed a virtual collapse in Indian populations in some parts of both nations. The Plains tribes in particular suffered drastic population losses. The Blood tribe in Alberta provided a stark example of this. In 1878 Canadian authorities recorded their population as 2,488 people. By 1885 they had dwindled to 1,776, and the 1920 census recorded only 1,111 of them still alive. Their high death rate and few births suggested that this group's future seemed grim indeed. For example, in 1884 the figures included 126 deaths and a mere 8 live births for these Indians. Obviously such a trend could not last for long if the tribe were to survive.[31]

Population figures for tribes in the United States showed a similar grim pattern, and in both societies thoughtful people began to wonder if the tribal peoples would survive as identifiable groups. Yet by the outbreak of World War I the downward population trend began to reverse, and since then the number of Indians in both countries has increased steadily. In Canada, for example, census figures from 1912 on showed a slow but steady increase in the number of registered Indians there. By 1924 Canadian Indian Department officials recognized and reported the turnaround. That year Duncan C. Scott noted that the increase proved "that the Indian race is not dying out, although there exists a popular misconception to this effect."[32]

An accurate idea of the number of Indians in the United States at the turn of the century is difficult to get because the Census Bureau and Indian Office did not cooperate fully. As a result, people may have appeared in the count twice or not at all. With the implementation of allotment after the 1887 passage of the Dawes Act, more Indians appeared in the census counts because now the bureaucrats began to include reservation dwellers in addition to those tribal people living within the general population. The 1900 figure of just over 237,000 proved to be the low-water mark for native peoples in the United States. The 1910 census staff made a determined effort to include all people who claimed Indian ancestry and found nearly 30,000 more people that year. After that the count continued to rise, and Indians could no longer be considered in danger of vanishing from either of the North American societies.[33]

INDIAN PARTICIPATION IN WORLD WAR I

As the populations in tribal communities increased and the reservation land bases shrank or remained static, it became obvious that difficulties lay ahead, but World War I interrupted further developments. That conflict had an immediate impact on Indian peoples as both societies focused their attention on war-related issues. By the time the fighting had ended, tribal groups across North America encountered significantly changed circumstances, and many reservation dwellers found themselves in worse straits than before the hostilities. Although Canada entered the war several years before the United States did, tribes in both nations had similar experiences. World War I brought them more public attention but little economic or social well-being. In fact, the large-scale diversion of funds from domestic concerns to war-related measures in both countries reduced programs for Indians drastically. Bureaucrats in Canada recognized that the war would sharply reduce the European market for Indian-trapped furs, and to offset the loss of income from trapping, the government encouraged people who depended on the fur business to increase their hunting—particularly for food animals. During 1914 Indian agents and Hudson's Bay Company traders received permission to issue modest amounts of ammunition and food to Indians in desperate straits.[34]

At the beginning of the war the government depended on volunteers to fill army needs. In 1914 Canada exempted all noncitizen Indians from military service and declined allowing them to enlist. Many young men had already joined local militia units, however, and some of those units went overseas. By late 1915 rising casualties and lagging numbers of volunteers persuaded Sir Sam

Hughes, then minister of militia and defense, to permit Indians to enlist. During the next several years officials held recruiting drives on or near many reserves. Often young men joined readily and, although accurate figures are lacking, it is possible that by 1917 as many as 35 percent of the eligible Indians had joined the army by the time the Military Service Act (the draft) became law.[35]

Most officials opposed creating segregated all-Indian units, but by late 1915 continuing shortages of men helped change that attitude. On 22 December 1915 officials authorized the organization of a battalion from the Six Nations Reserve in Ontario. About 350 reserve dwellers joined despite the continuing objections of Iroquois leaders, who insisted that they were independent allies of the king and not subject people. By 1916 the army dispersed the men, except for the Six Nations battalion, which remained intact for another year. Farther west, Chief Inspector of Indian Agencies Glen Lyon Campbell recruited some 500 Indians from various bands near Winnipeg. In other units the Indians often served as scouts or pioneers who worked on military construction projects both in Canada and in Europe.[36]

In 1916 young Canadian men had to register for conscription, which followed a year later. Some band and reserve leaders objected to the registration and to the enlistment drives taking place nearby. Eventually all male British subjects between ages twenty and forty-five had to register, including treaty or status Indians. This brought objections based on long-standing rights and the fact that as wards of the government reserve dwellers could not vote. Indians at Brantford, Ontario, and on Manitoulin Island complained, and support for the war effort varied widely among Canadian Indian groups. It is difficult to know just how many Indians served because some enlistment officials failed to record ethnic or racial data, and in parts of the Far North they kept few records at all. From existing data it is likely that between thirty-five hundred and four thousand Indians served with the Canadian Expeditionary Force in Europe.[37]

Some young men enlisted out of a feeling of loyalty to the king because of their treaties with representatives of the queen three or four decades earlier. Clearly any such loyalty existed toward Britain rather than Canada. It also seems likely that the continuing strength of tribal culture and the honor that went to successful warriors impelled some of the young men to join the army. Certainly the recruiters considered that the Indians' hunting skills and familiarity with firearms made them desirable candidates for military service. Some Indians may well have seen the military as an escape from the poverty or boredom of the reserves, with travel and adventure coming as a part of their enlistment. After 4 May 1916 the minister of justice ruled that Indians who served in the army obtained the right to vote without having to accept the often unpopular enfranchisement, with its individual land allotment and end of benefits as a band member on one's home reserve.[38]

In 1917 Parliament passed the Military Service Act, mandating the registration of all young men for the draft. Duncan Scott reported that by the end of that year most young Indians had registered, although on a few isolated reserves the tribal people still distrusted the government and cooperated grudgingly or not at all. Claiming that this resulted from misunderstandings of the conscription law, he said that Indian objections caused little "serious inconvenience or delay."[39] Despite his positive description, the situation proved more unsettled than calm. Some Indians objected to the draft because they lacked Canadian citizenship and demanded the same rights as other Canadians if they served. Petitions to the government raising this objection received prompt attention, and a 17 January 1918 order in council exempted Indians from having to serve in combat situations.[40] Nevertheless, objections to conscription remained the exception and followed the usual channels of Indian-government communications at the time.

The United States stayed out of the war until 1917, but its brief participation brought more discussion about Indian roles in the war effort than occurred in Canada. Since the 1890s some army officers and westerners had suggested creating separate, segregated Indian units, and this idea drew varied responses. All-Indian companies had existed for a short time during the 1890s, but military authorities soon rejected the idea. When the war broke out, however, the practice attracted renewed attention. Congressman Carl Hayden from Arizona, for example, claimed that hundreds of young men had experienced military discipline while attending the federal boarding schools, and they would prove most effective in all-Indian units. He pointed to such an Indian unit in his state's National Guard. Edward E. Ayer, a member of the Board of Indian Commissioners, supported the idea enthusiastically. He went so far as to suggest raising ten to fifteen Indian regiments.[41]

Within the War Department, where no solid support emerged for these schemes, the government listened to opponents, including various Indians. Leaders of the Society of American Indians, founded just a few years previously, joined the attack on efforts to start segregated all-Indian army units. Through the society's magazine, *American Indian*, writers such as Carlos Montezuma, Thomas Standing Bear, and Gertrude Bonnin denounced the proposed segregation, arguing that "much of the popular clamor for a spectacular Indian regiment or battalion arises from the showman's brand of Indian as seen in the circus."[42]

Others, including many of the Oklahoma Indians who joined the National Guard, claimed to prefer serving in segregated units. Whatever their ideas on this matter, Indian participation in the war effort was high.

Regardless of the arguments about having segregated units or integrating Indian men into the army, many tribes supported the United States enthusiastically. The Society of American Indians acted as a sort of cheerleading corps when backing the war effort and in demonstrating Indian contributions. During 1917 and 1918 leaders of the group used the *American Indian* to publicize Indian participation in military actions and on the home front. They continued to urge integrating young Indians within the armed forces and backed the war effort wholeheartedly. In an early 1918 editorial Gertrude Bonnin called on her readers to "stand by the flag, red men; it is your flag. Under it there is the only hope you may ever expect for yourself and your race."[43] What result this overheated rhetoric brought is uncertain, but the sentiments indicated how strongly some educated Indian leaders wanted to join the rest of American society.

Once the United States entered the war, it dealt with the issue of Indian enlistments and conscription in ways similar to those used north of the border. The Selective Service Act of 18 May 1917 applied to all citizens, which by then included at least a majority of Indians. Federal officials assigned the task of registering men to local Selective Service workers, although in remote areas, each agency got its own draft board. By the end of the war Commissioner Cato Sells bragged that at least six thousand of the eight thousand Indian men then in the service had enlisted. Not all of the young men welcomed military service with the same enthusiasm, however, and resistance to the draft occurred among the Gosiutes, Shoshones, Utes, Navajos, and some groups of Mission Indians in California. These incidents usually created more fear of violence than real danger, but officials on isolated reservations dreaded the worst, or at least they acted that way.

In a few cases actual violence appeared likely. For example, in western Utah and eastern Nevada Gosiute tribesmen refused to register and threatened to resist. After much confusion the commissioner of Indian affairs sent a special investigator to gather the facts, and by July 1917 most of the eligible men had registered. Nevertheless, antidraft agitation continued, and in early 1918 a platoon of soldiers and a sheriff's posse surprised the objectors and took them off to jail in Salt Lake City. Soon the excitement faded, as it became clear that Indian reluctance to registering came partially from some misunderstanding and partially from the certainty that they were not yet citizens and therefore should not have been declared eligible in the first place. Indian Office officials rejected that argument adamantly but later that same year came to accept the possibility that some of the young men were in fact not citizens.[44]

Not surprisingly, those most eager to get Indians into the military forces in both countries tended to stress skills that educators and missionaries had tried to eliminate. On some reservations and reserves tribal elders held ceremonies to bring spiritual power and blessings on the would-be soldiers. Individual Indian soldiers received much attention for their skills with firearms, and many of them became snipers once they reached the battle zones. At the same time, some officials in both nations claimed that military service would help to integrate the young men into their respective societies. Cato Sells described the army experience for U.S. soldiers as being something that would help them become more individualistic, hardly something to be expected from men participating in platoons and companies that stressed unit identity and solidarity. Sells concluded that the wartime service would serve as a "Civilizer" for the tribesmen. Exactly how this occurred he left vague, but his comments about the subject demonstrate the confusion whites exhibited whenever they dealt with tribal peoples.[45]

INCREASING AGRICULTURAL EFFORTS, DECREASING LAND

Not only did both nations benefit from Indians' service in the armed forces during the war, but at home bureaucrats looked to the tribes for increased food production. Canada's earlier entry into the war gave them a three-year head start in this respect. By late 1914 Duncan C. Scott instructed the agency personnel to persuade the Indians to increase their food and livestock production. Although apparently not certain that the agents could achieve this goal, Scott continued his urgings throughout the war. In 1918 he asked the boarding school principals to furlough all of the fifteen- and sixteen-year-old boys so that they could serve as laborers on nearby farms. With food production still not as large as expected, that same year he threatened to fire agents who failed to increase farm output on their reserves.[46]

Although agricultural production increased throughout Canada and reserve crops increased noticeably, the government remained dissatisfied. In 1917 it launched the Greater Production Effort to increase crop size even more. Aimed primarily at Indian reserve lands, the program waived tribal rights and treaty agreements in the name of helping the war effort. Claiming that many reserves included far more land than the Indians could farm effectively, the Department of Indian Affairs defended the amendments in the Indian Act vigorously. Under the new legislation, tribes that refused to sell their surplus land would have to lease it to white farmers or ranchers, who were then expected to use it effectively. The government also gave itself the authority to spend band funds to increase crop or livestock production even if the band or reserve leaders objected to that use of their money. Noting that "there are large areas of land on Indian reserves capable of pasturing cattle or producing wheat," the bureaucrats agreed "that all obstacles to the utilization of these lands should, in as far as possible, be removed."[47] When the discussion of this issue in Parliament brought questions about what might happen to the Indians if the whites got to farm their best land, Minister of the Interior Arthur Meighen replied, "I do not think we need waste any time in sympathy for the Indian, for I am pretty sure his interests will be looked after by the Commissioner."[48]

Had the Indian Department officials paid more attention to tribal rights rather than trying to show how smoothly their office functioned, the reserve dwellers might have suffered far less than they did. Unfortunately, William M. Graham, a longtime bureaucrat who thought of himself as abused because he did not direct the affairs of the department, decided to use the Greater Production Effort activities for his personal benefit. In January 1918 Graham proposed that his superiors authorize him to supervise agricultural production efforts on the reserves in the prairie provinces. He suggested that as many as 220,000 acres of Indian land still remained unused, and that by deploying this land and "idle" funds belonging to the Indians, grain and cattle production in the West might be tripled. Graham's suggestions brought him an appointment as commissioner for the Greater Production Effort in Manitoba, Saskatchewan, and Alberta.[49]

The new program and Graham's local authority gave him nearly unlimited power to regulate the use of tribal lands. Under existing treaties and previous legislation the band members had to vote their approval of new programs or for the use or sale of their lands. The wartime measure sidestepped those rights entirely, turning control of reserve lands to the bureaucrats with little check on their actions. For example, in early 1918 Indian Department officials tried to persuade the unwilling Blood tribe to sell up to ninety thousand acres of their reserve. Enraged that mere Indians dared oppose their plans, the officials turned to force, bribery, intimidation, and outright fraud to achieve their goal. The agent authorized underage boys to vote in the tribal election and gave presents to those who supported the sale. In the end the Indians voted reluctantly to accept the sale, but one of the chiefs soon charged the local officials with fraud, intimidation, and bribery. At that point the bureaucrats shifted their tactics and began leasing thousands of acres to nearby whites, using their powers under the recent amendments to the Indian Act. By the spring of 1918 this had been done, leading to overgrazing by the ranchers' cattle, and by 1919 a drop in Indian crop production.[50]

Losing some of their best land to leasing by their white neighbors hurt the Blood tribe for some years. Before the Greater Production Effort had gone into effect they had managed to increase their crop production substantially without much government help. Other dwellers on western reserves had done the same thing. Crops fell only after the bureaucrats began trying to regulate tribal farming and land use during the war. In 1916, for example, wheat production had climbed to 388,731 bushels among the western tribes, but just two years later it dropped to only 255,884 bushels. Some of this reduction may have resulted from bad weather, but the fact remains that the tribal people lost nearly a third of their wheat production within only two years. Once the forced leasing actions took place, wheat and other crops declined again. So while the government boasted of its successes, its own data convicted it of lying and mismanagement. Unfortunately, those two problems were the least of the Indians' worries. More significant for their future was their temporary land loss and the destruction visited upon several western reserves. Their own increased crops and larger livestock herds both added to the problems of overproduction and economic dislocation that followed the war. For the Canadian Indians, the war proved mostly negative. Their young men fought, and in some cases died, while those who stayed on the reserves saw their land base temporarily decreased and its economic potential damaged badly by the very officials who should have protected their interests.[51]

Even before the war ended, plans for demobilizing Canada's six hundred thousand military personnel began. With wounded and discharged men returning to Canada in February 1918, the government set into motion the Department of Soldiers' Civil Re-establishment. More important for the reserve Indians, however, was the 1917 Soldier Settlement Act, which resulted in further land losses, particularly for those groups inhabiting the southern parts of the prairie provinces. Under the settlement act, qualified veterans could receive grants of up to 160 acres of dominion-owned land, with accompanying loans for seed, equipment, and livestock should they want to move west and become farmers. When far more veterans responded to the program than anticipated, the government enlarged it. In early 1918 it authorized the Settlement Board to buy private lands for the veterans, through compulsion if necessary.

The act supposedly excluded Indian lands, but in fact parts of some reserves had been surrendered to the government and lay open for the veterans to settle. When discussions of changing this program occurred in Parliament, some MPs complained that the tribes monopolized large amounts of unused land. The Department of Indian Affairs proved only slightly stronger in its defense of tribal lands, and frequently it encouraged reserve dwellers to sell land to the government so groups of veterans could acquire acreage in the so-called Railway Belt. Most of the tribal lands sold to white farmers had passed out of Indian control by 1920, and during the last several years under the Soldier Settlement Act only modest amounts of Indian land changed hands.[52]

While most tribes lost little of their land, Indian veterans in Canada failed to get a fair share of the postwar benefits. Although the 1919 New Soldier Settlement Act authorized granting 160 acres of land to former servicemen, reserve dwellers found that officials used a 1906 amendment to the Indian Act to deny their applications for land. A few Indian veterans managed to get loans to buy land, but most of their holdings lay within their home reserves. In the prairie provinces only one in ten Indian applicants actually got loans for land purchases.[53] Ironically, the very year the veterans settled on the plains coincided with a serious drought there and with a worldwide drop in prices for farm goods. As a result, for much of the 1920s neither Indian nor white farmers had much success. The issue of selling Indian lands to veterans never came up in the United States because it developed no similar program for its veterans after the war.

There, no sooner had war been declared than President Wilson called upon the nation's farmers to do their part. The 250,000 or more Indians in the United States seemed to offer an excellent resource for increasing food production. After all, at least in the picture presented by the press, the tribal people could follow the lead of Bureau of Indian Affairs (BIA) officials to harness their largely unused lands to meet the country's needs. Commissioner of Indian Affairs Cato Sells pounced on the increased production effort to speed Indian incorporation into the national economy. Although acculturation had continued to lag during the early twentieth century, the war effort would allow the bureaucrats to apply renewed pressures on the tribes. Once Indians learned to farm successfully, it was hoped that they could be made self-sufficient and the government might escape its responsibilities and expenses for the vast wardship process.[54]

Sells focused much of his subordinates' energy on the farm production efforts. Indians heard lectures about soil conservation, proper choice of crops, and ways to raise more food per acre. Hints that farms had to become more profitable because federal monies usually allotted to Indian programs might well be diverted to wartime needs may have proved convincing. Notices in tribal languages announced the program, and local agents occasionally offered modest cash prizes to farmers with the most increased production. Many Indians responded favorably to the campaign. Medicine Owl, a Montana Blackfeet leader, promised that "we will plant more corn to feed your soldiers and we will raise more goats and sheep that your soldiers may be clothed."[55] Agents throughout the West reported increased interest, effort, and crop sizes by 1918, as the two-year-long campaign began to show results. Even some of the Nighthawks, a militantly antiacculturation group among the Oklahoma tribes, responded positively and farmed a few small plots as part of the campaign.[56]

Nevertheless, as in Canada, a perception persisted that much Indian land lay unused and that no matter how hard the tribal people worked they would be able to farm only a small part of their holdings. In fact, Commissioner Sells reported that "thousands of acres of uncultivated agricultural land on the different reservations" could be put into production, and he complained about "many able-bodied Indians not making their best effort toward self-support, many of whom should no doubt be farming."[57] The modest crops resulted from many causes, including large reservations with limited populations, Indian poverty, and a lack of agricultural equipment. Nevertheless, as agent after agent reported having more land than could be effectively used, calls for expanding the holdings of white lessees became common. Agents campaigned through direct letters to leaseholders as well as ads placed in local newspapers and farm journals. Responding to this effort and to war-driven inflation of crop prices, white farmers signed new leases as BIA officials interpreted the regulations liberally to encourage increased production. When some westerners urged the government to make fundamental changes in the leasing structure and regulations for Indian lands, however, tribal leaders objected and Congress declined to alter the system in any major ways.[58]

While white ranchers, farming companies, and sugar corporations hastened to increase both the food production and acres leased, Indians throughout the West contributed to the campaign as well. Commissioner Sells reported large-scale increases in Indian acreage. In 1917 he claimed that reservation farms added over 113,000 acres to their previous totals, and the next year his figures showed nearly 53,000 more acres under cultivation. Tribal efforts varied sharply across the country. Students at the Haskell Institute in Kansas raised vegetables between rows of trees in the school orchard. In several places Indian farmers planted a second crop on their land as soon as they harvested the first one. On the Rosebud Reservation the farmers sowed wheat between their rows of corn and put land lying fallow back into production.[59]

Despite all the effort, by the time the government and western farmers got their activities organized, the war had ended. Most of the additional production came in late 1918 and the next year. By that time both the demand and prices for farm products suffered a sharp downturn, bringing economic bad times to Indian and white farmers alike. In addition, during the years 1917–21 much of the West suffered from drought or at least greatly reduced rainfall, so that the farming effort produced little except higher debts. In the long run the increased leasing put additional burdens on the tribal land bases because the lessees tended to overgraze the Indian land. Pressing land that had been left vacant into production also further cut its fertility and lengthened the time needed to bring it back to usefulness. Although agents concluded that the Indians profited by becoming more involved in farming during the war years, the experience seems to have had few discernible positive outcomes.[60] As so often happened with government programs, the expectations remained high while the results failed to match. Certainly food production increased for both Indian and white farmers and ranchers, but it is unclear whether the modest short-term rise in crops offset the disruption of some reservations, the increased leasing of tribal lands to whites, and the heavy strain on the carrying capacity of the range.

By 1920 tribal people in both the United States and Canada had endured continued cultural, economic, and demographic battering by the societies in both countries. Government policies reduced the land base of many groups, as fraud and bribery often accomplished what formal actions did not. World War I led some Indians to leave their reservations for military service, but when the conflict ended they returned home to face increased poverty. Veterans' benefits helped many young men, but rarely did tribal members get much assistance. The continuing efforts of educators, missionaries, and bureaucrats hurt tribes more than helping them. As a result, the postwar decades would bring even more difficulties and problems for reserve dwellers.

10 Change, Depression, and War, 1920–1945

 THREE YEARS AFTER World War I had ended, an international cast of dignitaries gathered at Arlington National Cemetery. Their purpose on that 11 November 1921 afternoon was the burial of the unknown soldier. Representatives from seven nations awarded the unknown their highest military honors. A chaplain read the burial service, and people placed wreaths on the tomb. As the ceremonies drew to a close, the Crow chief Plenty Coups, now in his seventies and wearing a feathered war bonnet and Indian clothing, approached the sarcophagus. He placed the bonnet and his coup stick on it and raised both hands to the sky. "I feel it an honor to the red man that he takes part in this great event," he said in Crow, "because it shows that the thousands of Indians who fought in the great war are appreciated by the white man." When the chief ended his brief and unexpected remarks, an artillery salvo and taps ended the proceedings.[1]

The chief was correct. Thousands of Indians had fought for both the United States and Canada during World War I. Unfortunately, few citizens in either country realized that, and even fewer gave their contributions any thought. Once Indians stopped appearing in the Liberty Loan bond sale campaigns, they dropped from public view quickly. The crisis had ended, and each society focused on prompt economic recovery from the war. Soon both governments began thinking about and treating tribal people in ways that differed little from fifty-year-old practices. Yet at the same time, actions taken during the 1920s and 1930s laid the foundation for change. While that came slowly and unevenly, it led toward a vastly different Indian world.

At the time it seemed as if the tribes had sacrificed for nothing, and although that would not continue to be the case, it was true for a time. Continuing anti-Indian prejudices shaped relations between the races in rural and Western areas, while few people in the more settled parts of either nation dealt with any tribal people. Diamond Jenness, a Canadian anthropologist, traveled across that country visiting reserves and talking about Indian relations with whites living near them. "In every region I found a deep-rooted prejudice against them," he wrote. Most apparent in the West and least obvious in Quebec, it colored all aspects of interracial contact. Jenness credited widespread Indian poverty, their lack of education and poor use of English, and their limited contact with most English-speaking Canadians as the basic reasons for antipathy toward the tribal peoples. To westerners in particular he thought that Indians appeared as little more than "half-regenerate savages," and therefore the whites treated them "with hardly concealed contempt."[2]

Many Canadians considered Indians to be shiftless and unreliable, and along the Pacific Coast they ridiculed tribal people as "dirty Siwashes." Frequently, segregated schools accepted the children of recent Chinese or Japanese immigrants with little fuss while refusing to admit Indian children. Local regulations controlled white-Indian relations closely. For example, in the small western community of Hazelton a town ordinance decreed that "no Indian might walk beside a white man or woman, or sit on the same side of the village church."[3] At the same time farmers of the prairie provinces saw nothing wrong with paying $4.00 a day to Polish or Ukrainian immigrant laborers while offering only $2.50 to the few Indian workers they hired. Clearly, even though they had fought alongside other Canadians during the war, once they returned home the Indians faced widespread prejudice and enjoyed few benefits in their own country.

PANTRIBALISM AND PEYOTISM

The difficulties reserve dwellers experienced during the postwar era brought several responses. Some older Indians chose to ignore the intrusive white society as much as possible, drawing strength and pride from their tribal cultures. Despite their efforts, the constant battering by the change agents of the majority society left many tired and resigned to their status. Younger Indians, however, responded differently to their land loss, cultural destruction, and unequal treatment. Concluding that their poverty, illiteracy, inadequate diet, and poor health resulted from government bungling, they demanded that the bureaucrats begin to repair the damage their policies had caused.[4] When little changed, some people become apathetic, while others continued their grumbling. Gradually the latter led to the beginnings of the pan-Indian political and economic organizations that emerged during the early twentieth century.

Actually, Canadian Indians had begun organizing pantribal political organizations shortly after confederation. As early as the 1870s the Grand General Indian Council of Ontario began holding biannual meetings, and occasionally they sent copies of their resolutions to the Department of Indian Affairs. Apparently the bureaucrats had trouble deciding how to treat this group, but over the years they allowed bands to pay the travel expenses of their delegates to the meetings. Usually the council reflected the views of partially acculturated band groups in southern Ontario, and rarely did it act in anything but a calm and conservative manner. By the end of World War I its civility wore thin, however, as the council began to push the government for reasonable treatment. In 1919 the new president, Henry Jackson, raised issues that Indian veterans in both nations thought important. In particular he pointed to past treaty promises for fishing and hunting rights then being limited sharply by provincial laws. The 1911 Oliver Act, allowing expropriation of reserve lands adjacent to white communities, and a 1918 amendment to the Indian Act that authorized the government to lease vacant tribal lands to whites both received criticism. Despite this momentary burst of militancy, the group remained quiet, almost obsequious most of the time.[5]

Other pantribal groups sprang up across Canada during the early decades of the twentieth century, with the impetus coming from either Ontario or British Columbia tribes and spreading to the prairie provinces later. Most represented tribes or bands in a single province or even the scattered bands of a single tribe or nation, yet many reserve dwellers saw these organizations as a way to make their dissatisfaction known, to challenge the Department of Indian Affairs, or at least to focus some public attention on its actions. Some, such as the Nishga Council, began during a dispute over a single issue, in this case tribal land claims and the flat refusal of British Columbia to recognize them. Others included movements for religious or cultural revitalization of the kind seen in both countries for generations. The organizations came and went with startling rapidity, and white Canadians knew so little about their activities that considerable confusion over when some of the groups began, merged, or died out still exists.[6]

Federal officials responsible for dealing with the tribal peoples, viewing the emerging Indian groups that appeared after World War I as attacks on them or as moves by small groups of reserve dwellers to bring drastic changes to the system, watched the new associations and councils carefully. Indian men, however, had learned much through their wartime experience and, even though they won the right to vote and several other minor concessions, remained dissatisfied with their status within the country. Military service had brought them into contact with members of distant bands and tribes for the first time, and they began to share their complaints. Once they realized that many of them shared similar problems, it proved but a short step to the beginnings of intertribal organizations.

One of the most effective of the new groups got its start in December 1918 when Frederick O. Loft, a returning veteran from the Six Nations reserve in Ontario, became the first president of the League of Indians of Canada. Its founders began modestly but hoped to include all the tribal peoples of Canada in their organization. They mailed circulars to bands on many reserves, and within a year their influence had spread widely. One of their 1919 mailings reminded the readers that the time had passed when a single band or two could "free themselves from the domination of officialdom and from being ever the prey and victims of unscrupulous means of depriving us of our lands and homes and even deny us of the rights we are entitled to as free men under the British flag."[7] Appeals of this sort brought enthusiastic crowds to the "congresses," as the league called its large public meetings.

Loft, a skilled orator, spoke about gaining full rights of citizenship for Indians who had fought during the war. Despite the refusal of the Indian Department to allow bands to pay the cost of sending representatives to the league's meetings out of their own funds, the organization extended its membership and influence gradually. Wanting to disrupt the league's activities, Duncan Scott sent government spies to the group's meetings. Canadian authorities decided that the Indians brought this much surveillance on themselves because they publicly and repeatedly attacked the operations of the Department of Indian Affairs, gaining some public support through the newspapers and embarrassing the government by their rhetoric.[8]

During the early 1920s Loft traveled to Alberta and Saskatchewan, where the League of Indians of Canada held successful meetings and gathered considerable support. At these and other league meetings the Department of Indian Affairs encouraged local agents, teachers, missionaries, and even local law enforcement officials to observe—in effect, to spy on—the Indians' actions. Mounted Police officers patrolled the gatherings looking for drunkenness or other signs of public disorder, but with little success. Duncan Scott could brook no opposition and had little tolerance for public criticism; Loft's persistence in blaming the federal bureaucrats for tribal problems probably helped bring about the police interference. Because few misdeeds came to light, despite government surveillance, Scott could find no justification for halting the league meetings. When his wife got sick during the mid-1920s, Loft took her to Chicago and dropped out of organizing activities for some years. By the time he returned to active agitation for tribal rights, later in the decade, the League of Indians of Canada had faded, at least as a national organization. Only in the prairie provinces did it remain strong and active into the next decade.[9]

On the West Coast continuing agitation over tribal land claims and their complete rejection by British Columbia officials led to continuing Indian efforts to organize and present their claims to either Canadian federal officials or British judicial bodies. In 1909 some twenty British Columbia tribes formed the Indian Tribes of the Province of British Columbia. By 1916 other groups joined with these bands to form a new group, the Allied Tribes of British Columbia, led by Peter Kelly, a Haida, and Andrew Paull, a Squamish. This new group gained white supporters and a sympathetic attorney, Arthur E. O'Meara, who worked with them to present their claims to a wider audience and to the Canadian government. They led the negotiations with the Ottawa government, failing to get a settlement in 1923, but four years later managed to get a second set of hearings on the land question. In 1927 Paull and Kelly testified before a Senate and House of Commons special committee established to examine the British Columbia land claims issue. They got high marks for their presentation but again no settlement from the government. Instead, Parliament passed legislation to prohibit Indians from raising any more money to pay for the legal expenses of continuing their land claims.[10]

The Ontario Six Nations Iroquois proved most effective when dealing with Canadian officials. Having been offered land in Ontario by British authorities at the end of the American Revolution, these people insisted that they had never surrendered to anyone, and that rather than being subject people or wards of the government, they were, in fact, allies and thus independent equals with the government of Britain and therefore of Canada. Canadian officials dismissed such claims as nonsense, but the Indians maintained their position. For generations the Iroquoian groups had governed themselves through a council of hereditary chiefs, but once the 1876 Indian Act went into force, Canadian officials began tampering with this form of local government. The Indians objected repeatedly but with little success. Still, Ottawa bureaucrats chose not to force change because the majority of the Six Nations people opposed it. By World War I internal divisions on the reserves brought the conflict into sharp focus. So-called progressives known as the Dehorners wanted to replace the traditional chiefs with others to be elected, but they lacked widespread support. The hereditary chiefs remained divided too, however, as some wanted to continue their duties within the framework of Canadian regulations while others demanded total sovereignty for the tribes.[11]

Objecting repeatedly to the actions of the Department of Indian Affairs, the Six Nations Council established a committee to determine their tribal status within Canada. By 1919 the council faction most in favor of tribal sovereignty had taken the initiative. Led by Levi General, whom they called Chief Deske-heh, this group hired the lawyer A. G. Chisholm to gather evidence to support their position. Early in 1920 the House of Commons invited the Iroquois to send a representative to testify before the committee considering a compulsory enfranchisement bill; the Indians sent Chisholm, but he made little impact on the legislators' thinking, and the compulsory bill became law that summer. The Indians denounced this and petitioned the governor general, stating their view that they enjoyed sovereignty within Canada. By late that year the Justice Department claimed that an Indian suit on this issue would stand no legal chance of success, so the government declined to pay for such an action. It also rejected all Iroquois claims of independence or sovereignty or that they were "not subject to the legislative authority of the Dominion, or of the Province of Ontario."[12]

The Indians then hired an American lawyer, George Decker, who advised appealing to the king of England for publicity and sympathy. During the summer of 1921 Chief Deskeheh traveled to Britain and presented the tribal petition to the Colonial Office. Officials there promptly sent it back to Canada. Nevertheless, this action brought sympathetic publicity for the Iroquois. That same year a governmental change in Canada brought the repeal of the compulsory enfranchisement that lay at the base of the dispute, and it seemed as if the issue might die. That did not happen, however, and in 1922 Decker advised his clients to appeal their case to the newly formed League of Nations. Now the Iroquois launched their campaign on the international stage. They approached representatives of the Dutch government, who agreed to support their petition to League of Nations officials. In April 1923 the Dutch representative gave the Six Nations petition to the secretary general of the league—an embarrassing moment for Canada, not yet fully independent itself. To build support for the Indians' case, Chief Deskeheh headed to Europe and there issued a statement entitled "The Redman's Appeal for Justice," containing the tribal position on the sovereignty issue.[13]

In it Deskeheh asked for home rule for the reserves, an accounting of the use of band funds by both the British and Canadian governments, and the right to move across Canada to the borders. At this point Canadian officials persuaded Britain to intervene, and the British pressured the governments helping with the Six Nations claim to drop their support. Although League of Nations officials had accepted the Indian petition, they took no binding action, and in late 1923 the league secretariat informed Deskeheh that he could not appear before a plenary session to speak in support of the tribal petition. Although he remained in Europe into 1924 and later that year wrote an appeal directly to King George V, nothing came of his actions on behalf of the Iroquois.[14]

Not only did Canadian authorities manage to defeat the Six Nations abroad, but at home they forced the ouster of the hereditary chiefs on the reserves as well. In September 1924 an order in council directed that the Grand River Reserve be divided into six electoral districts and that two councillors be chosen in each of them. The new government was to take office on 21 October 1924. That same directive abolished the hereditary council of forty-nine chiefs, and the Mounties stationed on the reserve forcibly expelled the former chiefs from the Council House. Such action temporarily united the quarreling factions on the reserve, and in the election that followed, most of the population of some four thousand people boycotted the process, as fewer than one hundred people voted for the new chiefs. While that seemed hardly the best way to demonstrate the democratic process on the reserve, the government won at least a surface victory because the elected chiefs now ran the tribal council and the badly shaken Indians would never fully recover control of their local affairs. Intimidation, violence, and discord continued among the Iroquois of Ontario into the 1990s, and responsibility for at least some of that must be laid at the feet of Canadian officials determined to destroy tribal identity and to crush any vestige of resistance to their bureaucratic meddling in local tribal affairs.[15]

While Canadian tribal people appealed unsuccessfully for just treatment to their own government and even had the temerity to bring their difficulties to the attention of the League of Nations, Indians in the United States made fewer moves to express their discontent. Not that they settled down to quiet obscurity, but the conversion to peacetime activity had less apparent impact on the tribes or their reservations than was the case in Canada. There was no push to buy Indian land to provide farms for unemployed veterans, as there was no U.S. counterpart to the Canadian effort to force a new political status on returning veterans or their families. Instead, American Indians found themselves receiving credit for their patriotism and help with the war effort. True, a 1924 law granted all noncitizen tribal people citizenship, but that had no particular effect on their tribal membership or eligibility to receive federal benefits due them as Indians. Thus, on the surface the basic issues that caused the most concern in Canada did not appear south of the border.

Yet major problems continued for tribal people in the United States too. Even before the war progressive Indians, often educated and of mixed race, decided that they needed a national organization to present their ideas to both the tribes and to the general population as well. Meeting at Columbus, Ohio, on 11 November 1911, they organized what became the Society of American Indians. This group included leaders who stood apart from tribal Indians and from the white population too, and often the society found itself on the fringes of both. Announcing that Indianness went far beyond physical definition, they urged all tribal people to strive for ways to develop economically, to use their initiative, and to help each other in raising the Indian standard of living and educational attainments. Demonstrating strong cultural pride, the society's leaders strove to persuade other Indians that their identity and cultures went beyond tribal borders and that they shared common ideas and practices that made them unique in American society.[16]

Leaders of the new group included the physicians Charles Eastman (Sioux) and Carlos Montezuma (Yavapai), the Reverend Sherman Coolidge (Arapaho), the lawyers Thomas L. Sloan and Hiram Chase (both Omaha), as well as Henry Red Cloud (Winnebago), a recent Yale graduate. Obviously these men did not represent most Indians in the United States, but they thought that the time had come for tribal people to organize and gain support for changes in their social position. Other educated leaders followed, and by 1916 Arthur C. Parker, a Seneca, and Gertrude Bonnin, a Yankton Sioux, led the organization. While hoping to speak for Indians in general, these individuals never could avoid the issues that separated tribe from tribe or that divided people within a single reservation. Questions about the use of peyote, the need to work with or against the Bureau of Indian Affairs, and acculturation and education as opposed to the retention of tribal cultures divided and weakened the Society of American Indians. Its very existence, however, demonstrated that tribal people felt the need to work together for mutual protection of their rights and to redirect government programs into channels that Indians thought would be of most benefit to them.[17]

In both nations pantribal organizations fared badly throughout most of the first half of the twentieth century, and the Society of American Indians proved a classic example of that. Two issues rent the membership and alienated some of the leaders from each other. The dispute over working with and through the federal government or calling for the abolition of the Indian Office provided some of the most vitriolic exchanges between Indian leaders. Carlos Montezuma withdrew from the society and in 1916 founded his own monthly journal, *Wassaja*, using it as a forum to roast other Indian leaders while heaping scorn on the bureaucrats. He presaged the American Indian Movement of the post-1960 era by charging that tribal people who worked in a bureaucracy had sold out their kinsmen. He denounced the Bureau of Indian Affairs for killing tribal peoples' cultural pride and undermining their efforts to retain something of their aboriginal culture. "When you kill racial pride, you kill the Man," he wrote. By doing that "his high spirit of what is right and what is wrong; his relation of man with man and his abiding faith in the Great Spirit," are all destroyed.[18]

While Montezuma jousted openly with some pan-Indian leaders over political issues, others quarreled violently over social customs. The use of peyote in religious ceremonies drew increasing criticism and polarized would-be national leaders for decades. Well before the turn of the century, tribes native to the southern plains as well as those who had been forced west into present-day Oklahoma knew of peyote, and its use spread gradually across the southern plains region. Reports of early meetings described peyote ceremonies as family affairs with songs and prayers. Participants avoided alcohol and violence. Nevertheless, teachers and missionaries objected to the drug because they assumed that its use indicated the continuation of pagan and savage rites on the reservations. When Indians used the drug secretly, this persuaded the whites that their fears were justified. Gradually agents and then local governments began to ban its use, and it took a concerted effort when Oklahoma became a state, in 1907, to persuade the new legal authority not to legislate against the drug and its use there. By 1918 Oklahoma had issued a charter to the founders of the Native American Church, a group that used peyote for sacramental purposes. While that organization would become one of the most significant pantribal organizations among American Indians, the church's peyote ceremonies embroiled it in continuing legal challenges, and its members suffered intimidation and persecution for another generation.[19]

Not only did peyote use bring trouble with the whites, but some educated and partially acculturated Indian leaders saw it as a step backward, as a demonstration that tribal people lacked the stability and good sense to become equal members of American society. Up to 1920 Gertrude Bonnin served as the editor of the *American Indian*, the official journal of the Society of American Indians. Through its pages she stressed education, learning English, and living in a middle-class manner. She attacked failed government programs and incompetent, lazy, or corrupt bureaucrats too, but saved much of her energy and anger for peyote users and the bad image they gave to the Indian movement for self-respect. As early as 1914 the Society of American Indians leadership had condemned peyote use, and they joined forces with white reform groups such as the Indian Rights Association and the Lake Mohonk Conference in trying to outlaw the practice. Bonnin attacked those who employed peyote in religious ceremonies for "undermining the work of the churches and government to uplift the Indians."[20]

Bonnin was not alone among pan-Indian leaders in attacking what became the Native American Church. Disagreements over goals and methods continued to disrupt many national Indian organizations as the Society of American Indians faded quietly from the scene. By 1926 the disappointed reformers founded the National Council of American Indians, and Bonnin served as its president soon after its organization. Thus, in both the United States and Canada some educated Indians felt the need for regional or national organizations to present a unified front to their respective governments and societies. The general tenor of the times and the coming of world depression by the end of the 1920s, however, brought most of these efforts to their knees, and they failed to achieve any particular success in either country until well after World War II.

REFORM MOVEMENTS IN THE 1920S

Although Indian people in North America failed to alter their relationships with either the national government or the general population, changes did begin to occur, although they proved more striking in the United States than in Canada. During the immediate postwar decade, conditions on the reservations worsened as continuing allotment and widespread fraud combined to strip tribal people of most of their pre-1887 land base. Aimed at the same goal as the Canadian enfranchisement, allotment subdivided reservation lands, assigning specific plots to particular individuals or families and making the so-called unused land available for white purchase. During the early decades of the twentieth century large numbers of white farmers, ranchers, lumbermen, and miners moved onto the reservations, and often their resulting land purchases brought a checkerboard pattern of Indian and white property holdings. The Canadian experience differed because the reserves remained entirely Indian-owned, with whites being unable to purchase the land.

The eroding land base on western American reservations brought renewed calls for rethinking the system and its goals. During the 1920s few reformers objected to the general objective of acculturating tribal peoples, but many saw the methods then in use as exploitative and harmful. The Society of American Indians and the National Council of American Indians, as well as white reform groups, all helped keep the desperate plight of Indians before the public. While doing that they set into motion events leading to a major shift in the administration of Indian affairs. The first public crusade revolved around a dispute over Pueblo land rights in New Mexico. Although not subject to the allotment program, these villagers apparently lost their rights to sell or trade their land through a 1913 Supreme Court decision. In 1921 Senator Holm Bursom of New Mexico introduced a bill that would take control of Pueblo lands so squatters living on some of them might get clear title to the properties. The Bursum bill failed to get through Congress, however, and instead Congress passed the 1924 Pueblo Lands Act, setting out methods for settling the legal disputes. The effort to defeat the first bill and support the second brought the reform groups together, and they turned their attention to blocking other unwanted federal actions toward Indian lands.[21]

Continuing demands to change the management of Indian affairs brought the Committee of One Hundred into being. This group included tribal people such as Thomas L. Sloan, Charles Eastman, and Arthur C. Parker, already active in pantribal activities, as well as prominent whites including John Pershing, Bernard Baruch, William Allen White, and William Jennings Bryan. They organized in late 1923 and the next year issued their findings with the title *The Indian Problem*. The committee's report concentrated on education, health, and property issues while calling for careful study of the peyote question and urging more leeway for Indians to continue religious rites and dances still prohibited by federal action. The report triggered renewed demands for changes in federal administrative goals and practices, and in 1926 the Institute for Government Research, subsequently the Brookings Institute, signed a contract to study the issues raised earlier that decade.[22]

Dr. Lewis Meriam headed a staff of expert researchers in such fields as public health, economics, education, law, sociology, and Indian affairs. After gathering data all over the country, the group returned east, where his staff wrote *The Problem of Indian Administration*, often called simply the Meriam Report. That document provided evidence that the reformers had assumed was available, but that no one in or out of government had ever collected. It showed Indian schools to be badly staffed, greatly underfunded, overcrowded, and offering a poor education. According to the researchers, poverty was a daily way of life for many reservation dwellers, with Indian per capita income less than one-sixth that of the rest of the population. Inadequate diet brought disease, and reservation health facilities often proved as dangerous to health as the schools had. Understaffed, poorly equipped, and grossly underfunded, the medical units available to Indians could not provide the desperately needed services. Pointing to allotment as the single most important cause of the widespread poverty, the Meriam Report blamed the Bureau of Indian Affairs for the basic neglect of Indians in all parts of the country.[23] By the end of the 1920s, then, the reformers in the United States had made their case clearly to both the government and the general population. The reforms that swept American society during the New Deal era would bring fundamental changes to Indian-white relations for at least the next decade.

In Canada during the 1920s, no such reform groundswell appeared. Instead, under Duncan C. Scott the Department of Indian Affairs became increasingly authoritarian and negative about its charges. Although it is unclear how effective it was, the push for forcible enfranchisement was just an early example of that approach. Scott encouraged Indian Department employees to spy on tribal and regional associations and to report instances of the sun dance or potlatch observances. At the same time he directed the Mounted Police to restrict the religious dances. The Mounties feared subversion and, echoing the red scare then sweeping the United States, they considered pan-Indian ceremonies and meetings as suspicious gatherings. By 1921 the police attended dances, often disrupting the activities, sending the people home, and even arresting a few. Those convicted served jail sentences for having taken part in the ceremonies.[24]

Indians responded angrily as they denounced this continuing government oppression. The Cree chief Thunderchild asked, "Can things go well in a land where freedom of worship is a lie, a hollow boast? . . . Why has the white man no respect for the religion that was given to us, when we respect the faith of other nations?"[25] Although such complaints brought no respite, frequently Indians ignored or evaded the law. At times they refused to cooperate with the Indian Department, at others they held ceremonies away from the reserve headquarters to avoid being charged with breaking the law. Government persecution continued, and the 1927 amendments to the Indian Act outlawed fund-raising by Indian bands to pay the costs of litigation over land claims. These restrictions continued on the books until a 1951 set of amendments brought a major overhaul to Indian administration.[26]

Among the few positive things that happened during the 1920s, the 1922 revocation of compulsory enfranchisement undoubtedly most pleased those reserve dwellers who knew of the action. The other was 1924 legislation bringing the Inuit or Eskimos under the provisions of the Indian Act. Prior to this action, which paid only modest attention to the Inuits' situation, the government had given virtually no attention to the people of the Far North, and as economic development in the region continued, their needs became critical. These modest efforts characterized Canadian policy toward tribal peoples during the following decade. A set of instructions sent to each agent in September 1933 clearly demonstrates how the bureaucratic approach to tribal peoples left little room for them to maneuver, much less to have any significant say in the shaping of their own future. Item 5 on the first page states that "it is the policy of the Department to promote self-support among the Indians and not to provide gratuitous assistance to those Indians who can provide for themselves."[27] Obviously, assimilation lay in the future for the reserve dwellers if the government had its way.

A combination of callous treatment and frequent inattention pushed some tribal peoples into desperate straits. For example, Plains groups living near the Saskatchewan River had supported themselves at least partially by trapping beaver and muskrats in the vast marshes along that stream. Repeatedly, their increasing poverty forced these people to overtrap and nearly destroy the beaver population. When this, in turn, led to the collapse of the beaver dams that had helped control drainage in the region, the water levels in the marshes plummeted. With less water to support marsh vegetation, the muskrat population dropped, and Indian trappers gathered fewer pelts each year. Their annual crop of the furbearers had been 800,000 pelts in 1902, but by 1930 overtrapping and the marsh reductions destroyed virtually all of these animals. Showing surprising concern for that era, federal and provincial authorities launched a crash program to restore the beaver and muskrats to the marshes. In 1934 they reported some 135,000 acres of marsh as reclaimed, and by 1941 the local Indian trappers sold 190,000 pelts in a remarkable turnaround of local resources.[28]

Similar programs of resource conservation and regeneration occurred elsewhere. Federal and Quebec officials set aside some 13,000 square miles at the southeastern end of James Bay with a long-term lease to develop a substantial beaver population for the support of Indian trappers. In an ironic move, Alberta reserved another 400,000 acres near Wood Buffalo Park to encourage muskrat propagation. Fifty years earlier the local Indian population had faced actual starvation when the government established the Wood Buffalo sanctuary, forbidding them to hunt the few remaining animals while the people stumbled across the countryside in desperate need of food. On the West Coast the Indian workers in the salmon industry got no such direct help from the government, but at least it chose not to interfere with their efforts to unionize as canning-industry workers. Perhaps that leniency resulted from the Indians' shift from an "extreme militancy at the turn of the century to a conservative unionism" during the Great Depression.[29]

In spite of these modest efforts to help tribal groups in obvious need, Canadian authorities faced almost no public outcry demanding reform of the system. At the time, the Indian associations still had little impact on the situation either. Multitribal groups had developed in many provinces, with most occurring in Ontario and British Columbia. On the West Coast, in particular, Indian workers participated in unions and other groups from the earliest days of the twentieth century. At first this came about because growing numbers of low-wage Japanese workers moved into the salmon canneries and the hop fields of the region, displacing Indians. Soon tribal laborers joined with others in the bitter strikes early in the century, then gradually began their own organizations. In 1934 the Native Brotherhood of British Columbia had emerged to represent Indians as they sought to cooperate with the existing unions of the Fishermen's Joint Committee, then active on the coast. During the strike of 1936, however, their white colleagues left them to picket the strike-bound plants and went off to work elsewhere. The tribal laborers responded by establishing their own union, the Pacific Coast Native Fishermen's Association, that year. Other such organizations appeared in Saskatchewan and Alberta during the 1930s, but none had much long-term success.[30]

These modest Indian initiatives brought few dramatic changes, as the 1930s passed with existing goals, methods, and even public awareness still in place. What now appear as long-bankrupt policies, rigidly applied, continued in force while many bands sank into misery and despair. Even the families of dead Indian veterans suffered because of extreme poverty. When that led to placing the corpses of former servicemen in pauper's graves, protests erupted. As early as 1922 legislation had begun government funding of the Last Post Fund, monies used for keeping veterans' families from being forced to bury their loved ones in paupers' graves. When one veteran did get a pauper's burial in 1936, news of the event brought protests from the Canadian Legion and the British Empire Service League, the two leading veterans organizations in Canada at the time. After that the policies changed quickly.[31]

Despite such concerns, Indians remained outside Canadian society. As late as 1939 Canadian educators still deplored tribalism and feelings of group identification. Clearly, long-standing federal programs thought to encourage individualism among tribal people had failed. One commentator identified the "fear to transgress tribal ethics" as a major reason why Indians made so little "progress in civilization, and as the element that divided Indians from whites in Canadian society." In a perceptive comment he identified this aspect of tribal psychology "as a species of tribal nationalism which is a real divisive element in our effort to bring the Indian within the sphere of Canadian citizenship."[32] Federal officials had come to fear that acculturation and assimilation would take still more decades, as Indians continued to reject white Canadian ground rules for joining the national society. While recognizing this, however, the officials seem to have made little effort to alter their approach or programs.

THE INDIAN NEW DEAL

During the 1930s, when the Great Depression struck both countries, Indian affairs slipped further from public view in Canada, but the opposite occurred in the United States. There the reform pressures of the preceding decade intensified, resulting in the 1933 appointment of John Collier as the new commissioner of Indian affairs. One of the leading activists in the reform movement, he had toured, written, and spoken widely on the need to rethink the objectives and methods then in place for dealing with the tribal people. With his appointment to direct the Bureau of Indian Affairs, tribal people and reformers alike hoped for better days ahead. The new commissioner's ideas received widespread attention and considerable support from Secretary of the Interior Harold Ickes, but western congressmen, church groups, and some Indians opposed his approach. At first the BIA tried to create Indian divisions within federal relief programs such as the Civilian Conservation Corps or to get emergency food and clothing for destitute reservation dwellers. For example, during 1933–34 the bureau distributed surplus army clothing and shoes to as many as forty thousand needy Indians.[33]

After working to assure survival for the reservation dwellers, Collier turned to improving education and health care. Using the Meriam Report findings, the bureaucrats moved to build more day schools, hire well-qualified teachers, and promote local schools as community centers so the adults would benefit from training as well. Drawing funds from the Public Works Administration, Collier ordered the construction of one hundred new day schools. Then he set out to improve public health facilities by having new hospitals built, enlarging or remodeling others, and increasing existing staffs. He campaigned throughout the decade for increased funding for the Indian Medical Service but never secured satisfactory levels of support to make major, long-term improvements on many of the reservations.[34]

Once the immediate, emergency needs had been met, Collier turned his efforts to what he saw as his major achievement—a redirection of Indian-white relations. From independence to the 1930s American leaders had favored acculturating and assimilating Indian people. The 1887 Dawes Act, which brought allotment of tribal lands and broke up some of the reservations, was the logical capstone of the effort to force the Indians to accept individualism within a capitalist structure and disappear into the melting pot. By 1934, however, Collier had gotten legislation introduced that would halt some of the worst aspects of the assimilationist agenda. What became the Indian Reorganization Act (IRA) of that year suspended allotment, authorized the tribes to form local councils that would serve as tribal corporations, encouraged the use of tribal languages, and accepted Indian arts, crafts, and religious practices as worthwhile. The commissioner's general ideas and his determination to help tribal people retain and even rebuild their culture marked a distinct change in U.S. Indian policy. Unfortunately, within a decade his ideas about the position of Indians in American society came under vigorous attack, and the assimilationists regained control of tribal affairs after World War II. Nevertheless, his efforts during the early and mid-1930s proved both a watershed in the direction of Indian relations and a precursor of what would return as national policy several decades later.[35]

In the reform effort of the 1930s, Collier saw himself as helping the tribes to rebuild and strengthen their culture, but he also expected that they would gain local political control over their circumstances and through that be able to revitalize their societies economically. Coming during the worse depression in American history, those hopes had little realistic chance for success. In addition, his program established yet another set of regulations that came out of Washington, arousing almost instant suspicion among many tribal groups. Collier wanted the people of each tribe to organize politically, write a constitution, and proceed to elect officers as if they were running a local town or county government. In this fashion his plan resembled what Canadian officials had been trying to achieve among the Indians for several generations. Many Indians in both countries objected, however, some because they already lived as citizens on allotted lands or in towns and not on reservations and had no intention of "returning to the blanket," as they described the process. Others opposed electing leaders because they preferred having traditional chiefs and shamans direct their affairs. In short, the IRA offered Indians a copy of the white man's governmental structure without even bothering to ask if it might be suitable or even acceptable.[36]

Once Congress had passed the Wheeler-Howard Bill, also called the Indian Reorganization Act, and it had been signed into law, Collier visited many reservations speaking in favor of the new program, answering questions, and trying to drum up acceptance of his ideas. To his surprise and chagrin, many Indians rejected the chance to organize politically and economically. Of the 252 tribes and bands that voted on the new program, 174 accepted it while the other 78 voted against it. Thirteen other groups refused to vote at all or else had ceased to exist as functioning communities. Clearly, despite the wave of reform fervor sweeping over the society during the mid-1930s, some Indians saw the IRA and its white-style tribal council as just another program begun in Washington that would hurt the tribes when it went into action. When figures of Indians who rejected or were not eligible for the program are added together, it becomes clear that the majority of American Indians failed to welcome Collier's ideas or processes with enthusiasm. Of the 252 tribes and bands that had a choice on this matter, 150 either took no action or rejected political organization. Groups numbering 116,000 people in all adopted tribal constitutions, but at the same time, others with 194,000 did not take that step.[37]

Despite this negative reception, the New Deal Indian policies did score some impressive victories. Title III of the IRA dealt with trying to rebuild or enlarge the tribal land base and provided money to consolidate allotted and heirship lands into units large enough to be economically productive. Indians who owned their land could participate in the program, but their actions remained voluntary. The law also authorized the secretary of the interior to spend up to two million dollars each year to purchase former tribal lands and return them to the Indians. These actions brought considerable debate, as some Indians denounced them as steps backward while others welcomed the new policy. A few white critics of Collier pointed to the effort to restore tribal land bases as just the first step in a communist threat to the country, but while the debate took place, so did land purchases and consolidations. The Indian Division of the Civilian Conservation Corps worked on many reservations to improve existing landholdings through fire prevention and water conservation measures throughout the decade. It provided Indian workers desperately needed jobs as they built dams and bridges while helping to reforest some regions and repair badly eroded areas on some reservations.[38]

By encouraging Indian languages and tribal arts, crafts, and religious ceremonial activities, the new administration dropped the long-standing goal of acculturation and seemed to accept the possibility that tribal people could be Americans while retaining some of their own culture. This effort attracted much of the criticism eventually leveled at Collier's program, but it gave the tribal cultures a much-needed reinforcement and legitimacy after generations of government efforts to destroy them. In 1933 the BIA encouraged modest exhibits of weaving, pottery, and other items at the Chicago World's Fair, as well as in Atlanta and Washington DC. The Public Works of Art Project included Indian painters, weavers, and potters among its employees, and these artists and craftspersons produced artwork for the new community centers and schools then under construction on the reservations. In 1935 Congress established the Indian Arts and Crafts Board to help promote and market Indian-made products. It worked to help tribes develop their economic skills at the same time that they used traditional arts and crafts techniques. In Collier's eyes, economic success without cultural strength was not acceptable, and many Indians welcomed with enthusiasm his insistence on encouraging traditional cultural skills.[39]

In all of this activity Indians participated with varying degrees of interest. Many objected bitterly to what they saw as federal interference, while others welcomed BIA actions as critical for their survival. Collier occasionally asked for Indian advice, but he thought he knew best and that all tribal groups would welcome his programs. He was wrong. Nevertheless, most of his opposition in Congress came from those wanting to cut expenditures, from Western representatives whose constituents objected to what they saw as handouts for the Indians, and from many congressional leaders who came to detest the doctrinaire commissioner. Growing opposition to Collier as a person and to the programs he supported so vociferously grew each year. He supported the Navajo stock reduction plan, an effort in the mid-1930s to slaughter hundreds of sheep and goats to avoid further damage to rangeland already nearly ruined by drought, overgrazing, and erosion. His stance in that dispute brought much negative publicity. At the same time, his intervention in a dispute over peyote use at Taos Pueblo angered Indians and whites alike and received extensive criticism during the August 1936 hearings held by the Senate Committee on Indian Affairs. As a result, by the time World War II grabbed the headlines, Collier's effectiveness as commissioner of Indian affairs had been greatly reduced.[40]

Despite the commissioner's difficulties, his efforts helped change permanently the direction of Indian affairs in the United States. More effective as a reform spokesman and publicist than an administrator, he succeeded in getting legislation that enabled the tribes to create local governments and to begin the process of economic rehabilitation. His biggest failure resulted from his unwillingness to recognize that many Indians still did not think in terms of tribe but preferred to identify themselves by village or band. Others had moved to the cities and did not want to return to the reservation. Thus they objected to his efforts to create tribal governments or economic units as un-Indian, just another attempt by the government to meddle in their affairs. At the same time, most allotment of Indian land ceased once the Indian Reorganization Act passed, and although Congress never appropriated enough money to acquire as much tribal land as the Indians hoped, millions of dollars did buy acreage that the tribes added to their holdings throughout the West. Most present-day tribal governments came into being as the direct result of the IRA. These have given Indians a much stronger say about their lives on such matters as education, religion, local political action, and cultural activities.[41]

INDIAN PARTICIPATION IN WORLD WAR II

The coming of World War II deflected attention away from Indian affairs in both nations as the governments shifted money, manpower, and energy to issues seen as more immediate and significant. Certainly congressional and parliamentary committees continued their oversight, but wartime economic activities temporarily ended widespread poverty in both nations, and reforms took a backseat during the frantic wartime efforts to defeat the Axis powers. For tribal people in both nations the conflict brought significant and permanent changes— not during the war, necessarily, but because of their participation in it. In both countries citizens eventually faced the draft, and Indians were no exception. Few objected to entering the military, and the Iroquois of New York and Ontario formally declared war on the Axis nations to keep alive their claim of political sovereignty in both nations.

Canada's membership in the British Empire brought it into the war quickly. After the fall of France to German troops in June 1940 Parliament passed the National Resources Mobilization Act. This called for all young men to register and face conscription, although service overseas remained voluntary until near the end of the war. All males between the ages of nineteen and forty-five had to register, and many Indians served in the military either as enlistees or conscripts. When the government decided to send conscripts to Europe in November 1944, men on some reserves were spared because parts of treaties 3, 6, 8, and 11 exempted them from such duties. Nevertheless, nearly the same number of Indian men enlisted in World War II as had done so in World War I. The figures for how many Indians were conscripted remain vague. Few of those who entered the military forces from the reserves seem to have benefited much from their training or experiences. Yet in many cases their families and home communities enjoyed increased income and higher living standards as military spending ended much of the poverty resulting from the 1930s depression. Some families moved from the reserves to nearby cities for better jobs.[42]

In the United States the war reintroduced the long-standing issue of integrating Indians into the armed forces or of creating segregated units for them. As early as June 1940, fully a year and a half before the United States entered the conflict formally, the discussion began. John Collier estimated that some forty-two thousand men from the reservations might be eligible for the draft. He called for all-Indian units, hoping to foster feelings of tribalism. A few months later the Navajo Council chairman J. C. Morgan supported this idea. In fact, he wrote that "the Navajo will cheerfully accept any assignment of selective service, but it would seem wise to consider the advantages of maintaining the Navajo as an indigenous regiment."[43] Morgan, a long-time proponent of assimilation, saw segregated units as a way to get less-qualified members of the tribe into the army. He assumed that military service would expose the young men to white ideas and practices and hurry the process of acculturation. He also feared that if placed in regular units, many Indians would face severe difficulties because of their poor reading skills and the discrimination they might encounter. Despite these pleas, the Selective Service system integrated men from the reservations into all branches of the military.

As in World War I, some Indian individuals and groups balked as continuing questions about American citizenship arose. Some of the Utah Paiutes and the Mississippi Choctaws claimed that they were not citizens. In July 1941 one leader wrote that the "Choctaw Indians never vote or pay poll tax. The white friend here say we are not allowed to vote. . . . If we are not citizens, will it be right for" us to go to war?[44] In a few cases Indians rejected the draft on religious grounds. For example, men from Taos Pueblo in New Mexico considered their long hair as a significant religious symbol and did not want to have their braids shaved off. A small group of Hopi pacifists served time in federal prison when the government rejected their claims for exemptions on religious grounds. On the other hand, the elders at the Zuni Pueblo asked for an exemption for a twenty-six-year-old rain priest whom they considered necessary to bring rain for the entire world. After Collier's intervention, the man received the same treatment given to clergymen from other religious groups.[45]

Other motivations brought draft resistance too. Both the German-American Bund and some communists spread propaganda among tribal people, but their efforts failed to bring much organized opposition to the laws. The most serious complaints about the draft grew out of the long-standing Iroquois Confederacy claims to be independent, sovereign nations within the United States and Canada. The Tuscaroras, Mohawks, and Senecas all put forward their past treaties to claim that they were not citizens. In October 1940 the Saint Regis Mohawk tribal council passed a resolution stating that "under our treaties with the United States of America, we are a distinct race, nation and people owning and occupying and governing the lands of our ancestors and under the protection of the federal government in reciprocation for our friendship" and past services to that government.[46] One Tuscarora chief wrote to the president telling him that the Canadian government had recognized the existing treaties and did not require the Iroquois there to register for that nation's draft. John Collier urged these people to register as aliens and then get their claims into the courts. By late 1941 the U.S. Second Circuit Court of Appeals in *Ex parte Green* ruled against these tribes and their claims.[47]

Scattered objections notwithstanding, most tribal members enlisted quickly, and by mid-1942 about seventy-five hundred Indians had entered the armed forces, their numbers growing steadily to at least twenty-five thousand by the end of the war. This response had several causes. Genuine patriotism certainly impelled some young men and women into the military. Other motivations included the demands of the draft system, a chance for adventure, and at least a modest salary as opposed to the poverty and unemployment on the reservations. Among some groups the continuing warrior tradition played a role too. The Sioux on the northern plains and the Kiowa farther south still honored men for bravery, and although some of the traditional warrior societies had nearly died out, the traditional honors for successful warriors remained important. Thus, while young Indian men might gain some measure of status in white society through military service, they often received as much or more honor within their own communities. When veterans of World War II helped revive the warrior societies, they played a significant role in strengthening existing reservation culture, and their activities provided a degree of continuity with earlier tribal customs.[48]

Other Indians, as many as forty thousand of them, moved from the reservations into towns and cities to take jobs in munitions factories as well as other jobs that opened up because of the war-caused population drain and the frantic pace of the economy. These actions, of serving in the military and of leaving the reservations for good-paying jobs, became a twentieth-century watershed, bringing fundamental changes in Indian life. Thousands of tribal people left their homes to participate in mainstream American society or in the military. This brought unaccustomed travel, increased experience in dealing with whites, better jobs, steady incomes, and unaccustomed personal freedom to move about and to control their lives in ways never before experienced. Yet it also caused long-term problems. When the young, able-bodied adults left the reservations, those who remained included the elderly, children, and disabled and uneducated people. Those groups still represent most of the population on many reservations. Wartime exploits brought fame to some individuals and groups of Indians as well. The young Pima Ira Hayes caught the nation's imagination when photographed helping raise the flag on Iwo Jima. The government brought him back to speak at rallies for war bond sales, and for a brief time he came to personify Indian contributions to the war effort. The Navajo code talkers who served as radiomen mostly in the Pacific campaign also received widespread attention. Other Indians served around the world, and frequently the media used them to fan support for the war effort.[49]

While the war helped individual Indians and certainly ended some of the poverty on reservations at least temporarily, it brought a strong backlash to John Collier's reforms of the previous decade. His idea of accepting distinct minority enclaves within American society came under heavy fire as un-American and even dangerous during the wartime frenzy to achieve unity. At the same time, as a result of the explosive growth of federal agencies in Washington DC during the first year of the war, the BIA found itself removed west to Chicago. Thus by 1942 Collier had little chance to get his superiors' attention, and wartime issues clearly overshadowed federal Indian policies. Many experienced bureaucrats went into the military or shifted to more essential branches of the government, while funding for Indian programs dropped as all available funds flowed into the war effort. Reservation medical and educational programs withered as reduced populations got drastically less help from the government.[50]

Of more significance for the next generation, the groundswell of criticism on the reservations directed at Collier, the New Deal, and the Indian Recovery Act reached a crescendo during the war. Western senators in particular attacked Collier and his ideas repeatedly. As early as 1943 Senator Karl Mundt of South Dakota blasted the Bureau of Indian Affairs and called for its abolition. The next year others joined him to denounce the bureau as expensive, inept, and in need of major changes. Senator Elmer Thomas attacked Collier personally, and Senator Berton K. Wheeler, once a joint sponsor of the Wheeler-Howard Bill, joined in the denunciations. Some in Congress demanded that the IRA be repealed, while the Senate Subcommittee on Indian Affairs favored a return to the discredited allotment policy. Even the National Council of Churches joined the chorus, publicly supporting an end to the New Deal policy of tribal cultural independence and calling for renewed efforts to bring about the assimilation of tribal peoples. In January 1945 the rising tide of criticism persuaded Collier to resign as commissioner of Indian affairs. The immediate postwar reaction to his activities brought a temporary but significant shift in dealing with the tribes, but his reforms of the 1930s had taken hold strongly across the country.[51]

As the war neared its end, both governments began planning how to deal with veterans' matters and the social and economic issues raised by demobilization. In Canada as early as 1944 some groups asked that Indian reserve lands in the West be opened for purchase and settlement as they had been following World War I. This time, however, the minister of mines and resources, who oversaw Indian affairs, brushed aside the requests for tribal lands. He thought it unwise to strip any further land from the reserves. The later Veterans' Land Act did make some grants and loans available for Indian men who wanted to get land once the war ended. About eighteen hundred Indian veterans took advantage of these programs and got loans and land as well. A few received support for college, university, or vocational training.[52]

In Canada one can only surmise what effects the war had because scholars there have written little on the role of tribal people in the conflict. The issue of conscription and of sending draftees overseas divided politics sharply with voters in Quebec, who rejected it by margins of nearly 80 percent while the rest of the country favored it by nearly the same margin by late in the war. Those Indians who held citizenship became subject to the draft when it became law and served wherever Canadian troops did. Wartime mobilization in Canada proved somewhat less all-consuming than in the United States, but it seems likely that the impact on reserve dwellers must have been at least similar to that farther to the south. Governmental attention, personnel, and funds drained away, while some Indians went off to the military and others moved to nearby cities to accept employment. When the war ended, the tribal peoples had encountered many of the same experiences as their counterparts in the United States, and relations between the government and the tribes began to change permanently because of the war's long-term societal impact.[53] By 1945 governments and tribal peoples in each nation had reached a new era in their mutual relations. Both governments started a major overhaul of their bureaucracies and a rethinking of how to deal with the Indians, and those efforts helped to shape events down to the present.

"AFTER THE DEVASTATION in Europe, there was the Marshall Plan: Japan had its course set by MacArthur. For the Indians, on the other hand," charged the Sioux Benjamin Reifel, commissioner of Indian affairs, "there was House Concurrent Resolution 108. Soaring expectations began to plunge. Termination took on the connotation of extermination for many."[1] At least in the United States, that described the situation during the 1940s. Because the 1930s Indian Reorganization Act had encouraged tribal languages, religious practices, and cultural ceremonies for the first time in generations, many reservation dwellers expected their lives to continue improving. But that did not happen. Not only did World War II disrupt the course of Indian affairs, but once the conflict ended, some of the public and many governmental officials blamed the tribes for their poverty. So instead of meeting the Indians' new expectations, federal policies appeared to attack the reservation dwellers.

After the war native people in both countries experienced many changes. Around the world anticolonialism became the order of the day, and as a subjugated minority, Indians came to be identified by many with the dismantling of colonial empires. Indian veterans returned with dramatically altered self-perceptions, yet those reentering tribal communities faced restrictions on their right to purchase alcohol, to vote, or even to sell their livestock or other farm products. In Canada, people who had mobilized to fight racism and oppression soon recognized that their government's actions included some of those same things. In the United States the reaction to the war differed somewhat, in that people saw the fight against the Axis powers as one for personal freedom. As a result, public and governmental cries to free the Indians from the authority of the bureaucrats echoed across the land.

The changes in both societies during the immediate postwar years did not come at the same pace or move in the same directions. Canadians chose to revise and streamline the structure of federal dealings with the tribes without any consultation with the Indian peoples. In the United States political opponents of the New Deal and John Collier's policies joined spokesmen for western economic interests to support wholesale changes in dealing with the Indians. Widespread calls for undoing the damage Collier was thought to have caused echoed through Congress, while church groups continued their denunciations of the effort to encourage tribal cultural and religious practices. Although officials in the United States called for more consultations with the tribal people than did their Canadian counterparts, they ignored most of what the Indians told them or failed to find a consensus in the conflicting desires they heard. Clearly change was in the air. Only the question of its speed and direction remained.

Canadian governmental actions reflected a different set of attitudes. Indian affairs had never been a subject of much popular debate, and that silence had produced an almost apolitical approach to tribal peoples. In 1939 one authority noted that "the British traditions of reticence, of letting well enough alone, of hushing up 'scandals,' of trusting officials, are stronger [than in the United States], so that there is apparently not so much interest on the part of the public in the so-called Indian question."[2] This lack of interest would change once a 1946 special joint committee began its work. Its hearings would receive considerable publicity, drawing governmental attention to Indian affairs at a time when the Canadian public was developing a growing acceptance of enlarged state functions and more clearly articulated ideas about how individuals should be treated within the society. As the general level of expectations about governmental responsibilities rose, the growing disparity of services to the general population and to the Indians would become painfully obvious.

By 1946 Canadian government officials and church leaders had recognized that their assumptions about Indian policy and its goals needed changing. The feeling that something was wrong or that policy needed redirection persuaded the government to appoint a special joint committee of the Senate and the House of Commons for the purpose of examining the Indian Act and its amendments. An MP from Lethbridge, Alberta, voiced the general feeling that changes were necessary a year after the committee began its hearings. "The Canadian people as a whole are interested in the problem of Indians," he noted, commenting that "they are anxious to remedy our shortcomings" because the country was conscious of human rights issues.[3]

Beginning in 1946 and extending through 1948 the committee held frequent hearings on all aspects of Canadian Indian policy. The legislators heard a bewildering array of proposals and criticisms from many Indian bands and associations in its first major effort to solicit rather than ignore Indian wishes and ideas. Varying from band chiefs representing small groups in British Columbia to the North American Brotherhood, and from the Indian Association of Alberta to spokesmen for the various factions of the Six Nations people in Ontario, and even to representatives speaking for unaffiliated or nonstatus Indians, the lawmakers got more advice than they wanted or thought they needed. With the variety of proposals given to them, the MPs must have wanted to throw up their hands in frustration; the Indian comments included more disagreements than anything else. For example, some wanted traditional band councils reinstated, while others called for their removal. Despite vast differences in their visions for the future, most Canadian Indians opposed compulsory taxation and enfranchisement. On many other issues they disagreed.[4]

Instructed to consider all major aspects of Indian-white relations, the special committee worked for nearly three years gathering data, holding hearings, and preparing its recommendations. Because its members accepted the claims of the Department of Indian Affairs that efforts to acculturate and assimilate the Indians had made significant progress, their goals included giving the tribes additional time for the assimilation process to work, at the same time limiting the ability of bureaucrats to hinder changes on the reserves. After they had submitted their report it took until June 1950 for a bill to be introduced, and that one ignored many of the committee's recommendations. As a result, not until April 1951 did a revised bill gain a parliamentary hearing, and only in June of that year did the new Indian Act become law.[5]

After nearly five years of hearings, committee work, bill drafting, and debate, the 1951 Indian Act brought few basic changes for the Canadian tribes. It continued to protect their lands and retained the provision of Indian status through the male line. Because Indians had complained that bureaucratic meddling undermined their efforts at self-government and assimilation, the law reduced the number and variety of actions federal officials could take when dealing with each band. Still, the government retained most of the power in its relationship with the Indians.[6] The revised Indian Act of 1951 made significant alterations in dealings between the tribal people and the Canadian government, but on one fundamental issue little changed. The underlying assumption of this legislation continued the long-standing efforts to acculturate and assimilate Indians. By midcentury, then, the basic approach to ethnic affairs remained on the course set by legislation and ideas dating back to pre-Confederation days.

In the United States World War II also brought demands for changes in how the government dealt with the Indians. These, however, resulted from widespread disenchantment with the New Deal policies of the John Collier era. Western congressmen denounced the 1930s move away from the long-standing goals of acculturation and assimilation. The emphasis on tribalism, Indian arts and languages, and the halting of allotment angered important groups and people. Indians themselves presented no united front to the rest of the nation. Groups such as the Oklahoma-based American Indian Federation, representing mixed-race and assimilated people, supported repealing the Indian Reorganization Act and distributing tribal wealth on a per capita basis. Others living on or near reservations as widely scattered as the Colville Reservation in Washington and the Pine Ridge Reservation in South Dakota voiced similar demands. Their opposition to federal programs that supported or enhanced tribalism cut the ground out from under those trying to defend the New Deal–era programs.[7]

At the same time, those who had benefited from the Collier-era reforms objected bitterly to the proposed changes. The National Congress of American Indians attacked the continuing emphasis on acculturation and assimilation, demanding what it called self-determination. Some white reformers as well denounced the new approaches as a return to the discredited programs of allotment and forced acculturation. As Congress sought ways to cut costs and shrink programs and staff during the immediate postwar years, the pressures on existing programs continued, as did the debate over how tribal people should be treated. Regardless of what side of the argument people found themselves on, general agreement existed that the tribes had not always been treated justly and that some form of compensation seemed necessary.

This generally accepted idea resulted in the 1946 creation of the Indian Claims Commission, a body to hear and investigate the tribes' complaints and to propose monetary settlements for past wrongs. Proponents justified the commission and its charge by pointing out that among the 377 treaties signed by the government and the Indians, many included instances of fraudulent government actions, of failure to abide by the agreements, or of cases where tribal land and resources had not brought a reasonable payment. Indians who felt badly treated by the government raised few objections to the commission's goals, while reformers and anti-Indian conservatives alike found reasons to praise the new group. The latter in particular saw it as a way to pay off society's debts to the tribes and then to turn them loose to sink or swim in the general society.[8]

The law charged the three-person Indian Claims Commission with considering all Indian complaints against the federal government prior to its 1946 creation. Tribes and other groups had until 1951 to file their charges, and Congress gave the commissioners a decade to complete their business. This proved unduly optimistic, as hundreds of claims poured in and government lawyers opposed many of them. As a result, the process continued until 1978, when the commissioners turned over the remaining business to the long-operating U.S. Court of Claims. By 1978 the commission had received almost 850 separate claims, dismissing large numbers of them while settling only 285 of the cases. This modest completion rate resulted from several factors. The process included two basic steps, the title phase and the value phase. In the first, the tribe had to prove that it had exercised "exclusive occupancy" of a distinct area from "time immemorial." Because many tribal groups migrated frequently, it proved difficult for them to demonstrate that they even had a valid claim to a particular region. In the second phase of the hearings the tribe had to convince the commission of how much the land or other resource had been worth when the whites took it.[9]

This brought tribal lawyers into sharp conflict with Justice Department legal teams, which opposed each of the Indian claims. In fact, the government took such an active role in working to limit the number and size of the claims that it had to hire private law firms to plead for it in many cases. Thus for some years private attorneys represented both the tribes and the government before the commission. Petitions for delays, crowded dockets, and the grinding slowness of judicial and bureaucratic procedures all combined to limit the pace of settlement drastically. By the time the commission halted its operations, it had awarded some $818 million to those groups tenacious enough to have struggled through the bewildering maze of legal maneuvering. At times the seemingly endless process raised hopes for some groups only to have another series of delays dash them yet once more. For example, the Kalispel tribe of Washington State entered its claim in January 1951. It took until April 1958 for the commission to rule favorably on the validity of their claim, and then until March 1963 to settle disputes over the size of the judgment. Then, as the happy Kalispels looked forward to receiving their payment, several Western senators stepped into the picture, refusing to support the appropriations unless the tribe agreed to the termination of federal services. This delayed final settlement and payment in the case until July 1975, when the tedious process that had lasted nearly a quarter of a century ended.[10]

Having tried financial compensation as one means of settling Indian issues, the government turned to two other related programs, termination and relocation. The impetus for these grew out of wartime efforts to create patriotism and unity within American society. Termination grew out of the effort to settle the government's obligations to the tribes and was the next logical step after the Indian Claims Commission began its task of paying for past wrongs. In theory, the policy would free Indians from BIA restrictions that hindered their successful integration into the general society. In fact, the program as developed stripped treaty protections and rights from numerous groups and for some caused health, education, and economic problems to worsen. In essence the supporters of termination wanted to act as if the Indian Reorganization Act of 1934 had never happened. They sought the immediate withdrawal of federal services to the tribes and their forced assimilation. It was a full-scale return to the crude nineteenth-century philosophy of root hog or die, all in the guise of freeing Indians from the shackles of government bureaucracy.

By 1947 the move toward termination began to pick up speed when the Senate Civil Service Committee asked acting Commissioner of Indian Affairs William Zimmerman to start planning for ending federal services for select groups. Responding to the committee, the bureaucrats suggested ten groups scattered across the country from New York to California, including the Six Nations of New York, the Menominees, and the Klamaths. Termination supporters submitted bills for the termination of several individual tribes that same year, but no action took place. Nevertheless, other events helped push the growing demands to get the government out of the Indian business. That same year the Hoover Commission, then studying governmental efficiency, recommended that all special benefits to Indians be ended. In 1950 Dillon S. Myer, an outspoken supporter of termination, became the new commissioner of Indian affairs, and it would only be a matter of time before the new program swung into high gear.[11]

House Concurrent Resolution 108, passed in 1953, called upon the BIA to begin terminating the tribes. That same year Congress passed the first of what would be termination legislation for more than sixty Indian groups. In theory only the strongest, most economically stable tribes received this treatment, but mistakes occurred, and the federal reading of tribal stability often bore little relation to the actual situation. Tribes that suffered the most obvious damage from the new policy included the Menominees of Wisconsin and the Klamaths of Oregon. Both of those groups had substantial forest holdings, and apparently the planners assumed that their resources would help them succeed economically. In both cases that idea proved false, as the two tribes lost much of their land base and forest holdings and got little financial return. Even worse, the termination policy fostered deep and bitter divisions among the Indians as they argued over whether or not to accept the need for termination and then how the meager spoils should be divided. Within a decade those following the situation realized that termination had proven more than just another misguided policy. Instead, it meant disaster for many of the tribes experiencing it, and the program came to a halt. In fact, by 1970 President Richard Nixon formally repudiated it. The damage had been done, though, and much of it could not be adequately remedied.[12]

While the government tried to divest itself of long-term responsibility toward the tribes through the actions of the Indian Claims Commission and the termination policy, it used yet another device to bring rapid assimilation of the Indians. This third approach was to encourage individuals and families to leave the reservations and move to the major urban centers. The dual goal was to get tribal people away from the unemployment and poverty of the tribal enclaves and to help them ease into the general economy and society. Actually, what came to be called the relocation program had begun as early as 1948 when BIA officials began trying to help Hopi and Navajo people find employment in the Southwest. By 1951 the government claimed that it had helped twenty thousand Indians find off-reservation jobs, but what it neglected to say was that most of the new work remained seasonal and low-skilled positions. During the mid-1950s increasing numbers of native people moved through the BIA placement offices in a wide range of major cities, including San Francisco, Los Angeles, Seattle, Denver, Oklahoma City, and Chicago. Within a few years this list of cities grew. By 1957 the Adult Vocational Training Program, as relocation came to be known, offered minimal job training and placement to tribal immigrants to the cities. As a result of these federal efforts at least thirty-five thousand reservation dwellers left home, at least for a time.[13]

In the cities the newly arrived Indians experienced all of the usual problems that other urban immigrants did, as well as a few cultural problems of their own. For those who had never been a part of city life or the American economy, the need to pay rent on time, to keep regular hours at work, and to survive in a largely impersonal situation with few friends or relatives proved difficult. Many quit the cities and fled back to the reservations permanently. Others used holidays and tribal ceremonial times as excuses to leave for home, often neglecting to explain clearly to their employers and then losing their jobs. Certainly some did well and used their education or job skills successfully. Unfortunately many had little special training and so had to accept unskilled or semiskilled, low-paying jobs, making their stay in the city even more difficult. While the relocation program resulted from at least some thought to help poverty-stricken reservation dwellers, its results often fell far short of BIA claims. Nevertheless, it did encourage more Indians to try city life and off-reservation jobs than would likely have taken those steps themselves. As a result it provided some tribal people with experience and economic training that would help them in dealing with the majority society, but despite relocation, termination, and claims awards, many Indians still rejected assimilation.[14]

Although they had no similar large-scale program, Canadian officials hoped for the same results. Beginning in 1957 they encouraged native people to move into some of the western towns and cities, and by 1960 eight placement officers "worked to get selected recruits from the reserves adjusted into positions in the cities."[15] By that latter year the Indian Department planned to establish two northern recruitment centers, one in the Mackenzie District and the second in the Yukon. Those Indian and Métis who migrated to Saskatoon, Winnipeg, or Calgary encountered the same difficulties any rural person did moving to the city. Loneliness, economic problems, health and welfare difficulties, and discrimination made their transition to urban life a difficult one. Nevertheless, despite their obvious problems, in terms of "both income and housing" they were "vastly better off than their cousins on Indian reserves" in the north. In fact, one study notes that their cash incomes were at least a third higher than they would have been on the reserves or in the small Métis towns. Yet this assessment failed to take into account the higher cost of living in the cities and the basic lack of a social group or community, which the newly arrived urban immigrants desperately needed.[16]

Because of the poverty, crime, and alcohol abuse, local Indian organizations came into being in the cities, or at times provincial pantribal organizations moved in to sponsor what became the Friendship Centre Movement. Begun with federal funds, this effort strove to establish Indian social clubs, and the Friendship Centres soon came to offer other services as well. These included dealing with the immediate needs of newcomers to the city such as temporary housing, help in getting jobs, short-term small loans, and general social support. Begun as cultural support facilities, the centers moved quickly to meeting other obvious needs of the often transient urban Indian population. By 1976 the local facilities had established a National Association of Friendship Centres and had become well enough established as temporary care providers that the new association authorized an evaluation of their programs and operations to inform the staff across the country of what could be done to benefit tribal people moving into the cities.[17]

The flood of migrants from the reserves who visited those centers or joined the fledgling pantribal urban organizations faced many difficulties. By the early 1990s at least half of the registered Indians in both Manitoba and Saskatchewan resided in the towns or cities there, while in Alberta about 30 percent of them did. In some communities small numbers of former reserve dwellers held reliable jobs, often working for government agencies. Many, however, lacked the education and skills needed for successful long-term employment. Equally important, they may have needed far more remedial assistance than had been thought necessary to thrive in modern urban centers. One commentator described their position at the bottom of the educational and economic ladder as at least partly the result of long-term "psychological intimidation brought about by" their "almost complete dependence upon the state for the necessities of life" for years.[18] Clearly this overlooks the variety within and among differing bands, but having been an administered people for two or three generations certainly took a toll on the self-image and self-reliance of reserve populations.

Indians going from the reserves into town were generally of two types. Some moved permanently, intending to make a break with the near poverty they experienced on the home reserve. Most, however, tended to be young people, often teenagers leaving home for the first time. Usually they clustered in an Indian section of the community with old, cheap housing, where they could socialize with other tribal people at the neighborhood bars or an Indian culture center if one existed. Whenever possible they stayed with friends, neighbors, or relatives when they first got to the city, and their self-identification as Indians kept them from having more than minimal social contacts with whites. Because their migration was for economic reasons, usually they returned to the reserves if their jobs ended. That produced a continuing back-and-forth migration between reserve and town. Most of those in this migration tended to be between the ages of sixteen and twenty-five. Later many of them returned to the reserve, married, and raised families. Those who made white friends tended to remain in the town and retain only a minimal tribal identification.[19]

THE RISE OF MILITANT SELF-DETERMINATION MOVEMENTS

Whether or not Indians moved into the cities in Canada, during the postwar decades they strove to retain their cultural identity and, in many cases, to assert their rights more vigorously than earlier in the century. Efforts to obtain religious freedom, stated eloquently during the 1930s, achieved success when the Indian Act revisions of 1951 dropped the prohibitions of the sun dance and potlatch ceremonies. Pantribal organizations came and went in the 1950s and 1960s, but the worldwide decolonization movement and growing social unrest in the United States both helped to change Canadian attitudes toward ethnic issues. In particular the civil rights agitation and reforms south of the border demonstrated to Canadians the folly of not attending to social problems until they resulted in riots and bloodshed. Indian leaders in both nations learned quickly how to attract favorable media attention to their issues, making it easier to present their plight to the general public and making it more likely that they would receive a favorable response from the rest of society.

Clearly by the 1950s and 1960s Canadian society, government, and native peoples all realized that changes in the system were necessary. Indian leaders struggled to launch national organizations, and in 1961 they organized the National Indian Council. At the same time, government officials decided that they needed more data about their tribal wards; an extensive survey of Indian and Métis communities produced the 1966–67 Hawthorn Report. Although three decades later and having a different focus, the survey findings paralleled those of the 1928 Meriam Report in the United States. The investigators concluded that existing federal machinery for dealing with the Indians was inadequate. In fact, the survey noted that what it called the Indian Affairs Branch had taken on too much responsibility, as it oversaw education, health and welfare, local government, economic development, and general community change. Trying to do all of these jobs turned the offices dealing with Indian affairs into a "miniature government rather than an ordinary functional department," the investigators found. By 1965 it regulated the lives of some 217,864 individual Indians, who belonged to 511 distinct bands and lived on 2,267 reserves, under the administration of some 87 separate agencies. Whether the bureaucrats admitted it or not, their tasks extended beyond their competence, knowledge, or finances, and Indian affairs needed a major restructuring.[20]

With ethnic militancy rising sharply in both Canada and the United States during the 1960s and since, the native peoples demanded a larger role in deciding their own future. The Hawthorn Report noted that, in addition to deserving the full rights of other Canadian citizens, tribal peoples, as the original inhabitants in that land, should be considered as "citizens plus." That is, morally and legally, the rest of society owed Indians more than other groups within the country. While this finding brought little enthusiasm from the government, national Indian leaders pounced on it and used it repeatedly as they struggled to gain a more nearly sovereign position for individual bands and reserves. One basic difficulty for Canadian native groups was their division by the government into status, nonstatus, Métis, and Inuit categories. This made it hard to agree or to present a united front when dealing with the bureaucrats. Of those groups, only the status Indians had readily identifiable treaty rights. That problem caused a 1968 split of the National Council into two major groups, the National Indian Brotherhood, representing the status Indians, and the Canadian Métis Society, which spoke for the other native people.[21]

Since the 1960s pantribal groups have been at the center of much political controversy in both countries. In Canada this began during 1968 after Pierre Trudeau won the national election. The new government publicly supported what it described as fair treatment for disadvantaged groups in Canadian society, and this led to its working for a revision of existing Indian policy. The new prime minister called for full consultation with the tribes, but the effort had little chance for success. Because the continuing threat of secession by French Canadian nationalists in Quebec inclined Trudeau toward individualism and away from group rights, he proved totally unwilling to consider, much less accept, Indian claims to special treatment within the nation. "It's inconceivable I think that in a given society, one section of society have a treaty with the other section of the society," he said. "We must all be equal under the laws and we must not sign treaties amongst ourselves."[22] With that attitude being expressed by the head of the new government, it was not surprising that the consultations between the bureaucrats and Indian representatives failed to produce a lasting settlement.

Instead, after listening to Indian association representatives, the bureaucrats prepared a policy analogous to termination in the United States. *The Statement of the Government on Indian Policy, 1969*, usually referred to as the White Paper, called for sweeping changes in Indian-white relations, beginning with a dissolution of the department that supervised Indian affairs within five years. The government proposed repealing the Indian Act, giving Indians title to their lands, turning over to the provinces the administration of education, health, and other benefits, and making funds available for Indian economic development at least temporarily. The White Paper's authors claimed that the problems of Canadian Indians resulted from their peculiar legal status as wards of the government. Because they enjoyed a position legally different from that of other Canadians, they remained apart from and behind the rest of the society. That being the case, making them equal to other citizens would remove the fetters that had encumbered them and allow them to become fully equal.[23]

Just as the supporters of termination in the United States had done a decade and a half earlier, the Liberal government pushed its new policy over the vigorous objections of Indians throughout the country. Tribal leaders had asked for help in overcoming economic and social disabilities, but throughout the consultations that preceded the government's statement, they had insisted on retaining their tribal identities. The government completely ignored this basic demand. As far as Indians were concerned, the new policy agenda aimed at tribal destruction, and they began an all-out attack on it and the Trudeau government. Harold Cardinal, an articulate Cree then president of the Indian Association of Alberta, published his 1969 book *The Unjust Society*. In it he attacked the White Paper, characterizing its proposals as basically anti-Indian. He wrote that "the Americans to the south of us used to have a saying: 'The only good Indian is a dead Indian.' The MacDonald-Chrétien doctrine would amend this but slightly to 'The only good Indian is a non-Indian.' "[24]

Attacks on the policy proposal came from Indian groups throughout Canada, from concerned academics, and from interested citizens; within a year the Trudeau government had backed away from its termination proposal. Despite the government retreat, suspicion and ill will poisoned tribal-government relations for at least another decade. One of the few positive results of the bitter public debate of the White Paper was the strengthening of national and regional pan-tribal associations. When they learned that their objections had become newsworthy, Indian leaders began issuing press releases, even calling one a Brown Paper in reply to government initiatives. This attention gave many local and national leaders considerable experience in dealing with the media and the government and greatly strengthened their skills in doing so. Within a couple of years, pan-Indian organizations received an increased level of funding, and the Department of Indian Affairs even established an office to help tribes carry out legal research on their land claims and other treaty rights.[25]

Although Canadian tribes rarely used the term, they strove toward the same goal as their counterparts south of the border: self-determination. They began with demands for the closure of government- and church-supported residential schools, which had operated much like their counterparts in the United States, with a focus on acculturating the children and young people. In their efforts to change young Indians into good Canadians, however, the schools alienated both the students and their families. Figures from 1971, for example, show how badly the schools failed. All but a handful of students attending the schools in the prairie provinces—less than 1 percent—quit before completing secondary school.

The vast majority of students dropped out of what they saw as an unresponsive and irrelevant system. While in the north the Oblate fathers objected to the shutting down of their residential schools, most other religious groups felt the inflation that swept the country and came to accept the phasing out of the system. Often, more significant than financial difficulties for many was the sharp drop in clerics to staff or administer the schools; during the 1960s most church schools acquired lay teachers. By then the churches needed little persuasion to agree to surrender the operation of the schools. At the same time, provincial educational systems began accepting Indian students in the public schools.[26]

By 1970 just over 60 percent of all registered or status Indian children attended public schools throughout Canada. With this shift away from a missionary-dominated system to a public one came other changes as well. Provincial public schools, staffed by professional educators, continued efforts to displace the tribal culture so the children could be integrated successfully into the white community. Often Indian parents and tribal leaders protested having to place their children in nearby schools, which they saw as foreign, intrusive influences on their culture. While federal officials encouraged the use of Métis or Indians as teachers' aides, cultural awareness programs for the teachers, and even the use of Indian languages in some classrooms, their efforts failed to overcome parental objections. Some complained because of the long-distance busing their children faced, while others feared that the poorly dressed reserve children would be teased by the whites. Occasionally higher standards in provincial schools meant lower grades and more failures for native children than they had experienced at their own schools. Obviously, sending their children to nearby public schools did not seem all that positive for Indian parents, and in 1973, when the National Indian Brotherhood and the federal government agreed, the latter shifted funding and control of reserve schools to the Indian band governments.[27]

Throughout the 1970s Indian leaders kept up a drumbeat of criticism against the federal government and many of its programs. Gaining control of educational funding in 1973 proved to be only one of the results they achieved. Some reserve dwellers, such as the Six Nation Iroquois, continued to assert their independence from Canada, but despite several colorful episodes and considerable publicity, their claims failed to convince the legal authorities. While making little progress toward their political goals, they continued to agitate. During the intense reaction to the White Paper the government appointed a commissioner of claims, whose duties vaguely paralleled those of the U.S. Indian Claims Commission. This individual, however, had only modest authority, and the scope of his jurisdiction remained carefully limited. Still, by 1974 the government had expanded his position and set up an Office of Native Claims that was to help tribes and Indian associations carry out their claims research.[28]

Between 1960 and 1980 native groups in the United States demonstrated an unusual militancy as well. Earlier leaders of pantribal organizations may have grumbled about government policies or inaction, but they rarely had any strong following or influence. Then, during the bitter experience of termination, the mood shifted drastically. Influenced as well by African-American protesters and encouraged by the civil rights activism of the 1950s and 1960s, Indians soon learned that they could organize, protest, gain media attention, and even generate positive public responses to their grievances. This trend became public in 1961 when the leaders conducting the American Indian Chicago Conference proved too slow and cautious for the younger delegates at the meeting. The militants seceded, founded the National Indian Youth Council (NIYC), and issued a "Declaration of Indian Purpose." Meeting later that same year at Gallup, New Mexico, the new organization called on the government to accept Indian self-determination as the best method of settling tribal grievances. This term has remained at the center of tribal rhetoric.

In 1964 members of the National Indian Youth Council protested state limits on tribal fishing in the Pacific Northwest. The Indians of the region had treaty rights that allowed them to fish throughout the area, and in 1954 Congress had formally reaffirmed those rights, specifically exempting them from state and local regulations. Local officials and courts ignored the federal directives, arresting and fining Indians for fishing out of season or not having licenses. After repeated incidents where state game wardens arrested Indians, cut their nets, and seized their boats and catches, the local groups demanded legal treatment. In 1964, led by NIYC organizers, the Indians staged a series of "fish-ins," gaining national media attention when the comedian Dick Gregory and the film stars Marlon Brando and Jane Fonda joined their effort briefly. That same year civil rights activists participated in an NIYC protest at the Washington State capitol, and for several years tribal people held repeated fish-ins, protesting the illegal application of state regulations to them. Because of the continuing publicity, in 1966 the Justice Department intervened, defending several demonstrators.[29]

The Northwest fish-ins proved only the first of many demonstrations and campaigns to assert tribal rights during the following decade. In terms of publicity and likely long-term results, the 1969 occupation of Alcatraz Island in San Francisco Bay probably was the most significant action taken by militant Indians. Several years after the federal government closed its famous prison on the island, activists decided to occupy it. They seized upon the government declaration that Alcatraz was surplus property and under a provision of the Fort Laramie Treaty of 1868 claimed it as Indian land. On 9 November 1969 Indian students in the San Francisco area sailed out to the island, only to be removed by federal marshals the next day. Later that same month local people organized a new group, the Indians of All Tribes, and on 20 November they returned to the island. Their activities brought wide media coverage and apparent public support for a time, and the students tried to get funds for an Indian cultural center on Alcatraz. Instead the government proposed making the island a national park stressing Indian themes, but the occupiers rejected this option. After months of inaction and dwindling public attention and Indian support, the occupation ended on 11 June 1971, when federal marshals removed the last of the militants.[30]

Protests over unequal and violent treatment of tribal people and actions aimed at bringing public attention to lost Indian rights continued for several more years. In 1972 leaders of several militant groups joined forces for what they called the "Trail of Broken Treaties" caravan from Denver to Washington DC. In a move similar to the Canadian Caravan to Ottawa three years later, they drove east in a motley assortment of cars, trucks, buses, and vans, seeking all the media attention they could get. The protesters stopped in Minneapolis, where a large contingent of Ojibwas joined them. There they issued a statement entitled Twenty Points that included all of their demands. When they reached the capital they had more people than lodging, so after protesting in front of the BIA building they rushed in to occupy it. Their action caught the government by surprise as it came at the end of a presidential campaign. After some violence and considerable damage to the BIA building and its contents, on 8 November 1972 federal officials offered the protesters immunity from prosecution and provided funds for them to return home.[31]

The demonstrators' organization and determination showed how rapidly militancy had come to play a major role in Indian affairs. Leaders of the American Indian Movement (AIM) such as Dennis Banks and Russell Means, joined by others including the Indians of All Tribes, United Native Americans, and other groups, presented the country with a new spectacle—Indians who no longer came to the government humbly, hat in hand, to ask for things they had coming to them. Now loud, crude, articulate, and even armed leaders threatened the society. The culmination of these confrontations took place at Wounded Knee, South Dakota. In February 1973 AIM-led militants occupied the village, a symbol of white violence against the tribes nearly a century earlier. With Dee

Brown's popular best-seller *Bury My Heart at Wounded Knee* having made at least the name widely known, the militants settled down to challenge the federal government and, more important, to gain national media attention.

At first they got plenty of sympathy from groups across the nation, but the novelty soon wore off. Federal marshals and FBI agents surrounded the community, exchanging gunfire with the occupiers almost nightly for the entire seventy-two days. Two Indian men died from gunshot wounds and one marshal was paralyzed.[32] On 11 March 1973 Russell Means announced to a national TV audience that the Indians had established the Oglala Sioux Nation, declaring their independence from the United States. He declared that the new nation would establish its boundaries according to the Treaty of 1868, warning that it might order that people who violated the new borders be shot. While this may have encouraged Indian leaders across the country, such threats of violence quickly undermined popular support for the occupation. Although Wounded Knee continued to get media attention, from that point on it was mostly negative, as public support for militancy and armed confrontation had waned, and the occupation soon passed out of news accounts. After weeks of armed tension with federal marshals and FBI agents surrounding the village, on 8 May 1973 the militants left the tiny community. The Wounded Knee occupation demonstrated deep and permanent divisions among tribal groups, with some supporting and applauding militant actions while others deplored them as un-Indian and counterproductive.[33]

BATTLES FOR RESOURCES IN THE FAR NORTH

Despite these splits, the actions of the 1960s and early 1970s brought tribal matters to the point where they could no longer be ignored and permanently shifted Indian-government relations in the United States. This became apparent in 1975 when Peter MacDonald, Navajo tribal chairman, helped form the Council of Energy Resource Tribes (CERT). Patterned on the example of the OPEC oil cartel, this organization worked to bring reservation people better leverage in dealing with the government and corporations regarding the tribes' mineral, oil, and natural gas holdings. It offered advice, served as a clearinghouse for technical information, and helped in gaining higher payments for tribal resources. While not as successful as some might have wished, and seen as a tool of only the resource-rich tribes, CERT became an accepted part of government, business, and tribal relations in less than a decade.[34]

The Indians were not the only ones interested in resources and their management, as the experience of the Alaska native people demonstrated. The status of the tribal peoples there—Indians, Aleuts, and Eskimos, or Inuit—had not been clearly spelled out at any time since the United States acquired the region from Russia more than a century before. The 1884 establishment of civil government in Alaska had failed to recognize any native title to the land or resources, and although Congress occasionally established modest reservations for small groups, most of the native people had little relationship to the government. In 1906 Congress extended the provisions of the Dawes Act for land allotment to Alaska, but officials there made little effort to implement it. During the New Deal the Alaska Reorganization Act of 1936 allowed the native communities to organize formal local governments, and after that time the secretary of the interior began establishing some reservations; but Alaska proved distant from Washington, and not much happened. The native communities did organize several informal pantribal groups, of which the Alaska Federation of Natives, begun in the 1960s, proved to be the most effective.[35]

By the mid-twentieth century the Alaska native peoples faced challenges encountered by other Indians decades or even generations earlier. Commercial fishermen, mining and lumbering concerns, and the never-ending search for oil and natural gas brought thousands of outsiders into the region. Then, in 1959, Alaska achieved statehood and the pressures on the land and its resources increased sharply. In the next decade the new state government filed claims on nearly 20 million of the 102.5 million acres promised by the federal government. Much of this land, although considered a part of the "vacant, unappropriated, and unreserved" public domain within the state, proved to be settled upon or otherwise used by small groups of native people. As soon as they realized they faced possible dispossession, those people began objecting to the state claims and tied the land settlement process in knots. That prompted the federal government to examine the situation and move toward a settlement. What the agreement ignored was the continuing dependence of some Arctic peoples on a local subsistence economy. For many, fishing, hunting, trapping, and gathering remained both culturally and economically central to their lives. They had lived off the local resources for eons. When the representatives of government and corporations reached these people, the encounter tended to disrupt local relationships without much benefit to the local populations.[36]

Pressure from the oil companies to open parts of the state for exploration and drilling, along with the realization that any success they had at locating new oil fields would demand that a major pipeline be constructed to transport the oil, finally prodded the government into action. A 1962 Task Force on Alaska Native Affairs called for a resolution of disputes about land claims, while the native people themselves demanded the protection of their claims, retention of mineral rights, and compensation for lands lost. The discussions continued for several years, and in 1968 congressional hearings on these issues began. New major oil discoveries on the North Slope and increasing support for the positions taken by the Alaska Federation of Natives brought the dispute to a head. In December 1971 the Alaska Native Claims Settlement Act became law. It provided legal title to some 40 million acres of land in exchange for any existing claims and reserves held by native groups in the state. For the surrender of their lands the government paid some $462 million, with another $500 million to be paid for mineral rights to their lands. The legislation established numerous village corporations as well as another dozen regional corporations and yet another for nonresident natives. As might be expected, on paper the settlement looked better than it was in practice, but few could argue that the government had failed to consult with the native people, to heed their demands, and to deal equitably with them in this instance.[37]

The continuing search for mineral wealth, hydroelectric power, and just more land brought repeated clashes over these issues in Canada too. In British Columbia tribal peoples, the province, and the federal government had quarreled over native land title issues since Confederation. Land commissions, tribal suits, and bitter recriminations from all involved characterized the disputes for generations. During the early 1970s the Nisgha tribe from British Columbia turned to the courts while pressing its renewed claims to aboriginal land title. The province had continued to reject any such Indian rights for over a century, but despite losing their case in local courts the tribe persisted. In 1973 the Supreme Court of Canada ruled against them too. However, in this case, *Calder v. Attorney General of British Columbia*, the justices voted six to one to accept the Indians' land claims. Although the overall decision went against them, the ruling supported the tribal land claims and provided the basis for continuing legal and political maneuvering since then. Indians in British Columbia saw the outcome as favorable because it strengthened the position of tribal groups who had not signed treaties with either the British or the Canadian governments, and clearly made federal-provincial relations on the issue of aboriginal claims more difficult.[38]

The Calder decision came at a time when the ongoing push into the northern portions of existing provinces and into the Northwest Territories brought repeated contacts between the whites and tribal peoples still living in their traditional patterns in those areas. It caught political and economic leaders by surprise and threw developmental plans, particularly in the north, into confusion. By the early 1970s exploration and seismic testing for a major pipeline through the Mackenzie Valley in the Northwest Territories again brought Indians and whites into conflict. On 2 April 1973 the Mackenzie Valley chiefs filed a claim to nearly one-third of the land in the Northwest Territories, seeking to halt or slow pipeline construction. Later that same year a local judge ruled in favor of the chiefs, at least to the extent that he expressed doubt about earlier treaties having extinguished aboriginal title to much of the land in question. Two years later, in June 1975, the Canadian government won an appeal to overturn this ruling, but concern about the impact of pipeline workers and modern technology on the largely traditional peoples living in the region slowed economic expansion. An investigation by Justice Thomas Berger showed the severity of the cultural and economic changes the pipeline would bring to the region and predicted that it would take at least a decade to settle native claims in the region satisfactorily.[39]

While the oil companies pushed their construction and Justice Berger held his consultations with the Mackenzie Valley villagers, the tribes took the initiative. In July 1975 leaders of the Dene Indians of the area issued the "Dene Declaration," to the dismay of the government. Radical by Canadian standards, this document came close to being a declaration of Dene independence from Canada. Its first sentence set the tone for the document. "We the Dene of the N.W.T.," it began, "insist on the right to be regarded by ourselves and the world as a nation."[40] Continuing in the same vein, the declaration rejected Canadian authority and demanded a Dene government with control over education, justice, health and welfare, trade supervision, natural resources, transportation, culture, and even taxation. While local Indian leaders announced that they had no desire to separate from Canada, their declaration and a later expanded version of it sounded as if they had that goal in mind.[41]

Previously the Ottawa government had conducted its negotiations with native peoples through the Indian Association of the Northwest Territories and the Métis Association of the Northwest Territories. These two groups split soon after the declaration, however, and in September 1977 the Métis Association issued its own somewhat more modest statement, ignoring the Dene call for independence. The government responded positively to this moderate approach but now had two organizations with different agendas to face, slowing a settlement considerably. Negotiations continued sporadically for several years, and by 1981 the Denes and Métis had joined forces again. The urgency of these matters had waned somewhat by then because American oil firms chose to bypass the Mackenzie Valley and to build their pipeline elsewhere. While a shorter pipeline might still be built, the native peoples had fewer objections to this project.[42] By 1988 both the Denes and the Métis of the Mackenzie Valley had accepted a settlement of their claims giving them 180,000 square kilometers of land, $500 million, and a part of the royalties from oil and other minerals found on their land. This agreement followed the pattern set in 1984 when the Inuit of the Mackenzie River Delta settled their claims, and these accords predated one between the Yukon Territory native peoples and the government.[43]

Perhaps the most impressive settlement, at least as far as the size of the area being contested, was the 1975 James Bay Agreement in northern Quebec. In 1971 the government of Quebec began this enormous project. Planning to dam a series of rivers, forming several huge reservoirs that would then produce hydroelectric power for use in the south, the province established the James Bay Development Corporation. This entity received jurisdiction over 350,000 square kilometers, the traditional home of perhaps six thousand Cree hunters and another four thousand Inuit people. When the Crees heard rumors of the provincial government's plans for their homeland, they obtained federal funds to help protest the action. After Quebec authorities rejected the notion of any aboriginal title to the area, the Crees went to court in 1972 seeking an injunction to halt further construction. After seventy-one days of hearings, the court granted the injunction, but a higher court suspended it quickly.

Nevertheless, the very possibility that the issue of aboriginal title might disrupt the project eventually brought Quebec officials to the bargaining table. Following months of complicated negotiations between federal and provincial authorities and between Quebec officials and native leaders, in November 1975 the Cree and Inuit leaders signed the James Bay Agreement. It gave them $225 million over the next decade, title to just over 13,000 square kilometers of land, and exclusive hunting rights and environmental protection for another 65,000 square kilometers for the Crees and 90,000 more for the Inuit.[44] Signing the agreement brought much criticism. Whites objected to what they considered a giveaway of land and government funds, while some other native groups accused the Crees and Inuits of selling their land. Nevertheless, this agreement protected the people and lands in the region from further incursions. When provincial officials began planning for another such project, James Bay II or the Great Whale Project, native opposition helped persuade Quebec leaders to postpone it. In the late 1990s this effort remains stalled.

While the government, Indians, and Métis criticized each other and negotiated vast changes in their relationships, the Inuit peoples of the Arctic dwelt on the fringes of Canadian awareness. For decades the government refused to recognize them as another group of native people, and while officials of the Indian Department dealt with the Inuit sporadically, those people had no legal standing as a distinct group. They were citizens of Canada, but that was all. By 1950 the impact of traders, missionaries, and workers on the Alcan Highway combined with catastrophic results. Existing Inuit economic and social patterns changed rapidly, and by 1950 some observers feared that traditional Inuit culture would soon disappear. The people had shifted from a nomadic, land-based economy to a sedentary, settlement-based one, living near trading posts, missions, or other administrative centers. Basically many had come to live on the dole despite the best efforts of Canadian officials to avoid just that result.[45]

Despite their poverty and severe dietary problems the Inuit experienced sharply increased fertility rates, so that from 1951 to 1981 their population climbed from sixty-eight hundred to over seventeen thousand. This resulted in a preponderance of young people in Inuit settlements, a subsequent loss of traditional skills because few elders remained to pass on folk knowledge, and a heavy dependence on Canadian schools that offered an education little suited for dealing with issues faced in the region. Gradually, problems of unemployment and dependence on government programs became more critical, and during the past several decades both government officials and Inuit communities have grappled with these issues. Beginning in the 1960s the government abandoned its dangerous efforts to move villages of Inuit from one Arctic spot to another, and the native people themselves began organizing Inuit councils that have come to function well. Twenty years later federal officials and native leaders negotiated a series of claim settlements similar to those already discussed.[46]

More important for long-term Inuit affairs was their oft-stated desire for a northern political region they called Nunavut ("Our Land"), to be carved out of the existing Northwest Territories. In 1971 the Inuit Tapirisat of Canada, their multiband organization, began to propose the creation of Nunavut. Five years later they included the proposal as a part of their land claims to Ottawa. In 1979 they formally called for a division of the Northwest Territories, with the northern and easternmost portions becoming Nunavut, with its own legislature and potential provincial status to follow. During the next several years discussions took place with provincial authorities and both the Dene Nation and the Métis Association, organizations representing the other two major native groups in the region. As a result, in April 1982 the Northwest Territories held a referendum on this issue. Although the vote favored the division, desultory meetings for the next several years brought no result. Then in 1990 the Inuit and the federal government agreed on native land claims. Two years later a second plebiscite ratified the earlier vote.[47] In 1999 Nunavut is scheduled to come into being. The negotiations leading to this agreement indicate the continuing centrality of issues related to native people in Canadian public life. They also demonstrate clearly the growing divergence between U.S. and Canadian solutions to the problems of tribal peoples.

ORGANIZING FOR SELF-DETERMINATION

Militancy and negotiations brought basic changes in Indian-white relations within both nations. While Canadian officials conducted the negotiations and consultations that brought the agreements throughout the northern reaches of that country, the U.S. Congress responded to the continuing pressures of pan-tribal groups and the ongoing currents of the social reform still sweeping the United States. The twin goals of self-determination and full receipt of treaty and trust rights pulled the tribes and the governments in several directions simultaneously. In addition, continuing disputes between reservation dwellers, who made up less than half of the Indian population as of 1980, and their city relatives on the one hand, and between wealthy and poor tribes on the other, did little to calm the situation. A new problem also arose during the 1970s as a result of the Indian Claims Commission hearings. This dealt with groups of people claiming to be Indians but who, for various reasons, had no formal relationship to the federal government. Such people had no treaty rights, received no benefits from existing programs, and in general stood outside the existing framework of Indian-white relations.

During the 1960s and 1970s all of these issues faced Congress and the Bureau of Indian Affairs, and the two organizations responded with considerable energy if not always with wisdom. President Lyndon Johnson's War on Poverty extended the operations of many federal departments and programs to tribal people, whose dealings with the government thus came to extend far beyond the narrow borders of the BIA. At the same time, a preferential hiring program placed hundreds of young Indians into jobs within the BIA; one would think that their presence would have made the bureaucrats more willing to listen to tribal wishes, but this did not always occur. Militants and conservatives alike sought tribal control over the schools that taught their children, and following the publication of the 1969 Kennedy Report on Indian Education, the government took steps to bring this about.

For tribal people to succeed as a group they needed a trained leadership, and during the 1960–80s era several elements came together to help produce that result. By 1969 the federal government through the BIA provided some $3 million in scholarship assistance to about 3,500 Indian college students. Just five years later spending rose to some $47 million, aiding about 13,500 students. Two pieces of congressional legislation brought fundamental changes to the educational scene. The Indian Education Act of 1972 and the Indian Self-Determination and Educational Assistance Act of 1975 both made funds available to improve the amount, variety, and quality of education available to tribal people as part of their basic goals. In addition to providing additional funds for a multitude of programs, this legislation gave Indian leaders and communities a direct part in planning and administering school programs. It provided funds to help start community-operated schools, to create or enlarge adult education programs, and to establish an Office of Indian Education, to be controlled by a national advisory council consisting of Indians. Clearly, if money and legislation could help, the federal government seemed to be doing its part.[48]

Tribal communities also worked to help themselves. In 1966 the Navajo nation opened the Rough Rock Demonstration School, showing clearly that Native Americans could manage their own affairs. Three years later the tribe opened classes at its Navajo Community College with a three-sided curriculum. All students took the Navajo studies curriculum, whether enrolled in technical or academic courses. In 1971 Congress passed the Navajo Community College Act, which assured stable funding for the school. Other tribes followed the Navajo lead, taking charge of local schools or founding new ones. During the 1970s another eighteen tribally controlled colleges came into being from Michigan in the east to California in the west. Supported by various groups of Sioux, Ojibwa, Mandan, Omaha, Winnebago, Cheyenne, Blackfeet, Salish-Kootenai, Hopi, Hoppa Valley, and Soboba Indians, the new institutions offered training at the junior college level for people from many tribes. Since then the number of Indian colleges has continued to grow, and by 1995 the number of Indian colleges had climbed to thirty-one, with an enrollment of about sixteen thousand students. Most of the schools remained small, and their students attended only part-time, but their existence demonstrates the tribes' determination to direct their own future affairs and the obvious need for the services the schools offered.[49]

Despite progress of this sort, it seems unlikely that tribal people in the United States will escape the educational control of the rest of society. Assimilationist policies continued to conflict with their call for self-determination, and as recently as 1980 the BIA still operated 209 schools for over 43,000 Indian children. Another 176,000 attended other, nonfederal schools, but most of those were public schools in communities on or near the reservations. Obviously tribal people had little control or even influence in many of the public school systems their children attended, yet this did not stop them from demanding a larger say in school administration and curriculum. Gradually since the 1970s this came to pass as pantribal training programs instructed parents and tribal leaders how to deal with local school matters. As a result, Indians got the authority to review the use of federal funds in local school districts to make certain that the money allotted for Native American children actually went into programs for them and not into the general school budgets. In some areas Indians succeeded in getting tribal history and cultural materials added to the local school offerings.[50]

Continuing Indian demands for self-determination and for more control over their own affairs, while at the same time insisting that the government live up to treaties and other agreements, have kept the officials off balance for the past several decades. In trying to respond to these conflicting desires, Congress has moved back and forth from limiting tribal authority and rights to expanding them significantly. In 1968 it passed an Indian Bill of Rights meant to provide reservation dwellers the same basic civil rights as other American citizens enjoyed. However, this bill conflicted with the rights of tribal governments to regulate activities on the reservations. For example, in the 1950s the Navajo Tribal Council banned the use of peyote, bringing itself into direct conflict with practicing members of the Native American Church, who used peyote as a central part of their worship ceremonies. When church members challenged the tribal government in federal court, they lost because the court ruled that the U.S. Constitution did not apply to Indian tribes. Rather, their status as "domestic dependent nations" meant that they existed as legal bodies distinct from either the federal or the state governments. The court suggested that relief for the peyote users had to come from Congress, and in 1968 that body passed the Indian Civil Rights Act to deal with this issue.[51] In late 1994 the tribe legalized peyote use on the reservation, ending at least a half century of dispute over this matter.

On some issues federal and state officials discriminated against Indians or ignored their basic rights. For example, federal fish and game officials continue to enforce rigorously the prohibitions against the use of feathers from eagles and certain other protected species of birds. For some Indians, however, the feathers are central to their religious ceremonies. In addition, when Native Americans crossed into or out of the United States from either Canada or Mexico, Border Patrol agents regularly demanded to inspect sacred medicine bundles carried or worn by Indian men. In response to repeated objections from tribal officials and pantribal organizations, in 1978 Congress passed the American Indian Religious Freedom Act to halt such actions. Unfortunately, the provocations continued, often by federal officials themselves, and the law proved of only limited significance because it failed to provide any enforcement machinery. The issue has remained one of major contention between the tribal people and federal officials. As recently as 1986 the U.S. Supreme Court ruled that despite the use of eagle feathers in some Indian religious ceremonies, Native Americans' rights to obtain or possess such feathers fell under close federal supervision. It held that congressional legislation to protect certain birds demonstrated that the legislature wanted to restrict the past rights of some tribes to hunt the birds. This struck at the heart of time-honored ceremonies, and to the present neither subsequent legislation nor court rulings have settled the issue.[52]

Another issue of bitter dispute between tribal people and the government is over the Indian demands for the return to the tribes of skeletal burial remains and artifacts by museums and universities. The question has remained current, and in 1987 the *Legal Review*, the publication of the Native American Rights Fund, devoted its lead article to a discussion of federal burial policies. Contrasting the reverential treatment and reburial of the physical remains of a British soldier killed near Philadelphia during the American Revolution with the treatment accorded to the remains of Indian dead, the article castigated government policy and the selfish attitudes of archaeologists and museum curators for their cavalier treatment of Indian remains. Citing federal guidelines that call for maintaining collections of tribal remains "with the dignity and respect to be accorded all human remains," the report's author demanded an example of any other ethnic group in the country that had the graves of its dead treated in the same manner.[53]

On this issue the demands of the militants have had some effect, and sensibilities have become aroused. Several regional offices of the U.S. Forest Service have adopted a new policy that differs sharply with long-standing regulations of the Interior Department. The new policy calls for the rapid reburial of human remains but still accepts the assumption that the federal government, not the tribes, holds actual ownership of the burial remains. Museum personnel have become sensitized to the issue, too, and Robert McC. Adams, a past secretary of the Smithsonian Institution, commented in 1987 that curators, anthropologists, and archaeologists now "have an obligation to return skeletal remains in our collection to tribal descendants."[54] His comments, however, referred only to the remains of ancestors of individual Indians living today. Indian activists complained that such a position failed to accept the idea that skeletal and other remains should be returned to the tribes from which they were taken even when no lineage to living individuals can be established. For example, it took years of wrangling to persuade the State Historical Society of Nebraska to agree to the return of funerary materials to the Pawnee people of that state. Then in November 1990 President George Bush signed the Native American Grave Protection and Repatriation Act, a measure that overrode Adams's position and forced scholars, universities, and museums to make such materials available to the tribes whose ancestors had been exhumed in the first place.[55]

One last political issue remains a point of dispute. While Indians strove for tribal self-determination, as citizens they all possessed the right to vote in national, state, and local elections. In most of the country this caused little problem, but in western areas people on or near the reservations feared concerted Indian political action. This brought resistance to Indian voting and civil rights abuses in scattered areas. In Arizona, for example, state legislators hoped to divide one of the counties in order to reduce the impact of Navajo voters, but threats of legal action stopped that effort. Local officials in other states retreated to pre–civil rights era tactics to dilute Indian voting strength. Limiting the availability of voting registrars and the offices where people might register to one per county and holding at-large county elections kept many Indians away from the polls in lightly populated rural areas. When they did vote, their efforts brought vocal objections in some local political races. For example, in Big Horn County, Montana, during 1982 the Indian voters backed a single slate of candidates in the Democratic Party primary, helping those individuals win the election. This victory brought an immediate political backlash as the opposition organized to form the Bipartisan Campaign Committee and campaigned vigorously to defeat the Indian-backed Democrats. The Democrats carried the election, but not without bringing the latent anti-Indian feelings in the county to the surface in a bitter campaign.[56]

In Canada the past several decades have led in somewhat different directions. Nevertheless, native people there have worked toward two broadly similar goals, those of self-determination and of retaining their rights to the land and resources they claimed. By the end of the 1970s three major groups dominated the discussions between the government of Canada and the native peoples there. The National Indian Brotherhood represented the 289,000 status Indians in the country. The Inuit Tapirisat of Canada spoke for the nearly 22,000 Inuit people, while the Native Council of Canada saw itself as representing the Métis and the nonstatus Indians, perhaps as many as 750,000 people. Other pantribal organizations operate as well, but these three proved most widely accepted at the time. Generally they agreed about their relationship with the Canadian federal government. They denounced the existing legal and constitutional situation as unacceptable and claimed that their special status comes from their having been the original people in Canada.[57]

All three organizations sought recognition of their independent nationhood within the Dominion of Canada. The Indian Brotherhood insists that its members are distinct and separate nations and that each retains its own sovereignty. The other groups claim distinct national status as well. In their view they are more than just ethnic minorities within Canadian society. "Our homeland is here," they state. "We must survive here as a people or we cease to survive at all." Rejecting the concept of two founding people of Canada—the English and the French—they objected strongly to constitutional discussions in the 1979–82 era, fearing that any new agreement would continue to stress assimilation for them. As in the claims of tribal peoples in the United States, demands for self-determination and for a protected land base dominated the thinking of all three of the major associations. With that in mind they demanded that their ideas on aboriginal rights be written into the new constitutional agreement. While the discussions with the federal government continued, the Indian Brotherhood reconstituted itself as the Assembly of First Nations to reflect its political agenda. After intense pressure the native groups got the government to include a clause that recognized their "existing aboriginal and treaty rights" and defining the Métis as an aboriginal people in the 1982 Constitutional Act.[58]

The political and constitutional maneuvering that has occurred in Canada since the early 1980s has tended to accept the native peoples as part of the mainstream debates in ways that have not occurred in the United States. Beginning in 1983 and lasting sporadically until 1987, spokesmen representing Canadian aboriginal groups met repeatedly with federal authorities to discuss getting a secure financial base for tribal governments, adjudicating Métis land claims, and obtaining guarantees for the participation of native peoples in the ongoing constitutional reform. Although the government sponsored three conferences in four years, these meetings failed to reach any mutually acceptable agreements. In fact, by the last of the three meetings many tribal leaders opposed the government proposals because they hoped for immediate results, while the national political leaders expected minimal changes at the time.[59]

Then in 1987 federal and provincial leaders drew up a series of proposals they called the Meech Lake Accord. This document aimed at bridging some of the gaps between the demands of Quebec separatist leaders and the ongoing work on constitutional revision. After considerable discussion the accord failed. During the summer of 1992 the political leaders tried again; this time they produced the Charlottetown Accord. It, too, focused on political compromise. Representatives from the four major native groups took part in the meetings and at first seemed to accept the basic ideas put forth there. The agreement dealt with Métis land claims and recognized Indian demands for self-government. However, because it also called for future negotiations, when the national voting took place in October 1992 reserve dwellers joined a majority of Canadians in voting against this set of proposals as well.[60]

While federal, provincial, and pantribal talks sputtered, parliamentary committees strove to settle the outstanding disputes. In 1983 a Special Committee of the House of Commons on Indian Self-Government reported strongly in favor of Indian self-government. The Penner Report, as the committee's findings came to be called, supported aboriginal rights including land claims and self-determination. In fact, Penner's committee proposed that the federal and provincial governments should recognize band and tribal governments and that the Indian right to self-government be added to the constitution. Among these surprising findings, the report stated that the "Indian First Nations" should "form a distinct order of government in Canada."[61]

By no means did all government actions or court rulings during the 1980s or 1990s bring favorable reactions from the tribal peoples. The 1982 Charter of Rights and Freedoms, in some ways similar to the 1978 Indian Bill of Rights in the United States, created at least as many problems as it solved. The Indian Act had excluded Indian women who married non-Indians and their offspring from tribal membership or treaty rights for over a century, and during the 1980s a United Nations committee ruled that the Canadian practice had to change. Indian groups proved less than enthusiastic about enlarging their band rolls, particularly those with large or potentially large mineral holdings. After considerable discussion and some ill will, the government repealed the discriminatory parts of the law and asked the individual bands to set up criteria for deciding what, if any, portion of band resources people who had lost status before the 1985 settlement might get.[62]

Having had their basic position on aboriginal rights and tribal self-government upheld strongly by the Penner Commission in 1983 may have made the native peoples overconfident, because several years later they received another rude shock. After its 1984 election victory the new government of Brian Mulroney appointed yet another committee to review government-Indian relationships. Headed by Erik Nielsen from the Yukon Territory, the new committee sought ways to increase government efficiency and cut expenses. They recommended giving the provincial governments the responsibility for most Indian services, proposed cutting funding and phasing out much of what had become the Department of Indian Affairs and Northern Development, and urged that the government launch a media campaign to reduce harmful political criticism. Indian groups responded with anger, and a sharp political tug-of-war between the major pantribal associations and the government continued for several years. The tribes feared a return to the discredited termination policy called for by the 1969 White Paper, while the new government claimed that its major interest lay in cutting costs and reducing bureaucratic inefficiency.[63]

Continuing suggestions of the same sort followed as a result of the Mulroney government's stress on cutting costs and improving government efficiency. Clearly the 1985–86 Nielsen task force proposals fit that mold. While Nielsen and his associates considered new approaches to dealing with the tribes, the bureaucrats continued along well-worn paths. In 1985 the Department of Indian Affairs worked to get tribal acceptance of its plan to organize reserves as municipal units of local government. This scheme had been considered for many decades because such a designation might be used to end federal responsibilities or at least to cut costs. While the plan looked inviting to the bureaucrats, the Indians objected loudly because they viewed municipal government as less effective than their existing band councils. Not only did such governments lack enough jurisdiction, but even more important, they dealt directly with the provincial rather than the federal government, something few Indian leaders wanted to consider. So although a few bands did agree to accept such an arrangement, most balked.[64]

While the Canadian government and tribal people continued to grope toward solutions of their disputes, bureaucrats in the United States encountered similar difficulties. During the public attention that Indian affairs generated during the Indian Claims Commission hearings of the 1960s and 1970s, tribal groups long thought to have vanished reappeared. People such as the Pequots in New England or the Poosepatucks of Long Island emerged to claim a place as Indians, asking for federal recognition as tribes. In some ways these groups resembled the nonstatus peoples in Canada. They existed but received no benefits.[65] In 1971 the Passamaquoddy Indians of Maine sued the United States, trying to force the government to help them in legal action against Maine to gain compensation for their 1794 loss of some twelve million acres of land, which the tribe had challenged at the time. The tribe won its case against the federal authorities when the federal appeals court ruled that "the absence of specific federal recognition in and of itself provides little basis for concluding that the

Passamaquoddies are not a 'tribe' within the act."[66] This allowed the tribe to continue its suit against Maine, and in 1980 they concluded an agreement with both the state and the federal governments.

The Passamaquoddy victory brought funds for a tribal land base, but more important, it set a major precedent for other groups seeking recognition as tribes. In an extended 1976 report, the American Indian Policy Review Commission focused attention on the position of the more than one hundred groups that lacked federal tribal recognition. Their findings and several related court rulings prodded the bureaucrats into action, and in 1978 the BIA started the Federal Acknowledgment Project. When it became apparent that over one hundred groups sought recognition, the government created the Branch of Acknowledgment within the BIA. This office now deals with Indian groups and receives, evaluates, and either accepts or rejects claims for tribal status from the applicants. During the first ten years after the acknowledgment process began, 111 separate groups filed for federal acknowledgment. This keen interest caught the bureaucrats by surprise, and they have moved at a snail's pace thus far. As of June 1988 the Branch of Acknowledgment reported that it had completed action on only twenty-two of the petitions. Of those, only half of the decisions resulted in the award of formal tribal status, so considerable disappointment still exists.[67]

As Indians became increasingly active and vocal in securing their rights, some citizens and politicians objected. In a 1979 letter to the Senate Select Committee on Indian Affairs, a member of the Sanders County, Montana, Board of Commissioners wrote to the committee suggesting that the government abolish all Indian reservations. Grumbling that the government had "been taking care of RED MEN long enough," he complained because he thought that the tribal people had received special rather than equal treatment.[68] That opinion remains strong, as a 1986 incident illustrates. In January of that year the Mobil Oil Corporation announced that it had removed a Denver company from its list of potential subcontractors for a project on the Navajo Reservation in Arizona. The reason for this action was a letter from the company president, Ronald Vertrees, in which he objected to a Navajo requirement that employers on the reservation give Navajo workers preference. Writing to the Office of Navajo Labor Relations, Mr. Vertrees said, "We hereby inform you that we do not recognize the legal existence of the so-called Navajo Preference in Employment Act of 1985 or any other part of the so-called Navajo Tribal Code." After labeling the Indians as "members of the vanquished and inferior race," he refused to comply with any of the tribal regulations.[69]

During the 1980s and 1990s other issues also disrupted Indian-white relations in the United States. Some people living near reservations perceived favoritism toward Indians at the expense of whites. In the Pacific Northwest bitter reactions continued long after the 1974 Boldt decision awarded half of the annual salmon catch to the coastal tribes there. That ruling had upheld tribal fishing rights guaranteed under their 1854–55 treaties with the United states. In doing so it brought into public view some of the most virulent anti-Indian actions and statements in the past several decades. Under heavy pressure from commercial and sport fishing groups in the state, Washington officials did all they could to obstruct and delay implementation of the decision. It took until 1979 before they finally accepted the court orders and made the necessary changes in their regulations and their enforcement. The controversy reemerged because of a December 1995 ruling by Judge Edward Rafeedie of the federal district court in Los Angeles. His decision extended the 1974 Boldt ruling to cover Indian harvesting of up to one-half of the shellfish from Puget Sound. When the Squamish and other tribes moved to begin harvesting the shellfish, someone fired gunshots over their heads. Clearly this issue has yet to be resolved satisfactorily.[70]

Anti-Indian forces objected to other exercises of treaty rights for Indians during the past several decades. In 1974 Wisconsin state game officials arrested several Ojibwa men for spearfishing out of season. The tribal people sued, basing their claims on earlier treaty cessions that had preserved their hunting, fishing, and gathering rights. A 1983 federal district court ruled in their favor, setting off an uproar among sport fishermen throughout the state. Anti-Ojibwa spokesmen charged that the treaties lacked validity, claiming that the courts practiced a sort of reverse discrimination in favor of the Indians. Some people displayed bumper stickers with hate phrases such as "Spear an Indian, Save a Walleye." Despite this vociferous opposition, federal courts ruled in favor of the Indians, who continue spearfishing. For a while protesters ignored the decision, lining the stream banks and lakeshores, shouting racial slurs and pelting the Indians with rocks. One of the many short-lived anti-Indian groups lost a 1992 decision when the Lac du Flambeau tribe sued them in federal court.[71]

Another sensitive issue resulted from the 1988 Indian Gaming Regulation Act. That law made it legal for tribes to operate bingo halls and gambling casinos in many parts of the country. In Connecticut the Mashantucket Pequots have such a successful operation that Donald Trump has tried to use the federal courts to halt their competition with his Atlantic City casinos. The legislation authorizing gaming allows gambling to the extent that a state already has it, leading dozens of groups across the country to establish casinos. Many of these have operated profitably for some years. The casinos provide much-needed funds for local improvements, better housing, community health clinics, and a variety of other causes. Their apparent success has created jealousy and anger in some regions. Several states have used these feelings to try to limit present and future casino operations. Both Kansas and Arizona fought Indian gaming vigorously, but in the long run to little avail.[72]

In 1989 and 1990 gambling disputes combined with other quarrels to turn the Mohawk lands of New York and Quebec into a virtual war zone. As part of the Six Nations Confederacy, the Mohawks had always claimed their independence from both the United States and Canada. In New York bitter divisions separated the traditional chiefs, the elected tribal council, and an active and aggressive Warriors Society over cooperating with the federal and state governments and over gambling on tribal lands. In 1989 isolated violence escalated into an open fight between the pro- and anti-gambling groups. This in turn led to raids by the New York State Police and bitter divisions among the Indian factions. Their continuing disagreements spilled over into Canada by early 1990, when town officials in Oka, near Montreal, moved to expand the local country club golf course. Because the site they chose included an Indian burial ground, the proposal brought immediate and heated objections. These, in turn, became intermixed with the gambling dispute and led to road blockages that brought the Quebec and Canadian governments into the disputes. After an unsuccessful attack on one Indian roadblock, in which a Quebec lawman died, both sides backed away from each other slightly. In September 1990 Canadian officials removed the last Mohawk protesters from their barricaded camp. These events brought intense press coverage in both countries, but more than anything they demonstrated the deep and bitter divisions in these tribal communities. Many of the central issues here remain unsolved.[73]

Despite those events, Indian affairs and the amount of public attention paid to them in the United States have diminished. A 1989 Senate investigation into the conduct of Indian affairs brought forth a new proposal to accept Indian demands for self-determination. In fact, it went beyond that and suggested that any tribe that chose to do so be allowed "to exit the current bureaucracy of federal Indian programs and, instead, receive and use at its own discretion a proportional share of the current federal Indian budget."[74] This call for a new federalism under which the tribes would exercise their rights and duties without veto power from the Department of the Interior or the BIA seems to offer what many tribal people have advocated. It also signals continuing federal hopes to escape having to deal with the "Indian question."

Some distrust certainly lingers over anything that might be taken as just another call to abolish the BIA and turn the Indians loose. Obviously the committee report is only a proposal, not concrete legislation, but it seems to move American leaders in the same direction that Canadian officials have taken, if only hesitantly. As both nations struggle with the concept of semi-independent tribes, disputes continue between and among native peoples. Still, the message seems clear. Indian people who dominated the continent from the Saint Lawrence to Florida and from Virginia to Alaska have not disappeared. Rather, during the most recent generation their numbers grew and their competence developed, and because of those trends their survival is assured. How their future niche in either society will evolve as we enter the twenty-first century remains unclear, but certainly they will play an increasingly independent role in the years ahead.

Conclusion

 BY THE 1990S, after nearly five centuries of facing the Europeans, native peoples in the United States and Canada share many concerns and experiences. They have passed through the stages set out earlier in this text, moving downward from independence to equality, dependency, and marginality before emerging with renewed cultural strength and political awareness. Although the details and timing of the changes differed in the two nations, the general pattern held with only modest variations. Indians in the United States and First Nations people in Canada now have many of the same objectives. Increasingly they demand self-determination, tribal sovereignty, and near independence, and they are moving toward some of those goals, if only slowly. In addition, they have become increasingly aware of the actions of other native peoples in both countries as the century comes to a close.

Meanwhile, both the U.S. and Canadian governments and societies continue to deal with Indian-related issues with considerable hesitation. For example, during the past century south of the border the federal government has conducted many studies of the tribal situation. Still, only modest and incremental changes have resulted. The same thing continues to occur in Canada. There, as recently as 21 November 1996, the Royal Commission on Aboriginal Peoples presented its four-thousand-page report, some five years in the making, to Parliament. It called for fundamental changes in policies and their implementation in dealing with the native peoples. If the legislators fail to heed its recommendations, the commission predicted, existing practices would "condemn many of the more than 800,000 indigenous Canadians to worsened poverty, disease and anger."[1]

Canadian officials responded cautiously to the report, for several reasons. First, because it called for steeply increased government spending needed to implement programs for better housing and education, as well as improved job training and placement—things that few who know anything about the present situation would argue against. Yet this recommendation for more government programs and increased expenditures comes at a time when Prime Minister Jean Chrétien's Liberal government has worked for over three years to cut federal spending in virtually all departments to reduce Canada's crushing federal deficit. Second, First Nations' calls for more assistance, for full nationhood, and for a new, thorough review of all past land claims come at a time when many Canadians fear that their nation may be crumbling. Thus Indian demands focus largely on issues that have contributed to the sense that Canadian society is threatened with collapse. In this situation it appears unlikely that the First Nations' needs will be met soon.

While officials and social commentators agree that the situation must change, there appears to be little agreement on how to proceed. Some Canadian leaders are at least cautiously optimistic and are taking limited steps to move in new directions. For example, in the late 1960s federal officials forced the Innu Indians from their traditional homes to Davis Inlet, Newfoundland, a barren, rocky island. There the tribe experienced serious unemployment, alcoholism, and a rapid social breakdown. After years of misery these people persuaded federal officials to help them move to a site of their own choosing. Minister of Indian Affairs and Northern Development Ronald A. Irvin claimed that the recently signed agreement with the Innu reflected "a new spirit of partnership and working together."[2] Given the muted response to the November 1996 Royal Commission Report, however, this prediction appears to be mostly rhetorical flourishes.

In the United States similar difficulties bedeviled decision makers. The past decade brought huge budget deficits and widespread demands to cut federal expenditures. Like the Department of Indian Affairs and Northern Development in Canada, the Bureau of Indian Affairs is generally regarded as hopelessly tied in bureaucratic knots. To many observers both agencies lack the skill and the desire to bring about fundamental changes. Leaders of individual tribes and bands as well as those who represent multitribal organizations often call for the abolishment of both bureaucracies in the hope that whatever might replace them will be more receptive to change and innovation than the existing structures.

At present one finds striking similarities in the positions of the native peoples. In both countries multitribal groups work closely with the government and the media to keep native peoples' concerns in the news. Many people in each of the two societies now recognize the value of Indian cultural distinctiveness. Large numbers of native people moved into the cities in each country during the past several decades. In the United States well over one-half of the recognized Indians now live somewhere other than on the reservations. In Canada the towns and cities also attract reserve dwellers by offering jobs, possibly improved education, and better health care. Yet most tribal people find themselves among the poorest in either society. Theoretically the governments in each society now accept having a multiethnic and multiracial population. In each, Indians have a specific part of the federal government directly responsible for them, something they share with no other ethnic or racial group. Nevertheless, strong antipathy toward reservation and reserve dwellers permeates many communities.

These similarities do not mask the variety of issues that distinguish both the long-term experiences and present situations of native groups in each of the two countries. The most significant difference is the mythic role of the frontier experience and the numerous clashes between pioneers and Indians in the American past. These elements simply do not play a similar role in Canadian thought or history. In fact, people north of the border often looked smugly at their better record of dealing with tribal people when contrasted with that of the United States. Such different attitudes help explain some of the variations that exist. In Canada the Inuit people have negotiated virtual self-government with the promised 1999 establishment of Nunavut in the eastern Arctic. Such an action is beyond possibility in the United States at present. In western Canada the continued refusal of British Columbia authorities to recognize anything more than minimal native land title claims for over a century is distinct. In the United States, despite their bitter complaints, the states had little impact on such matters because the federal constitution assigned responsibility for Indian affairs to the central government. That was supposed to occur in the north too, but Ottawa did not follow through on its responsibilities. There, mixed-race people, Métis, have a recognized and separate status, something that does not exist in the United States.

While American officials have faced the issue of nonrecognized tribes and established a process for some groups to gain tribal status, the tribes themselves have moved to assert control over many aspects of their lives. In education they have sought to determine curricular content at their children's schools. Bilingual classes, materials with Indian cultural ideas, and more Indian teachers and classroom aides all mark the present situation. Reservation dwellers in the United States now have access to thirty-one tribally supported colleges. To pay for this and finance other needed facilities and programs, many tribes have launched reservation-based gaming enterprises. Some of these are spectacularly successful, and many bring substantial revenue into the tribal treasuries. Since the U.S. Congress passed the 1990 Native American Grave Protection and Repatriation Act, major changes related to the handling, storage, and return of human relics and cultural funerary items have occurred. At the same time, Indian issues have faded from the headlines and the speeches of policy makers there, while in Canada native affairs appear to be getting more attention as central to the major issues that nation faces.

Looking at the implications of the historical record for the present is risky at best. Supposedly each of the two societies now sees itself as a mix of racial and ethnic groups, but neither appears comfortable with that circumstance. Politically, demands for reducing government services and thus the tax burden of the citizens are popular everywhere. If such policies are carried out, then Indians will fail to see their circumstances change dramatically. In addition, for many tribal people their culture remains important enough that they reject or ignore much of what the rest of society expects. At this point it appears likely that the existing antigovernment mood in each nation and the Indians' understandable efforts to retain their distinct identity outside the mainstream cultures will delay or even block major changes in their status, economic position, or general well-being.

The population statistics in the two countries tend to reinforce this view. In Canada tribal groups, excluding the Métis, number about 2.5 percent of the population, while in the United States they make up only about 0.8 percent. With their numbers that small, these people are going to have a difficult time bringing about much change without the solid backing of the political, economic, and cultural leaders. That is not happening in either society at the moment.

What has occurred results largely from the distinct nature of the two societies and the differing paths each has followed to the present. Canadian society at this point appears to be slightly more receptive to Indian demands, but at the same time it is less confident of its own stability. For the tribal people in either society the future looks better than the past, perhaps only because the past is already on record while what is to come remains little more than conjecture. Because of differing past actions and ideas in each country and the differing issues that will capture the attention and support within the two societies, it seems likely that tribal groups will continue to experience similar but not identical treatment.

Notes

INTRODUCTION

1   For a careful discussion of this use of the term *frontier* see Lamar and Thompson, *The Frontier in History*, 3–13; and Wilbur R. Jacobs, "The Fatal Confrontation: Early Native-White Relations on the Frontiers of Australia, New Guinea, and America: A Comparative Study," *Pacific Historical Review* 40 (August 1971): 283–309.

2   W. Turrentine Jackson, "A Brief Message for the Young and/or Ambitious: Comparable Frontiers as a Field for Investigation," *Western Historical Quarterly* 9 (January 1978): 5–18; Deloria, *Custer Died for Your Sins*; and Cardinal, *The Unjust Society*.

3   One example for each country offers a glimpse of the bulk of the literature. In the United States, the University of Oklahoma Press's Civilization of the American Indian series includes well over 150 titles, with new ones being added regularly. The volume of Canadian scholarship may be seen from Alber and Weaver's *A Canadian Indian Bibliography, 1960–1970*, which for that single decade lists 3,082 items. In both countries, the volume of both popular and scholarly literature on Native American issues continues to rise dramatically.

1. INDIANS MEET THE SPANISH, FRENCH, AND DUTCH, 1513–1701

1   Trigger, *Natives and Newcomers*, and Weber, *Spanish Frontier*, both give broad accounts of the colonial era, and I use them heavily in this chapter.

2   The most accessible sources for these generalization include chapters 2–3 in Wilcomb E. Washburn, *The Indian in America* (New York: Harper & Row, 1975); chapters 2–4 in Dickason, *Canada's First Nations*; and Alice B. Kehoe, *North American Indians: A Comprehensive Account*, 2d ed. (Englewood Cliffs NJ: Prentice Hall, 1992).

3   Weber, *Spanish Frontier*, 33–55.

4   Cartier, *Voyages*, 51.

5   Cartier, *Voyages*, 60; Bailey, *Conflict*, 7; Trigger, *Natives and Newcomers*, 130.

6   Trigger, *Natives and Newcomers*, 131.

7   Cartier, *Voyages*, 152–72; Trigger, *Natives and Newcomers*, 131–33.

8   Goldstein, *French-Iroquois Diplomacy*, 18–19; Trigger, *Natives and Newcomers*, 133–34; Dickason, *Canada's First Nations*, 98–102.

9   Weber, *Spanish Frontier*, 50–55; De Soto, *Narratives of the Career of Hernando De Soto*.

10 Weber, *Spanish Frontier*, 45–49. A full account of the explorer's career is given in Bolton, *Coronado*. Primary accounts are in Coronado, *Narratives of the Coronado Expedition of 1540–1542*.

11 Weber, *Spanish Frontier*, 38–42; Kelsey, *Juan Rodriquez Cabrillo*, 123–63.

12 Quoted in Weber, *Spanish Frontier*, 74.

13 Lowery, *Spanish Settlements*, 244–63, 339–66; Dobyns, *Their Numbers Become Thinned*, 7–44. See also Eugene Lyon, *The Enterprise of Florida: Pedro Menedez de Aviles and the Spanish Conquest of 1565–1568* (Gainesville: University of Florida Press, 1976).

14 Weber, *Spanish Frontier*, 77–87; Hammond and Rey, *Don Juan de Oñate*; and Simmons, *The Last Conquistador*.

15 Eccles, *France in America*, 12–13; Innis, *Fur Trade*, 12–15.

16 Eccles, *Canadian Frontier*, 20; Axtell, *Invasion Within*, 33–34; Trigger, *Natives and Newcomers*, 172–74.

17 Eccles, *Canadian Frontier*, 22; Axtell, *Invasion Within*, 34.

18 Trigger, *Children* 1:62–64, 243.

19 Chrestien Le Clercq, *New Relation of Gaspesia*, 227.

20 Trigger, *Children* 1:244.

21 Trigger, *Children* 1:244.

22 Quoted in Miller, *Skyscrapers*, 37.

23 Quoted in Innis, *Fur Trade*, 32.

24 Miller, *Skyscrapers*, 37; Trigger, *Natives and Newcomers*, 186–89.

25 Trigger, *Children* 1:229.

26 Eccles, *Canadian Frontier*, 23.

27 Axtell, *Invasion Within*, 35–36; Trigger, *Natives and Newcomers*, 174–75.

28 Quoted in Brebner, *Canada*, 32; see also Trigger, "Champlain Judged," 87–88.

29 James Douglas, *New England and New France*, 99–100; Trigger, *Natives and Newcomers*, 177–81.

30 Eccles, *France in America*, 45–46.

31 Trigger, *Children* 1:223–24.

32 Quoted in Jaenen, "Amerindian Views," 289–90.

33 Bailey, *Conflict*, 14; Jaenen, "Amerindian Views," 277, 280–84; Trigger, *Children* 2:566–67.

34 Eccles, *France in America*, 27; Brebner, *Canada*, 35–36.

35 Trelease, "Indian-White Contacts."

36 Jennings, *Ambiguous Iroquois Empire*, 48–49.

37 Trelease, *Indian Affairs*, 60–84.

38 Quoted in Macleod, *American Indian Frontier*, 229.

39 Trelease, *Indian Affairs*, 138–68.

40 W. Morton, *The Kingdom of Canada*, 32; Eccles, *France in America*, 34.

41 Quoted in Jaenen, *Friend and Foe*, 155. See also Stanley, "Policy of 'Francisation,'" 334;
    Trigger, *Children* 1:325.
42 Trigger, *Children* 1:325, 378.
43 Trigger, *Children* 1:378–80; Eccles, *Canadian Frontier*, 26–27; Jaenen, *Friend and Foe*, 153,
    166.
44 Jaenen, *French Relationship*, 68.
45 Quoted in Jaenen, *Friend and Foe*, 163.
46 Stanley, "Policy of 'Francisation,'" 335–37; Axtell, *Invasion Within*, 56–57.
47 Chalmers, *Education behind the Buckskin Curtain*, 30; Axtell, *Invasion Within*, 57.
48 Quoted in Jaenen, "Amerindian Views," 286.
49 Chalmers, *Education behind the Buckskin Curtain*, 30; Axtell, *Invasion Within*, 57–58.
50 Quoted in Axtell, *Invasion Within*, 58.
51 Bidney, "The Idea of the Savage," 323; Trigger, *Children* 2:468.
52 Jaenen, "Problems of Assimilation," 280; Stanley, "First Indian 'Reserves,'" 180–81; Ronda,
    "Sillery Experiment," 4–5.
53 Jaenen, *French Relationship*, 84; Ronda, "Sillery Experiment," 6–7.
54 Stanley, "First Indian 'Reserves,'" 181–83; Ronda, "Sillery Experiment," 10–11.
55 Villeneuve, *Historical Background of Indian Reserves*, 6; Stanley, "First Indian 'Re-
    serves,'" 184–85; Ronda, "Sillery Experiment," 8–9.
56 Axtell, *Invasion Within*, 46; Trigger, *Natives and Newcomers*, 227–31.
57 Eccles, *Canadian Frontier*, 46; Trigger, *Natives and Newcomers*, 227–29. Dickason, *Can-
    ada's First Nations*, 122–30.
58 Trigger, *Children* 2:567–68.
59 Jaenen, "Amerindian Views," 274–75.
60 Trigger, "French Presence," 129; Trigger, *Children* 2:597–98, 700.
61 Trigger, "French Presence," 133–37; Jaenen, *Friend and Foe*, 65.
62 Weber, *Spanish Frontier*, 96–98, 100.
63 Weber, *Spanish Frontier*, 100–104.
64 Weber, *Spanish Frontier*, 133–41.
65 Jennings, *Amibiguous Iroquois Empire*, 89–100.
66 Dickason, *Canada's First Nations*, 130–35.
67 Quoted in Innis, *Fur Trade*, 31.
68 Quoted in Eccles, *Canada under Louis XIV*, 4; see also Eccles, *France in America*, 36–37;
    Eccles, "Fur Trade Imperialism," 342; and W. Smith, "Fur Trade and the Frontier," 21.
69 W. Smith, "Fur Trade and the Frontier," 28; Stanley, "Policy of 'Francisation,'" 334; Jaenen,
    Friend and Foe, 162–63.
70 Quoted in Jaenen, *Friend and Foe*, 162.
71 Bailey, *Conflict*, 10.
72 Jaenen, *Friend and Foe*, 162–63; Jaenen, *French Relationship*, 68.
73 Eccles, *France in America*, 39; Trigger, *Children* 2:455–56.
74 Trigger, "Champlain Judged," 98–99.
75 Jaenen, "Amerindian Views," 278–88.
76 Quoted in Jaenen, *Friend and Foe*, 158.
77 Jaenen, *Friend and Foe*, 158–59.

78 Eccles, *Canadian Frontier*, 106–08.

79 Eccles, *Canadian Frontier*, 108–10.

80 Eccles, *Canadian Frontier*, 113–15; Jennings, *Ambiguous Iroquois Empire*, 173–75.

81 Jennings, *Ambiguous Iroquois Empire*, 176–77.

82 For an excellent discussion of this practice see Richter, "War and Culture."

83 Eccles, *Canadian Frontier*, 116–17; Jennings, *Ambiguous Iroquois Empire*, 175–76, 184–85.

84 Eccles, *Canadian Frontier*, 119–20.

85 Eccles, *Canadian Frontier*, 120–25; Jennings, *Ambiguous Iroquois Empire*, 195–212.

86 Jennings, *Ambiguous Iroquois Empire*, 128–30. For a thoughtful discussion of the fur trade see White, *Middle Ground*, 94–141.

87 Eccles, *Canada under Louis XIV*, 124; Jaenen, *Friend and Foe*, 136.

88 Stanley, "Policy of 'Francisation,' " 334; Jaenen, *Friend and Foe*, 160–61.

89 Jaenen, *French Relationship*, 32.

2. INDIANS AND ENGLISH NEAR THE CHESAPEAKE, 1570S–1670S

1 Quinn, *New American World* 3:282.

2 Quinn, *Set Fair for Roanoke*, 39.

3 Quinn, *Set Fair for Roanoke*, 70–72.

4 Harriot, *A Briefe and True Report*, 381–82.

5 Quinn, *Set Fair for Roanoke*, 114.

6 Quinn, *Set Fair for Roanoke*, 127, 138.

7 Quinn, *Set Fair for Roanoke*, 150–52.

8 Quinn, *Set Fair for Roanoke*, 341–78.

9 Quinn, *North America from Earliest Discovery*, 447.

10 Fausz, "Fighting 'Fire,' " 36.

11 Lurie, "Indian Cultural Adjustment," 40; Fausz, "Fighting 'Fire,' " 34.

12 Fausz, "Fighting 'Fire,' " 38–39.

13 Fausz, "Fighting 'Fire,' " 40.

14 Quoted in Vaughan, "Expulsion," 65; Fausz, "Fighting 'Fire,' " 39.

15 Quoted in Vaughan, "Expulsion," 65.

16 Quoted in Vaughan, "Expulsion," 65–66.

17 Kingsbury, *Records of the Virginia Company* 3:14–15, 18–19.

18 Kingsbury, *Records of the Virginia Company* 3:14.

19 Kingsbury, *Records of the Virginia Company* 3:27.

20 Kingsbury, *Records of the Virginia Company* 3:14–15.

21 Vaughan, "Expulsion," 67.

22 Fausz, "The Powhatan Uprising of 1622," gives details of this era. See also Fausz, "Fighting 'Fire,' " 40.

23 Fausz, "Fighting 'Fire,' " 40.

24 Quoted in Pearce, *The Savages of America*, 13.

25 Quoted in Pearce, *The Savages of America*, 15.

26 Quoted in Vaughan, "Expulsion," 70.

27 Robinson, "Indian Education," 154–55.

28 Vaughan, "Expulsion," 69; Robinson, "Indian Education," 155–56; Craven, *Southern Colonies in the Seventeenth Century*, 453–98.

29 Robinson, "Indian Education," 158; Stith, *History*, 162–63.

30 Vaughan, "Expulsion," 70; Robinson, "Indian Education," 158.

31 Quoted in Vaughan, "Expulsion," 65.

32 Vaughan, "Expulsion," 71, 73.

33 Quoted in Smits, "Abominable Mixture," 160.

34 Quoted in Vaughan, "Expulsion," 72; see also Smits, "Abominable Mixture," 161–64.

35 Vaughan, "Expulsion," 73–74.

36 Quoted in Vaughan, "Expulsion," 74.

37 Quoted in Vaughan, "Expulsion," 74.

38 Fausz, "Fighting 'Fire,'" 41.

39 Fausz, "Fighting 'Fire,'" 41–42.

40 Fausz, "Fighting 'Fire,'" 41–42; Vaughan, "Expulsion," 75–76.

41 Lurie, "Indian Cultural Adjustment," 42.

42 Lurie, "Indian Cultural Adjustment," 41–50; Vaughan, "Expulsion," 75.

43 Quoted in Vaughan, "Expulsion," 75.

44 Fausz, "Fighting 'Fire,'" 42–44; Vaughan, "Expulsion," 75–76.

45 Fausz, "Fighting 'Fire,'" 43–44.

46 Quoted in Fausz, "Fighting 'Fire,'" 43.

47 Kingsbury, *Records of the Virginia Company* 3:98–99, 102, 221–22; Vaughan, "Expulsion," 77.

48 Powell, "Aftermath of the Massacre"; Shea, *Virginia Militia*.

49 Kingsbury, *Records of the Virginia Company* 3:556–57.

50 Examples of this include Nash, "Image of the Indian"; Vaughan, "Expulsion"; Jennings, "Virgin Land and Savage People"; Smits, "Abominable Mixture"; and Lurie, "Indian Cultural Adjustment."

51 Quoted in Robinson, "Indian Education," 159.

52 Hening, *Statutes at Large* 1:410.

53 Hening, *Statutes at Large* 1:396, 455; Lauber, *Indian Slavery in Colonial Times*, 197–98; and Robinson, "Indian Education," 158–60.

54 Robinson, *Southern Colonial Frontier*, 48.

55 Shea, *Virginia Militia*, 51–72.

56 Quoted in Robinson, *Southern Colonial Frontier*, 50.

57 Robinson, *Southern Colonial Frontier*, 49–50.

58 Robinson, "Legal Status of the Indian"; Robinson, "Tributary Indians in Colonial Virginia."

59 Robinson, "Legal Status of the Indian," 251–52.

60 Nash, *Red, White and Black*, 65; Lurie, "Indian Cultural Adjustment," 44; and Crosby, "Virgin Soil Epidemics," 189–99.

61 Washburn, *Governor and Rebel*, 20–21; Morgan, *American Slavery, American Freedom*, 250–51.

62 Washburn, *Governor and Rebel*, 21–33; Morgan, *American Slavery*, 251–52.

63 Washburn, *Governor and Rebel*, 23–27; Morgan, *American Slavery*, 252–54.

64 Washburn, *Governor and Rebel*, 40–76; 153–66; Morgan, *American Slavery*, 252–70; and Shea, *Virginia Militia*, 97–121, provide more details for these events.

3. INDIANS AND ENGLISH IN NEW ENGLAND, 1600–1670S

1 Salisbury, *Manitou and Providence*, 90.

2 Salisbury, *Manitou and Providence*, 95–96; Vaughan, *New England Frontier*, 16.

3 Cook, "Significance of Disease"; Crosby, "God . . . Would Destroy Them"; Duffy, *Epidemics in Colonial America*, 140–41; Stern and Stern, *Effect of Small Pox*, 21–22.

4 Quoted in Vaughan, *New England Frontier*, 22

5 Cook, "Significance of Disease," 487–89; Crosby, "Virgin Soil Epidemics."

6 Salisbury, *Manitou and Providence*, 101–9; Vaughan, *New England Frontier*, 21–23.

7 Salisbury, *Manitou and Providence*, 22–30; Vaughan, *New England Frontier*, 50–63. For discussions of each local group see the tribal entries in Trigger, *Handbook*.

8 Vaughan, *New England Frontier*, 50–56.

9 Bradford, *Of Plymouth Plantation*, 26.

10 Vaughan, *New England Frontier*, 66.

11 Bradford, *Of Plymouth Plantation*, 69; Vaughan, *New England Frontier*, 67; Salisbury, *Manitou and Providence*, 113.

12 Vaughan, *New England Frontier*, 69.

13 Vaughan, *New England Frontier*, 69–70; Salisbury, *Manitou and Providence*, 114.

14 Vaughan, *New England Frontier*, 70–72; Salisbury, *Manitou and Providence*, 114–16.

15 Salisbury, *Manitou and Providence*, 115–16.

16 Vaughan, *New England Frontier*, 73; Salisbury, *Manitou and Providence*, 117.

17 Quoted in Vaughan, *New England Frontier*, 74.

18 Quoted in Vaughan, *New England Frontier*, 74.

19 Vaughan, *New England Frontier*, 75–77.

20 Vaughan, *New England Frontier*, 82–87; Salisbury, *Manitou and Providence*, 125–33; Jennings, *Invasion*, 186–87.

21 Vaughan, *New England Frontier*, 94. This chronology follows Vaughan, although I question some of his conclusions.

22 Quoted in Salisbury, *Manitou and Providence*, 180.

23 Vaughan, *New England Frontier*, 98–99.

24 Salisbury, *Manitou and Providence*, 205–6, 209–10.

25 Jennings, *Invasion*, 189–90; Salisbury, *Manitou and Providence*, 217–18; Vaughan, *New England Frontier*, 123–25.

26 Vaughan, *New England Frontier*, 124–25.

27 Jennings, *Invasion*, 202–4; Salisbury, *Manitou and Providence*, 203–15; Vaughan, *New England Frontier*, 126.

28 Jennings, *Invasion*, 187–201; Salisbury, *Manitou and Providence*, 211–15; Vaughan, *New England Frontier*, 126–27.

29 Vaughan, *New England Frontier*, 128–29; Salisbury, *Manitou and Providence*, 218.

30 Vaughn, *New England Frontier*, 132–33; Salisbury, *Manitou and Providence*, 219.

31 John Underhill, "Newes from America," quoted in Salisbury, *Manitou and Providence*, 222.

32 Bradford, *Of Plymouth Plantation*, 296.

33 Salisbury, *Manitou and Providence*, 220–25; Vaughan, *New England Frontier*, 144–45.

34 Vaughan, *New England Frontier*, 147–51.

35 Vaughan, *New England Frontier*, 150–51.

36 Roger Clap, "Memoirs," in Young, *Chronicles*, 364.

37 Vaughan, *New England Frontier*, focuses on Indian-Indian and Indian-white relations, while Salisbury, *Manitou and Providence*, and Jennings, *Invasion*, include intercolonial and international rivalry too. Although they disagree sharply in method and conclusions, taken together the three offer a clear picture of the situation.

38 Vaughan, *New England Frontier*, 161–67; Salisbury, *Manitou and Providence*, 230–35.

39 Gary B. Nash, "Red, White, and Black: The Origins of Racism in Colonial America," in Nash and Weiss, *The Great Fear*, 7.

40 Shurtleff, *Records of Governor and Company* 3:96–97.

41 Quoted in Young, *Chronicles*, 133.

42 Bowden, *American Indians and Christian Missions*, 113–14.

43 Canny, " Ideology of English Colonization"; Bowden, *American Indians and Christian Missions*, 114–16.

44 Beaver, "Methods in American Missions," 148; Pearce, *Savagism and Civilization*, 20.

45 Salisbury, "Red Puritans," 30.

46 Salisbury, "Red Puritans," 31; Bushnell, "Treatment of Indians in Plymouth Colony," 208.

47 Vaughan, *New England Frontier*, 242–44.

48 Vaughan, *New England Frontier*, 246–51.

49 Vaughan, *New England Frontier*, 257.

50 Quoted in Jordan, *White over Black*, 211.

51 Jordan, *White over Black*, 212.

52 Beaver, "Methods in American Missions," 131–32; Vaughan, *New England Frontier*, 266–67.

53 Salisbury, "Red Puritans," 35.

54 Salisbury, "Red Puritans," 35–36; Tanis, "Education in Eliot's Indian Utopias," 316; Vaughan, *New England Frontier*, 303.

55 Salisbury, "Red Puritans," 42–43, 46.

56 Vaughan, *New England Frontier*, 285–87.

57 Quoted in Vaughan, *New England Frontier*, 281.

58 Salisbury, "Red Puritans," 46–47; Vaughan, *New England Frontier*, 281–82.

59 Beaver, "Methods in American Missions," 137–38.

60 Beaver, "Methods in American Missions," 137; Vaughan, *New England Frontier*, 262; Salisbury, "Red Puritans," 40–41.

61 Beaver, "Methods in American Missions," 135–36.

62 Vaughan, *New England Frontier*, 294–95; Kawashima, "Jurisdiction of the Colonial Courts," 540; Koehler, "Red-White Power Relations."

63 For Plymouth see Ronda, "Red and White at Bench."

64 Kawashima, "Jurisdiction of the Colonial Courts," 538.

65 Quoted in Vaughan, *New England Frontier*, 201.

66 Salisbury, *Manitou and Providence*, 186–87; Vaughan, *New England Frontier*, 188–90.

67 Ronda, "Red and White at Bench," 203–5.

68 Koehler, "Red-White Power Relations," 24–30; Ronda, "Red and White at Bench," 206–10.

69 Quoted in Vaughan, *New England Frontier*, 193.

70 Leach, *Flintlock and Tomahawk*, gives the most complete discussion of this conflict. For differing interpretations of the causes and nature of the war see Jennings, *Invasion*, and Vaughan, *New England Frontier*.

71 Leach, *Flintlock and Tomahawk*, 22–24.

72 Leach, *Flintlock and Tomahawk*, 26–27.

73 Leach, *Flintlock and Tomahawk*, 30–33.

74 Russell Bourne, *The Red King's Rebellion: Racial Politics in New England, 1675–1678* (New York: Atheneum, 1990), 85–205, provides a fresh look at these events.

75 Bourne, *The Red King's Rebellion*, 3, 38.

76 Vaughn, *New England Frontier*, 319; V. Anderson, "King Philip's Herds."

4. TRADE, DIPLOMACY, WARFARE, AND ACCULTURATION, 1670S–1750S

1 Rule, "Jerome Phelypeaux," 190–91; Robinson, *Southern Colonial Frontier*, 68; Daniel H. Usner Jr., *Indians, Settlers, and Slaves in a Frontier Exchange Economy: The Lower Mississippi Valley before 1783* (Chapel Hill: University of North Carolina Press, 1992), 16–18.

2 Rich, *The Fur Trade and the Northwest*, 19–23.

3 Rich, *The Fur Trade and the Northwest*, 23–36.

4 Ray, *Indians in the Fur Trade*, discusses the trade and its impact on these tribes.

5 Van Kirk, *Many Tender Ties*, focuses on how the relationships of Indian women and English traders altered tribal life.

6 White, *Middle Ground*. See also Brown, *Strangers in Blood*; Van Kirk, *Many Tender Ties*; and Peterson and Brown, *The New Peoples*.

7 Quoted in Robinson, *Southern Colonial Frontier*, 84.

8 Merrell, *The Indians' New World*, 30–32, 34–38.

9 Merrell, *The Indians' New World*, 84; Crane, *Southern Frontier*, 16–17.

10 Crane, *Southern Frontier*, 19–21; Robinson, *Southern Colonial Frontier*, 87.

11 Crane, *Southern Frontier*, 24–31.

12 Weber, *Spanish Frontier*, 141–45; Boyd, Smith, and Griffin, *Here They Once Stood*.

13 Robinson, *Southern Colonial Frontier*, 98–99; Woods, *French-Indian Relations*, 13–22.

14 P. Wood, "The Changing Population of the Colonial South," 38–39.

15 White, *Roots of Dependency*, 34–36, 40–45.

16 Woods, *French-Indian Relations*, 5.

17 Merrell, "Our Bond of Peace," 198–203.

18 Robinson, *Southern Colonial Frontier*, 100–102; Crane, *Southern Frontier*, 17–19, 109–114.

19 Robinson, *Southern Colonial Frontier*, 99–100; Crane, *Southern Frontier*, 78–81, 88–91.

20 Wright, *Only Land*, 117–18; Parramore, "Tuscarora Ascendancy."

21 Parramore, "Tuscarora Ascendancy," 322–26.

22 Quoted in Wright, *Only Land*, 120.

23 Crane, *Southern Frontier*, 158–61; Wright, *Only Land*, 118–21; Thomas C. Parramore, "With Tuscarora Jack on the Back Path to Bath," *North Carolina Historical Review* 64 (April 1987): 115–38.

24 Quoted in Crane, *Southern Frontier*, 166.

25 Merrell, *The Indians' New World*, 68–73.

26 Wright, *Only Land*, 121–23; Haan, "The Trade Do's Not Flourish as Formerly."

27 Quoted in Merrell, *The Indians' New World*, 68. See also Wright, *Only Land*, 123.

28 Merrell, *The Indians' New World*, 75–80; Reid, *A Better Kind of Hatchet*, 52–72; Wright, *Only Land*, 123–25; Crane, *Southern Frontier*, 167–86.

29 Robinson, *Southern Colonial Frontier*, 115–18; Weber, *Spanish Frontier*, 178–81.

30 Robinson, *Southern Colonial Frontier*, 118–19.

31 Woods, *French-Indian Relations*, 55–56.

32 Woods, *French-Indian Relations*, 57–60.

33 Woods, *French-Indian Relations*, 62–63, 71–74; Usner, *Indians, Settlers, and Slaves*, 65–70.

34 Woods, *French-Indian Relations*, 75–78.

35 Woods, *French-Indian Relations*, 62–63; Usner, *Indians, Settlers, and Slaves*, 70–72.

36 Usner, *Indians, Settlers, and Slaves*, 77–104, 244–75.

37 For a rich and detailed consideration of these issues see White, *Middle Ground*, 1–49, 142–85. See also McConnell, *A Country Between*, 1–60, and Aquila, *Iroquois Restoration*, 85–128.

38 Edmunds and Peyser, *The Fox Wars*, gives a clear discussion of these events.

39 McConnell, *A Country Between*, 61–112; Aquila, *Iroquois Restoration*, 129–45.

40 Quoted in Axtell, *Invasion Within*, 78.

41 Axtell, *Invasion Within*, 83–86.

42 Axtell, *Invasion Within*, 119.

43 Quoted in Axtell, *Invasion Within*, 94

44 Stanley, "First Indian 'Reserves,'" 185–95, 203–5; Villeneuve, *Historical Background of Indian Reserves*, 6–9.

45 Quoted in Jaenen, *Friend and Foe*, 177.

46 Quoted in Jaenen, *Friend and Foe*, 177.

47 Stanley, "Policy of 'Francisation,'" 344–47; Ralston, "Religion, Public Policy, and Education of Micmac Indians," 474–75.

48 J. Jones, "Established Virginia Church," 14–15.

49 Quoted in Goodwin, "Christianity, Civilization and the Savage," 103.

50 Quoted in Klingberg, *Anglican Humanitarianism*, 55.

51 Quoted in Robinson, "Indian Education," 161.

52 Quoted in Robinson, "Indian Education," 163.

53 Quoted in Szasz, *Indian Education*, 72.

54 Quoted in Robinson, "Indian Education," 166.

55 Szasz, *Indian Education*, 72–74; Byrd, *Histories of the Dividing Line*, 118.

56 Byrd, *Histories of the Dividing Line*, 163–70.

57 Bushnell, "Treatment of Indians in Plymouth Colony," 209–10; Jordan, *White over Black*, 204; Szasz, *Indian Education*, 174–76.

58 Quoted in Szasz, *Indian Education*, 182.

59 Quoted in Szasz, *Indian Education*, 182. See also Ronda, "We Are Well as We Are."

60 Beaver, "American Missionary Motivation," 220.

61 Lawson, *A New Voyage to Carolina*, 192.

62 Quoted in Jaenen, *Friend and Foe*, 165

63 Jaenen, *Friend and Foe*, 187.

64 Jordan, *White over Black*, 143, 163; Lauber, *Indian Slavery in Colonial Times*, 204.

65 Byrd, *Histories of the Dividing Line*, 3–4.

66 Brebner, "Subsidized Intermarriage with the Indians," 25–36.

67 Jaenen, *French Relationship*, 37–38.

68 Quoted in Jaenen, *French Relationship*, 34.

69 Quoted in Jaenen, *French Relationship*, 41.

70 Trelease, *Indian Affairs*, 225–26.

71 Robinson, "Legal Status of the Indian"; Kawashima, "Jurisdiction of the Colonial Courts," 533; Koehler, "Red-White Power Relations."

72 Quoted in Robinson, "Legal Status of the Indian," 258.

73 Robinson, "Legal Status of the Indian," 251–53.

74 Kawashima, "Jurisdiction of the Colonial Courts," 541–44.

75 Kawashima, "Jurisdiction of the Colonial Courts," 545, 547.

5. STRIVING FOR INDEPENDENCE, 1750–1790S

1 Edmunds, "Old Briton."

2 The best discussions of these issues are found in White, *Middle Ground*; McConnell, *A Country Between*; Dowd, *Spirited Resistance*; and Usner, *Indians, Settlers, and Slaves*. See also Lewis, "Shamans and Prophets."

3 Dowd, *Spirited Resistance*, 31–35.

4 Corkran, *The Cherokee Frontier*, 156–81.

5 Robinson, *Southern Colonial Frontier*, 217–22.

6 Quoted in Peckham, *Pontiac and the Indian Uprising*, 81.

7 Quoted in Peckham, *Pontiac and the Indian Uprising*, 101; Axtell, "The White Indians of Colonial America," discusses the issue of captivity and returns.

8 Jaenen, "French Sovereignty and Native Nationhood," 83–93.

9 Quoted in Peckham, *Pontiac and the Indian Uprising*, 104. The rest of this discussion of the war comes from this source.

10 Jaenen, *French Relationship*, 36.

11 Jensen, *American Colonial Documents*, 640–43.

12 Surtees, *Indian Land Surrenders*, 2–3.

13 Clinton, "The Proclamation of 1763," 356–58.

14 Clinton, "The Proclamation of 1763," 363.

15 Francis, *History of the Native Peoples of Quebec*, 8–9; Milloy, "Early Indian Acts," 56–57.

16 Sosin, *Whitehall and the Wilderness*, 73–78.

17 Sosin, *Whitehall and the Wilderness*, 128–64.
18 Sosin, *Whitehall and the Wilderness*, 169–80.
19 Allen, *History of the British Indian Department*, 20.
20 Sosin, *Revolutionary Frontier*, 82–83.
21 Dowd, *Spirited Resistance*, 37–38.
22 Dowd, *Spirited Resistance*, 83–87.
23 Sosin, *Revolutionary Frontier*, 90–92; Wise, "American Revolution and Indians," 192–93; Dowd, *Spirited Resistance*, 47–54.
24 Sosin, *Revolutionary Frontier*, 105–10, 112–23.
25 Horsman, *The Frontier in the Formative Years*, 9–11.
26 Horsman, *The Frontier in the Formative Years*, 13.
27 Green, "Alexander McGillivray," 80–83.
28 Quoted in Green, "Alexander McGillivray," 54; Martin, *Sacred Revolt*, 83–84.
29 Martin, *Sacred Revolt*, 55–57.
30 Horsman, "American Indian Policy in the Old Northwest," 35–38.
31 "Articles of Confederation," in J. Richardson, *Compilation of Messages and Papers of the Presidents* 1:5–13; Ford, et al., *Journals of the Continental Congress* 31:490–93.
32 Allen, *History of the British Indian Department*, 28.
33 Carter, *Life and Times of Little Turtle*, 88–97; Dowd, *Spirited Resistance*, 99–103.
34 Carter, *Life and Times of Little Turtle*, 55–57. For a detailed analysis see Eid, "American Indian Military Leadership."
35 Horsman, *The Frontier in the Formative Years*, 44; Horsman, *Matthew Elliott*, 69–74.
36 *American State Papers: Indian Affairs* 1:356–57; hereafter cited as ASP:IA.
37 Downes, *Council Fires on the Upper Ohio*, 320–24.
38 Horsman, *The Frontier in the Formative Years*, 45–49; and Nelson, "Never Have They Done So Little."
39 Carter, *Life and Times of Little Turtle*, 145–53; Dowd, *Sprinted Resistance*, 112–15.
40 Quoted in Allen, *History of the British Indian Department*, 28.
41 Allen, *History of the British Indian Department*, 35.
42 Quoted in Allen, *History of the British Indian Department*, 43.
43 Wise, "Indian Diplomacy of Simcoe," 38.
44 Surtees, *Indian Land Surrenders*, 1–12; D. Smith, *Sacred Feathers*, 17–27.
45 D. Smith, "Dispossession of the Mississauga," 71–72; Surtees, *Indian Land Surrenders*, 14–18; Stanley, "Significance of the Six Nations," 218.
46 Surtees, *Indian Land Surrenders*, 20–24; and Allen, *His Majesty's Indian Allies*, 57–59.
47 Quoted in D. Smith, *Sacred Feathers*, 27.
48 Quoted in D. Smith, "Dispossession of the Mississauga," 75.
49 D. Smith, *Sacred Feathers*, 27–31.
50 C. Johnson, "Joseph Brant."
51 C. Johnson, "Outline of Early Settlement," 48–53.
52 Harper, "Canada's Indian Administration: The Treaty System," 133–34; Surtees, *Indian Land Surrenders*, 9–13.
53 Knox to Washington, 15 June 1789, ASP:IA 1:13.
54 Jefferson to James Monroe, 17 April 1791, in Jefferson, *Writings*, ed. Ford, 5:319.

55 Knox to Cornplanter, Half-Town, and Big Tree, 8 February 1791, in ASP:IA 1:145.

56 Washington to Ohio Tribes, 29 November 1796, in Washington, *Writings* 35:194–95; Washington to Cherokee Nation, 24 August 1796, in Washington, *Writings* 35:301.

57 Washington to Secretary of State, 1 July 1796, in Washington, *Writings* 35:112.

58 Hutton, "Indian Affairs in Nova Scotia," 49–50.

59 Hutton, "Indian Affairs in Nova Scotia," 9.

60 Fingard, "New England Company," 30–31.

61 Chalmers, *Education behind the Buckskin Curtain*, 38–41.

6. OLD THREATS, NEW RESOLVE, 1795–1820S

1 Washington to James Duane, 7 September 1783, in Washington, *Writings* 27:137–38.

2 The best short discussion of these issues is in Prucha, *Great Father* 1:115–34. For a full treatment of the system see Peake, *History of the United States Indian Factory System*.

3 Jefferson to Harrison, 27 February 1803, in Jefferson, *Writings*, ed. Lipscomb, 10:369–71.

4 Dowd, *Spirited Resistance*, 116–22, and White, *Middle Ground*, 469–502, discuss these events in some detail.

5 Dowd, *Spirited Resistance*, 124–25; Wallace, *Death and Rebirth of the Seneca*, 230.

6 Wallace, *Death and Rebirth of the Seneca*, 239–41.

7 Wallace, *Death and Rebirth of the Seneca*, 249–53.

8 Edmunds, *Shawnee Prophet*, 32–41.

9 Quoted in Edmunds, *Shawnee Prophet*, 47.

10 Edmunds, *Shawnee Prophet*, 43–48.

11 Edmunds, *Shawnee Prophet*, 68–70.

12 Edmunds, *Shawnee Prophet*, 70–71.

13 Edmunds, *Shawnee Prophet*, 74–78.

14 Edmunds, *Shawnee Prophet*, 80–83.

15 Quoted in Horsman, *Matthew Elliot*, 179.

16 Edmunds, *Shawnee Prophet*, 107–8.

17 Edmunds, *Shawnee Prophet*, 108–13.

18 Edmunds, *Shawnee Prophet*, 59.

19 Prucha, *Sword of the Republic*, 106–7.

20 Stanley, "Significance of the Six Nations," 220–24, 230–31.

21 Prucha, *Sword of the Republic*, 110–12.

22 Prucha, *Sword of the Republic*, 114–18.

23 Kappler, *Indian Affairs* 2:114; Prucha, *Great Father* 1:82.

24 Prucha, *Broadax and Bayonet*, 1–22.

25 Prucha, *Great Father* 1:125–33.

26 Rollings, *The Osage*, 185–237; Gibson, *The Chickasaws*, 143–45; McLaughlin, *Cherokee Renascence*, 145–60.

27 Quoted in Parsons, "A Perpetual Harrow upon My Feelings," 340.

28 Surtees, "Indian Land Cessions," 70–73.

29 Surtees, *Indian Land Surrenders*, 67; Miller, *Skyscrapers*, 92.

30 Miller, *Skyscrapers*, 69–70.

31 Miller, *Skyscrapers*, 71–73.

32 Hutton, "Indian Affairs in Nova Scotia," 51–52; Upton, "Indian Policy in Nova Scotia," 13.

33 Upton, "Indian Policy in Nova Scotia," 13–15; Hutton, "Indian Affairs in Nova Scotia," 52–53.

34 Quoted in Upton, "Colonists and Micmacs," 44.

35 Clark and Guice, *Frontiers in Conflict*, 41–65; Remini, *Andrew Jackson*, 76–88.

36 Bowden, *American Indians and Christian Missions*, 167–69.

37 Bodo, *The Protestant Clergy*, 88–89.

38 Berkhofer, "Model Zions for the American Indians," 178–89.

39 Quoted in Berkhofer, "Model Zions for the American Indians," 185.

40 Horsman, "Scientific Racism."

41 Morse, *A Report to the Secretary of War*, 65–66.

42 Quoted in Morse, *A Report to the Secretary of War*, 74.

43 Quoted in Morse, *A Report to the Secretary of War*, 73–74.

44 Quoted in Morse, *A Report to the Secretary of War*, 76–80.

7. CULTURAL PERSISTENCE, PHYSICAL RETREAT, 1820S–1860S

1 Quoted in D. Smith, *Sacred Feathers*, 66.

2 Quoted in Surtees, *Original People*, 38.

3 D. Smith, "Dispossession of the Mississauga," 82.

4 Quoted in Leslie, *Commissions of Inquiry*, 21.

5 Quoted in Leslie, *Commissions of Inquiry*, 21.

6 Upton, "Origins of Canadian Indian Policy," 55–57.

7 Allen, *The British Indian Department and the Frontier*, 100; Upton, "Origins of Canadian Indian Policy," 59–60.

8 Upton, "Indian Affairs in New Brunswick," 4–5.

9 Chalmers, *Education behind the Buckskin Curtain*, 42–43.

10 Quoted in Fingard, "New England Company," 36.

11 Prucha, *Great Father* 1:151–52.

12 Quoted in Prucha, *Great Father* 1:187.

13 Quoted in McLaughlin, *Cherokee Renascence*, 353.

14 Horsman, *Origins of Indian Removal*, 11–13.

15 McLaughlin, *Cherokee Renascence*, 424; Satz, *American Indian Policy*, 44–48.

16 Satz, *American Indian Policy*, 99–101.

17 Quoted in Gibson, *The Chickasaws*, 164.

18 Quoted in Gibson, *The Chickasaws*, 169.

19 Quoted in Gibson, *The Chickasaws*, 174; for details of these events see 152–78.

20 Quoted in Hering, *Kenekuk*, 53. Details of this story are on 37–75.

21 Wallace, "Prelude to Disaster."

22 Nichols, *General Henry Atkinson*, 156–73; Nichols, *Black Hawk*, 101–45.

23 Mahon, *History of the Second Seminole War*.

24 Clifton, *A Place of Refuge*, 34–90.

25 Quoted in Horsman, "Scientific Racism," 154.

26 Quoted in Horsman, "Scientific Racism," 155.

27 Horsman, "Scientific Racism," 162, 164–65.

28 Satz, *American Indian Policy*, 133–43.

29 Leslie, *Commissions of Inquiry*, 24–25.

30 Leighton, "Compact Tory as Bureaucrat," 40–42.

31 Surtees, *Original People*, 36–37.

32 Chalmers, *Education behind the Buckskin Curtain*, 48; Scott, "Indian Affairs, 1840–1867," 349.

33 Quoted in Scott, "Indian Affairs, 1840–1867," 349.

34 C. Johnson, *Valley of the Six Nations*, 49–50.

35 D. Smith, *Sacred Feathers*, 105–6; Miller, *Skyscrapers*, 101–2.

36 Quoted in Hogkins, *Documentary History* 5:298.

37 Wilson, "No Blanket to Be Worn in School," 71.

38 Chalmers, *Educations behind the Buckskin Curtain*, 51–54.

39 D. Smith, *Sacred Feathers*, 15–16.

40 Quoted in Scott, "Indian Affairs, 1840–1867," 338.

41 Scott, "Indian Affairs, 1840–1867," 337; Clifton, *A Place of Refuge*, 52.

42 Quoted in D. Smith, *Sacred Feathers*, 162–63.

43 Upton, "Origins of Canadian Indian Policy," 57–58; Leslie, *Commissions of Inquiry*, 41–42.

44 Quoted in Upton, "Origins of Canadian Indian Policy," 58.

45 Quoted in D. Smith, *Sacred Feathers*, 164.

46 Leslie, *Commissions of Inquiry*, 42–43.

47 Quoted in Leighton, "Manitoulin Incident," 114.

48 Leighton, "Manitoulin Incident," 115–16; Scott, "Indian Affairs, 1840–1867," 335, 350.

49 Quoted in Scott, "Indian Affairs, 1840–1867," 335, 350.

50 Quoted in Scott, "Indian Affairs, 1840–1867," 332.

51 Quoted in Harring, "The Liberal Treatment of Indians," 305; this case and related issues are discussed on 299–305.

52 Leslie, "The Bagot Commission," 48–50.

53 Leslie, "The Bagot Commission," 51.

54 Surtees, *Indian Land Surrenders*, 94–96.

55 Quoted in Surtees, *Indian Land Surrenders*, 96.

56 Surtees, *Indian Land Surrenders*, 96–98.

57 Upton, "Indian Policy in Nova Scotia," 18–20.

58 Upton, "Indian Policy in Nova Scotia," 21–22.

59 Villeneuve, *Historical Background of Indian Reserves*, 15–16.

60 Francis, *History of the Native Peoples of Quebec*, 1–3, 21.

61 McNab, "Herman Merivale," 96–99; Harper, "Canada's Indian Administration: The Treaty System," 135–36; and Robin Fisher, *Contact and Conflict: Indian-European Relations in British Columbia, 1774–1890* (Vancouver: University of British Columbia Press, 1977), 1–48.

62 Fisher, *Contact and Conflict*, 48–68; Barman, *The West beyond the West*, 52–54.

63 Fisher, *Contact and Conflict*, 150–55.

64 Quoted in Fisher, *Contact and Conflict*, 156.

65 Fisher, *Contact and Conflict*, 156–57.

66 Milloy, "Early Indian Acts," 58–59.

67 Quoted in Milloy, "Early Indian Acts," 59.

68 Milloy, "Early Indian Acts," 59–60.

69 Harper, "Canada's Indian Administration: Basic Concepts and Objectives," 131–32; Leslie, *Commissions of Inquiry*, 149–54.

70 Quoted in Trennert, *Alternative to Extinction*, 7.

71 Phillips, *The Enduring Struggle*, 42–44.

72 Hurtado, *Indian Survival on the California Frontier*, 132–35.

73 Hurtado, *Indian Survival on the California Frontier*, 136–48.

74 Prucha, *Great Father* 1:397–402.

75 Richards, *Isaac I. Stevens*, 181–312.

76 Quoted in Richards, *Isaac I. Stevens*, 164–65.

77 Richards, *Isaac I. Stevens*, 180–90.

8. SOCIETIES UNDER SIEGE, 1860s–1890

1 McWorter, *Yellow Calf*, 40; this is an eyewitness account recorded later.

2 O. Howard, *Nez Perce Joseph*, 64–65.

3 Milloy, "Early Indian Acts," 60.

4 Leighton, "Manitoulin Incident," 116–17. Milloy, "Early Indian Acts," 60.

5 Leighton, "Manitoulin Incident," 117–23.

6 Hewlett, "Chilcotin Uprising," 50–51, 53–58, 71–72.

7 Fisher, *Contact and Conflict*, 105–9.

8 Quoted in D. Morton, "Cavalry or Police," 28.

9 Stanley, *Birth of Western Canada*, 187.

10 Quoted in Milloy, "Early Indian Acts," 61.

11 [Canada, Department of Indian Affairs] (hereafter DIA), Indian Branch, *Annual Report*, 1870, 4.

12 Canada, *Statutes of Canada*, 1869, 31 Vic, c. 6, 22 June, 664–65.

13 Quoted in Leslie and Maguire, *Historical Development of the Indian Act*, 54.

14 Canada, *Statutes of Canada*, 1869, 31 Vic, c. 6, 12–13.

15 G. Anderson, *Little Crow*, 116–65.

16 Hoig, *Sand Creek Massacre*, chronicles these events.

17 U.S. Congress, Senate, *Condition of the Indian Tribes*, 156; Kelsey, "Doolittle Report"; Chaput, "Generals, Indian Agents, Politicians"; Utley, *Indian Frontier*, 91–100, 118–20.

18 D. Jones, *Treaty of Medicine Lodge*, discusses these negotiations in detail.

19 Quoted in D. Jones, *Treaty of Medicine Lodge*, 116.

20 Quoted in D. Jones, *Treaty of Medicine Lodge*, 124.

21 Quoted in D. Jones, *Treaty of Medicine Lodge*, 127.

22 D. Jones, *Treaty of Medicine Lodge*, 127–29; Kappler, *Indian Affairs* 2:977–89.

23 Quoted in Olson, *Red Cloud*, 74–75.

24 Olson, *Red Cloud*, 75–82; Kappler, *Indian Affairs* 1:998–1003.

25 Olson, *Red Cloud*, 75–79.

26 Quoted in Utley, *Indian Frontier*, 130.

27 Utley, *Indian Frontier*, 129–34.

28 Utley, *Indian Frontier*, 178–89.

29 Stanley, *Birth of Western Canada*, 68–124; W. Morton, *Manitoba*, 94–150.

30 Johansen, "To Make Some Provision."

31 Harper, "Canada's Indian Administration: The Treaty System"; Friesen, *Canadian Prairies*, 137–49.

32 D. Morton, "Cavalry or Police," 27–37.

33 Quoted in H. Dempsey, *Big Bear*, 63.

34 Quoted in H. Dempsey, *Crowfoot*, 89.

35 Quoted in Lamour, "Edgar Dewdney," 15.

36 Tobias, "Canada's Subjugation of the Plains Cree."

37 Of the many studies of this rebellion, see Stanley, *Birth of Western Canada*; Flanagan, *Riel and the Rebellion*; and H. Dempsey, *Big Bear*.

38 Milloy, "Early Indian Acts," 57–63; Deloria and Lytle, *American Indians, American Justice*, 220–22.

39 Canada, *Statutes of Canada*, 1876, 39 Vic, c. 18, 12 April, 68–70.

40 Chalmers, *Education behind the Buckskin Curtain*, 160; [DIA], Deputy Superintendent of Indian Affairs, *Annual Report*, 1875, 9.

41 U.S. Department of Interior, *Annual Report*, 1877, 4–5.

42 Quoted in DIA, *Annual Report*, 1886, 156. See also Chalmers, *Education behind the Buckskin Curtain*, 148.

43 Quoted in DIA, *Annual Report*, 1882, 134. See also Gresko, "Creating Little Dominions," 97–102.

44 Scott, "Indian Affairs, 1867–1912," 602; DIA, *Annual Report*, 1881, 131.

45 Gresko, "White 'Rites' and Indian 'Rites,'" 174–76.

46 Chalmers, *Education behind the Buckskin Curtain*, 148; Tobias, "Protection, Civilization, Assimilation," 21.

47 DIA, *Annual Report*, 1896, 210.

48 Trant, "Treatment of the Canadian Indians," 524.

49 Wilson, "No Blanket to Be Worn in School," 74–80.

50 DIA, *Annual Report*, 1890, 138.

51 Abbott, "Commendable Progress"; Mihesuah, "Out of the 'Graves of the Polluted Debauches.'"

52 U.S. Congress, House, *Annual Report of the Secretary of the Interior*, 1884, House Executive Document no. 1, serial 2286, 111–13.

53 Quoted in Prucha, *Great Father* 1:690.

54 Utley, *Battlefield and Classroom*; Eastman, *Pratt*; D. Adams, "Education in Hues." For a detailed look at one school see Robert A. Trennert, *The Phoenix Indian School: Forced Assimilation in Arizona, 1891–1935* (Norman: University of Oklahoma Press, 1988).

55 Quoted in Ahern, "Returned Indians," 105.

56 Ahern, "Returned Indians," 110.

57 Quoted in Ahern, "An Experiment Aborted," 8.

58 I am indebted to Wilbert H. Ahern for acquainting me with the source of this data in "An Experiment Aborted," appendix. See also Emmerich, "Right in the Midst of My Own People."

59 Usher, *Duncan of Metlakatla*, 61–135.

60 Rettig, "Nativist Movement."

61 Miller, *Skyscrapers*, 192–94.

62 DIA, *Annual Report*, 1900, 33.

63 Quoted in Nock, "Canadian Indian Research and Aid Society," 32.

64 Prucha, *American Indian Policy in Crisis*, 132–68.

65 Prucha, *Great Father* 2:658–73.

66 Dunlay, *Wolves for the Blue Soldiers*, considers the use of Indian auxiliaries throughout the West. See also Hagan, *Indian Police and Judges*, 113–16; and Prucha, *Great Father* 2:678–79.

67 U.S. Department of Interior, *Annual Report*, 1874, 6.

68 Tobias, "Protection, Civilization, Assimilation," 16–19.

69 U.S. Department of Interior, *Annual Report*, 1882, 65; Tobias, "Protection, Civilization, Assimilation," 19.

70 Clifford Sifton to Governor General, 27 September 1897, quoted in D. Hall, "Clifford Sifton," 139.

71 DIA, *Annual Report*, 1883, 133. See also U.S. Department of Interior, *Annual Report*, 1875, 5–6; 1879, x–xi; and DIA, *Annual Report*, 1880, 55–56.

72 Quoted in Buckley, *From Wooden Ploughs to Welfare*, 52.

73 Buckley, *From Wooden Ploughs to Welfare*, 51–58, 61–66; Samek, *Blackfoot Confederacy*, 75–77; Titley, *Narrow Vision*, 51–53.

74 DIA, *Annual Report*, 1882, 55–56; 1883, x; 1888, lvi; 1895, xix.

75 Schurz, "Present Aspects of the Indian Problem," 10–11; Bowles, *Our New West*.

76 Hagan, "Kiowas, Comanches, and Cattlemen," 336, 340–41.

77 Quoted in D. Morton, "Cavalry or Police," 32; Leighton, "A Victorian Civil Servant at Work." For the United States see Kvasnicka and Viola, *Commissioners of Indian Affairs*, 89–211.

78 Mooney, *Ghost Dance*, 711–16.

79 Mooney, *Ghost Dance*.

80 Mooney, *Ghost Dance*, gives the best account of this event.

9. SURVIVING MARGINALIZATION, 1890S–1920

1 Standing Bear, *Land of the Spotted Eagle*, 244.

2 Quoted in D. Hall, "Clifford Sifton," 134.

3 Quoted in D. Hall, "Clifford Sifton," 133.

4 Scott, "Indian Affairs, 1867–1912," 610.

5 Quoted in Surtees, *Original People*, 74.

6 DIA, *Annual Report*, 1905, 100.

7 Blair Jaekel, "The Corn Dance at Santo Domingo," *Colliers* 49 (17 August 1912): 15.

8 Stoddard, *Rising Tide of Color*, 126.

9 Greska, "White 'Rites' and Indian 'Rites,'" 173.
10 DIA, *Annual Report*, 1900, 226; 1902, xxv; Chalmers, *Education behind the Buckskin Curtain*, 161.
11 Chalmers, *Education behind the Buckskin Curtain*, 161.
12 DIA, *Annual Report*, 1924, 16.
13 Scott, "Indian Affairs, 1867–1912," 615.
14 Woodsworth, "Problems of Indian Education," 273.
15 Trennert, "From Carlisle to Phoenix."
16 G. Hall, "Principles of Education," 365, 367; G. Hall, *Adolescence* 2:699.
17 Francis E. Leupp, "Back to Nature for the Indians," *Charities and the Commons* 20 (6 June 1908): 336–37.
18 Quoted in Hoxie, *A Final Promise*, 193.
19 Trennert, "Educating Indian Girls," 282; Hoxie, *A Final Promise*, 195–200.
20 Quoted in Hoxie, *A Final Promise*, 202.
21 Quoted in Hoxie, *A Final Promise*, 204.
22 Trennert, "From Carlisle to Phoenix," 283; Hoxie, *A Final Promise*, 204–6.
23 Hoxie, *A Final Promise*, 204–5, 207–9.
24 DIA, *Annual Report*, 1900, 36.
25 Dion, *My Tribe the Crees*, 145.
26 Quoted in Tennant, *Aboriginal Peoples and Politics*, 39.
27 Tennant, *Aboriginal Peoples and Politics*, 39–41.
28 Tennant, *Aboriginal Peoples and Politics*, 43–44, 55–56. See also Fisher, *Contact and Conflict*, 175–211.
29 Quoted in Raby, "Indian Land Surrenders," 46.
30 Hoxie, *A Final Promise*, 154–61; Clark, *Lone Wolf v Hitchcock*.
31 H. Dempsey, "Blood Indians," 5–6; Chalmers, *Education behind the Buckskin Curtain*, 145.
32 DIA, *Annual Report*, 1914, xxiv; 1925, 26; Hoey, "Economic Problems of the Canadian Indian," 199.
33 U.S. Bureau of the Census, *Historical Statistics* 1:3–4, 14.
34 DIA, *Annual Report*, 1914, xxviii; 1915, xxx.
35 Tate, "From Scout to Doughboy," 425–26; Gaffen, *Forgotten Soldiers*, 20.
36 Gaffen, *Forgotten Soldiers*, 21–23.
37 DIA, *Annual Report*, 1915, xxx; 1916, xxxv; J. Dempsey, "Indians and World War One," 2.
38 J. Dempsey, "Indians and World War One," 2.
39 DIA, *Annual Report*, 1918, 16.
40 J. Dempsey, "Indians and World War One," 2.
41 Tate, "From Scout to Doughboy," 423.
42 Tate, "From Scout to Doughboy," 426.
43 Quoted in Tate, "From Scout to Doughboy," 428.
44 D. Wood, "Gosiute-Shoshone Draft Resistance"; Ellis, "Indians at Ibapah in Revolt"; Prucha, *Great Father* 2:771.
45 J. Dempsey, "Indians and World War One," 4–5.
46 Titley, *Narrow Vision*, 39–40.

47 DIA, *Annual Report*, 1918, 20.

48 Quoted in Titley, *Narrow Vision*, 41.

49 Titley, *Narrow Vision*, 40.

50 J. Dempsey, "Indians and World War One," 6–7; Samek, *Blackfoot Confederacy*, 116–18.

51 J. Dempsey, "Indians and World War One," 6–7; Titley, *Narrow Vision*, 41–43.

52 Titley, *Narrow Vision*, 43–47.

53 Gaffen, *Forgotten Soldiers*, 38.

54 D. Wood, "American Indian Farmland," 249–50.

55 Quoted in D. Wood, "American Indian Farmland," 252.

56 D. Wood, "American Indian Farmland," 154.

57 Quoted in Prucha, *Great Father* 2:884.

58 D. Wood, "American Indian Farmland," 254–56.

59 D. Wood, "American Indian Farmland," 260–61.

60 D. Wood, "American Indian Farmland," 263–65.

10. CHANGE, DEPRESSION, AND WAR, 1920–1945

1   Quoted in Ewers, "A Crow Chief's Tribute," 34–35.

2   Jenness, "Canada's Indians Yesterday," 95–96.

3   Quoted in Jenness, "Canada's Indians Yesterday," 97.

4   Jenness, "Canada's Indians Yesterday," 98.

5   Titley, *Narrow Vision*, 95.

6   Pelletier, "For Every North American Indian," 112–13; Patterson, "Andrew Paull."

7   Quoted in Titley, *Narrow Vision*, 103.

8   Titley, *Narrow Vision*, 102–7.

9   Daugherty, *Guide to Native Political Associations*, 16–17; Titley, *Narrow Vision*, 102–8.

10 Daugherty, *Guide to Native Political Associations*, 14–15; Patterson, "Andrew Paull," 48–50.

11 Titley, *Narrow Vision*, 112–14.

12 Montgomery, "Legal Status of the Six Nations," 97.

13 Titley, *Narrow Vision*, 117–21.

14 Montgomery, "Legal Status of the Six Nations," 98–100; Titley, *Narrow Vision*, 122–23.

15 Montgomery, "Legal Status of the Six Nations," 101–2; Cork, *The Worst of the Bargain*, 2–3.

16 Hertzberg, *The Search for an American Indian Identity*, 59–75.

17 Hertzberg, *The Search for an American Indian Identity*, 111–35, 155–78; D. Johnson and Wilson, "Gertrude Simmons Bonnin," 29–30; Iverson, "Carlos Montezuma," 210–14.

18 Quoted in Iverson, "Carlos Montezuma," 213.

19 Steward, *Peyote Religion*, is the most recent and through discussion of this issue.

20 Quoted in D. Johnson and Wilson, "Gertrude Simmons Bonnin," 31.

21 G. Taylor, "The Divided Heart," 241–42.

22 Olson and Wilson, *Native Americans in the Twentieth Century*, 99–100.

23 Olson and Wilson, *Native Americans in the Twentieth Century*, 100–101.

24 Titley, *Narrow Vision*, 177.

25 Quoted in Titley, *Narrow Vision*, 177–78.

26 J. Taylor, *Canadian Indian Policy*, 135–41, 146–52; Titley, *Narrow Vision*, 162–83.

27 DIA, "General Instructions of Indian Agents in Canada," 1 September 1933, Form no. 1024, 1.

28 Allan, "Indian Land Problems in Canada," 189–90.

29 Gladstone, "Native Indians and the Fishing Industry," 26; Hoey, "Economic Problems of the Canadian Indian," 203–4.

30 DIA, *Annual Report*, 297–98; Gladstone, "Native Indians and the Fishing Industry," 26–32; Pelletier, "For Every North American Indian," 112–13.

31 Gaffen, *Forgotten Soldiers*, 38

32 Woodsworth, "Problems of Indian Education," 268.

33 Olson and Wilson, *Native Americans in the Twentieth Century*, 110–11.

34 Olson and Wilson, *Native Americans in the Twentieth Century*, 111–12.

35 Kelly, "The Indian Reorganization Act."

36 Kelly, "The Indian Reorganization Act," 296–99.

37 Kelly, "The Indian Reorganization Act," 301–5.

38 Brombert, "The Sioux and the Indian CCC"; Quinten, "Oklahoma Tribes"; Olson and Wilson, *Native Americans in the Twentieth Century*, 116–21.

39 Schrader, *Indian Arts and Crafts Board*.

40 Prucha, *Great Father* 2:1007; Holm, "Fighting a White Man's War," 72–73.

41 Prucha, *Great Father* 2:1007.

42 Gaffen, *Forgotten Soldiers*, 66–68, 79.

43 Quoted in Bernstein, *American Indians and World War II*, 22.

44 Quoted in Bernstein, *American Indians and World War II*, 24.

45 Bernstein, *American Indians and World War II*, 26, 33; Parman, *Indians and the American West*, 111–12.

46 Quoted in Bernstein, *American Indians and World War II*, 29.

47 Bernstein, *American Indians and World War II*, 25–33.

48 Holm, "Fighting a White Man's War," 70, 75; Prucha, *Great Father* 2:1006; J. Howard, "Dakota Victory Dance."

49 Olson and Wilson, *Native Americans in the Twentieth Century*, 125–27.

50 Prucha, *Great Father* 2:1009–12.

51 Olson and Wilson, *Native Americans in the Twentieth Century*, 127.

52 Gaffen, *Forgotten Soldiers*, 71–72.

53 Creighton, *Forked Road*, 15–61; McNaught, *Penguin History of Canada*, 254–69. Canadian Indians' participation in the war gets so little attention that neither J. L. Granatstein (*Canada's War*) nor C. P. Stacey (*Arms, Men and Governments*) includes Indians or related topics in the index.

11. TRIBES AND THE MODERN STATE, 1945–1990S

1 Statement in Kenneth R. Philp, ed., *Indian Self Rule: First-Hand Accounts of Indian-White Relations from Roosevelt to Reagan* (Salt Lake City: Howe, 1986), 112.

2 Loram and McIlwraith, *The North American Indian Today*, 4–5.

3   Quoted in Leslie and Maguire, *Historical Development of the Indian Act*, 133.
4   The hearings are found in Canada, Parliament, *Minutes of Proceedings*.
5   Leslie and Maguire, *Historical Development of the Indian Act*, 132–45.
6   Leslie and Maguire, *Historical Development of the Indian Act*, 132–45.
7   Olson and Wilson, *Native Americans in the Twentieth Century*, 134–35.
8   Olson and Wilson, *Native Americans in the Twentieth Century*, 137.
9   Lurie, "Indian Claims Commission Act"; Prucha, *Great Father* 2:1019–23.
10 Carriker, "Kalispel Tribe"; Olson and Wilson, *Native Americans in the Twentieth Century*, 141–42.
11 The most complete discussion of termination is Fixico, *Termination and Relocation*.
12 For specific examples of the policy, see Hood, "Termination of the Klamath Tribe," and Lurie, "Menominee Termination."
13 Prucha, *Great Father* 2:1081–84.
14 Margon, "Indians and Immigrants"; Neils, *Reservation to City*; Ablon, "American Indian Relocation."
15 Dunning, "Some Aspects of Governmental Indian Policy," 215.
16 Davis, "Urban Indians in Western Canada," 225.
17 National Association of Friendship Centres, *Survey of Migrating Native People*; Price and McCaskill, "Urban Integration of Canadian Native People"; Nagler, *Indians in the City*.
18 Quoted in Buckley, *From Wooden Ploughs to Welfare*, 151.
19 Denton, "Migration from a Canadian Indian Reserve," 55–60.
20 Hawthorn, *Survey of Contemporary Indians of Canada* 1:207.
21 Miller, *Skyscrapers*, 233.
22 Quoted in Purich, *Our Land*, 52.
23 Canada, Parliament, *Statement of the Government*, 6.
24 Cardinal, *Unjust Society*, 1.
25 Weaver, *Making Canadian Indian Policy*, is the best study of this controversy.
26 Chalmers, "Federal, Provincial, and Territorial Strategies"; Dosman, *Indians*, 40–41; Buckley, *From Wooden Ploughs to Welfare*, 97–101.
27 Chalmers, *Education behind the Buckskin Curtain*, 317–24.
28 Daniel, *History of Native Claims Processes*, 220–23.
29 Olson and Wilson, *Native Americans in the Twentieth Century*, 160; Josephy, *Now That the Buffalo's Gone*, 177–211; Hagan, "Tribalism Rejuvenated."
30 Blue Cloud, *Alcatraz Is Not an Island*; Costo, "Alcatraz."
31 The two most informative accounts of this are Burnette and Koster, *Road to Wounded Knee*, and Deloria, *Behind the Trail*.
32 Deloria, *Behind the Trail*, 79–80.
33 Deloria, *Behind the Trail*, 77–79. See also Matthiesen, *In the Spirit of Crazy Horse*; and U.S. Congress, Senate, Subcommittee on Indian Affairs, *Occupation of Wounded Knee*.
34 O'Gara, "Canny CERT Gets Respect"; Olson and Wilson, *Native Americans in the Twentieth Century*, 189–91.
35 Naske and Slotnik, *Alaska*, and Arnond, *Alaska Native Land Claims*, offer solid general discussions of these issues.
36 Prucha, *Great Father* 2:1129–30; Berger, *Long and Terrible Shadow*, 126–32.

37   Lazarus and West, "Alaska Native Claims Settlement Act"; Prucha, *Great Father* 2:1131–35; Berger, *Long and Terrible Shadow*, 126–32.

38   Daniel, *History of Native Claims Processes*, 221.

39   Sanders, "Native People"; Berger, *Northern Frontier, Northern Homeland*; Daniel, *History of Native Claims Processes*, 222–23.

40   Quoted in Morrison, *Survey of the History and Claims*, 69.

41   Morrison, *Survey of the History and Claims*, 70–72; Coates, *Best Left as Indians*, 239–43.

42   Morrison, *Survey of the History and Claims*, 72–76.

43   Miller, *Skyscrapers*, 260.

44   Morrison, *Survey of the History and Claims*, 87–93; B. Richardson, *Strangers Devour the Land*; La Rusic, *Negotiating a Way of Life*.

45   Roberts, "Becoming Modern," 301–6.

46   Roberts, "Becoming Modern," 307–11; Diubaldo, *Government of Canada and the Inuit*.

47   Abel, *Drum Songs*, 260–63.

48   Gross, *Federal Policy toward American Indians*, 51–52; Szasz, *Education and the American Indian*, 199–200.

49   Oppelt, "Tribally Controlled Colleges."

50   Olson and Wilson, *Native Americans in the Twentieth Century*, 203–4.

51   Deloria and Lytle, *American Indians, American Justice*, 232–33.

52   Michaelsen, "Civil Rights, Indian Rites"; *United States v. Dion*, 106 S. Ct. 2216 (1986). For an examination of many constitutional issues see Wunder, *Retained by the People*.

53   Quoted in Native American Rights Fund, *Legal Review* 12 (spring 1987): 4.

54   R. Adams, "Smithsonian Horizons."

55   Native American Rights Fund, *Legal Review*, 7.

56   Svingen, "Jim Crow, Indian Style."

57   Moss, "Native Proposals for Constitutional Reform," 85–86.

58   Quoted in Miller, *Skyscrapers*, 239; see also Moss, "Native Proposals for Constitutional Reform," 86–88.

59   Webber, *Reimagining Canada*, 122–23.

60   Webber, *Reimagining Canada*, 127–33, 162–74.

61   Quoted in Miller, *Skyscrapers*, 241.

62   Miller, *Skyscrapers*, 241–42.

63   Weaver, "Indian Policy in the New Conservative Government."

64   Purich, *Our Land*, 225–26.

65   Porter, *Strategies for Survival*, 1–42; Henderson, *The Road*.

66   Passamaquoddy v. Morton, 388 F. Supp 649 (F.D. Maine 1975).

67   Greenbaum, "In Search of Lost Tribes"; *Federal Register* 47, no. 61 (30 March 1982): 133326–28; T. Anderson, "Federal Recognition."

68   George W. Wells to John Melcher, 31 August 1979, in U.S. Congress, Senate, *Montana Water Rights Hearings*, 585.

69   Quoted in *Arizona Daily Star*, 16 January 1986.

70   Parman, *Indians and the American West*, 164–65, 176; *New York Times*, 27 January 1996.

71   Parman, *Indians and the American West*, 179–81.

72   Parman, *Indians and the American West*, 176–77.

73 The best discussion of these complex events is in Hornung, *One Nation under the Gun*, and York and Pindera, *People of the Pines*.

74 U.S. Congress, Senate, Special Committee on Investigations of the Select Committee on Indian Affairs, *Final Report and Legislative Recommendations*, 213.

CONCLUSION

1 *New York Times*, national edition, 26 November 1996, A6.

2 Quoted in *New York Times*, national edition, 22 November 1996. A6.

Selected Bibliography

This book is meant to inform the nonspecialist and be of use to interested scholars. Therefore the annotations cite almost no archival collections. Scholars know where such material is, and others can find repeated references to it in any of the monographs included below. While about three thousand items were consulted for this study, the bibliography is limited almost entirely to materials actually cited in the text.

Abbott, Devon. " 'Commendable Progress': Acculturation at the Cherokee Female Seminary." *American Indian Quarterly* 11 (summer 1987): 187–201.

Abel, Kerry. *Drum Songs: Glimpses of Dene History*. Montreal: McGill–Queen's University Press, 1993.

Abler, Thomas S., and Sally Weaver, comps. *A Canadian Indian Bibliography, 1960–1970*. Toronto: University of Toronto Press, 1974.

Ablon, Joan. "American Indian Relocation: Problems of Dependency and Management in the City." *Phylon* 24 (winter 1965): 362–71.

Adams, David Wallace. "Education in Hues: Red and Black at Hampton Institute, 1878–1893." *South Atlantic Quarterly* 76 (spring 1977): 159–76.

Adams, Robert McC. "Smithsonian Horizons." *Smithsonian*, May 1987, 12.

Ahern, Wilbert H. "An Experiment Aborted: Returned Students in the Indian Service, 1881–1908." Unpublished paper, NEH Summer Seminar for College Teachers, 1988.

——. " 'The Returned Indians': Hampton Institute and Its Indian Alumni, 1879–1893." *Journal of Ethnic Studies* 10 (winter 1983): 101–24.

Allan, D. J. "Indian Land Problems in Canada." In *The North American Indian Today*, ed. Charles T. Loram and T. F. McIlwraith, 184–98. Toronto: University of Toronto Press, 1943.

Allen, Robert S. *The British Indian Department and the Frontier in North America, 1755–1830*. Canadian Historic Sites: Occasional Papers in Archaeology and History, no. 14. Ottawa: National Historic Parks and Sites Board, 1973.

——. *His Majesty's Indian Allies: British Indian Policy in the Defence of Canada*. Toronto: Dundurn Press, 1992.

——. *A History of the British Indian Department*. Ottawa: Indian Affairs and Northern Development, 1971.

American State Papers: Indian Affairs. 2 vols. Washington DC: 1832–34.

Anderson, Gary Clayton. *Little Crow: Spokesman for the Sioux*. St. Paul: Minnesota Historical Society Press, 1986.

Anderson, Terry. "Federal Recognition: The Vicious Myth." *American Indian Journal* 4 (May 1978): 7–19.

Anderson, Virginia DeJohn. "King Philip's Herds: Indians, Colonists and the Problem of Livestock in Early New England." *William and Mary Quarterly* 3d ser., 51 (October 1994): 601–24.

Aquila, Richard. *The Iroquois Restoration: Iroquois Diplomacy on the Colonial Frontier, 1701–1754*. Detroit: Wayne State University Press, 1983.

Arnond, Robert D. *Alaska Native Land Claims*. Anchorage: Alaska Native Foundation, 1976.

Axtell, James. *The Invasion Within: The Contest of Cultures in Colonial North America*. New York: Oxford University Press, 1985.

——. "The White Indians of Colonial America." *William and Mary Quarterly* 3d ser., 32 (January 1975): 55–88.

Bailey, Alfred G. *The Conflict between European and Eastern Algonkin Cultures, 1504–1700: A Study in Canadian Civilization*. 1937. 2d ed. Toronto: University of Toronto Press, 1969.

Barman, Jean. *The West beyond the West: A History of British Columbia*. Toronto: University of Toronto Press, 1991.

Barman, Jean, Yvonne Hebert, and Don McCaskill, eds. *Indian Education in Canada*. 2 vols. Vancouver: University of British Columbia Press, 1986.

Beaver, R. Pierce. "American Missionary Motivation before the Revolution." *Church History* 31 (June 1962): 216–26.

——. "Methods in American Missions to the Indians in the Seventeenth and Eighteenth Centuries: Calvinist Models for Protestant Foreign Missions." *Journal of Presbyterian History* 47 (June 1969): 124–48.

Berger, Thomas R. *A Long and Terrible Shadow: White Values, Native Rights in the Americas*. Vancouver: Douglas & McIntyre, 1991.

——. *Northern Frontier, Northern Homeland: The Report of the Mackenzie Valley Pipeline Inquiry*. 2 vols. Ottawa: Supply and Services, 1977.

Berkhofer, Robert F., Jr. "Model Zions for the American Indians." *American Quarterly* 15 (summer 1963): 178–89.

Bernstein, Alison R. *American Indians and World War II*. Norman: University of Oklahoma Press, 1991.

Bidney, David. "The Idea of the Savage in North American Ethnohistory." *Journal of the History of Ideas* 15 (April 1954): 322–27.

Blue Cloud, Peter, ed. *Alcatraz Is Not an Island*. Berkeley CA: Wingbow Press, 1972.

Bodo, John R. *The Protestant Clergy and Public Issues, 1812–1848*. Princeton NJ: Princeton University Press, 1954.

Bolton, Herbert E. *Coronado: Knight of Pueblos and Plains*. Albuquerque: University of New Mexico Press, 1949.

Bowden, Henry Warner. *American Indians and Christian Missions: Studies in Conflict*. Chicago: University of Chicago Press, 1981.

Bowles, Samuel. *Our New West*. Hartford CT: Hartford Publishing Co., 1869.

Boyd, Mark F., Hale G. Smith, and John W. Griffin. *Here They Once Stood: The Tragic End of the Apalachee Missions*. Gainesville: University of Florida Press, 1951.

Bradford, William. *Of Plymouth Plantation, 1620–1647*. Edited by Samuel Eliot Morison. New York: Knopf, 1966.

Brebner, John B. *Canada: A Modern History*. Ann Arbor: University of Michigan Press, 1960.

Brebner, John B., ed. "Subsidized Intermarriage with the Indians: An Incident in British Colonial Policy." *Canadian Historical Review* 6 (March 1925): 35–36.

Brombert, Roger. "The Sioux and the Indian CCC." *South Dakota History* 8 (fall 1978): 340–56.

Brown, Jennifer S. H. *Strangers in Blood: Fur Trade Families in Indian Country*. Vancouver: University of British Columbia Press, 1980.

Buckley, Helen. *From Wooden Ploughs to Welfare: Why Indian Policy Failed in the Prairie Provinces*. Montreal: McGill–Queens University Press, 1992.

Burnette, Robert, and John Koster. *The Road to Wounded Knee*. New York: Bantam, 1974.

Bushnell, David. "The Treatment of the Indians in Plymouth Colony." *New England Quarterly* 26 (June 1953): 193–218.

Byrd, William. *Histories of the Dividing Line betwixt Virginia and North Carolina*. Introduction and notes by William K. Boyd. New York: Dover, 1967.

Canada. *Statutes of Canada*. 1869, 31 Vic, c. 6, 42; 1876, 39 Vic, c. 18.

Canada. Department of Indian Affairs. *Annual Report*. 1868–present.

Canada. Parliament. *Minutes of Proceedings and Evidence of the Special Joint Committee of the Senate and the House of Commons Appointed to Examine and Consider the Indian Act*. Ottawa: King's Printer, 1946–48.

——. *Statement of the Government of Canada on Indian Policy, 1969*. Ottawa: Queen's Printer, 1969.

Canny, Nicholas P. "The Ideology of English Colonization: From Ireland to America." *William and Mary Quarterly* 3d ser., 30 (October 1973): 575–98.

Cardinal, Harold. *The Unjust Society: The Tragedy of Canada's Indians*. Edmonton: Hurtig, 1969.

Carriker, Robert C. "The Kalispel Tribe and the Indian Claims Commission Experience." *Western Historical Quarterly* 9 (January 1978): 19–31.

Carter, Harvey Lewis. *The Life and Times of Little Turtle: First Sagamore of the Wabash*. Urbana: University of Illinois Press, 1987.

Cartier, Jacques. *The Voyages of Cartier*. Edited by Henry P. Biggar. Ottawa: Acland, 1924.

Cass, Lewis. "Service of Indians in Civilized Warfare." *North American Review*, 24 April 1827, 382–83.

Chalmers, John W. *Education behind the Buckskin Curtain: A History of Native Education in Canada*. Edmonton: University of Alberta Press, 1972.

——. "Federal, Provincial, and Territorial Strategies for Canadian Native Education, 1960–1970." *Journal of Canadian Studies* 11 (August 1976): 39–43.

Chaput, Donald. "Generals, Indian Agents, Politicians: The Doolittle Survey of 1865." *Western Historical Quarterly* 3 (July 1972): 269–82.

Clark, Blue. *Lone Wolf v Hitchcock: Treaty Rights and Indian Law at the End of the Nineteenth Century.* Lincoln: University of Nebraska Press, 1994.

Clark, Thomas D., and John D. W. Guice. *Frontiers in Conflict: The Old Southwest, 1795–1830.* Albuquerque: University of New Mexico Press, 1989.

Clifton, James A. *A Place of Refuge for All Time: The Migration of the American Potawatomi into Upper Canada, 1835–1845.* Mercury Series. Ottawa: National Museum of Man, 1975.

Clinton, Robert N. "The Proclamation of 1763: Colonial Prelude to Two Centuries of Federal-State Conflict over the Management of Indian Affairs." *Boston University Law Review* 69 (March 1989): 329–85.

Coates, Ken. *Best Left as Indians: Native-White Relations in the Yukon Territory, 1840–1973.* Montreal: McGill–Queen's University, 1991.

Coates, Ken, ed. *Aboriginal Land Claims in Canada: A Regional Perspective.* Toronto: Copp Clark Pitman, 1992.

Cook, Sherburne F. "The Significance of Disease in the Extinction of the New England Indians." *Human Biology* 45 (September 1973): 485–508.

Cork, Ella. *"The Worst of the Bargain": Concerning the Dilemmas Inherited from Their Forefathers along with Their Lands by the Iroquois Nation of the Canadian Grand River Reserve.* San Jacinto CA: Foundation for Social Research, 1962.

Corkran, David H. *The Cherokee Frontier: Conflict and Survival, 1740–62.* Norman: University of Oklahoma Press, 1962.

Coronado, Francisco Vasquez. *Narratives of the Coronado Expedition of 1540–1542.* Edited and translated by George P. Hammond and Agapito Rey. 2 vols. Albuquerque: University of New Mexico Press, 1940.

Costo, Rupert. "Alcatraz." *Indian Historian* 3 (winter 1970): 4–12.

Crane, Verner W. *The Southern Frontier, 1670–1732.* 1928. Reprint, Ann Arbor: University of Michigan Press, 1956.

Craven, Frank Wesley, *The Southern Colonies in the Seventeenth Century.* Baton Rouge: Louisiana State University Press, 1949.

Creighton, Donald G. *The Forked Road: Canada, 1939–1957.* Toronto: McClelland & Stewart, 1976.

Crosby, Alfred W. "God . . . Would Destroy Them, and Give Their Country to Another People. . . ." *American Heritage* 29 (October/November 1978): 38–43.

———. "Virgin Soil Epidemics as a Factor in the Aborignal Depopulation in America." *William and Mary Quarterly* 3d ser., 33 (April 1976): 189–99.

Dailey, R. C. "The Role of Alcohol among North American Indians as Reported in the Jesuit Relations." *Anthropologica* 10, no. 1 (1968): 45–59.

Daniel, Richard C. *A History of Native Claims Processes in Canada, 1867–1979.* Ottawa: Department of Indian and Northern Affairs, 1980.

Daugherty, Wayne. *A Guide to Native Political Associations in Canada.* Ottawa: Treaties and Historical Research Centre, 1982.

Davis, Arthur K. "Urban Indians in Western Canada: Implications for Social Theory and Social Policy." *Transactions of the Royal Society of Canada* 6th ser., 4 (June 1968): 217–28.

Deloria, Vine, Jr. *Behind the Trail of Broken Treaties: An Indian Declaration of Independence.* New York: Delacorte, 1974.

——. *Custer Died for Your Sins: An Indian Manifesto.* New York: Macmillan, 1969.

Deloria, Vine, Jr., and Clifford M. Lytle. *American Indians, American Justice.* Austin: University of Texas Press, 1983.

Dempsey, Hugh A. *Big Bear: The End of Freedom.* Lincoln: University of Nebraska Press, 1984.

——. "The Blood Indians." *Glenbow* 5 (May/June 1972): 3–8.

——. *Crowfoot: Chief of the Blackfeet.* Edmonton: Hurtig, 1976.

Dempsey, James. "The Indians and World War One." *Alberta History* 31 (summer 1983): 1–8.

Denton, Trevor. "Migration from a Canadian Indian Reserve." *Journal of Canadian Studies* 7 (May 1972): 54–62.

De Soto, Hernando. *Narratives of the Career of Hernando De Soto. . . .* Edited by Edward G. Bourne. Translated by Buckingham Smith. 2 vols. New York: Allerton, 1912. Reprint, New York: AMS, 1973.

Dickason, Olive Patricia. *Canada's First Nations: A History of Founding Peoples from Earliest Times.* Norman: University of Oklahoma Press, 1992.

Dion, Joseph F. *My Tribe the Crees, 1888–1860.* Edited by Hugh A. Dempsey. Calgary: Glenbow Museum, 1979.

Diubaldo, Richard. *The Government of Canada and the Inuit, 1900–1967.* Ottawa: Indian and Northern Affairs, 1985.

Dobyns, Henry F. *Their Numbers Become Thinned: Native American Population Dynamics in Eastern North America.* Knoxville: University of Tennessee Press, 1983.

Dosman, Edgar J. *Indians: The Urban Dilemma.* Toronto: McClelland & Stewart, 1972.

Douglas, James. *New England and New France: Contrasts and Parallels in Colonial History.* New York: Putnam, 1913.

Dowd, Gregory Evans. *A Spirited Resistance: The North American Indian Struggle for Unity, 1745–1815.* Baltimore: Johns Hopkins University Press, 1992.

Downes, Randolph C. *Council Fires on the Upper Ohio: A Narrative of Indian Affairs in the Upper Ohio Valley to 1795.* 1940. Reprint, Pittsburgh: University of Pittsburgh Press, 1969.

Duffy, John. *Epidemics in Colonial America.* Baton Rouge: Louisiana State University Press, 1953.

Dunlay, Thomas W. *Wolves for the Blue Soldiers.* Lincoln: University of Nebraska Press, 1982.

Dunning, R. W. "Some Aspects of Governmental Indian Policy and Administration." *Anthropologica* 4, n.s., no. 2 (1962): 209–31.

Eastman, Elane Goodale. *Pratt: The Red Man's Moses.* Norman: University of Oklahoma Press, 1935.

Eccles, William J. *Canada under Louis XIV, 1663–1701.* Toronto: McClelland & Stewart, 1964.

——. *The Canadian Frontier, 1534–1760.* New York: Holt, Rinehart & Winston, 1969.

——. *France in America.* New York: Harper & Row, 1972.

Edmunds, R. David. "Old Briton." In *American Indian Leaders: Studies in Diversity*, ed. R. David Edmunds, 1–20. Lincoln: University of Nebraska Press, 1980.

——. *The Shawnee Prophet.* Lincoln: University of Nebraska Press, 1983.

Edmunds, R. David, ed. *American Indian Leaders: Studies in Diversity.* Lincoln: University of Nebraska Press, 1980.

Edmunds, R. David, and Joseph L. Peyser. *The Fox Wars: The Mesquakie Challenge to New France.* Norman: University of Oklahoma Press, 1993.

Eid, Leroy V. "American Indian Military Leadership: St. Clair's 1791 Defeat." *Journal of Military History* 57 (January 1993): 71–88.

Ellis, Richard N. "Indians at Ibapah in Revolt: Goshutes, the Draft, and the Indian Bureau, 1917–1919." *Nevada Historical Society Quarterly* 19 (fall 1976): 163–70.

Emmerich, Lisa E. " 'Right in the Midst of My Own People': Native American Women and the Field Matron Program." *American Indian Quarterly* 15 (spring 1991): 201–16.

Ewers, John C. "A Crow Chief's Tribute to the Unknown Soldier." *American West* 8 (November 1971): 30–35.

Fausz, J. Frederick. "Fighting 'Fire' with Firearms: The Anglo-Powhatan Arms Race in Early Virginia." *American Indian Culture and Research Journal* 3, no. 4 (1979): 33–50.

——. "The Powhatan Uprising of 1622: A Historical Study of Ethnocentrism and Cultural Conflict." Ph.D. diss., William and Mary, 1977.

Federal Register 47, no. 61 (30 March 1982): 133326–28.

Fingard, J. "The New England Company and the New Brunswick Indians, 1786–1826: A Comment on the Colonial Perversion of British Benevolence." *Acadiensis* n.s., 1 (spring 1972): 29–42.

Fixico, Donald L. *Termination and Relocation: Federal Indian Policy, 1945–1960.* Albuquerque: University of New Mexico Press, 1986.

Flanagan, T. *Riel and the Rebellion: 1885 Reconsidered.* Saskatoon: Western Producer Prairie, 1983.

Ford, Worthington, et al., eds. *The Journals of the Continental Congress, 1774–1789.* 34 vols. Washington DC: GPO, 1903–37.

Francis, Daniel. *A History of the Native Peoples of Quebec, 1760–1867.* Ottawa: Indian Affairs and Northern Development, 1983.

Franklin, Benjamin. *Writings.* Edited by J. A. Leo Lemay. New York: Library Association of America, 1987.

Frideres, James S., ed. *Canada's Indians Contemporary Conflicts.* Scarborough ON: Prentice Hall, 1974.

Friesen, Gerald. *The Canadian Prairies: A History.* Toronto: University of Toronto Press, 1984.

Gaffen, Fred. *Forgotten Soldiers.* Penticton BC: Theytus, 1985.

Getty Ian A. L., and Antoine S. Lussier, eds. *As Long as the Sun Shines and Water Flows: A Reader in Canadian Native Studies.* Vancouver: University of British Columbia Press, 1983.

Gibson, Arrell M. *The Chickasaws.* Norman: University of Oklahoma Press, 1971.

Gladstone, Percy, "Native Indians and the Fishing Industry." *Canadian Journal of Economics and Political Science* 19 (February 1953): 20–34.

Goldstein, Robert A. *French-Iroquois Diplomacy and Military Relations, 1609–1701.* The Hague: Mouton, 1969.

Goodwin, Gerald J. "Christianity, Civilization and the Savage: The American Mission to the American Indian." *Historical Magazine of the Protestant Episcopal Church* 42 (June 1973): 93–110.

Granatstein, J. L. *Canada's War: The Politics of the Mackenzie King Government, 1939–1945.* Toronto: Oxford University Press, 1975.

Green, Michael D. "Alexander McGillivray." In *American Indian Leaders: Studies in Diversity,* ed. R. David Edmunds, 41–63. Lincoln: University of Nebraska Press, 1980

Greenbaum, Susan D. "In Search of Lost Tribes: Anthropology and the Federal Acknowledgment Process." *Human Organization* 44 (winter 1985): 361–67.

Gresko, Jacqueline. "Creating Little Dominions within the Dominion: Early Catholic Indian Schools in Saskatchewan and British Columbia." In *Indian Education in Canada*, ed. Jean Barman, Yvonne Hebert, and Don McCaskill, 1:88–109. Vancouver: University of British Columbia Press, 1986.

——. "White 'Rites' and Indian 'Rites': Indian Education and Native Responses in the West, 1870–1910." In *Western Canada, Past and Present*, ed. Anthony W. Rasporich, 163–86. Calgary: McClelland and Stewart, 1975.

Gross, Emma R. *Federal Policy toward American Indians*. Westport CT: Greenwood, 1989.

Haan, Richard L. "'The Trade Do's Not Flourish as Formerly': The Ecological Origins of the Yamassee War of 1715." *Ethnohistory* 28 (fall 1982): 341–58.

Hagan, William T. *Indian Police and Judges: Experiments in Acculturation and Control*. New Haven CT: Yale University Press, 1966.

——. "Kiowas, Comanches, and Cattlemen, 1867–1906: A Case Study of the Failure of U.S. Reservation Policy." *Pacific Historical Review* 40 (August 1971): 333–55.

——. "Tribalism Rejuvenated: The Native American since the Era of Termination." *Western Historical Quarterly* 12 (January 1982): 4–15.

Hall, David J. "Clifford Sifton and Canadian Indian Administration, 1896–1905." *Prairie Forum* 2 (November 1977): 127–51.

Hall, G. Stanley. *Adolescence: Its Psychology and Its Relations to . . . Education*. 2 vols. New York: Appleton, 1904.

——. "How Far Are the Principles of Education among Indigenous Lines Applicable to American Indians?" *Pedagogical Seminary* 15 (September 1908): 365–69.

Hammond, George P., and Agapito Rey, eds. & trans. *Don Juan Oñate: Colonizer of New Mexico, 1595–1628*. 2 vols. Albuquerque: University of New Mexico Press, 1953.

Harper, Allan G. "Canada's Indian Administration: Basic Concepts and Objectives." *American Indigena* 5 (April 1945): 119–32.

——. "Canada's Indian Administration: The Treaty System." *American Indigena* 7 (April 1947): 129–48.

Harring, Sidney L. "'The Liberal Treatment of Indians': Native People in Nineteenth Century Ontario Law." *Saskatchewan Law Review* 56, no. 2 (1992): 297–371.

Harriot, Thomas. *A Briefe and True Report of the New Found Land of Virginia* (1588). Reprint in *The Roanoke Voyages, 1554–1590*, ed. David Beers Quinn. Hakluyt Society Publications 104. London: Hakluyt Society, 1955.

Hawthorn, Harry B., ed. *A Survey of Contemporary Indians of Canada: A Report on Economic, Political, Educational Needs and Policies*. 2 vols. Ottawa: Queen's Printer, 1966–67.

Henderson, James Y. *The Road: Indian Tribes and Political Liberty*. Berkeley and Los Angeles: University of California Press, 1980.

Hening, William W., ed. *The Statutes at Large . . . of Virginia*. 13 vols. Richmond VA: Bartow, 1819–23.

Hering, Joseph B. *Kenekuk, the Kickapoo Prophet*. Lawrence: University Press of Kansas, 1988.

Hertzberg, Hazel W. *The Search for an American Indian Identity: Modern Pan-Indian Movements*. Syracuse NY: Syracuse University Press, 1971.

Hewlett, Edward S. "The Chilcotin Uprising of 1864." *BC Studies* 19 (autumn 1973): 50–72.

Hoey, R. A. "Economic Problems of the Canadian Indian." In *The North American Indian Today*, ed. Charles T. Loram and T. F. McIlwraith. Toronto: University of Toronto Press, 1943.

Hogkins, John G., ed. *Documentary History of Education in Upper Canada.* . . . 28 vols. Toronto: Warwick Brothers & Rutter, 1894–1910.

Hoig, Stan. *The Sand Creek Massacre*. Norman: University of Oklahoma Press, 1961.

Holm, Tom. "Fighting a White Man's War: The Extent and Legacy of American Indian Participation in World War II." *Journal of Ethnic Studies* 9 (summer 1981): 69–81.

Hood, Susan. "Termination of the Klamath Tribe in Oregon." *Ethnohistory* 19 (fall 1972): 379–92.

Hornung, Rick. *One Nation under the Gun*. New York: Pantheon, 1991.

Horsman, Reginald, "American Indian Policy in the Old Northwest, 1783–1812." *William and Mary Quarterly* 3d ser., 18 (January 1961): 35–53.

——. *The Frontier in the Formative Years, 1783–1815*. New York: Holt, Rinehart and Winston, 1970.

——. *Matthew Elliott, British Indian Agent*. Detroit: Wayne State University Press, 1964.

——. *The Origins of Indian Removal, 1815–1824*. East Lansing: Michigan State University Press, 1970.

——. "Scientific Racism and the American Indian in the Mid-Nineteenth Century." *American Quarterly* 27 (May 1975): 152–68.

Howard, James H. "The Dakota Victory Dance, World War II." *North Dakota History* 18 (January 1951): 31–40.

Howard, Oliver Otis. *Nez Perce Joseph*. Boston: Lee & Shepard, 1881.

Hoxie, Frederick E. *A Final Promise: The Campaign to Assimilate the Indians, 1880–1920*. Lincoln: University of Nebraska Press, 1984. Reprint, New York: Cambridge University Press, 1989.

Hurtado, Albert L. *Indian Survival on the California Frontier*. New Haven CT: Yale University Press, 1988.

Hutton, Elizabeth A. "Indian Affairs in Nova Scotia, 1760–1834." In *Collections of the Nova Scotia Historical Society*, 34:33–54. Halifax: Kentville, 1963.

Innis, Harold A. *The Fur Trade in Canada*. 1930. Reprint, New Haven CT: Yale University Press, 1962.

Iverson, Peter. "Carlos Montezuma." In *American Indian Leaders: Studies in Diversity*, ed. R. David Edmunds, 206–21. Lincoln: University of Nebraska Press, 1980.

Jaenen, Cornelius J. "Amerindian Views of French Culture in the Seventeenth Century." *Canadian Historical Review* 55 (September 1974): 261–91.

——. *The French Relationship with the Native Peoples of New France and Acadia*. Ottawa: Research Branch, Indian and Northern Affairs, 1984.

——. "French Sovereignty and Native Nationhood during the French Regime." *Native Studies Review* 2 (1986): 83–113.

——. *Friend and Foe: Aspects of French-Amerindian Conflict in the Sixteenth and Seventeenth Centuries*. Toronto: McClelland & Stewart, 1976.

——. "Problems of Assimilation in New France." *French Historical Studies* 4 (spring 1966): 280.

Jefferson, Thomas. *The Papers of Thomas Jefferson*. Edited by Julian P. Boyd. 2 vols. Princeton
   NJ: Princeton University Press, 1950–.
——. *The Writings of Thomas Jefferson*. Edited by Paul L. Ford. 10 vols. New York: Putnam,
   1892–99.
——. *The Writings of Thomas Jefferson*. Edited by Andrew A. Lipscomb. 20 vols. Washington DC:
   Thomas Jefferson Memorial Association, 1903–4.
Jenness, Diamond. "Canada's Indians Yesterday: What of Today?" *Canadian Journal of Eco-
   nomics and Political Science* 20 (February 1954): 95–100.
Jennings, Francis. *The Ambiguous Iroquois Empire*. New York: Norton, 1984.
——. *The Invasion of America: Indians, Colonialism, and the Cant of Conquest* Chapel Hill:
   University of North Carolina Press, 1975.
——. "Virgin Land and Savage People." *American Quarterly* 23 (October 1971): 519–41.
Jensen, Merrill, ed. *American Colonial Documents to 1776*. Vol. 9 of *English Historical Docu-
   ments*. New York: Oxford University Press, 1955.
Johansen, Gregory J. " 'To Make Some Provision for Their Half-Breeds': The Nemaha Half-Breed
   Reserve, 1830–1866." *Nebraska History* 67 (spring 1986): 8–29.
Johnson, Charles M. "Joseph Brant, the Grand River Lands and the Northwest Crisis." *Ontario
   History* 55 (December 1963): 267–82.
——. "An Outline of Early Settlement in the Grand River Valley." *Ontario History* 54 (March
   1962): 43–67.
Johnson, Charles M., ed. *The Valley of the Six Nations: A Collection of Documents on the
   Indian Lands of the Grand River*. Toronto: Champlain Society, 1964.
Johnson, David L., and Raymond Wilson. "Gertrude Simmons Bonnin, 1876–1938: 'America-
   nize the First Americans.' " *American Indian Quarterly* 12 (winter 1988): 27–40.
Jones, Douglas C. *The Treaty of Medicine Lodge*. Norman: University of Oklahoma Press, 1966.
Jones, Jerome W. "The Established Virginia Church and the Conversion of Negroes and Indians,
   1620–1760." *Journal of Negro History* 46 (January 1961): 12–23.
Jordan, Winthrop D. *White over Black: American Attitudes toward the Negro, 1550–1812*.
   Chapel Hill: University of North Carolina Press, 1968.
Josephy, Alvin M., Jr. *Now That the Buffalo's Gone: A Study of Today's American Indians*. New
   York: Knopf, 1982.
Kappler, Charles J., comp. *Indian Affairs: Laws and Treaties*. 5 vols. Washington DC: GPO, 1904–
   41.
Kawashima, Yasu. "Jurisdiction of the Colonial Courts over the Indians in Massachusetts,
   1689–1763." *New England Quarterly* 42 (December 1969): 532–50.
Kelly, Lawrence C. "The Indian Reorganization Act: The Dream and the Reality." *Pacific Histor-
   ical Review* 44 (August 1975): 291–312.
Kelsey, Harry. "The Doolittle Report of 1867: Its Preparation and Shortcomings." *Arizona and
   the West* 17 (summer 1975): 107–20.
——. *Juan Rodriguez Cabrillo*. San Marino CA: Huntington Library, 1986.
Kingsbury, Susan M., ed. *Records of the Virginia Company of London*. 4 vols. Washington DC:
   GPO, 1906–35.
Klingberg, Frank J. *Anglican Humanitarianism in Colonial New York*. Philadelphia: The
   Church Historical Society, 1940.

Koehler, Lyle. "Red-White Power Relations and Justice in the Courts of Seventeenth Century New England." *American Indian Culture and Research Journal* 3, no. 4 (1979): 1–31.

Kvasnicka, Robert M., and Herman Viola, eds. *The Commissioners of Indian Affairs, 1824–1977.* Lincoln: University of Nebraska Press, 1979.

Lamar, Howard R., and Leonard Thompson, eds. *The Frontier in History: North America and Southern Africa Compared.* New Haven CT: Yale University Press, 1981.

Lamour, Jean. "Edgar Dewdney: Indian Commissioner in the Transition Period of Indian Settlement, 1884." *Saskatchewan History* 33 (winter 1980): 105–17.

Land, Robert H. "Henrico and Its College." *William and Mary Quarterly* 2d ser., 16 (October 1938): 453–98.

La Rusic, Ignatius E. *Negotiating a Way of Life: Initial Cree Experience with the Administrative Structure Arising from the James Bay Agreement.* Ottawa: Department of Indian and Northern Affairs, 1979.

Lauber, Almon W. *Indian Slavery in Colonial Times within the Present Limits of the United States.* New York: Columbia University, Longmans, Green, 1913.

Lawson, John. *A New Voyage to Carolina.* Edited by Hugh T. Lefler. Chapel Hill: University of North Carolina Press, 1967.

Lazarus, Arthur, Jr., and W. Richard West Jr. "Alaska Native Claims Settlement Act: Long-Term Prospects." *American Indian Journal* 3 (May 1977): 10–17.

Leach, Douglas E. *Flintlock and Tomahawk: New England in King Philip's War.* New York: Norton, 1958.

Le Clercq, Chrestien. *New Relation of Gaspesia: With the Customs and Religion of the Gaspesian Indians.* Edited by William W. Ganong. Toronto: Champlain Society, 1910.

Leighton, Douglas. "The Compact Tory as Bureaucrat: Samuel Peters Jarvis and the Indian Department, 1837–1845." *Ontario History* 73 (March 1981): 40–53.

——. "The Manitoulin Incident of 1863: An Indian-White Confrontation in the Province in Canada." *Ontario History* 69 (June 1977): 113–24.

——. "A Victorian Civil Servant at Work: Lawrence Vankoughnet and the Canadian Indian Department, 1874–1893." In *As Long as the Sun Shines and Water Flows,* ed. Ian A. L. Getty and Antoine S. Lussier, 104–19. Vancouver: University of British Columbia Press, 1983.

Leslie, John. "The Bagot Commission: Developing a Corporate Memory for the Indian Department." *Historical Papers/Communications Historiques.* Ottawa: Canadian Historical Association, 1982.

——. *Commissions of Inquiry into Indian Affairs in the Canadas, 1828–1858: Evolving a Corporate Memory for the Indian Department.* Ottawa: Indian Affairs and Northern Development, 1985.

Leslie, John, and Ron Maguire, eds. *The Historical Development of the Indian Act.* Ottawa: Indian and Northern Affairs, 1978.

Lewis, James R. "Shamans and Prophets: Continuities and Discontinuities in Native American New Religion." *American Indian Quarterly* 12 (summer 1988): 221–28.

Loram Charles T., and T. F. McIlwraith, eds. *The North American Indian Today.* Toronto: University of Toronto Press, 1943.

Lowery, Woodbury. *The Spanish Settlements within the Present Limits of the United States: Florida, 1562–1574.* New York: Russell & Russell, 1959.

Lurie, Nancy O., "The Indian Claims Commission Act." *Annals of the American Academy of Political and Social Science* 311 (May 1957): 56–70.

———. "Indian Cultural Adjustment to European Civilization." In *Seventeenth Century America: Essays in Colonial History*, ed. James M. Smith, 33–60. Chapel Hill: University of North Carolina Press, 1959.

———. "Menominee Termination: From Reservation to Colony." *Human Organization* 31 (fall 1972): 257–70.

Macleod, William C. *The American Indian Frontier.* New York: Knopf, 1928.

Mahon, John K. *History of the Second Seminole War, 1835–1842.* Gainesville: University of Florida Press, 1967.

Margon, Arthur. "Indians and Immigrants: A Comparison of Groups New to the City." *Journal of Ethnic Studies* 4 (winter 1977): 17–28.

Marton, Joel W. *Sacred Revolt: The Muskogees' Struggle for a New World.* Boston: Beacon, 1991.

Matthiesen, Peter. *In the Spirit of Crazy Horse.* New York: Viking, 1983.

McConnell, Michael N. *A Country Between: The Upper Ohio Valley and Its Peoples, 1724–1774.* Lincoln: University of Nebraska Press, 1992.

McDermott, John Francis, ed. *Frenchmen and French Ways in the Mississippi Valley.* Urbana: University of Illinois Press, 1969.

McLaughlin, William G. *Cherokee Renascence in the New Republic.* Princeton NJ: Princeton University Press, 1986.

McNab, David T. "Herman Merivale and Colonial Office Indian Policy in the Mid-Nineteenth Century." In *As Long as the Sun Shines and Water Flows: A Reader in Canadian Native Studies*, ed. Ian A. L. Gett and Antoine S. Lussier, 85–103. Vancouver: University of British Columbia Press, 1983.

McNaught, Kenneth. *The Penguin History of Canada.* 1969. Reprint, New York: Viking Penguin, 1988.

McWorter, Lucullus Virgil. *Yellow Calf: His Own Story.* Caldwell ID: Caxton, 1940.

Mercredi, Ovide, and Mary Ellen Turpel. *In the Rapids: Navigating the Future of First Nations.* Toronto: Viking, 1993.

Merrell, James H.. *The Indians' New World: Catawbas and Their Neighbors from European Contact through the Era of Removal.* Chapel Hill: University of North Carolina Press, 1989.

———. "Our Bond of Peace: Patterns of Intercultural Exchange in the Colonial Piedmont, 1650–1750." In *Powhatan's Mantle: Indians in the Colonial Southeast*, ed. Peter H. Wood, Gregory A. Waselkov, and M. Thomas Hately. Lincoln: University of Nebraska Press, 1989.

Michaelsen, Robert S. "Civil Rights, Indian Rites." *Society* 21 (May/June 1984): 42–46.

Mihesuah, Devon Abbott. "Out of the 'Graves of the Polluted Debauches': The Boys of the Cherokee Male Seminary." *American Indian Quarterly* 15 (fall 1991): 503–21.

Miller, J. R. *Skyscrapers Hide the Heavens: A History of Indian-White Relations in Canada.* Toronto: University of Toronto Press, 1989.

Milloy, John S. "The Early Indian Acts: Development Strategy and Constitutional Change." In *As Long as the Sun Shines and Water Flows: A Reader in Canadian Native Studies*, ed. Ian A. L. Getty and Antoine S. Lussier, 39–64. Vancouver: University of British Columbia Press, 1983.

Moir, John S., ed. *Character and Circumstances: Essays in Honour of Donald Grant Creighton*. Toronto: Macmillan, 1970.

Montgomery, Malcolm. "The Legal Status of the Six Nations in Canada." *Ontario History* 55 (June 1963): 93–105.

Mooney, James. *The Ghost Dance and the Sioux Outbreak of 1890*. 14th Annual Report of the Bureau of American Ethnology, 1892–93, pt. 2. Washington DC: GPO, 1896.

Morgan, Edmund S. *American Slavery, American Freedom: The Ordeal of Colonial Virginia*, New York: Norton, 1975.

Morrison, William R. *A Survey of the History and Claims of the Native Peoples of Northern Canada*. Ottawa: Treaties and Historical Research Centre, 1983.

Morse, Jedidiah. *A Report to the Secretary of War of the United States on Indian Affairs*. New Haven CT: Howe and Spalding, 1822.

Morton, Desmond. "Cavalry or Police: Keeping the Peace on Two Adjacent Frontiers, 1870–1900." *Journal of Canadian Studies* 12 (spring 1977): 27–37.

Morton, William L. *The Kingdom of Canada*. Toronto: McClelland & Stewart, 1963.

——. *Manitoba: A History*. 1957. Reprint, Toronto: University of Toronto Press, 1967.

Moss, John E. "Native Proposals for Constitutional Reform." *Journal of Canadian Studies* 15 (winter 1980–81): 85–92.

Nagler, Mark. *Indians in the City: A Study of the Urbanization of Indians in Toronto*. Ottawa: St. Paul University, 1970.

Nash, Gary B. "The Image of the Indian in the Southern Colonial Mind." *William and Mary Quarterly* 3d ser., 29 (April 1972): 197–230.

——. *Red, White, and Black: The Peoples of Early America*. Englewood Cliffs NJ: Prentice-Hall, 1974.

Nash, Gary B., and Richard Weiss, eds. *The Great Fear: Race in the Mind of America*. New York: Holt, Rinehart, & Winston, 1970.

Naske, Claus M., and Herman E. Slotnik. *Alaska: A History of the 49th State*. Grand Rapids MI: Eerddmans, 1979.

National Association of Friendship Centres. *A Survey of Migrating Native People*. Ottawa: NAFC, 1977.

Native American Rights Fund. *Legal Review* 12 (spring 1987): 1–7.

Neils, Elaine M. *Reservation to City*. Chicago: University of Chicago Department of Geography, 1971.

Nelson, Larry L. " 'Never Have They Done So Little': The Battle of Fort Recovery and the Collapse of the Miami Confederacy." *Northwest Ohio Quarterly* 64 (spring 1992): 43–55.

Nichols, Roger L. *Black Hawk and the Warrior's Path*. Arlington Heights IL: Davidson, 1992.

——. *General Henry Atkinson: A Western Military Career*. Norman: University of Oklahoma Press, 1965.

Nock, David A. "The Canadian Indian Research and Aid Society: A Victorian Voluntary Association." *Western Canadian Journal of Anthropology* 6 (special issue; 1976): 31–48.

O'Callaghan, Edmund B., ed. *Documents Relative to the Colonial History of the State of New York*. 15 vols. Albany NY: Weed, Parsons, 1853–87.

O'Gara, Geoffrey. "Canny CERT Gets Respect, Money Problems." *Wassaja/Indian Historian* 13 (June 1980): 24–28.

Olson, James C. *Red Cloud and the Sioux Problem.* Lincoln: University of Nebraska Press, 1965.

Olson James S., and Raymond Wilson, *Native Americans in the Twentieth Century.* Urbana: University of Illinois Press, 1984.

Oppelt, Norman T. "The Tribally Controlled Colleges in the 1980s: Higher Education's Best Kept Secret." *American Indian Culture and Research Journal* 8, no. 4 (1984): 27–45.

Parman, Donald L. *Indians and the American West in the Twentieth Century.* Bloomington: Indiana University Press, 1994.

Parramore, Thomas C. "The Tuscarora Ascendency." *North Carolina Historical Review* 59 (October 1982): 307–22.

Parsons, Lynn Hudson. "A Perpetual Harrow upon My Feelings: John Quincy Adams and the American Indian." *New England Quarterly* 46 (September 1973): 339–79.

Passamaquoddy v. Morton, 388 F. Supp 649 (F.D. Maine 1975).

Patterson, E. Palmer, II. "Andrew Paull and the Early History of British Columbia Indian Organizations." In *One Century Later: Western Canadian Reserve Indians since Treaty 7*, ed. Ian A. L. Getty and Donald B. Smith, 63–82. Vancouver: University of British Columbia Press, 1978.

Peake, Ora Brooks. *A History of the United States Indian Factory System, 1795–1822.* Denver: Sage, 1954.

Pearce, Roy H. *The Savages of America: A Study of the Indian and the Idea of Civilization.* Baltimore: Johns Hopkins University Press, 1953.

——. *Savagism and Civilization: A Study of the Indian and the American Mind.* Rev. ed. Baltimore: Johns Hopkins University Press, 1967.

Peckham, Howard H. *Pontiac and the Indian Uprising.* Princeton NJ: Princeton University Press, 1947.

Pelletier, Wilfred. "For Every North American Indian That Begins to Disappear I Also Begin to Disappear." In *Canada's Indians Contemporary Conflicts*, ed. James S. Frideres, 101–13. Scarborough ON: Prentice Hall, 1974.

Percy, George. *Observations of George Percy* (1607). Reprinted in *Narratives of Early Virginia*, ed. Lyon G. Tyler. New York: Scribner's, 1907.

Peterson, Jacqueline, and Jennifer S. H. Brown, eds. *The New Peoples: Being and Becoming Métis in North America.* Winnipeg: University of Manitoba Press, 1985.

Phillips, George H. *The Enduring Struggle: Indians in California History.* San Francisco: Boyd & Fraser, 1981.

Porter, Frank E., III, ed. *Strategies for Survival: American Indians in the Eastern United States.* Westport CT: Greenwood, 1986.

Powell, William S. "Aftermath of the Massacre: The First Indian War, 1622–1632." *Virginia Magazine of History and Biography* 56 (January 1958): 44–75.

Price, John A., and Don N. McCaskill. "The Urban Integration of Canadian Native People." *Western Canadian Journal of Anthropology* 4, no. 2 (October 1974): 29–47.

Prucha, Francis Paul, *American Indian Policy in Crisis: Christian Reformers and the Indian, 1865–1900.* Norman: University of Oklahoma Press, 1976.

——. *Broadax and Bayonet: The Role of the United States Army in the Development of the Northwest, 1815–1860.* Madison: State Historical Society of Wisconsin, 1953.

——. *The Great Father: The United States Government and the American Indians.* 2 vols. Lincoln: University of Nebraska Press, 1984.

——. *The Sword of the Republic: The United States Army on the Frontier, 1783–1846.* 1969. Reprint, Bloomington: Indiana University Press, 1977.

Purich, D. *Our Land: Native Rights in Canada.* Toronto: Lorimer, 1986.

Quinn, David Beers. *North America from Earliest Discovery to First Settlements: The Norse Voyages to 1612.* New York: Harper & Row, 1975.

——. *Set Fair for Roanoke: Voyages and Colonies, 1584–1606.* Chapel Hill: University of North Carolina Press, 1985.

Quinn, David Beers, ed. *New American World: A Documentary History of North America to 1612.* 5 vols. New York: Arno Press & Hector Bye, 1979.

——. *The Roanoke Voyages, 1554–1590.* Hakluyt Society Publications, 104. London: Hakluyt Society, 1955.

Quinten, B. T. "Oklahoma Tribes, the Great Depression, and the Indian Bureau." *Mid-America* 49 (January 1967): 29–43.

Raby, Stewart. "Indian Land Surrenders in Southern Saskatchewan." *Canadian Geographer* 17 (spring 1973) : 46.

Ralston, Helen. "Religion, Public Policy, and the Education of Micmac Indians of Nova Scotia, 1605–1872." *Canadian Review of Sociology and Anthropology* 18 (November 1981): 470–98.

Rasporich, Anthony W., ed. *Western Canada, Past and Present.* Calgary: McClelland & Stewart, 1975.

Ray, Arthur J. *Indians in the Fur Trade: Their Role as Trappers, Hunters, and Middlemen in the Lands Southwest of Hudson's Bay, 1660–1870.* Toronto: University of Toronto Press, 1974.

Reid, John Phillip. *A Better Kind of Hatchet: Law, Trade, and Diplomacy in the Cherokee Nation during the Early Years of Euorpean Contact.* University Park: Pennsylvania State University Press, 1976.

Remini, Robert V. *Andrew Jackson.* New York: Twayne, 1966.

Rettig, A. "A Nativist Movement at Metlakatla Mission." BC *Studies* 46 (summer 1980): 28–39.

Rich, Edwin E. *The Fur Trade and the Northwest to 1857.* Toronto: McClelland & Stewart, 1967.

Richards, Kent D. *Isaac I. Stevens: Young Man in a Hurry.* Provo UT: Brigham Young University Press, 1979.

Richardson, Boyce. *Strangers Devour the Land: The Cree Hunters versus Premier Bourassa and the James Bay Development Corporation.* Toronto: Macmillan, 1975.

Richardson, James D., ed. *A Compilation of the Messages and Papers of the Presidents.* 11 vols. Washington DC: Bureau of National Literature and Art, 1911.

Richter, Daniel K. "War and Culture: The Iroquois Experience." *William and Mary Quarterly* 3d ser., 40 (October 1983): 528–59.

Roberts, Lance W. "Becoming Modern: Some Reflections on Inuit Social Change." In *As Long as the Sun Shines and Water Flows: A Reader in Canadian Native Studies,* ed. Ian A. L. Getty and Antoine S. Lussier, 299–314. Vancouver: University of British Columbia Press, 1983.

Robinson, W. Stitt. "Indian Education and Missions in Colonial Virginia." *Journal of Southern History* 18 (May 1952): 152–68.

——. "The Legal Status of the Indian in Colonial Virginia." *Virginia Magazine of History and Biography* 61 (July 1953): 249–59.

——. *The Southern Colonial Frontier, 1607–1763*. Albuquerque: University of New Mexico Press, 1979.

——. "Tributary Indians in Colonial Virginia." *Virginia Magazine of History and Biography* 67 (January 1959): 49–64.

Rollings, Willard H. *The Osage: An Ethnohistorical Study of Hegemony on the Prairie-Plains*. Columbia: University of Missouri Press, 1992.

Ronda, James P. "Red and White at the Bench: Indians and the Law in Plymouth Colony, 1620–1691." *Essex Institute Historical Collections* 110 (July 1974): 200–215.

——. "The Sillery Experiment: A Jesuit-Indian Village in New France, 1637–1663." *American Indian Culture and Research Journal* 3, no. 1 (1979): 1–18.

——. " 'We Are Well as We Are': An Indian Critique of Seventeenth-Century Christian Mission." *William and Mary Quarterly* 3d ser., 34 (January 1977): 66–82.

Rule, John C. "Jerome Phelypeaux, Comte de Pontchartrain, and the Establishment of Louisiana." In *Frenchmen and French Ways in the Mississippi Valley*, ed. John Francis McDermott, 179–97. Urbana: University of Illinois Press, 1969.

Salisbury, Neal. *Manitou and Providence: Indians and the Making of New England, 1500–1643*. New York: Oxford University Press, 1982.

——. "Red Puritans: The 'Praying Indians' of Massachusetts Bay and John Eliot." *William and Mary Quarterly* 3d ser., 31 (January 1974): 27–54.

Samek, Hana. *The Blackfoot Confederacy: A Comparative Study of Canadian and U.S. Indian Policy*. Albuquerque: University of New Mexico Press, 1987.

Sanders, Douglas E. "Native People in Areas of Internal National Expansion." *Saskatchewan Law Review* 38, no. 1 (1973–74): 63–87.

Satz, Ronald N. *American Indian Policy in the Jacksonian Era*. Lincoln: University of Nebraska Press, 1975.

Schrader, Robert F. *The Indian Arts and Crafts Board: An Aspect of New Deal Indian Policy*. Albuquerque: University of New Mexico Press, 1983.

Schurz, Carl. "Present Aspects of the Indian Problem." *North American Review* 133 (July 1881): 1–24.

Scott, Duncan C. "Indian Affairs, 1840–1867." In *Canada and Its Provinces*, ed. Adam Shortt and Arthur G. Doughty, 5:331–62. Toronto: Publishers Association of Canada, 1913–17.

——. "Indian Affairs, 1867–1912." In *Canada and Its Provinces*, ed. Adam Shortt and Arthur G. Doughty, 7:593–626. Toronto: Publishers Association of Canada, 1913–17.

Shea, William L. *The Virginia Militia in the Seventeenth Century*. Baton Rouge: Louisiana State University, 1983.

Shortt, Adam, and Arthur G. Doughty, eds. *Canada and Its Provinces*. 23 vols. Toronto: Publishers Association of Canada, 1913–17.

Shurtleff, Nathaniel B., ed. *Records of Governor and Company of the Massachusetts Bay in New England*. 5 vols. in 6. Boston: White, 1853–54.

Simmons, Marc. *The Last Conquistador: Juan de Oñate and the Settling of the Far Southwest*. Norman: University of Oklahoma Press, 1991.

Smith, Donald B. "The Dispossession of the Mississauga Indians: A Missing Chapter in the Early History of Upper Canada." *Ontario History* 73 (June 1981): 67–87.

——. *Sacred Feathers: The Reverend Peter Jones (Kahkewaquonaby) and the Mississauga Indians*. Lincoln: University of Nebraska Press, 1987.

Smith, Wallis M. "The Fur Trade and the Frontier: A Study of Inter-Cultural Alliance." *Anthropologica* 5, no. 1 (1973): 21–35.

Smits, David. "'Abominable Mixture': Toward the Repudiation of Anglo-Indian Marriage in Seventeenth Century Virginia." *Virginia Magazine of History and Biography* 95 (April 1987): 157–92.

Sosin, Jack M. *The Revolutionary Frontier, 1763–1783.* New York: Holt, Rinehart & Winston, 1967.

——. *Whitehall and the Wilderness: The Middle West in British Colonial Policy, 1760–1775.* Lincoln: University of Nebraska Press, 1961.

Stacey, C. P. *Arms, Men and Governments: The War Policies of Canada, 1939–1945.* Ottawa: Information Canada, 1970.

Standing Bear, Luther. *Land of the Spotted Eagle.* Boston: Houghton Mifflin, 1933.

Stanley, George F. G. *The Birth of Western Canada: A History of the Riel Rebellions.* Toronto: University of Toronto Press, 1936. 2d ed. 1960.

——. "The First Indian 'Reserves' in Canada." *Revue d'histoire de l'Amerique française* 4 (September 1950): 178–210.

——. "The Policy of 'Francisation' as Applied to the Indians during the Ancien Régime." *Revue d'histoire de l'Amérique française* 3 (December 1949): 333–48.

——. "The Significance of the Six Nations in the War of 1812." *Ontario History* 55 (December 1963): 215–31.

Stern, Esther Wagner, and Allen E. Stern. *The Effect of Small Pox on the Destiny of the Amerindian.* Boston: Humphries, 1945.

Steward, Omer C. *Peyote Religion: A History.* Norman: University of Oklahoma Press, 1987.

Stith, William. *The History of the First Discovery and Settlement of Virginia.* Williamsburg VA: William Parks, 1747. Reprint, New York: Joseph Sabin, 1865.

Stoddard, T. Lathrop. *The Rising Tide of Color against White World-Supremacy.* New York: Scribner's, 1921. Reprint, Westport CT: Negro University Press, 1971.

Surtees, Robert J. "Indian Land Cessions in Upper Canada, 1815–1830." In *As Long as the Sun Shines and Water Flows: A Reader in Canadian Native Studies,* ed. Ian A. L. Getty and Antoine S. Lussier, 65–84. Vancouver: University of British Columbia Press, 1983.

——. *Indian Land Surrenders in Ontario 1763–1867.* Ottawa: Indian Affairs and Northern Development, 1983.

——. *The Original People.* Toronto: Holt, Rinehart & Winston, 1971.

Svingen, Orlan. "Jim Crow, Indian Style." *American Indian Quarterly* 11 (fall 1987): 275–86.

Szasz, Margaret Connell. *Education and the American Indian: The Road to Self-Determination, 1928–1973.* Albuquerque: University of New Mexico Press, 1974.

——. *Indian Education in the American Colonies, 1607–1783.* Albuquerque: University of New Mexico Press, 1988.

Tanis, Norman E. "Education in John Eliot's Indian Utopias, 1646–1675." *History of Education Quarterly* 10 (fall 1970): 308–23.

Tate, Michael L. "From Scout to Doughboy: The National Debate over Integration of American Indians into the Military. 1891–1918." *Western Historical Quarterly* 17 (October 1986): 417–37.

Taylor, Graham D. "The Divided Heart: The Indian New Deal." In *The American Indian Experience: A Profile,* ed. Philip Weeks, 240–59. Arlington Heights IL: Forum, 1988.

Taylor, John Leonard. *Canadian Indian Policy during the Inter War Years, 1918–1939.* Ottawa: Indian Affairs and Northern Development, 1984.

Tennant, Paul. *Aboriginal Peoples and Politics: The Indian Land Question in British Columbia, 1849–1989.* Vancouver: University of British Columbia Press, 1990.

Titley, E. Brian. *A Narrow Vision: Duncan Campbell Scott and the Administration of Indian Affairs in Canada.* Vancouver: University of British Columbia Press, 1986.

Tobias, John L. "Canada's Subjugation of the Plains Cree, 1879–1885." *Canadian Historical Review* 64 (December 1983): 519–48.

——. "Protection, Civilization, Assimilation: An Outline History of Canada's Indian Policy." *Western Canadian Journal of Anthropology* (special issue; 1976): 13–30.

Trant, William. "The Treatment of the Canadian Indians." *Westminster Review* 144 (November 1895): 506–27.

Trelease, Allen W. *Indian Affairs in Colonial New York.* Ithaca NY: Cornell University Press, 1960.

——. "Indian-White Contacts in Eastern North America: The Dutch in New Netherland." *Ethnohistory* 9 (spring 1962): 137–46.

Trennert, Robert A., Jr. *Alternative to Extinction: Federal Indian Policy and the Beginnings of the Reservation System, 1846–1851.* Philadelphia: Temple University Press, 1975.

——. "Educating Indian Girls at Nonreservation Boarding Schools, 1878–1920." *Western Historical Quarterly* 13 (July 1982): 271–90.

——. "From Carlisle to Phoenix: The Rise and Fall of the Indian Outing System, 1878–1930." *Pacific Historical Review* 52 (August 1983): 267–91.

Trigger, Bruce G. "Champlain Judged by His Indian Policy: A Different View of Early Canadian History." *Anthropologica* 13 n.s. (special issue; 1971): 85–114.

——. *The Children of Aataentsic: A History of the Huron People to 1600.* 2 vols. Montreal: McGill–Queen's University Press, 1976.

——. "The French Presence in Huronia: The Structure of Franco-Huron Relations in the First Half of the Seventeenth Century." *Canadian Historical Review* 49 (June 1968): 107–41.

——. *Natives and Newcomers: Canada's "Heroic Age" Reconsidered.* Montreal: McGill–Queen's University Press, 1985.

Trigger, Bruce G., ed. *Handbook of North American Indians.* Vol. 15. *Northeast.* General ed. William T. Sturtevant. Washington DC: Smithsonian Institution, 1978.

United States v. Dion, 106 S. Ct. 2216 (1986).

Upton, L. S. F., "Colonists and Micmacs." *Journal of Canadian Studies* 10 (August 1975): 44–56.

——. "Indian Affairs in Colonial New Brunswick." *Acadiensis* n.s., 3 (spring 1974): 3–26.

——. "Indian Policy in Colonial Nova Scotia." *Acadiensis* n.s., 5 (autumn 1975): 11.

——. "The Origins of Canadian Indian Policy." *Journal of Canadian Studies* 8 (November 1973): 51–61.

U.S. Bureau of the Census. *Historical Statistics of the United States: Colonial Times to 1970.* 2 parts. Washington DC: GPO, 1975.

U.S. Congress. Senate. *Condition of the Indian Tribes.* Report no. 1, 39th Cong., 2d sess., 1866.

——. *Montana Water Rights Hearings.* 96th Cong., 1st sess., 1979.

——. Special Committee on Investigations of the Select Committee on Indian Affairs. *Final Report and Legislative Recommendations.* 101st Cong., 1st sess., 1989.

——. Subcommittee on Indian Affairs. *Occupation of Wounded Knee*. 93 Cong., 1st sess., 1973.

U.S. Department of Interior. *Annual Report*. 1849–present.

Usher, J. *Duncan of Metlakatla*. Ottawa: National Museum of Man, 1974.

Utley, Robert M., ed. *Battlefield and Classroom: Four Decades with the American Indian, 1876–1904*. New Haven CT: Yale University Press, 1964.

——. *The Indian Frontier of the American West, 1846–1890*. Albuquerque: University of New Mexico Press, 1984.

Van Kirk, Sylvia. *Many Tender Ties: Women in Fur Trade Society, 1670–1870*. Norman: University of Oklahoma Press, 1983.

Vaughan, Alden T. "'Expulsion of the Savages': English Policy and the Virginia Massacre." *William and Mary Quarterly* 3d ser., 35 (January 1978): 57–84.

——. *New England Frontier: Puritans and Indians, 1620–1675*. Rev. ed. New York: Norton, 1979.

Villeneuve, Larry. *The Historical Background of Indian Reserves and Settlements in the Province of Quebec*. Revised and updated by Daniel Francis. Ottawa: Indian and Northern Affairs Canada, 1984.

Wallace, Anthony F. C. *The Death and Rebirth of the Seneca*. New York: Knopf, 1970.

——. "Prelude to Disaster: The Course of Indian-White Relations Which Led to the Black Hawk War of 1832." In *The Black Hawk War, 1831–1832*, vol. 1, *Illinois Volunteers*, ed. Ellen M. Whitney, 1–51. Collections of the Illinois Historical Library, vol. 35. Springfield: Illinois State Historical Library, 1970.

Washburn, Wilcomb E. The Governor and the Rebel: A History of Bacon's Rebellion in Virginia. Chapel Hill: University of North Carolina Press, 1957.

Washington, George. *Writings of George Washington*. Edited by J. C. Fitzpatrick. 39 vols. Washington DC: GPO, 1931–44.

Way, Royal B. "The United States Factory System for Trading with the Indians, 1796–1822." *Mississippi Valley Historical Review* 6 (September 1919): 220–35.

Weaver, Sally M. "Indian Policy in the New Conservative Government, Part I: The Nielsen Task Force of 1985." *Native Studies Review* 2, no. 1 (1986): 1–43.

——. *Making Canadian Indian Policy: The Hidden Agenda, 1968–1970*. Toronto: University of Toronto Press, 1981.

Webber, Jeremy. *Reimaging Canada: Language, Culture, Community, and the Canadian Constitution*. Montreal: McGill–Queen's University Press, 1994.

Weber, David J. *The Spanish Frontier in North America*. New Haven CT: Yale University, 1992.

Weeks, Philip, ed. *The American Indian Experience: A Profile*. Arlington Heights IL: Forum, 1988.

White, Richard. *The Middle Ground: Indians, Empires, and Republics in the Great Lakes Region, 1650–1815*. New York: Cambridge University Press, 1991.

——. *The Roots of Dependency: Subsistence, Environment, and Social Change among the Choctaws, Pawnees, and Navajos*. Lincoln: University of Nebraska Press, 1983.

Wilson, J. Donald. "'No Blanket to Be Worn in School': The Education of Indians in Early Nineteenth Century Ontario." *Histoire sociale/Social History* 7 (November 1974): 74–80. Reprint in *Indian Education in Canada*, ed. Jean Barman, Yvonne Hebert, and Don McCaskill. 2 vols. Vancouver: University of British Columbia Press, 1986.

Wise, S. F. "The American Revolution and the Indians." In *Character and Circumstances: Essays in Honour of Donald Grant Creighton*, ed. John S. Moir, 172–90. Toronto: Macmillan, 1970.

——. "The Indian Diplomacy of John Graves Simcoe." In *Canadian Historical Association, Report, 1953*, 36–44. Toronto: Tribune, 1954.

Wood, David L. "American Indian Farmland and the Great War." *Agricultural History* 55 (July 1981): 249–65.

——. "Gosiute-Shoshone Draft Resistance, 1917–18." *Utah Historical Quarterly* 49 (spring 1981): 173–88.

Wood, Peter H. "The Changing Population of the Colonial South: An Overview by Race and Region, 1685–1790." In *Powhatan's Mantle: Indians in the Colonial Southeast*, ed. Peter H. Wood, Gregory A. Waselkov, and M. Thomas Hately. Lincoln: University of Nebraska Press, 1989.

Woods, Patricia Dillon. *French-Indian Relations on the Southern Frontier, 1699–1762*. Ann Arbor MI: UMI Research Press, 1980.

Woodsworth, J. F. "Problems of Indian Education in Canada." In *The North American Indian Today*, ed. Charles T. Loram and T. F. McIlwraith, 265–74. Toronto: University of Toronto Press, 1943.

Wright, J. Leitch, Jr. *The Only Land They Knew: The Tragic Story of the American Indians in the Old South*. New York: Free Press, 1981.

Wunder, John R. *"Retained by the People": A History of American Indians and the Bill of Rights*. New York: Oxford University Press, 1994.

York, Geoffrey, and Loreen Pindera. *People of the Pines: The Warriors and the Legacy of Oka*. Toronto: Little, Brown, 1991.

Young, Alexander, ed. *Chronicles of the Pilgrim Fathers of the Colony of Plymouth, from 1602–1625*. Boston: Little and Brown, 1841.

Index

157–58; definition of "Indian," 194; establishment of Dominion of, 210–11, 252; and ethnocentrism, 148–49, 167, 230, 236, 244, 245, 277–78; fear of Indians by, 142; fear of U.S. by, 142, 211; and frontier violence, 145; and land cessions, 143–47, 164–65, 251, 252; and Métis, 222; and refugee Indians, 183, 219; suppression of native ceremonies by, 233–34; and War of 1812, 159

Canada East, 194

Canadian Expeditionary Force, 255

Canadian Indian (journal), 234

Canadian Indian Research and Aid Society, 234

Canadian Legion, 277

Canadian Métis Society, 297

Canonchet (Narragansett), 86

Caravan to Ottawa, 301

Cardinal, Harold (Cree), xiv, 298

Carleton, Guy, 142

Carlisle Indian School, 230, 250; and outing system, 102

Cartier, Jacques, 4, 5, 6

Carver, Gov. John, 65

Cass, Lewis, 184

Catawbas, 102

Catholic Church, 28, 197

Caughnawaga Reserve, 111, 160

Celoron, Capt. Pierre Joseph de Blainville, 108

A Century of Dishonor (Jackson), 235

Champlain, Samuel de, 10, 15, 17, 20; and assimilation, 31, 32; founds Quebec, 14; and hostages, 32; and missionaries, 22, 26; and Mohawk defeat, 14

Charleston SC, 99

Charlottetown Accord, 314

Charter of Rights and Freedoms, 314

Chase, Hiram (Omaha), 271

Chepart, Captain de, 106

Cherokees, 95, 133; and American Revolution, 134; and education, 230; and English, 97; in French and Indian War, 125; and removal, 134; and Yamassee War, 101, 103

Cherokee v. Georgia, 180

Cheyennes, 201, 214

Chickahominys, 51, 52

Chickamaugas, 134, 163

Chickasaws, 102, 180, 181; and English, 97; and French, 106; and Spanish, 136

Chicken, Capt. George, 102

Chilcotins, 210

Chippewas. *See* Ojibwas

Chisholm, A. G., 269

Choctaws, 30, 181, 283; and French, 97, 98, 104; and Spanish, 136; and Tecumseh, 158

Chowans, 40

Chretien, Jean P., 321

"Citizens Plus," 296

Civilian Conservation Corps, 278

civilization policy, 169, 184–85

Clark, William, 182

Claus, William, 156

Clay, Sen. Henry, 184

Cochran, John, 102

Code of Handsome Lake, 154

Colbert, Levi (Chickasaw), 180, 181

Colborne, Sir John, 188

Collier, John, 278–81, 283, 284; attacks on reforms of, 285; resigns, 286

Colville Reservation, 290

Colyer, Vincent, 218

Comanches, 201, 239

Commissioner of Claims, 299

Commissioners of the United Colonies of New England, 77

Committee of One Hundred, 274

Company of New France (Hundred Associates), 20, 24, 25, 31, 32

confederacies, 123, 139–41

Congregationalists, 169

Connolly, John, 133

Constitutional Act of 1791, 142

Constitutional Act of 1982, 313

Cook, Capt. James, 197

Coolidge, Rev. Sherman, 271

Coosas, 1

Copeland, Patrick, 47

Corbitant (Wampanoag), 67

Cornplanter (Seneca), 148, 154

Coronado, Francisco Vasquez de, 7, 28

Corporation for the Propagation of the Gospel in New England, 76–77

Council of Energy Resource Tribes, 302

country-born, 92, 93, 207, 221. *See also* Métis

country wives, 116. *See also* intermarriage

Course of Study for the Indian Schools, 249

court of oyer and terminer, 120

Cradock, Matthew, 75

Craven, Gov. Charles, 102, 103

Crawford, T. Harley, 201

Crazy Horse (Lakota), 219

Crees, 92, 93, 223, 306

Creeks, 95, 96, 103, 181; and English, 97; and Spanish, 136; and Tecumseh, 158; and Yamassee War, 103

Croatoans, 39

Croghan, George, 126, 131

Crook, Gen. George, 236

Crooks, Ramsay, 163

Crowfoot (Blackfoot), 224

Custer, Col. George A., 219

Custer Died For Your Sins (Deloria), xiv

Cutshamekin (Massachusets), 79

Darling, Gen. Henry C., 176

Dawes, Sen. Henry L., 235

Dawes Act, 235, 252–53

Decker, George, 269

"Declaration of Indian Purpose," 300

Dehorners, 269

de la Ware, Gov. Thomas, 44, 45

Delaware Indians, 108, 128, 134, 157; and Osages, 163, and witchcraft, 155

Deloria, Vine, Jr., xiv

De Meulles, 111

"Dene Declaration," 305

Denes, 305, 306, 307

Denonville, Marquis de, 35–36

Department of Indian Affairs, 237, 266, 315

Deseronto, John (Mohawk), 114

Deskeheh (Cayuga), 269

Dewdney, Lt. Gov. Edgar, 224

d'Iberville, Pierre Le Moyne, 91

disease. *See* epidemics

Doegs, 58

Donnacona (Iroquois), 4, 5

Doolittle Commission, 215

Douglas, Gov. James, 198

Downs, Richard, 47

draft resistance: in Canada, 255–57; in U.S., 257, 283–84

Dragging Canoe (Chickamauga), 134

Drake, Sir Francis, 40

Dreamer religion, 240

Duncan, William, 232–33

Dunmore, Governor, 133

Dutch, 19, 38; defeated by Mohawks, 18; ideas about landholding, 37; missionary actions of, 20

Eastman, Charles (Sioux), 271, 274

education, 226. *See also* schools

Eliot, John, 77, 78, 79–82

Elk v. Wilkins, 226

Elliot, Matthew, 158

Endicott, John, 68, 75; attacks Pequots, 71

Eneah Miko (Creek), 136

Enfranchisement Act of 1869, 212, 225

enfranchisement program, 226, 235, 236–37; opposition to, 289; revoked, 276

English in Carolina: at Charleston, 94; and Cherokees, 97, 124–25; and Chickasaws, 97; and Creeks, 97; and education, 116; in fur trade, 98–99; and intermarriage, 116, 117; and land, 118, 129–33; and law, 119–20; and missions, 112–13; in slave trade, 99

English in New England: and acculturation, 77–79; ethnocentrism of, 66, 74–76, 78; in King Philip's War, 84–88; and land, 69; and law, 82–84; and missions, 75–79, 115; and Pequots, 69–73

English in Virginia, 39, 40; and acculturation, 47–48, 113–14; as aggressors, 41; ethnocentrism of, 41, 48, 55; and missions, 44, 55, 114; and settlement, 52; and treachery, 54

Epenow (Algonkian), 61

epidemics, 25, 26, 27, 38, 62, 97; cholera, 205. *See also* measles, smallpox

Eries, 31

Eskimos. *See* Inuit

Esopus, 19

ethnocentrism, 246, 248–49, 316; of Indians, 109, 124

Evans, Gov. John, 214

Ex Parte Green, 284

factory system, 152, 163

Fallen Timbers, Battle of, 141

Feast of the Dead, 33

Federal Acknowledgment Project, 316

Fetterman, Capt. William, 215

Field Matron Service, 232

First Anglo-Powhatan War, 45

First Puritan Conquest (Pequot War), 71–73, 87

Fishermen's Joint Committee, 277

"fish-ins," 300

Fitzpatrick, Thomas, 204, 205

Ford Motor Company, 250

Fort Atkinson, 163

Fort Christanna, 114

Fort Dearborn, 160

Fort Frontenac, 34, 35

Fort Hall, 205

Fort Jackson, 161

Fort Kearney, 215

Fort Laramie, 205, 216, 217

Fort Loudoun, 124, 125

Fort Mackinac, 132, 160

Fort Malden, 158, 159, 161

Fort Meigs, 160

Fort Miami, 141

Fort Mims, 161

Fort Niagara, 118, 128, 132, 142; refugees at, 143

Fort Orange, 18

Fort Pitt, 127, 128

Fort Prince George, 124, 125

Fort Recovery, 141

Fort Rosalie, 105, 106

Fort San Marcos, 104

Fort San Mateo, 8

Fort Sault Ste. Marie, 163

Fort Saybrook, 71

Fort Sill, 239

Fort Smith, 163

Fort Snelling, 163

Fort Stanwix Treaty: of 1768, 132; of 1784, 138, 144

Fort St. Marks, 168

Fort Toulouse, 104

Fort Vancouver, 198

Fort Victoria, 198

Fort Washington, 139

Fort Wayne, 157

fountain of youth, 3

Four Winds, 154

Foxes. *See* Mesquakies

Fox Wars, 107–8

Franciscans: in Florida, 29, 38, 96, 109; methods of, 110; in New France, 21, 22, 38

Franklin, state of, 135

French and Indian War, 124

French in Canada: and acculturation, 22; and discrimination, 33; in Fox Wars, 107–8; goals of, 16–17, 37; and intermarriage, 116–17; and land, 118; and missions, 110–11

French in Louisiana, 91; and Chickasaws, 98, 106; and Choctaws, 97, 98; and genocide, 108; and Natchez, 104, 105, 106

Friendship Centre Movement, 294

friends of the Indian, 234, 235

Frontenac, Louis, 34, 36

fur trade, 11; methods of, 12; in South, 98

Gage, Gen. Thomas, 127

Gaines, Gen. Edmund P., 182

Gall (Lakota), 219

gambling, 317–18

Ganeodiyo (Seneca), 154

Gates, Sir Thomas, 44

General, Levi (Cayuga), 269

General Allotment Act, 235, 252–53

237; in 1884, 233; in 1890, 228; in 1951, 289–90, 296

Indian Arts and Crafts Board, 281

Indian Association of Alberta, 289, 298

Indian Association of the Northwest Territories, 305

Indian Bill of Rights, 310, 314.

Indian Civilization Fund, 169, 201

Indian Civil Rights Act, 310

Indian Claims Commission, 290–91, 292, 308, 315

Indian Country, 130

Indian Department, 130

Indian Education Act of 1972, 309

Indian Gaming Regulation Act, 317

Indian Homestead law (1875), 238

Indian Medical Service, 279

Indian Ordinance of 1786, 138

The Indian Problem, 274

Indian Removal Act, 181

Indian Reorganization Act, 279, 287; tribal responses to, 280–82

Indian Republics, 123

Indian Rights Association, 234, 273

Indian Self-Determination and Educational Assistance Act, 309

Indian Shaker religion, 241

Indians of All Tribes, 301

Indian Tribes of the Province of British Columbia, 268

Indian-White relations: stages of, xiv

Ingham, Benjamin, 114

Innus, 321

Institute for Government Research, 274

intermarriage, 31, 32, 90, 92, 93, 116

Inuit, 222, 276, 303, 306, 307

Inuit Tapirisat, 307, 312

Ipais, 7

Ironcutter, John, 132

Iron Nation (Lakota), 232

Ironside, George, 195

Iroquois, 226–27; and Beaver Wars, 25, 35–36; confederacy of, 15, 132, 284; and French, 30; and fur trade, 13, 16; and independence,

118, 284; migration of, 108; and Yamassee War, 103

Irvin, Ronald A., 321

Itopan (Powhatan), 50

Jack of the Feathers, 51, 52–53

Jackson, Andrew, 161, 168, 179

Jackson, Helen Hunt, 234–35

Jackson, Henry, 266

James Bay Agreement, 306

James Bay Development Corporation, 306

James Bay II, 306

James I, 44, 47

Jamestown, 41

Jay's Treaty, 141

Jefferson, Pres. Thomas, 147–48, 152

Jenness, Diamond, 265

Jesuits, 9, 24, 38; and acculturation, 109, 110; and assimilation, 22; and education, 23, 25; in Florida, 28; and Hurons, 26–28; and Mohawks, 34–35

Johnson, Pres. Lyndon B., 308

Johnson, Sir William, 126, 131, 132

Jolliet, Louis, 34

Jones, Rev. Peter, 174, 194

justice systems of Indian groups, 32–33, 82

Kalispels, 291

Kelly, Peter (Haida), 268

Kenekuk (Kickapoo), 175, 181, 182

Kennedy Report on Indian Education, 308

Keokuck (Sauk), 182

Kickapoos, 160, 181, 182, 208

Kieft, Gov. Willem, 19

Kilcrease, Simon, 100

King George's War, 108, 122

King Philip (Metacom), 84, 85, 86

King Philip's War, 63, 84; causes of, 84–87; results of, 86–88

Kiowas, 239, 284

Kirke, Lewis, 17

Kirke, Thomas, 17

Klamaths, 292

Knox, Henry, 147, 148

Wovoka (Paiute), 241
Wright, John, 102
Wyandots, 34, 108

Yakimas, 203
Yamacraws, 114, 115
Yamasees, 96, 101

Yamasee War, 101–3
Yeardley, Sir George, 47, 51, 52
York Factory, 92

Zimmerman, William, 292
Zunis, 1, 283